D0855889

**A National Bureau
of Economic Research
Conference Report**

Social Security Programs
and Retirement around
the World
The Relationship
to Youth Employment

Edited by **Jonathan Gruber and
David A. Wise**

The University of Chicago Press

Chicago and London

JONATHAN GRUBER is professor of economics at the Massachusetts Institute of Technology and director of the Program on Health Care at the National Bureau of Economic Research, where he is a research associate. DAVID A. WISE is the John F. Stambaugh Professor of Political Economy at the Kennedy School of Government, Harvard University. He is area director of the Health and Retirement programs, director of the Program on the Economics of Aging, and a research associate at the NBER.

The University of Chicago Press, Chicago 60637
The University of Chicago Press, Ltd., London
© 2010 by the National Bureau of Economic Research
All rights reserved. Published 2010
Printed in the United States of America

19 18 17 16 15 14 13 12 11 10   1 2 3 4 5
ISBN-13: 978-0-226-30948-4 (cloth)
ISBN-10: 0-226-30948-7 (cloth)

Library of Congress Cataloging-in-Publication Data

Social security programs and retirement around the world : the
    relationship to youth employment / edited by Jonathan Gruber and
    David A. Wise
        p. cm.— (National Bureau of Economic Research conference
    report)
    Includes bibliographical references and index.
    ISBN-13: 978-0-226-30948-4 (alk. paper)
    ISBN-10: 0-226-30948-7 (alk. paper)
    1. Social security. 2. Old age pensions. 3. Older people—
Employment. 4. Youth—Employment. 5. Labor supply.
6. Retirement—Government policy. 7. Early retirement incentives.
I. Gruber, Jonathan. II. Wise, David A. III. Series: National Bureau
of Economic Research conference report.
HD7091.S67 2010
368.4'3—dc22
                                                        2009025779

Relation of the Directors to the
Work and Publications of the
National Bureau of Economic Research

1. The object of the NBER is to ascertain and present to the economics profession, and to the public more generally, important economic facts and their interpretation in a scientific manner without policy recommendations. The Board of Directors is charged with the responsibility of ensuring that the work of the NBER is carried on in strict conformity with this object.

2. The President shall establish an internal review process to ensure that book manuscripts proposed for publication DO NOT contain policy recommendations. This shall apply both to the proceedings of conferences and to manuscripts by a single author or by one or more co-authors but shall not apply to authors of comments at NBER conferences who are not NBER affiliates.

3. No book manuscript reporting research shall be published by the NBER until the President has sent to each member of the Board a notice that a manuscript is recommended for publication and that in the President's opinion it is suitable for publication in accordance with the above principles of the NBER. Such notification will include a table of contents and an abstract or summary of the manuscript's content, a list of contributors if applicable, and a response form for use by Directors who desire a copy of the manuscript for review. Each manuscript shall contain a summary drawing attention to the nature and treatment of the problem studied and the main conclusions reached.

4. No volume shall be published until forty-five days have elapsed from the above notification of intention to publish it. During this period a copy shall be sent to any Director requesting it, and if any Director objects to publication on the grounds that the manuscript contains policy recommendations, the objection will be presented to the author(s) or editor(s). In case of dispute, all members of the Board shall be notified, and the President shall appoint an ad hoc committee of the Board to decide the matter; thirty days additional shall be granted for this purpose.

5. The President shall present annually to the Board a report describing the internal manuscript review process, any objections made by Directors before publication or by anyone after publication, any disputes about such matters, and how they were handled.

6. Publications of the NBER issued for informational purposes concerning the work of the Bureau, or issued to inform the public of the activities at the Bureau, including but not limited to the NBER Digest and Reporter, shall be consistent with the object stated in paragraph 1. They shall contain a specific disclaimer noting that they have not passed through the review procedures required in this resolution. The Executive Committee of the Board is charged with the review of all such publications from time to time.

7. NBER working papers and manuscripts distributed on the Bureau's web site are not deemed to be publications for the purpose of this resolution, but they shall be consistent with the object stated in paragraph 1. Working papers shall contain a specific disclaimer noting that they have not passed through the review procedures required in this resolution. The NBER's web site shall contain a similar disclaimer. The President shall establish an internal review process to ensure that the working papers and the web site do not contain policy recommendations, and shall report annually to the Board on this process and any concerns raised in connection with it.

8. Unless otherwise determined by the Board or exempted by the terms of paragraphs 6 and 7, a copy of this resolution shall be printed in each NBER publication as described in paragraph 2 above.

Contents

Preface

This is the fourth volume presenting results of an ongoing project on social security and labor supply organized through the Program on the Economics of Aging at the National Bureau of Economic Research.

Funding for the project was provided by the National Institute on Aging, grants P01-AG05842 and P30-AG12810 to the National Bureau of Economic Research. Funding for individual papers is noted in specific chapter acknowledgments.

Any opinions expressed in this volume are those of the respective authors and do not necessarily reflect the views of the National Bureau of Economic Research or the sponsoring organization.

Introduction and Summary

Jonathan Gruber, Kevin Milligan, and David A. Wise

Several years ago we began an international project to study the relationship between social security program provisions and retirement. Under pay-as-you-go social security systems, most developed countries have made promises they cannot keep. The systems in their current forms are not financially sustainable. What caused the problem? It has been common to assume that the problem was caused by aging populations. The number of older persons has increased very rapidly relative to the number of younger persons and this trend will continue. Thus, the proportion of retirees has increased relative to the number of employed persons who must pay for the benefits of those who are retired. In addition, persons are living longer so that those who reach retirement age are receiving benefits longer than they used to. The effect of aging populations and increasing longevity has been compounded by another trend: until recently, older persons had been leaving the labor force at younger and younger ages, further increasing the ratio of retirees to employed persons. What has not been widely appreciated is that the provisions of social security programs themselves often provide strong incentives to leave the labor force. By penalizing work, social security systems magnify the increased financial burden caused by aging populations and thus contribute to their own insolvency.

Why countries introduced plan provisions that encouraged older persons

Jonathan Gruber is professor of economics at the Massachusetts Institute of Technology and director of the Program on Health Care at the National Bureau of Economic Research, where he is a research associate. Kevin Milligan is associate professor of economics at the University of British Columbia and a faculty research fellow of the National Bureau of Economic Research. David A. Wise is the John F. Stambaugh Professor of Political Economy at the Kennedy School of Government, Harvard University. He is area director of the Health and Retirement programs, director of the Program on the Economics of Aging, and a research associate at the NBER.

to leave the labor force is unclear. After the fact, it is now often claimed that these provisions were introduced to provide more jobs for the young, assuming that fewer older persons in the labor force would open up more job opportunities for the young. In some cases this may have been a motivation for the provisions but in other instances it was not, as shown by illustrations presented following. Now, the same reasoning is also often used to argue against efforts in the same countries to reduce or eliminate the incentives for older persons to leave the labor force, claiming that the consequent increase in the employment of older persons would reduce the employment of younger persons. Here are a few examples:

- "The Job Release Scheme is a measure which allows older workers to retire early in order to release jobs for the registered unemployed." (The United Kingdom 1977 Labour Government)
- "We will extend the voluntary Job Release Scheme to men over 60 so that those who want to retire early vacate jobs for those who are currently unemployed. This could take as many as 160,000 people out of unemployment and into work." (The United Kingdom 1987 Labour Party manifesto)
- "And I would like to speak to the elders, to those who have spent their lifetime working in this region, and well, I would like them to show the way, that life must change; when it is time to retire, leave the labor force in order to provide jobs for your sons and daughters. That is what I ask you. The Government makes it possible for you to retire at age 55. Then retire, with one's head held high, proud of your worker's life. This is what we are going to ask you . . . This is the "contrat de solidarité" [an early retirement scheme available to those fifty-five and over who quit their job]. That those who are the oldest, those who have worked, leave the labor force, release jobs so that everyone can have a job." (France: Pierre Mauroy, French Prime Minister, in Lille 27th September 1981, quoted in Gaullier (1982), L'avenir à reculons, 230)
- "The lowering of the retirement age strengthens the positive effects on employment that early retirement policies made possible. It even widens these positive effects as a larger share of the population is concerned." (France: Ministry of Employment, in La retraite à 60 ans, Droit social n°4—avril 1983)
- "Unemployment among the youth is perhaps the most serious problem of today, because we cannot hide from the fact that we risk losing a whole generation of young persons from the labour market and from society as a whole." (Denmark, with respect to the Post Employment Wage: The Minister of Labour, Svend Auken, Proceedings of Parliament, 1978)

The validity of such claims is addressed in this volume. It presents the results of analyses of the relationship between the labor force participation of older persons and the labor force participation of younger persons in twelve countries.

This is the fourth phase of the ongoing project. The first phase described the retirement incentives inherent in plan provisions and documented the strong relationship across countries between social security incentives to retire and the proportion of older persons out of the labor force (Gruber and Wise 1999). The second phase, based on microeconomic analysis of the relationship between a person's decision to retire and the program incentives faced by that person, documented the large effects that changing plan provisions would have on the labor force participation of older workers (Gruber and Wise 2004). The third phase demonstrated the consequent fiscal implications that extending labor force participation would have on net program costs—reducing government social security benefit payments and increasing government tax revenues (Gruber and Wise 2007). The analyses in the first two phases, as well as the analysis in the third phase, are summarized in the introduction to the third phase.

The results of the ongoing project are the product of analyses conducted for each country by analysts in that country. Researchers who have participated in the project are in the following list. The authors of the country papers in this volume are listed first; others who have participated in one or more of the first three phases are listed second and shown in italics.

Belgium	Alain Jousten, Mathieu Lefèbvre, Sergio Perelman, Pierre Pestieau, *Raphaël Desmet, Arnaud Dellis,* and *Jean-Philippe Stijns*
Canada	Michael Baker, Jonathan Gruber, and Kevin Milligan
Denmark	Paul Bingley, Nabanita Datta Gupta, and Peder J. Pedersen
France	Melika Ben Salem, Didier Blanchet, Antoine Bozio, Muriel Roger, *Ronan Mahieu, Louis-Paul Pelé,* and *Emmanuelle Walraet*
Germany	Axel Börsch-Supan, Reinhold Schnabel, *Simone Kohnz,* and *Giovanni Mastrobuoni*
Italy	Agar Brugiavini and Franco Peracchi
Japan	Takashi Oshio, Satoshi Shimizutani, Akiko Sato Oishi, and *Naohiro Yashiro*
Netherlands	Adriaan Kalwij, Arie Kapteyn, and Klaas de Vos
Spain	Michele Boldrin, Sergi Jiménez-Martín, Pilar Garcia Gomez, and *Franco Peracchi*
Sweden	Mårten Palme and Ingemar Svensson
United Kingdom	James Banks, Richard Blundell, Antoine Bozio, Carl Emmerson, *Paul Johnson, Costas Meghir,* and *Sarah Smith*
United States	Jonathan Gruber, Kevin Milligan, *Courtney Coile,* and *Peter Diamond*

An important goal of the project has been to present results that were as comparable as possible across countries. Thus, the papers for each phase were prepared according to a detailed template that we prepared in consultation with country participants.

In this introduction, we summarize the collective results of the country analyses. In large part, the results presented in the introduction could only be conveyed by combined analysis of the data from each of the countries. The country papers themselves present much more detail for each country and, in addition to template analyses performed by each country, often present country-specific analysis relevant to a particular country.

The proposition that more work by older persons reduces the job opportunities for younger persons is put forth in many different forms. It is sometimes referred to by economists as the "lump of labor" theory. Taken literally, this statement of the theory says that if an additional older worker is employed, one younger worker must be displaced. The implication is that economies are boxed and that the box cannot be enlarged.

In this volume, we emphasize the relationship between the employment rate of older persons and the unemployment and employment rates of younger persons, youth in particular. We emphasize employment and unemployment rates because public discourse about the relationship is typically in terms of these rates—that the unemployment rate of youth, for example, will be increased if incentives for older persons to leave the labor force are eliminated.

The Context

At first glance, it seems clear that economies are not boxed. The flow of women into the labor force in the past few decades has increased the size of the labor force enormously in many countries. For example, the number of women in the labor force in the United States increased by almost 48 million between 1960 and 2007, from about 34 percent to 46 percent of the labor force. But the employment rate of men changed little as the proportion of women employed increased. Figure 1 shows the percent change in the employment rate of men compared to the percent increase in the female employment rate in the twelve countries participating in this project. In this figure, the number of years over which the change occurred varies from country to country. The longest period is from 1960 to 2006 (in Germany) and the shortest from 1983 to 2004 (in Belgium). Two features of the data stand out. First, there was a small decline in the employment rate of men over this time period in all but one of the countries, but second, on average, the *smallest* of the small declines were in the countries with the *largest* increase in the employment rate for women. For example, in the Netherlands, the employment rate of women increased by 54 percentage points, but the employment rate of men declined by only 1 percentage point. Very similar results are obtained if the same span of years is used for all countries—1983 to 2004.

The results are summarized more succinctly in figure 2 that compares the

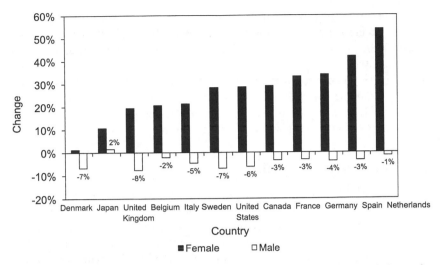

Fig. 1   Relationship between the increase in female employment rates and change in male employment rates, years vary by country

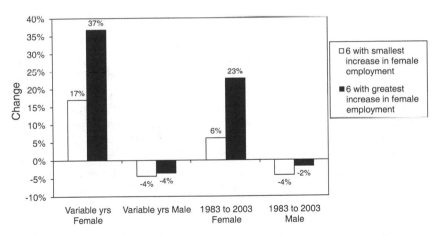

Fig. 2   Compare the six countries with smallest increase with the six with the greatest increase in female employment, variable and same years

six countries with the smallest to the six countries with the largest increase in the employment rate of women. The results are shown both for the variable-years version and the same-years version. The smallest of the small decreases in the employment of men are in the countries with the greatest increase in the employment rate of women. For example, for the same years (1983 to 2003) the average increase in the employment rate of women was 23 percentage points in the countries with the greatest increase and in these countries the decline in the employment rate of men was only 2 percentage points. On the other hand, the average increase in the employment rate of women was only 6 percentage points in the countries with the smallest increase in the employment rate of women and the decline in the employment rate of men in these countries was 4 percentage points. It seems clear that the small decline in the employment rate of men was not tied to the increase in the employment of women. The boxed economy proposition seems quite inconsistent with these data. Could there be another relationship between the old and the young? That is the question we address in this volume.

The Country Papers and the Data

Each of the country papers begins with an historical summary of the changes in social security program provisions over the past three or four decades. The key question is whether social security plan provisions, which provide incentives for older persons to leave the labor force, were prompted by concerns about youth unemployment in particular. The evidence is based on a review of legislation, press coverage, and other public discussion preceding program changes. The evidence gained in this way is further checked against corresponding empirical evidence. For each country, the relationship between the timing of program reforms and the trends in the employment of older persons and the employment and unemployment of youth is described graphically. For example, if public discussion suggests the program changes may have been prompted by increasing youth unemployment, does the data show an increase in youth unemployment prior to the program reform?

The reason for emphasizing the extent to which the program provisions (which induce older persons to leave the labor force) were prompted by youth unemployment is to help to interpret the key relationships that are estimated in the country papers, as explained later. The core analyses presented in each of the country papers are regression estimates of the relationship between the employment rates of persons fifty-five to sixty-four on the one hand, and the employment and unemployment of youth twenty to twenty-four and prime age persons twenty-five to fifty-four on the other hand. Several different estimation specifications of these relationships are presented.

These estimates follow on the estimates in previous phases of the project. As noted before, the first phase of the project documented the strong relationship across countries between program provisions that induce retirement and the proportion of older persons out of the labor force. The second phase was based on micro-estimation of the relationship between the retirement incentives faced by individuals and their retirement decisions. The central finding is the strong relationship between social security program provisions that penalize work and departure from the labor force. Now, the question is whether the departure of older persons from the labor force expands the job opportunities of youth.

The trends in the employment of older persons, however, reflect all determinants of the employment of older persons, not only the social security program incentives to leave the labor force. Thus, in addition to the template components of the country analyses that are common to each of the country papers, a few of the country papers also present additional information that helps to explain the developments in that country. For example, while the estimates (of the "direct" effect of the employment of the old on the employment of the young) are the central focus of the analysis in this phase, we have also considered whether it was feasible to estimate the relationship between changes over time in the incentives inherent in social security plan provisions and the employment of the young. The reason for considering this question was to address more directly the effects of plan provisions that are the subject of public discussion. This goal turned out to be very difficult to accomplish on a comparable basis across countries. In particular, we were unable, on a consistent basis across countries, to obtain a reliable measure of the average incentives faced by persons retired in a given year. Perhaps most important, even if the average were measured well, the average may not adequately capture the wide range of incentives faced by individuals. In short, the procedure we explored was not replicable across countries. Thus, such estimates are presented in only a few of the country papers.

The illustrations and the cross-country analyses presented in this introduction are based on data provided by each country. Key data series are shown here. Much of the answer to the central question posed in this volume can be seen in the data themselves.

Figures 3 to 14 show the data for each country. The first panel of each figure shows the actual data for three series—the employment of persons fifty-five to sixty-four (E 55–64), the employment of youth twenty to twenty-four (E 20–24), and the unemployment of youth twenty to twenty-four (UE 20–24).[1] To simplify the figures, we have not shown data for prime age persons (age twenty-five to fifty-four). The employment and unemployment rates for the prime age group typically parallel closely the rates of youth and both series are shown in the country papers. In the analysis following we present results for prime age persons, as well as for youth.

The following figures show two versions of the data for each country. The first panel shows the actual data as reported for each country. The second panel shows the data adjusted for changes in gross domestic product (GDP) per capita, GDP growth, and the proportion of GDP generated by manufacturing.[2] The years for which data are available varies from country to country. The longest period is from 1960 to 2006 (in Germany) and the shortest period from 1983 to 2004 (in Belgium).

To obtain the adjusted data for a given country, we first determine how

1. In Sweden the data for youth are for the age range sixteen to twenty-four.
2. The adjustment in the United States, Japan, Spain, and Sweden is based on GDP per capita and GDP growth only because the proportion of GDP generated by manufacturing is not available in all years for these countries.

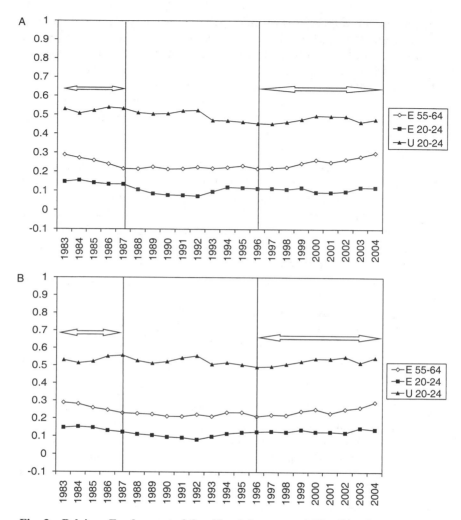

Fig. 3   Belgium: Employment of the old and the young: *A*, **Unadjusted data;** *B*, **Adjusted data**

each of the three employment series varies with GDP per capita, GDP growth, and the "manufacturing share" in that country. Then beginning with the first year of data for that country, the data for each subsequent year is adjusted based on the change in the predictor variables between the first year and the subsequent year. The same procedure is followed for each of the countries. (The details are shown in the appendix.) Thus, the adjusted series eliminates the movement in each of the series that can be predicted by the change over time in the adjustment variables in that country. In particular, each of the employment series is adjusted for macroeconomic shocks to the economy that tend to affect each of the series. Of course, the employment

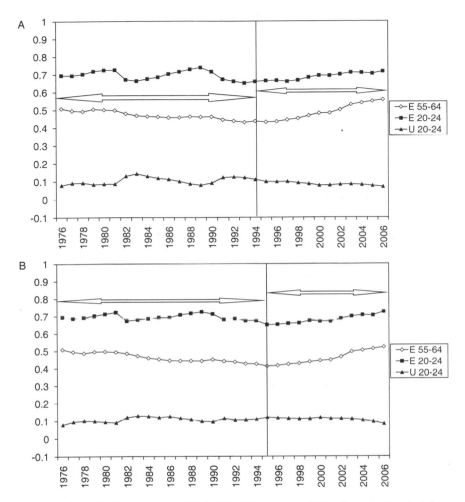

Fig. 4   Canada: Employment of the old and the young: *A*, Unadjusted data; *B*, Adjusted data

series may be affected by other influences imperfectly controlled for by the adjustment variables. Some such influences are mentioned in the country papers.[3]

In the subsequent analyses, we often show results based on both unadjusted and adjusted data. Both are shown for two reasons. One is that we often want to observe youth employment or unemployment rates prior to a given reform in a country. For this purpose we want to use the unadjusted data. The second reason is that it is not clear that estimates based on the

3. For example, in France there was a change in the Labor Force Survey in 2002 and a change in the work week schedule in 2000.

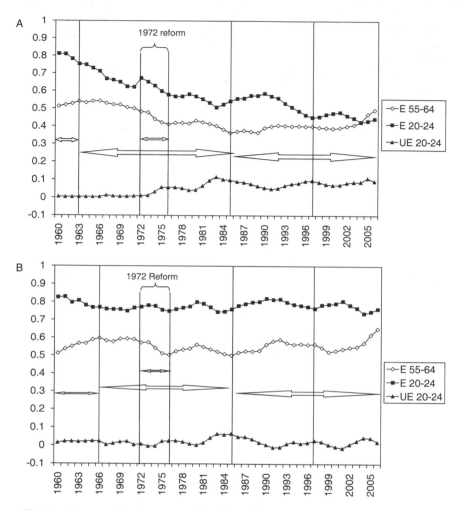

Fig. 5   **Germany: Employment of the old and the young:** *A*, **Unadjusted data;** *B*, **Adjusted data**

adjusted data always yield the best estimate of the effect of employment of the old on the employment of the young.

In addition, prolonged upward and downward trends in the employment of persons fifty-five to sixty-four are marked by left-right arrows in each of the figures. The arrows' positions are determined on the basis of the unadjusted data and are in the same positions on the adjusted data figures. These prolonged upward and downward intervals are used in subsequent analysis.

Three features of the data stand out. First, in each country, the unadjusted data show substantial correlation among the series. As might be expected, the employment of youth is positively correlated with the employment of

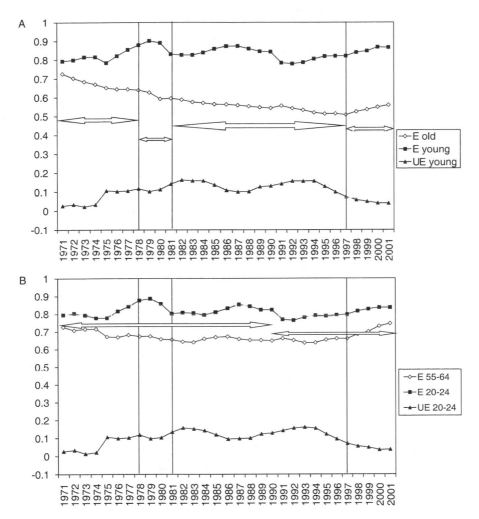

Fig. 6   Denmark: Employment of the old and the young: *A*, Unadjusted data; *B*, Adjusted data

older persons. The unemployment of youth is negatively correlated with the employment of older persons. That is, macro "shocks" to the economy affect employment at all ages and in the same direction. Second, the variation over time in each of the series is typically reduced when the change associated with economic output per capita is controlled for. In some countries, the smoothing of the series trends is substantial. Third, and most important for our analysis, even after adjusting for economic growth and the manufacturing share, much of the relationship between the employment of the old and the young remains.

Simple perusal of the data reveals no evidence that increases in the

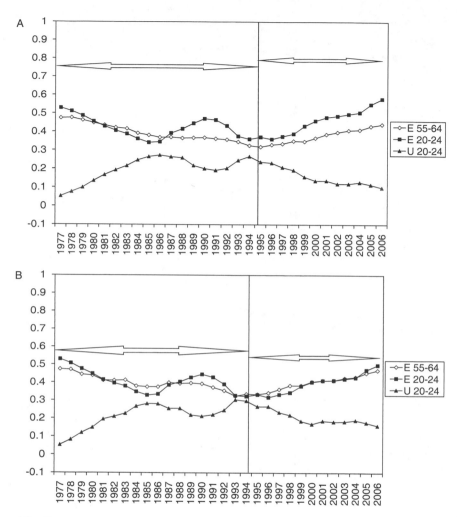

Fig. 7   Spain: Employment of the old and the young: *A*, **Unadjusted data;** *B*, **Adjusted data**

employment of older persons are related to a reduction in the employment of younger persons, or that decreases in the employment of older persons are associated with increases in the unemployment of younger persons.

We next consider a series of estimates of the relationship between the employment of older persons and the employment of youth and we show key results for prime age persons as well. In section 3 we begin by showing how the tax force to retire—emphasized in the first phase of the project—is related to the employment of youth and prime age persons. In section 4 we show illustrative within-country "natural experiment" comparisons that help to demonstrate the relationship between within-country reforms and

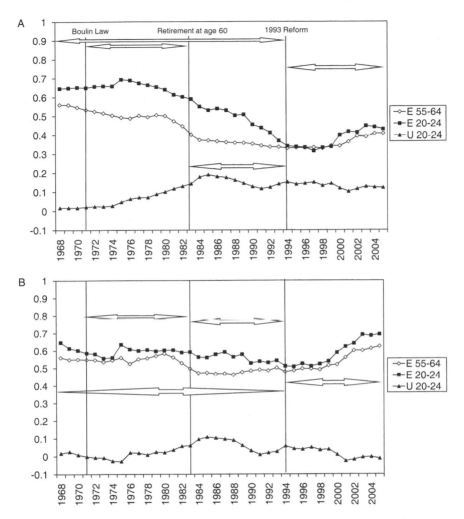

Fig. 8   France: Employment of the old and the young: *A*, Unadjusted data; *B*, Adjusted data

the consequent changes in the employment of the old on the one hand, and changes in the employment of the young on the other hand. In section 5, we show cross-country comparisons based on various comparison methods. To simplify the presentations in sections 4 and 5 we show results only for youth. In section 6, we show more formal estimates based on panel regression analysis. In this section we show estimates for prime age persons, as well as for youth. As it turns out, all of the various estimation methods yield very consistent results. In particular, there is no evidence that reducing the employment of older persons provides more job opportunities for younger persons. And, there is no evidence that increasing the labor force participa-

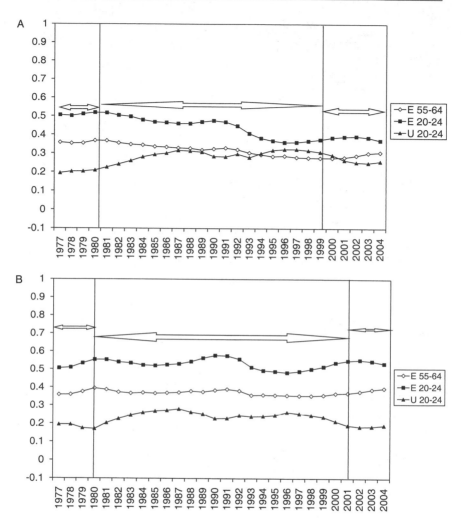

Fig. 9   Italy: Employment of the old and the young: *A*, Unadjusted data; *B*, Adjusted data

tion of older persons reduces the job opportunities of younger persons. In section 7 we summarize the results.

The Employment of Youth and the Tax Force to Retire

We begin by recalling the key finding from the first phase of the project in which we considered the "tax force to retire." The tax force to retire can be explained in this way: compensation for working another year, say at age sixty, can be divided into two parts—the wage earnings for an additional year of work and the change in the present value of future social security

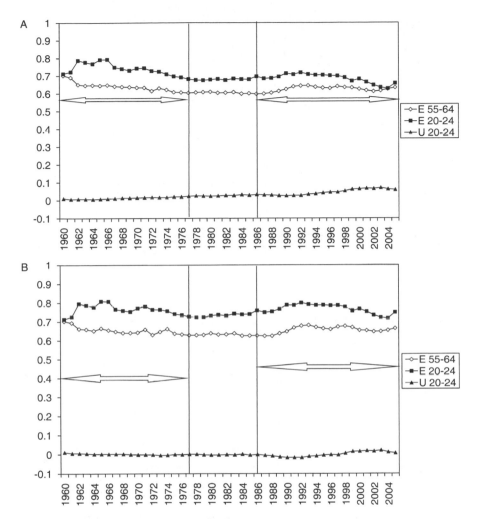

Fig. 10   Japan: Employment of the old and the young: *A*, Unadjusted data; *B*, Adjusted data

benefits. One might suppose that if benefits will be received for one fewer years, then annual benefits will be increased enough to offset their receipt of one fewer years. This is typically not the case, however. The present value of benefits declines in most countries. In some countries, the reduction in benefits is greater than 80 percent of wage earnings. We then consider the sum of these percents (the ratio of the loss in benefits to wage earnings) from the early retirement age in a country to age sixty-nine. We call this sum the tax force to retire.

The relationship between the tax force to retire and the proportion of men fifty-five to sixty-five was shown in the summary to the Phase I volume

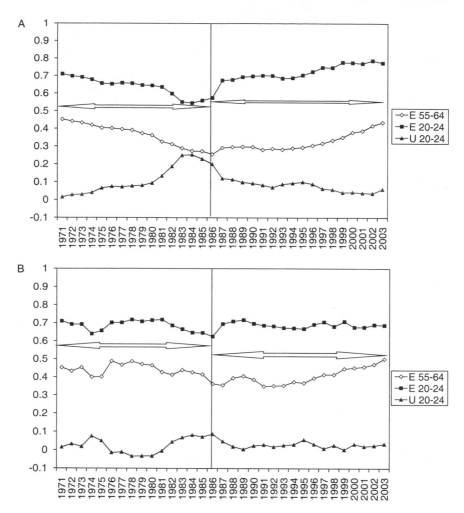

Fig. 11   Netherlands: Employment of the old and the young: *A*, **Unadjusted data;** *B*, **Adjusted data**

(Gruber and Wise 1999). One version of that relationship is reproduced as figure 15. The strong relationship between the tax force to retire and the proportion of older men out of the labor force is apparent.

If the incentives that reduced the proportion of older persons in the labor force—that is, increased the proportion out of the labor force—increase the job opportunities of young persons, then the tax force to retire should be related to youth employment. The greater the tax force to retire, the lower youth unemployment should be and the greater youth employment should be. And analogous relationships should be true for prime age persons. But this is not the case.

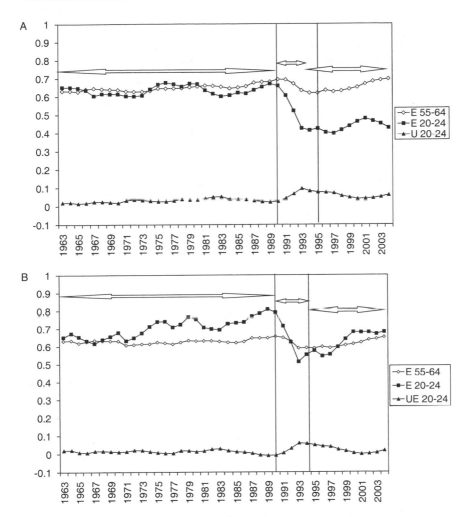

Fig. 12   Sweden: Employment of the old and the young: *A*, Unadjusted data; *B*, Adjusted data

Figure 16 is the same as figure 15 but with the addition of the unemployment rate of young men twenty to twenty-four. Essentially there is no relationship across countries between the tax force for older persons to retire and the unemployment of young men. Indeed, the actual relationship is slightly positive—the greater the tax force to retire the greater is youth unemployment.

Figure 17 shows the unemployment rate of all youth, male and female combined. Again, there is a slightly positive relationship between the tax force to induce older persons to leave the labor force and the unemployment rate of youth twenty to twenty-four.

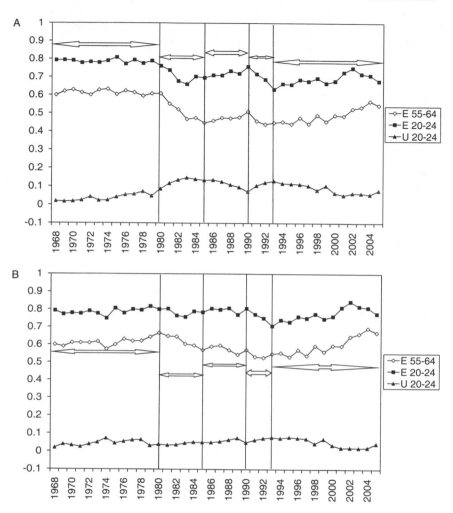

Fig. 13   United Kingdom: Employment of the old and the young: *A*, Unadjusted data; *B*, Adjusted data

Figure 18 shows the relationship between the tax force for older persons to leave the labor force and the employment of youth twenty to twenty-four. If inducing older persons to leave the labor force provides more jobs for the young, then the tax force to retire—which is strongly related to the proportion of older persons out of the labor force—should also be strongly related to the employment of youth. But in fact the opposite is true. The greater the tax force to retire, the lower the employment rate of youth.

Figures 19 and 20 show the relationship between the tax force for older persons to leave the labor force and the unemployment and employment of

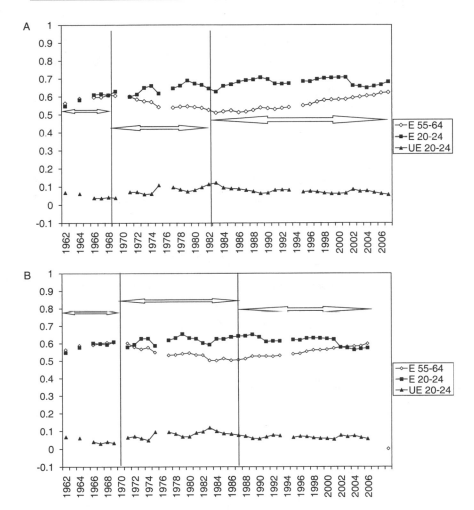

Fig. 14   United States: Employment of the old and the young: *A*, Unadjusted data; *B*, Adjusted data

prime age persons twenty-five to fifty-four. Like the results for youth, the greater the tax force to retire the greater the unemployment and the lower the employment of prime age persons twenty-five to fifty-four.

In short, these results provide no evidence that inducing older persons to leave the labor force frees up jobs for the young. If anything, the opposite is true; paying for old persons to leave the labor force reduces the employment rate and increases the unemployment rate of youth and of persons in their prime age working years.

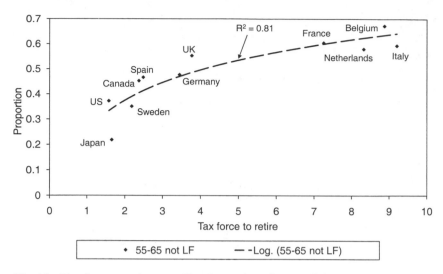

Fig. 15   Tax force to retire, men fifty-five to sixty-five out of the labor force

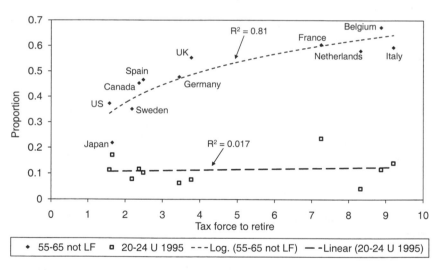

Fig. 16   Tax force to retire, men fifty-five to sixty-five out of the labor force, men twenty to twenty-four unemployed (1995)

Within-Country Estimates of the Relationship between the Employment of the Old and the Young

In many instances it is possible to trace employment trends for both young and older workers that preceded a social security reform in a country and then to trace the effect of the reform on the labor force participation of older

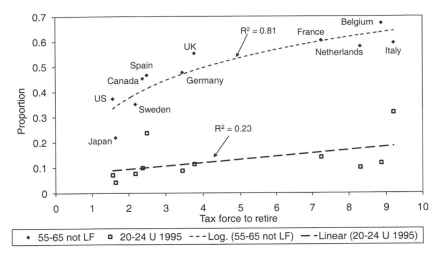

Fig. 17   Tax force to retire, men fifty-five to sixty-five out of the labor force, youth twenty to twenty-four unemployed (1995)

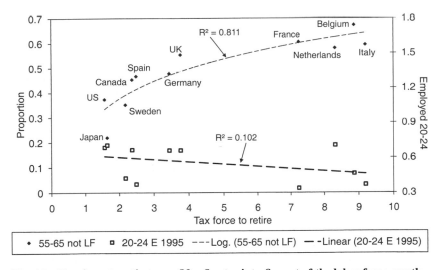

Fig. 18   Tax force to retire, men fifty-five to sixty-five out of the labor force, youth twenty to twenty-four employed (1995)

workers and, in turn, the relationship between the effect on older workers and the effect on younger workers. Several such illustrations are presented here. The illustrations serve two important purposes. The first reason is simply to demonstrate—as we have in prior phases of the project—the effects of reform on the labor force participation of older workers, and then to show the corresponding effect on younger persons.

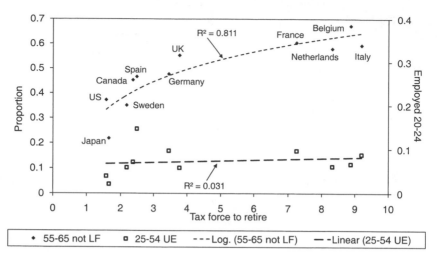

Fig. 19   Tax force to retire, men fifty-five to sixty-five out of the labor force, prime age twenty-five to fifty-four unemployed (1995)

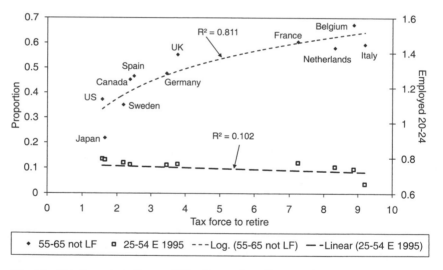

Fig. 20   Tax force to retire, men fifty-five to sixty-five out of the labor force, prime age twenty-five to fifty-four employed (1995)

The second reason to present the illustrations is to help to judge the extent to which the further results shown following are affected by an important issue that complicates estimation of the causal relationship between employment of the old and the young. Suppose—as is now often claimed—that the program provisions that induced older persons to leave the labor force were prompted by increasing youth unemployment. In this case, a decline in youth unemployment following the introduction of retirement incentives could simply have been a continuation of the preincentive decline, and not caused by the incentive-induced decline in the employment of older persons. To address this issue, we have selected some examples in which specific reforms were apparently not prompted by concerns about youth unemployment (or employment). We call these "natural experiment" or sometimes "natural experiment like" examples. We want examples where the reform that induced older persons to leave the labor force was "exogenous." That is, not motivated by the employment or unemployment of youth. Or, we want examples that are not contaminated by the "endogeneity" problem. There is no sure way to correct for the problem, to the extent that it exists. But, as comparison with subsequent results show, the "natural experiment" results—that are not contaminated by endogeneity—are very similar to the findings from comparisons in which we are less sure of the extent of endogeneity. Thus, the fact that later results are much like the findings from these and other natural experiments lends credence to the results obtained by other estimation methods.

We have emphasized the "endogeneity" issue. The natural experiment illustrations also address an additional and closely related issue. Economic shocks to the economy are likely to induce parallel movements in both the employment of the old and the employment of the young. We would like to evaluate the effect of precipitating events that are intended to induce older persons to leave the labor force, without a contemporaneous influence on the employment of the young—unlike macro economic shocks that tend to affect both simultaneously. The following illustrations also avoid the confounding effect of economic shocks. Thus, the fact that later results are much like the natural experiment findings also adds credence to later results that could be confounded by imperfect control for macro shocks.

Consider first an example for Germany. Before 1972, the social security retirement age in Germany was sixty-five, except for disability, and there was no social security early retirement age. But legislation in 1972 provided for early retirement at age sixty for women and at age sixty-three for men (given the accumulation of thirty-five required social security work years). In addition, increased liberal use of disability and unemployment benefits effectively expanded the early retirement option. Beginning in 1972 (with further provisions over the next twenty years), social security early retirement benefits were made available with no actuarial reduction in benefits available at the normal retirement age; benefits if taken at the early retirement age were the same as if they were taken at the normal retirement age. Delayed benefits were increased only through years of service, about 2.2 percent each year, well below an actuarially fair adjustment. The 1972 reform greatly increased the incentive to leave the labor force early. Over the next four years the employment rate of persons fifty-five to sixty-four fell by about 7 percentage points, a decrease of over 17 percent.

Looking at the unadjusted data in figure 5, panel A, it seems clear that this change could not have been motivated by an increase in the unemployment rate of youth, since this rate had been very low throughout the prior decade. The employment rate of youth had been falling in previous years, however. The adjusted data show essentially no change in either the unemployment or the employment rate over the prior six years, however.

The 1992 reform introduced actuarial adjustment of benefits, to be phased in *beginning in 1998.* In addition, benefits were based on net wages, rather than gross wages, which further reduced the incentive to leave the labor force. Since this reform reduced the incentive for older persons to leave the labor force, it could not have been motivated by the desire to provide jobs for the young by inducing older persons to leave the labor force. Indeed, the labor force of older persons increased following this reform. Between 1997 and 2006, the employment rate of older persons increased from about 0.40 to 0.49, an increase of about 23 percent.

What was the effect of these reforms on the employment of youth? The results are shown in figure 21, panels A and B. Panel A shows results based on the unadjusted data. A 7 percentage point reduction in the employment rate of older persons between 1972 and 1976 was associated with a 2 percentage point *reduction* in the employment of youth, not an increase, and was associated with a 1.7 percentage point *increase* in the unemployment rate of youth, not a reduction. The 15 percentage point increase in the employment rate of older persons following the 1998 actuarial adjustment phase-in was associated with *no change,* not a decrease, in the employment rate of youth and a slight *reduction,* not an increase, in the unemployment rate of youth. The results based on the adjusted data, shown in panel B, are essentially the same. Thus, the effect of these reforms was quite inconsistent with the boxed economy view of the German economy.

The experience in France provides another, but somewhat more complex, illustration. Prior to 1972, the French normal social security retirement age was sixty-five and early retirement provisions were uncommon. Beginning in the early 1970s there was a series of reforms that provided early retirement incentives, including more generous benefits and guaranteed income for persons age sixty and over who lost their jobs. The first of the series of reforms was encoded in the Loi Boulin of 1971. A further series of reforms was put in place between 1977 and 1983. In 1983, age sixty became the *normal* retirement age.

Prior to 1972, the youth employment rate was rising and the youth unemployment rate had increased only slightly. Thus, it seems unlikely that the 1971 reform was prompted by youth employment concerns. By the time of the reforms beginning in 1977, however, the youth unemployment rate was rising and the youth employment rate had begun to fall. Even though it appears that the fall in youth employment and rise in youth unemployment were tied to the reforms in the early 1970s, some proponents of the 1977 and

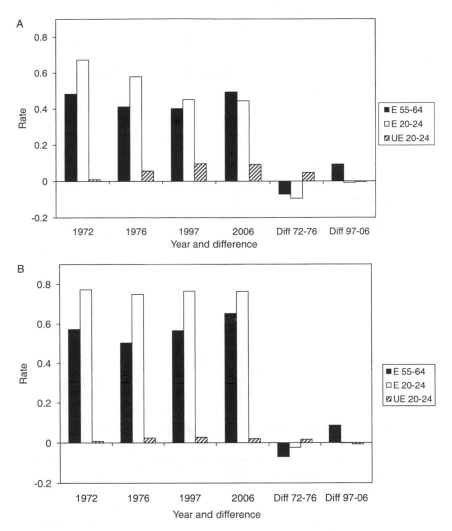

Fig. 21   Response to reforms in Germany, 1972 and 1998 to 2006: *A*, Unadjusted data; *B*, Adjusted data

1983 reforms used the (by then) deteriorating youth employment and unemployment trends to justify the reforms. That is, while the first of the series of reforms—which induced older persons to leave the labor force—could not have been justified by adverse trends in youth employment and unemployment, by the time of the later reforms in the series, after the youth trends had deteriorated on the heels of the early reforms, the deterioration was used to justify further inducement for older persons to retire. Thus, while the first of the long series reforms seems exogenous with respect to youth employment, the exogeneity of the later reforms in the series is unclear.

In 1993, there was a reversal. The number of years of work required to earn full benefits was raised from 37.5 to forty years and the rules for computing the replacement rate became less generous. It seems evident that the 1993 reform could not have been prompted by the continuing adverse trends in youth employment.

Here we consider the combined effects of the 1971 and subsequent reforms, using the period 1972 to 1993. (In the next section we compare reforms in France and the United Kingdom and use a somewhat different range of years.)

The results of these reforms can be seen in figure 22, panels A and B. Panel A, based on unadjusted data, shows that as the employment of older persons *fell* by about 21 percentage points between 1971 and 1993, the employment of youth also *fell* by approximately an equal percent, and the youth unemployment rate *increased.* In short, the series of reforms was very successful in inducing older persons to leave the labor force. But to the extent that the reforms were prompted by hope of providing more job opportunities for youth (only the later reforms in the series), they failed. There is no evidence that the reforms provided more jobs for youth.

On the other hand, when the employment of older persons *increased* between 1993 and 2005, the employment of youth also *increased* and the unemployment of youth *declined.* The adjusted employment series for France show substantially reduced fluctuations in the employment trends over time, as can be seen by comparing the unadjusted and the adjusted series in figure 8. Nonetheless, the direction of the changes are the same when based on adjusted data, as shown in panel B of figure 22. Again, the results show no evidence of the boxed economy proposition.

A reform in Denmark provides a very striking example. In 1979, the Post Employment Wage (PEW) program was introduced. It induced an almost immediate 28 percent drop in the labor force participation rate of men sixty-one to sixty-five. Prior to the 1979 reform, the employment rate of youth had been increasing and the unemployment rate of youth had changed little since 1975. Thus, it seems unlikely that the reform was prompted by a fall in the employment rate or an increase in the unemployment rate of youth. The response to this reform is shown in panel A of figure 23, based on unadjusted data. Between 1978 and 1983 the employment rate of men sixty-one to sixty-five fell by almost 23 percentage points, a decline of 35 percent. Over the same period the employment rate of all youth twenty to twenty-four fell by about 4 percentage points and the unemployment rate of youth increased by about 4 percentage points. The results based on adjusted data are shown in panel B of figure 23 and tell the same story. Again, this "natural experiment" shows no evidence of the boxed economy proposition.

In short, each of these "natural experiments" is consistent one with the other, and none of them is consistent with the boxed economy proposition.

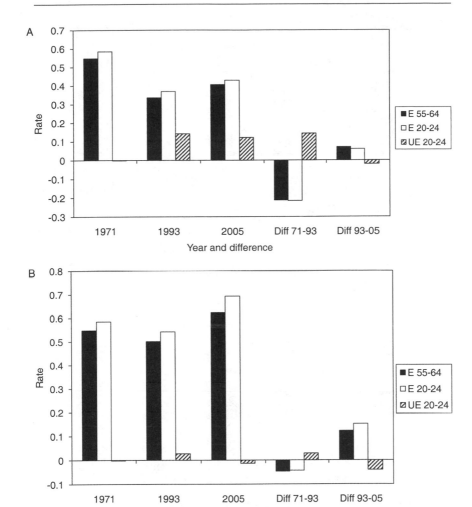

Fig. 22   Response to reforms in France, 1971 to 1983 and 1993: *A*, **Unadjusted data;** *B*, **Adjusted data**

Cross-Country Estimates of the Relationship between the Employment of the Old and the Young

The examples in the previous section are "natural experiment" estimates of the effects of reforms in selected countries. The results in this section are based on cross-country comparisons.

Before considering comparisons across all countries, we begin by comparing the employment trends in two countries—the United Kingdom and France—and then by comparing natural experiment estimates of the

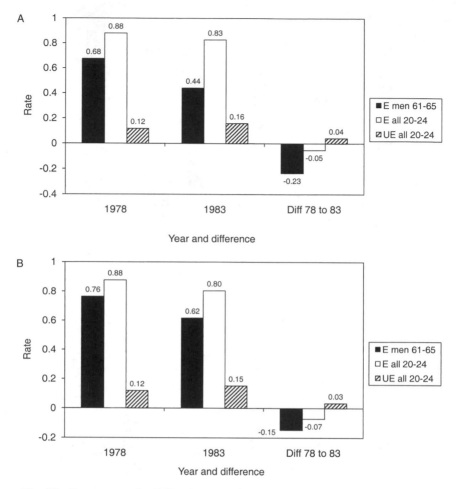

Fig. 23   **Response to the 1979 reform in Denmark:** *A*, **Unadjusted data;** *B*, **Adjusted data**

responses to reform in the two countries. These two countries provide an illustration of the effect of differences in reform on the employment of older persons and, in turn, on the consequent tie between the employment of older persons and the employment of youth.

Figure 24 is abstracted from figure 11.8 in the United Kingdom chapter that shows trends for four age groups. Figure 24 shows employment trends for the sixty to sixty-four age group only. Between 1968 and 1983, the trends were similar in both countries. Prior to 1972, the French normal social security retirement age was sixty-five and early retirement provisions were uncommon. In the early 1970s "early retirement provisions" were introduced by way of guaranteed income for persons age sixty and over who lost their jobs. (Provisions to facilitate early retirement began with provisions in

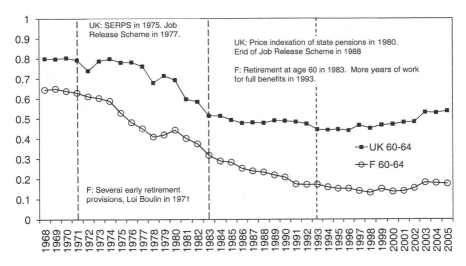

Fig. 24   Comparison of the proportion of older men employed in the United Kingdom and in France, 1968 to 2005

specific industries in the private sector in the late 1960s.) In 1983, age sixty became the *normal* retirement age in France. In addition, guaranteed income was provided for persons age fifty-seven and older who lost their jobs. The downward trend in the employment of the sixty to sixty-four age group was continuous over the whole 1968 to 1983 interval in France. The downward trend in the United Kingdom began at the time of the 1975 State Earnings Related Pension Scheme (SERPS) reform and continued until the end of the interval. The downward trend was also facilitated by the 1977 Job Release Scheme.

After 1983, however, there was a striking divergence in the trends in the two countries. With the 1983 reform establishing age sixty as the normal retirement age in France, the downward trend in the employment of older men in France continued and was long-lasting, continuing until 1998. The eventual reversal was facilitated by the 1993 reform that increased the number of years of work required to get full benefits and reduced the replacement rate. On the other hand, the downward trend in the United Kingdom changed abruptly. The Job Release Scheme was terminated in 1988. (In addition, private sector firms were converting from defined benefit [DB] plans—which typically have large early retirement incentives—to defined contribution [DC] plans without such incentives. But in the late 1980s most older workers were not yet affected by this shift.) The employment of men sixty to sixty-four turned upward in 1993. In essence, the difference between the post-1983 trends in France and the United Kingdom arise because the reforms in France remained in effect for many years, while the reforms in the United Kingdom were short-lived.

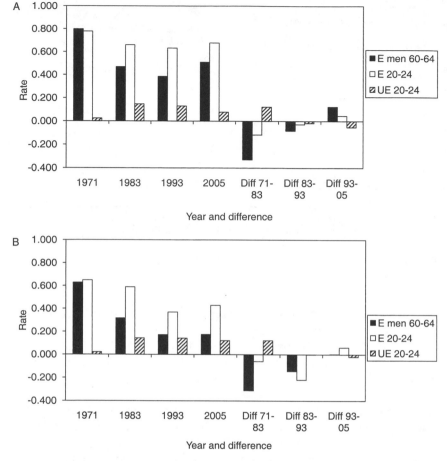

Fig. 25   Comparison of employment trends in the United Kingdom and France, 1971 to 2005, unadjusted data: *A*, United Kingdom; *B*, France

To capture as closely as possible the differences in the reforms ongoing in the two countries in different time intervals, we show data for four time periods—1971, 1983, 1993, and 2005—and the corresponding three intervals.

In the years between 1968 and the early 1970s, there was little change in the employment or the unemployment of youth in either country. Thus, it is unlikely that the early reforms in either country were prompted by decline in the employment or increases in the unemployment of youth in either country (as emphasized for France in the prior section).

Figure 25 and figure 26 summarize the differences in the two countries, both with respect to the employment of older persons and with respect to the employment and unemployment of the young. The comparisons in these

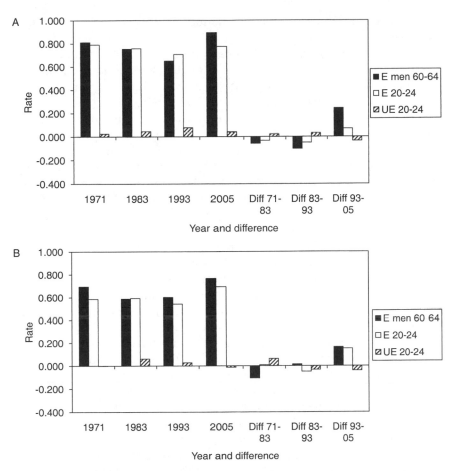

Fig. 26   Comparison of employment trends in the United Kingdom and France, 1971 to 2005, adjusted data: *A*, United Kingdom; *B*, France

figures are based on men only in the sixty to sixty-four age group, but all youth in the twenty to twenty-four age group.

Consider first the results based on the unadjusted data in figure 25. In the years between 1971 and 1983 the employment of older persons was declining in both countries. The employment of youth was also *declining* in both countries and the unemployment of youth was increasing in both countries. The differences in all three trends are very similar in the two countries. But after 1983 when the employment trends of older persons diverged in the two countries, the employment trends for young persons also diverged. In the United Kingdom, with only a small decline in the employment of older men between 1983 and 1993, there was little change in the employment and unemployment of youth during this period. Between 1993 and 2005, the employment of men increased substantially and there was an increase in the employment and a decrease in the unemployment of youth. On the other hand, in France, where the employment of the older group continued to decline, the employment of youth also declined substantially. The employment of men continued to decline in the United Kingdom until 1998 but then began to increase. By 2005 the employment of youth had increased substantially and the unemployment of youth had declined slightly.

The results based on the adjusted data are shown in figure 26. The general pattern of change in both countries is the same as the pattern based on the unadjusted data. For both the United Kingdom and France, however, the trends in the adjusted data differ substantially from the trends in the unadjusted data, as shown in figure 8, panel A. The adjusted data suggest, for example, that in both countries much of the fall in the employment of older men between 1971 and 1983 may be explained by macro shocks to the economies; the differences in the adjusted trends are smaller than the differences in the unadjusted trends in both countries. By 2005, the adjusted data show a substantial increase in the employment of older men in both countries and a corresponding increase in the employment and a decrease in the unemployment of youth in both countries.

Like the previous country-specific examples, this comparison shows natural experiment-like estimates of the effect of the reforms in each country on the employment of older persons and on the relationship between the employment of the old and the young. These differences between the employment trends in the two countries correspond closely to the differences in their reforms. The findings are clearly inconsistent with the boxed economy proposition.

Now consider a comparison across all participating countries. In each of the twelve countries, the employment of persons fifty-five to sixty-four increased over the last ten or fifteen years.[4] This can be seen in figures 3 to 14 in section 2. In most countries, the increase began between the mid-1980s and the mid-1990s, but the beginning date varied from country to country— between 1983 in the United States and 1999 in Italy. In many countries the increase can be ascribed to a particular reform that limited early retirement, as illustrated in some of the previous country-specific illustrations. But even if a precipitating reform cannot be narrowly identified, it is implausible that a reform (or other event) that precipitated the increase in the employment

---

4. In prior phases of the project, we emphasized the dramatic decline in the labor force participation of men sixty to sixty-four between the 1960s and the mid-1990s (Gruber and Wise 1999). We also emphasized the reversal to an increase in the labor force participation of men sixty to sixty-four in most of the countries beginning in the mid-1990s and noted that the increase could be attributed to specific reforms in many countries (Gruber and Wise 2007). Here we focus on men and women combined and on a broader age interval, fifty-five to sixty-four for all persons, instead of sixty to sixty-four for men.

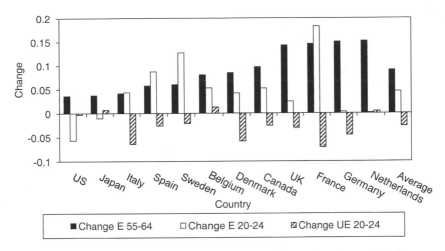

Fig. 27   Change in the employment of persons fifty-five to sixty-four and in the employment and unemployment of persons twenty to twenty-four, from beginning of last upturn in fifty-five to sixty-four employment to data end, adjusted data

of older persons was motivated by a desire to increase the employment—or reduce the unemployment—of youth. Thus, these increases provide a good natural experiment—not plagued by the endogeneity problem—to judge the effect of the increase in the employment of older persons on the employment of youth.

The results are presented in a series of figures. Most of the figures are based on adjusted data, although some comparison figures are shown for unadjusted data as well. Figure 27 shows the difference in the employment rate of older persons from the beginning of the upturn to the end of the data in each country, together with the difference in the employment and unemployment rate of youth. The countries are ordered by the increase in the employment of older persons, from least to greatest. It is apparent that a greater increase in the employment of older persons is not associated with a decrease in the employment of youth and is not associated with an increase in the unemployment of youth. On average, across all countries the increase in the employment of older persons is 8.1 percentage points, the increase in the employment of youth is 4.7 percentage points, and the decrease in the unemployment of youth is 2.6 percentage points.

Figure 28 shows the fit of the relationship between the employment of older persons and the employment of youth. Figure 29 shows the fit of the relationship between the employment of older persons and the unemployment of youth. It is clear that if anything, the relationship to youth employment is slightly positive and the relationship to youth unemployment slightly negative. A boxed economy view would suggest exactly the opposite.

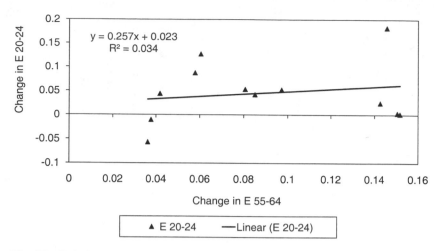

Fig. 28   **Relationship between the increase in fifty-five to sixty-four employment and twenty to twenty-four employment, from beginning of last upturn in fifty-five to sixty-four employment to data end, adjusted data**

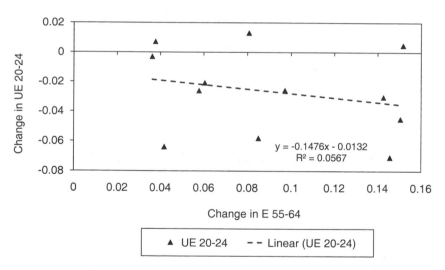

Fig. 29   **Relationship between the increase in fifty-five to sixty-four employment and twenty to twenty-four unemployment, from beginning of last upturn in fifty-five to sixty-four employment to data end, adjusted data**

Figure 30 compares the six countries (in figure 27) with the least increase to the six countries with the greatest increase in the employment of the old. The six countries with the greatest increase in the employment of the old had the greatest increase in the employment of youth and the greatest decrease in the unemployment of youth.

Because the change in youth employment depends in part on when the

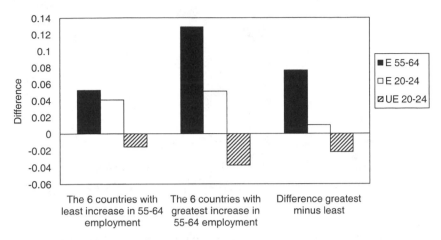

Fig. 30   Comparison of the six countries with the least to the six with the greatest increase in the fifty-five to sixty-four employment, from beginning of last upturn in fifty-five to sixty-four employment, adjusted data—difference

upturn for older persons began, we have scaled the differences by the ratio of the value at the end of the period (the last observation in the data) to the value at the beginning of the upturn. Using this measure, the six countries with the least increase are compared to the six with the greatest increase in figure 31. Based on this measure, there is essentially no difference between change in the employment and unemployment of youth in the two groups of countries.[5]

As a further check on the comparison, consider the change over the same time period for all countries—1995 to 2003. Again, the six countries with the least increase are compared with the six with the greatest increase in the employment of older workers. Figure 32 shows the results measured in differences and figure 33 the results measured in ratios.[6] Both measures show that the six countries with the greatest increase in employment of the older group had a slightly greater increase in the employment of youth. Based on either measure, the difference in the unemployment of youth was close to zero. Based on the ratio measure (figure 10), a 1 percent increase in the employment of older persons leads to a 0.51 percent increase in the employment of youth and a 0.06 percent decline in the unemployment of youth. Based on the difference measure (figure 9), a 1 percentage point increase in the employment of older persons leads to a 0.173 percentage point increase

5. France is excluded from the average ratio for unemployment of youth because the adjusted unemployment rate for France declined from a positive to a negative value between the beginning and end of the period. Japan is excluded for the same reason.

6. The ratio averages for youth unemployment exclude France, Germany, and Japan because the adjusted unemployment values for these countries go from positive values at the beginning of the period to negative values at the end of the period.

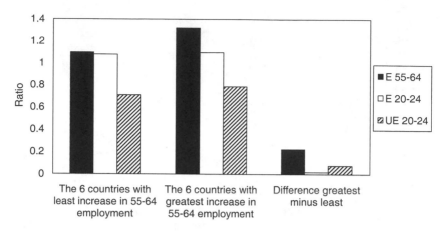

Fig. 31   Comparison of the six countries with the least to the six with the greatest increase in the fifty-five to sixty-four employment, from beginning of last upturn in fifty-five to sixty-four employment to data end, adjusted data—ratio

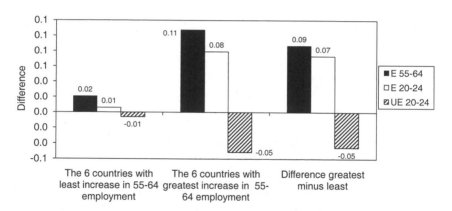

Fig. 32   Comparison of the six countries with the least and the greatest increase in fifty-five to sixty-four employment, 1995 to 2003 in each country, adjusted data—difference 2003 to 1995

in the employment of youth and a 0.036 percentage point increase in the unemployment of youth. (These estimates can be compared to panel regression estimates shown later.)

Thus we conclude that based on this comparison, there is no evidence that increasing the employment of older persons reduces the employment, or increases the unemployment, of youth.

The other side of the comparison of upturns across countries is the comparison of downturns. Most downturns were long-terms and occurred prior to the upturns discussed before, as can be seen in figures 3 to 14 in section 2. One country has two separate downturn intervals and we consider both. As

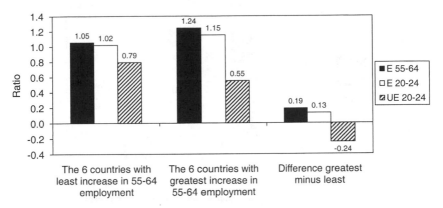

Fig. 33   Comparison of the six countries with the least and the greatest increase in fifty-five to sixty-four employment, 1995 to 2003 in each country, adjusted data— ratio 2003/1995

already shown, many of the downturns were precipitated by specific reforms, or by a series of reforms. In this case, we compare the countries with the greatest decreases with the countries with the smallest decreases. We show results based on the ratio measure only. The results are shown in figures 34 and 35 for unadjusted and adjusted data, respectively. The figures show the averages over the six countries with the smallest decreases in the employment of older persons and the average over the seven "countries" with the greatest decreases—the seven instead of six—to indicate that one country had two separate downward intervals.

Both figures show that the countries with the greatest decline in the employment of the older age group have the greatest decline in the employment of the young as well. The differences are somewhat smaller when based on the adjusted data.

Like the previous results, these comparisons show no evidence that reductions in the employment of older persons provides more job opportunities for the young. The results are inconsistent with the boxed economy proposition.

Panel Regression Estimates

Perhaps the most common way to summarize data series across many countries is by way of panel regression estimation. The panel estimates allow control for country-specific attributes that affect the employment and the unemployment of the young, but that are not included as covariates in the analysis. Although this method presents a concise estimate of results, it is subject to several limitations. First, taken on its own, this method masks the results of "natural experiments" like those discussed previously. Second, in

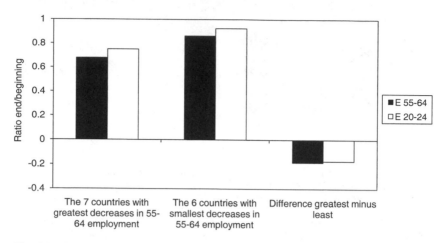

Fig. 34   Comparison of countries with the greatest and least declines in E fifty-five to sixty-four, ratio—unadjusted data

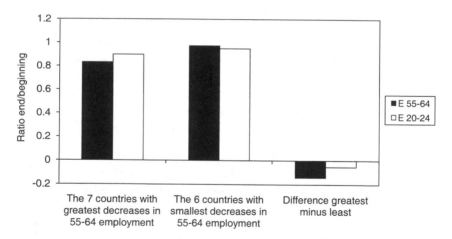

Fig. 35   Comparison of countries with the least and greatest declines in E fifty-five to sixty-four, ratio—adjusted data

the simple specification we have used, the effect of covariates is presumed to be the same in all countries. The results based on adjusted data, presented before, allow the effects of the covariates on each of the employment time series to vary from country to country. It is clear that the effect of the covariates differs from country to country. Third, judging by the "natural experiment" segments in the data, it seems evident that the most relevant year intervals for comparison—whether differences, or percent changes, or another measure—are not common to all countries.

We present panel estimates based on several different specifications. The

Table 1   **Panel estimates of the effect of the LFP of persons fifty-five to sixty-four on the unemployment rate, employment rate, and schooling of younger persons**

Specification	Youth 20 to 24			Prime age 25 to 54	
	UE	EMP	SCH	UE	EMP
	No controls				
Levels	−0.367	0.663	−0.451	−0.267	0.279
	(0.039)	(0.076)	(0.073)	(0.019)	(0.042)
3-year lag on elderly	−0.092	0.321	−0.391	−0.158	0.065
employment	(0.044)	(0.084)	(0.073)	(0.023)	(0.046)
5-year difference	−0.437	0.835	−0.285	−0.282	0.466
	(0.062)	(0.078)	(0.053)	(0.030)	(0.037)
5-year log difference	−1.868	0.611	−0.721	−2.186	0.238
	(0.268)	(0.063)	(0.160)	(0.253)	(0.021)
	With controls				
Levels	−0.232	0.912	−0.911	−0.191	0.416
	(0.055)	(0.090)	(0.094)	(0.027)	(0.053)
3-year lag on elderly	0.110	0.541	−0.804	−0.056	0.136
employment	(0.056)	(0.098)	(0.089)	(0.029)	(0.057)
5-year difference	−0.193	0.573	−0.179	−0.115	0.288
	(0.081)	(0.094)	(0.072)	(0.039)	(0.044)
5-year log difference	−0.905	0.486	−0.619	−0.960	0.144
	(0.329)	(0.090)	(0.240)	(0.260)	(0.028)

Notes: Reported is the coefficient on elderly employment. Controls include GDP per capita, growth in GDP per capita, and manf. share. Each specification also includes country fixed effects and year fixed effects. Levels regression means that we regress levels on levels. 3-year lag means that we regress the dependent variable on a 3-year lag of elderly employment. 5-year difference means that we take 5th differences for the RHS and the LHS variables. 5-year log difference means that we take the log of each X and Y variable, then take 5-year differences. UE = unemployment rate; EMP = employment rate; SCH = schooling.

method followed is set out in detail in the appendix. The key right-hand variable is the employment rate of persons fifty-five to sixty-four. We also control directly for GDP, the growth in GDP, and the proportion of the economy in manufacturing. In addition we include country-specific effects, which control for country-specific attributes that, in addition to the covariates, affect the employment and the unemployment of youth. We also include year effects that capture attributes that are common to all countries in a given year.

The results are shown in table 1. The table shows the estimated effect of the employment of persons fifty-five to sixty-four on the unemployment and the employment of youth twenty to twenty-four, and on the unemployment and employment of prime-age persons twenty-five to fifty-four. The table also shows the estimated effect of the employment of older persons on the proportion of youth in school. Estimates are reported for several specifications. The first is "levels," which means that levels of employment and unemployment rates are regressed on contemporaneous levels of the explanatory variables, including the employment rate of persons fifty-five to sixty-four. The second is "3-year lag," which means that the employment and unemployment rates of youth and prime-age persons in a given year are regressed on the employment of older persons three years earlier. (The other covariates are measured in the same year as the youth and prime-age employment and unemployment rates.) The third is "5-year difference," which means that we consider, for example, the difference between youth unemployment in a given year to youth unemployment five years earlier. We relate this difference to the comparable five-year difference in employment of older persons, and five-year difference in the other explanatory variables. The fourth specification is "5-year log difference," which is the same as the third specification, but the logarithm of unemployment, for example, in a given year is compared to the logarithm of unemployment five years earlier. In this case, the estimates represent the percent difference in the unemployment of youth associated with a percent difference in the employment of older persons.

Estimates are shown with and without controlling for the covariates— GDP per capita, growth in GDP, and the manufacturing proportion.

The key result is that in each specification but one, an increase in the employment of older persons is estimated to *decrease* the unemployment rate of youth (and prime age persons) and to *increase* the employment rate of youth (and prime-age persons). Each estimate is statistically different from zero. The only estimate that does not follow this pattern is the estimated effect of employment of older persons on the unemployment rate of youth in the "3-year lag on elderly" specification, with controls. And in this case, the estimated effect is not statistically different from zero.

More precisely, with respect to the unemployment of youth the estimates for youth suggest this: with controls, a 1 *percentage point* increase in the employment of older persons changes the unemployment rate of youth between +0.11 and –0.23 percentage points. Without controls the decrease is between 0.09 and 0.44 percentage points. For the log difference specification with controls, a 1 *percent* increase in the employment of older persons is associated with a 0.91 percent decrease in the unemployment rate of youth. Without controls the decrease is 1.87 percent.

With respect to the employment of youth: with controls, a 1 *percentage point* increase in the employment of older persons increases the employment rate of youth between 0.54 and 0.91 percentage points. Without controls the increase is between 0.32 and 0.84 percentage points. For the log difference specification with controls, a 1 *percent* increase in the employment of older persons is associated with a 0.49 percent increase in the unemployment rate of youth. Without controls the increase is 0.61 percent. Comparable estimates for prime-age persons can be seen in the table.

The estimates for each specification also indicate that an increase in the employment of older persons is associated with a decrease in the schooling of youth, and each of these estimates is significantly different from zero. Across all specifications, a 1 percentage point increase in the employment of older persons reduces the proportion of youth in school by between 0.17 and 0.70 percentage points. A 1 percent increase in the employment of older persons is associated with about a 0.70 percent reduction in the proportion of youth twenty to twenty-four in school. This result is consistent with findings elsewhere that the greater the employment rate of youth (or the greater the opportunity for employment) the lower school attendance will be.

In short, the panel regression results are consistent with the "natural experiment" results as well as the results based on increasing and decreasing employment intervals for older persons. The findings provide no support for the boxed economy proposition. Indeed, the weight of the evidence suggests that increasing the employment of older persons provides more job opportunities for younger persons and reduces the unemployment rate of younger persons. The positive relationship is, of course, not consistent with the boxed economy proposition. We have not, however, emphasized the possible mechanisms—such as lower earnings tax rates—that could produce the positive relationship.

Summary and Conclusions

In this volume, we direct attention to the oft-claimed proposition that incentives to induce older persons to retire—inherent in the provisions of social security systems—were prompted by youth unemployment. And that if the incentives to retire were removed, and older persons stayed longer in the labor force, the job opportunities of youth would be reduced. We find no evidence to support this boxed economy proposition. We find no evidence that increasing the labor force participation of older persons reduces the job opportunities of young persons. Indeed, the evidence suggests that greater labor force participation of older persons is associated with greater youth employment and with reduced youth unemployment.

The results shown in this summary are based on data from the individual country papers. Some of the data in the papers was borrowed to use in natural experiment illustrations. The data from all of the country papers was also pooled to obtain estimates based on the collective information from all of the countries combined. We began the introduction by showing that the enormous waves of women entering the labor force over the past several decades varied substantially across countries and were unrelated to the small changes in the labor force participation of men across countries.

We ask whether the economic world might be different for young versus old employees. We presented results based on several different methods of inference. A striking feature of the results is the strong similarity of the findings based on these quite different methods of estimation.

In short, the overwhelming weight of the evidence, as well as the evidence from each of the several different methods of estimation, is contrary to the boxed economy proposition. We find no evidence that increasing the employment of older persons will reduce the employment opportunities of youth and no evidence that increasing the employment of older persons will increase the unemployment of youth.

Appendix
Adjusted Data

We want to adjust the employment series for macro changes that may affect each of the employment series. The variables we use to make the adjustment are GDP per capita, growth in GDP, and the percent of the economy in manufacturing. This is the procedure we follow: suppose the employment series is Y and the adjuster variables are X_1, X_2, and X_3. Then, for *each series* in *each country* we estimate

$$Y_t = \beta_0 + \beta_1 X_{1t} + \beta_1 X_{1t} + \beta_1 X_{1t} + \varepsilon_t,$$

and obtain the estimated values β_1, β_2, and β_3. We let the first year, Y_1, of each employment series be the base. Then each subsequent year is adjusted based on the change in the X variables between period 1 and period t. The adjusted value of Y in period t is given by

$$Y(A)_t = Y_t + \beta_1(X_{1t} - X_{11}) + \beta_2(X_{2t} - X_{21}) + \beta_3(X_{3t} - X_{31}).$$

Panel Estimates

We follow a standard panel estimation procedure, with

$$Y_{(20-24)it} = \beta_0 + \beta_1(E_{55-64})_{it} + \beta_2 X_{it} + c_i + y_t + u_{it},$$

where i indexes countries and t indexes years, Y is youth employment or youth unemployment (or prime age employment or unemployment, or schooling), X represents the covariates, the c_i are country-fixed effects, and the y_t are year effects. As explained in the text, we estimate several different specifications of this general model.

Incentive to Leave the Labor Force

The text presents the results of several different ways to assess the effect of the employment of older persons on the employment of youth. In principle, this approach provides an all-inclusive estimate of the relationship between the employment rates of the two groups. In particular, in addition to the strong relationship between the provisions of social security programs and the labor force participation of older workers—which has been demonstrated in earlier phases of the project—the employment of older workers depends on other economic influences as well. For example, macroeconomic shocks to the economy can affect the employment of older persons, as can be seen in the comparison of the unadjusted and adjusted employment trends in each of the countries.

Much public discussion, however, is focused on the need for the incentives to induce older persons to retire so that the job prospects for younger people will be improved. This is often used both as an explanation for the introduction to the incentive in the first place and, now, as a reason for not removing the incentives. Thus, we believe it would be useful to present evidence on the direct relationship between the incentives for older persons to leave the labor force and the employment of youth. We approached this question by calculating a time series index of the average incentives faced by persons who were retired in each year.

The index, as well as potential estimation methods, is described below. In practice, however, the approach was not replicable across countries. There are several possible reasons for this. One reason is that it is unclear whether an accurate measure of the incentives faced by all persons retired in a year can be obtained. A second reason is that even if an accurate average can be calculated, the average may not be sufficient; it is the broad range of incentives faced by individuals that matters. The extremes may be more important than the average, for example. We have shown in earlier phases of the project that the incentives faced by individuals matter.

The incentive faced by persons of age a in year y is given by

$$I(a, y) = \{W(a, y) + \alpha[W(a, y) - PV(a, y)]\}\, q(a, y).$$

Here, $W(a, y)$ is the social security wealth (the present discounted value of future benefits) that a person would receive at age a in year y and $q(a, y)$ is a weight explained following; $[W(a, y) - PV(a, y)]$ is the gain that could be obtained if a person delayed retirement to the age at which benefits would be at their "peak value" $PV(a, y)$.

Persons who are retired in a given year are different ages and the incentive they faced when approaching retirement depends on the person's age at that time. So to get the average incentive, we must average over the ages of persons retired in year y. Here we assume, for illustration, that the possible ages are from fifty-five to fifty-nine. The youngest, age fifty-five, is assumed to be the earliest age that any benefits are available. Now the average for year y is obtained by weighting each age by the proportion of persons that age.

$$\bar{I}(y) = \sum_{a=55}^{a=59} \left[\frac{P(a, y)}{\sum_{a=55}^{59} P(a, y)} \right] [I(a, y)].$$

But we do not know at what age a person retired. A person who is fifty-nine, for example, could have retired at fifty-five, fifty-six, fifty-seven, fifty-eight, or fifty-nine. A person who is fifty-five must have retired at fifty-five. Thus we must consider the incentive the person would have faced at each of the possible ages the person could have retired. If the person is fifty-five, there is only one term in the second bracket. If the person is fifty-nine, there are five terms.

If the weight given to age a in year y is $q(a, y)$, then the average can be written as

$$\bar{I}(y) = \sum_{a=55}^{a=59} \left[\frac{P(a, y)}{\sum_{a=55}^{59} P(a, y)} \right] \left[\sum_{t=0}^{a-55} I(a - t, y - t) \frac{q(a - t, y - t)}{\sum_{t=0}^{a-55} q(a - t, y - t)} \right].$$

If accurate, this could be interpreted as "the tax force to retire" that was faced by persons who were observed to be retired in year y, the term we used to describe the incentive to retire faced by persons between the early retirement age and age sixty-nine in phase one of the project, and as used in section 3 in this introduction.

Now we need to determine an appropriate way to approximate the relative weight to give to each possible age of retirement. We assume that the weight is proportional to the proportion of persons in the labor force in the year before the retirement age. That is, the assumption is that the likelihood that a person faced a particular incentive depends on the proportion of persons in the labor force the year before the person attained that age. If, for example, as the labor force participation (LFP) was declining over the years the person aged from fifty-five to fifty-nine, we assume that the person was most likely to face the incentive appropriate to fifty-five, less likely to face the incentive appropriate to fifty-six, and so forth. Now we have

$$q(a - t, y - t) = \text{LFP}(a - t, y - t - 1),$$

and

$$\overline{I(y)} = \sum_{a=55}^{a=59} \left[\frac{P(a,y)}{\sum_{a=55}^{59} P(a,y)} \right]$$

$$\times \left[\sum_{t=0}^{a-55} I(a-t, y-t) \frac{\text{LFP}(a-t, y-1-t)}{\sum_{t=0}^{a-55} \text{LFP}(a-t, y-t-1)} \right],$$

where

$$I(a - t, y - t) = \{1 \cdot W(a - t, y - t) + \alpha \cdot [W(a - t, y - t) - PV(a - t, y - t)]\}.$$

To estimate $\overline{I(y)}$ we need to determine α; that is, we need to determine the relative weight given to the two components of the index. Suppose we set the weight on $W(a - t, y - t)$ equal to 1, as set out in the previous equation. Then we need only determine the relative weight α on $[W(a - t, y - t) - PV(a - t, y - t)]$. There are at least two ways to do this. One way is to regress the proportion of older persons in the labor force in a year on the index $\overline{I(y)}$, where the index value is based on different values of α, and then choose the α that maximizes the regression r-squared value.

Estimation can also be based on independently estimated averages of the two components of the index I. The two components are

$$
\overline{W}(y) = \sum_{a=55}^{a=59} \left[\frac{P(a, y)}{\sum_{a=55}^{59} P(a, y)} \right]
$$
$$
\times \left[\frac{\sum_{t=0}^{a-55} W(a - t, y - t) \cdot \text{LFP}(a - t, y - t - 1)}{\sum_{t=0}^{a-55} \text{LFP}(a - t, y - t - 1)} \right]
$$

$$
\overline{[W - PV]}(y) = \sum_{a=55}^{a=59} \left[\frac{P(a, y)}{\sum_{a=55}^{59} P(a, y)} \right]
$$
$$
\times \left[\frac{\sum_{t=0}^{a-55} [W(a - t, y - t) - PV(a - t, y - t)] \cdot \text{LFP}(a - t, y - t - 1)}{\sum_{t=0}^{a-55} \text{LFP}(a - t, y - t - 1)} \right].
$$

Notice that these means are obtained by calculating the measures at the individual age-year levels and then averaging over the individual age-year measures. In this case, the value of α is determined by a time series regression of the labor force participation of older workers on these two components, setting the coefficient on $\overline{W}(y)$ equal to 1 and estimating the α coefficient on $\overline{[W - PV]}(y)$.

References

Gruber, J., and D. A. Wise. 1999. *Social security and retirement around the world.* Chicago: University of Chicago Press.
———. 2004. *Social security programs and retirement around the world: Micro-estimation.* Chicago: University of Chicago Press.
———. 2007. *Social security programs and retirement around the world: Fiscal implications of reform.* Chicago: University of Chicago Press.

1

The Effects of Early Retirement on Youth Unemployment
The Case of Belgium

Alain Jousten, Mathieu Lefèbvre, Sergio Perelman, and Pierre Pestieau

1.1 Introduction

Belgium is characterized by a very low labor force participation rate at older ages. According to Eurostat, in 2001, Belgium was in the leading group of European countries with respect to early retirement. On average, workers dropped out of the labor force at an average age of 57.9 years. Since then, the long-standing trend toward lower retirement ages tapered off. By 2005, the number increased to 59.6 years of age—and thus remains at a rather low level by international standards. Another indicator is the employment rate among the elderly workers, which is also far from satisfying the Lisbon criteria in terms of labor force activity rates of the elderly—and this in spite of the fact that more than half the time imparted by the EU has passed by without much action.[1]

Following the studies of Blondal and Scarpetta (1999) and Gruber and Wise (1999, 2003), there is a widespread recognition by academics and policymakers alike that the generosity of the social security and retirement

Alain Jousten is professor of economics at HEC–University of Liège and an IZA research fellow. Mathieu Lefèbvre is a post-doctoral researcher at HEC–University of Liège. Sergio Perelman is professor of economics at HEC–University of Liège. Pierre Pestieau is a professor emeritus of economics at HEC–University of Liège and a CORE faculty member.

The authors wish to thank for financial support under the "Communauté Française de Belgique" ARC contract (ARC 05/10-332) and FRFC (2.4501.05).

1. The Lisbon strategy was adopted for a ten-year period in 2000. It broadly aims to "make Europe, by 2010, the most competitive and the most dynamic knowledge economy in the world." One of the goals is to achieve a 50 percent employment rate of the elderly population (people age fifty-five to sixty-four). In Belgium, the elderly employment rate was 25 percent in 2000 and only 30 percent in 2005, which is far from the objective at half period.

systems has had a potentially decisive role in shaping the retirement patterns. Beyond the sheer generosity of the systems in terms of their benefit levels, it is by now recognized that marginal incentives toward exiting work play a decisive role in individual and collective decision making. By imposing explicit or implicit taxes on continued work, the systems favor early retirement and thus early exit from the labor force.

While reasons for such incentives toward early retirement can be multiple, one prominent justification often encountered is that giving older workers an incentive to leave the labor market frees up space for younger workers.[2] This chapter addresses this issue from several perspectives within the Belgian context. Our aim is to derive a conclusive answer on the often cited potential for substitutability of employment of the old with that of the younger age groups.

The chapter is structured as follows. In section 1.2 we give some institutional background on the systems and regimes applicable to the older workers, as well as some specificity applicable to the young. Section 1.3 gives some theoretical arguments regarding both early retirement and youth unemployment. Section 1.4 proceeds on to a description of the data. Section 1.5 estimates the effect of incentive variables on activity rates, and documents the overall weak impact of parameters regarding the old on behavior of the young. Section 1.6 contains an alternative and more comprehensive specification for the existing difference between sex groups and section 1.7 concludes.

1.2 Institutional Background

The aim of this section is to describe the most important social protection schemes that provide for some form of replacement income when retiring from the labor market and when young and inactive. This chapter focuses on the wage earners. For the treatment of the young, this does not represent a significant limitation, as unemployment benefits are not accessible to the public sector anyway. For retirement, it thus exclusively models the wage earner pension and early retirement systems and does not consider the regimes applicable to either civil servants or the self-employed. The reason for this selective treatment lies in the severe data limitations, which do not allow us to identify which system a person belongs to (see section 1.4). Therefore, this chapter opts for a selective but detailed modeling strategy focusing on the single most important regime covering a wide majority of Belgian workers—while emphasizing the multitude of options available to these wage earners.

---

2. As an example, see the headline of a Belgian biweekly union newsletter: "More early retirement also means more jobs for young people!" (*Syndicats,* August 29, 2005).

1.2.1   The Policy Framework Regarding the
          Withdrawal from the Labor Force

Anticipated Retirement under the Private Sector Wage-Earner Scheme

The public pension system is financed by tax-deductible employer and employee contributions and by contributions from the federal government's budget on a pay-as-you-go (PAYG) basis. Social security benefits are indexed to the cost of living and from time to time adjusted on a purely discretionary basis to the growth rate of the economy.

A pivotal year in the pension systems of the private sector wage earners is the year 1967. As a result of the merger of several existing pension schemes for different categories of workers the pension system takes on its current form. The basic attributes of the scheme are its PAYG financing mechanism, and the determination of a normal age of retirement set at sixty-five for men and at sixty for women. Anticipated retirement is allowed up to five years before the normal retirement age. Early retirement is accompanied by an actuarial reduction of 5 percent of the benefits by year of anticipation to compensate for the longer period of benefit claiming and the shorter period of contributions. The pension benefit is calculated on the basis of a forty-five-year career for men and forty-year career for women. In this framework, retirement at the age of sixty-four, without reduction of the benefits, is allowed for men who have already forty-five years of career or who have been employed in severe work conditions. A special treatment is applicable to veterans, resistance fighters, and deported people who benefited from a national recognition. As of 1969, they can anticipate the date of retirement by a maximum of five years without any reduction of benefits. Special regimes also remain in place for some specific sectors, such as most notably for coal mining and the maritime sector.

In 1977, a first step is taken to allow for early retirement within the aforementioned general pension system. The special early retirement schemes ("Régimes de prépension spéciale") give disabled workers or long-term unemployed at least sixty years of age for men and of fifty-five for women a bonus equal to the difference between the actual pension and the one they would receive if it was not reduced by the "5 percent rule." This specific early retirement system is rather short-lived and is only applicable for a few years. It is formally terminated in 1979 for disabled workers and in 1982 for unemployed.

In 1983, a new scheme of early retirement is introduced within the framework of the pension system. The program of "Prépension de retraite" allows for male workers retiring with a maximum of five years of anticipation without reduction of the benefits if the employer commits to replacing the worker by an unemployed who is benefiting from a full-time compensation from the unemployment insurance. This second early retirement scheme will only end in 1991 with the introduction of the concept of a flexible retirement age in the pension system. Since 1987 (for women) and 1991 (for men), workers can freely choose the age of retirement without reduction of benefits as soon as age sixty, while maintaining separate normal retirement ages and full-career requirements for the two sexes. This means that the system has become significantly more flexible and generous as both the "prépension de retraite" and the "5 percent rule" are no longer applicable. As a consequence, early retirement possibilities for women are significantly worsened, as before 1987 they could retire at a minimum age of fifty-five, which is now no longer possible.

The last reform affecting workers in our analysis dates back to 1997. Following up on a ruling by the European court of Justice requiring Belgium to put an end to the discrimination against men in the wage-earner pension system, the government decides to align the treatment of men and women by raising the female full career condition and the associated normal retirement age to the one applicable to men. Since 1997, the compulsory age of retirement for women has gradually been raised to sixty-one in 1997, sixty-two in 2000, sixty-three in 2003, sixty-four in 2006, and will attain sixty-five in 2009, with the corresponding increase in the full-career requirement from forty to forty-five years. While aimed at eliminating discrimination, the measure has also a clearly beneficial impact in budgetary terms and contributes positively to the longer term viability of the regime.

Finally, the most recent reform to retirement incentives is introduced into the system in early 2007. As a result of the Intergenerational Solidarity Pact[3] negotiated between the social partners and the government in late 2005, workers working beyond the age of sixty-two or beyond forty-four years of career can benefit from a pension supplement. The pension bonus of an amount of two euros per day worked beyond these limits augments the annual benefit payable, and this independently of the wage earned or the contributions accumulated. As such, it can be seen as a much stronger relative incentive for lower-wage earners than for higher-wage earners.

Conventional Early Retirement

Next to the wage-earner pension system, a parallel system of supplementary benefits for early retirement is created in 1973 for the old workers in case of firing: the conventional early retirement ("la Prépension conventionelle"). The announced goal of the scheme—which is not run by the pension administration—is to contribute toward a better distribution of

---

3. The Belgian Intergenerational Solidarity Pact includes some thirty measures aimed at reducing early retirement without changing the legal retirement age or current benefits already granted. Measures include limiting the number of people taking early retirement, stimulating employers to retain or hire older workers as well as making early retirement less attractive for both workers and employers.

jobs between young and old. The program intends to achieve this goal by insuring a decent income to old workers that are forced to retire earlier than the normal pension age.

At the beginning, workers of age sixty and above who lose their job are eligible for the benefits of the system. One condition to be eligible for the regime is that the worker has been laid off by his employer, and a further condition stipulates that the employer has to recruit a person benefiting from full-time unemployment benefits as a replacement for the worker. The laid off elderly worker is then, in his turn, entitled to unemployment benefits with a top-up complementary benefit paid by the employer. This complementary benefit is equal to half the difference between the net wage and the unemployment benefit. A particularity of the system is that these early retirees are exempted from job search and—as for all unemployed—the time spent in the early retirement program is fully credited in the earnings file for pension purposes. As the crediting in the earnings history is done at a constant real value, it means that the worker's only financial loss is the immediate loss of purchasing power due to the lower level of the combined benefits with respect to the net wage previously earned.

If initially the age of early retirement is set at sixty, the limit is rapidly lowered by means of collective bargaining agreements within industries. As a result, there ultimately exists a variety of different regimes with different career requirements, minimum ages, replacement of the worker, and so forth, for different sectors and companies. In front of this imbroglio, the legislation is harmonized in 1986 by setting the minimum age at fifty-eight years. However, numerous exceptions persist with respect to the general rules. For example, while workers below the age of sixty do in theory have to be replaced when they are put onto early retirement, this is not the case for companies that are considered in economic difficulty or in restructuring, or if the company is closing or unable to find a suitable replacement. Similarly, while the age of fifty-eight is a priori the minimum access age, a lower age is possible in some sectors (steel, glass, textile, etc.) at the ages of fifty-five, fifty-six, or fifty-seven, depending on more stringent career conditions. Similar exceptions exist for some workers in the construction sector and some who work in shifts. Even more pronounced reductions in the minimum age are possible when the company is recognized as being in economic difficulty, under which case the age can be brought down to fifty-two years, or even fifty in special circumstances.

As a consequence of the Intergenerational Solidarity Pact of 2005, the conditions for access to the conventional early retirement scheme are becoming more stringent for all cases of early retirement before the age of sixty but not directly linked to companies in economic difficulties. As of January 2008, the access to the conventional early retirement route at age fifty-eight is restricted to people with long working careers in a limitative list of "exhausting" occupations. The access to routes opening up at ages fifty-five, fifty-six, and fifty-seven will also progressively be tightened and the reference ages increased over the next five years.

Legal Early Retirement

Between 1976 and 1982, another program of early retirement coexists with those exposed previously. The so-called system of legal early retirement ("Prépension légale") holds that the workers have access to the same status as the one provided by the conventional early retirement system, with the major difference being that the worker did not need to be laid off by his employer but could freely opt into the system. As a consequence of this different setting, the cost of the complementary benefit is not supported by the employer but by the social security budget with the restriction that the employer has to hire a young unemployed aged less than thirty and benefiting from full-time unemployment compensation. Access to this scheme is possible under an age condition of sixty for men and fifty-five for women.

Part-Time Early Retirement and the System of Career Breaks

In 1993 the possibility of work and half-time early retirement is introduced into the Belgian landscape. Access to the status is conditional on a written agreement between the worker and his employer. Further conditions relate to the age of the worker (no lower than fifty-five) as well as the replacement of the worker by a fully indemnified unemployed for the reduced portion of his schedule. This path is complex and is chosen by very few people—less than 1,000 people are registered in 2005.

Another route to early retirement is opened by the career break scheme, which is originally introduced in 1985 but later modified in 2001 to make it more flexible for early retirement. It allows workers to reduce their working hours or take a career break for any reason, while maintaining their social insurance protection and even usually getting a career break benefit. The scheme specifically attempts to allow workers age fifty and above to reduce their working hours and thus permit a progressive shift into retirement. It allows both a reduction to a four-fifth schedule and a reduction to a half-time schedule.

Aged Unemployed Exempted from Job Search

The last exit path out of the labor market is known as the regime for the "Old aged unemployed," a status that is introduced in 1985 into the Belgian social insurance landscape. According to this regime, an unemployed person aged at least fifty-five and who is out of his job for at least two years is exempted of job search and continues to receive the unemployment benefits without any restrictions in time or in availability for the job market. In 1996, the age of admission to the system is lowered to the age of fifty and the period of joblessness is lowered to one year. As a result, this scheme is widely used in the Belgian retirement landscape. In its most extreme version, employers use it to separate from older workers by compensating them with (large) lump sum compensations/side payments—this way avoiding the more complicated and stringent conventional early retirement route. The latter mechanism is also known in the Belgian context by the name of "Canada Dry" retirement arrangements, as it looks and tastes like early retirement but it formally is none.[4]

Faced with the growing importance of these arrangements, the government progressively introduces changes to the legislation to slow down the spread of its use and abuse. Since July 2004, new entrants to the system have to satisfy more stringent conditions to access the waiver with respect to the availability for job search. Under the new rules, only workers age fifty-eight and above or with very long careers can still benefit from the full job search waiver, while those below fifty-eight still have to be available for the labor market. However, while the younger jobless are increasingly subject to stricter controls of their availability for the job market, these same rules are not enforced on those age fifty and above—hence, making the changes less dramatic than they may seem at first sight.

Figures 1.1 and 1.2 present early exit routes over the period 1980 to 2005. They show for each year, at January 31, the percentage of men and women recorded as beneficiaries of each program. On both figures, we see how the structure changed over time with the introduction of new exit paths to retirement, namely the aged unemployed scheme in 1985 and its extension in 1996.

1.2.2   Specific Unemployment Policies Targeted Toward the Young

A specificity of the Belgian social insurance system is the generalized availability of unemployment benefits (called "waiting allowance") for young people on the pure basis of education. As of 1945 unemployment benefits are given on the basis of studies. Initially it is only implemented for people that have followed vocational schooling. Formally, there is no age limit but the individual has to claim benefits in the first year following the end of his studies. In 1951, the status is extended to people having completed apprenticeships. The waiting period before claiming the first benefit is set at seventy-five days. In 1968, the list of admissible graduates is extended to all secondary education levels (technical or general) and the age limit was generally set at twenty-five years of age. In 1980, the maximum age is pushed up to twenty-six, the waiting period increased from seventy-five days to 150 days, and in 1983 the one-year deadline on first claiming is eliminated. In 1985, the possibility of first claiming these benefits is introduced for people aged between twenty-six and thirty subject to a waiting period of 300 days. The

---

4. This alludes to an old European commercial for Canada Dry ginger ale that was said to have the color of beer without being it.

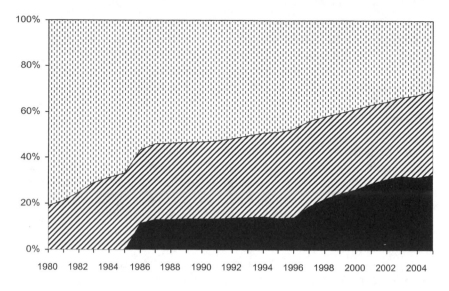

■ Aged unemployed ☑ Conventional early retirement ☐ Anticipated retirement

Fig. 1.1   Exit paths to early retirement—Men
Source: Belgostat and National Office of Pension (ONP-RVP).

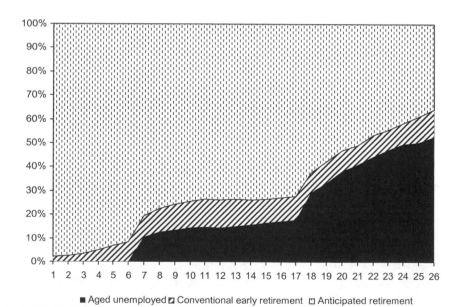

■ Aged unemployed ☑ Conventional early retirement ☐ Anticipated retirement

Fig. 1.2   Exit paths to early retirement—Women
Source: Belgostat and National Office of Pension (ONP-RVP).

year 1994 is the last major reform of the system with waiting periods further increased for people belonging to different age brackets below the age of thirty. The new standards are 155 days for those aged less than eighteen, 233 days between eighteen and twenty-five, and 310 days between twenty-six and thirty, corresponding to six, nine, and twelve months, respectively.

Currently, almost every young person leaving school in Belgium is entitled to unemployment benefits without any work requirement. It is common for young people aged less than thirty to sign up with the regional Public Employment Service as a job seeker immediately upon receiving one's school diploma (usually high school or college/university). This enrollment entitles the graduate to an unemployment benefit awarded after the above-mentioned age-dependent waiting period. This unemployment benefit—which is awarded for an indefinite period of time—was at first based on the level of education attained by the graduate. Over time, it has progressively evolved into a lump sum amount, which is purely a factor of the family status of the person claiming the benefit. Administratively, the young unemployed receiving the "waiting allowance" is considered a job seeker and technically enters the category of persons benefiting from full-time unemployment benefits.

A number of jobs benefiting from tax and contributions exemptions are open to the young unemployed at the end of the waiting period. Consequently, when the waiting period increases one observes a similar increase in the rate of youth unemployment (ONEM 2001).

1.3   Lump of Labor Fallacy and Youth Unemployment in Belgium

The idea that forcing elderly workers out of the labor market before the statutory age of retirement would provide jobs for the unemployed young has been for a long time widely accepted in several European countries, particularly in Belgium, where youth unemployment is particularly high both in absolute and in relative terms. For most economists and (fortunately) an increasing number of Belgians, this view is based on the erroneous belief in a fixed amount of work, what is sometimes dubbed a "boxed economy." Economists call this allegedly widespread view the "lump of labor fallacy."

Those who make the fallacy claim fail to offer specific evidence of the supposed belief in a fixed amount of work. Yet it is too convenient to yield the burden of the proof on the advocates of the lump of labor fallacy.[5] In this study we revisit the question of whether pre-retirement is a means to free up jobs for the young. Boldrin et al. (1999) have started to do so by comparing

5. This view is also called the lump-of-output fallacy since it assumes that output is unaffected by the job reallocation. While it seems that labor force exiting will affect the wage rate and inflation and then output (Layard, Nickell, and Jackman 1991).

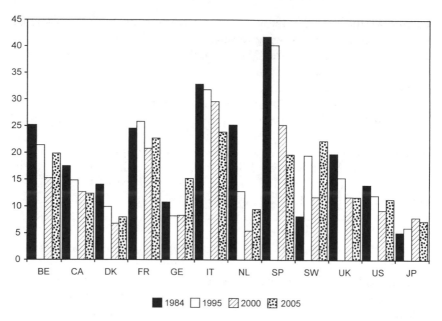

■ 1984 ☐ 1995 ▨ 2000 ⬚ 2005

Fig. 1.3   Youth fifteen to twenty-four unemployment rates in OECD countries
Source: OECD labor force database (2006a).

for several countries and several periods the relation between pre-retirement and youth unemployment. Their conclusion is negative but their methodology is questionable. They plot the exit rates from the labor force of older workers and the variation in the unemployment rate of young workers and do not find any negative link between the two variables.

What we want to do in this section is to look at the main characteristics of youth unemployment in Belgium over the last decades and to see whether such unemployment would decrease with an increase in the demand of labor. Implicitly, we assume that pre-retirement policies imply an increased demand for labor and that such a demand is relevant for the unemployed young. In other words, for the sake of the argument, we follow the reasoning of the advocates of the lump of labor.

Belgian youth unemployment is high and has tended to increase in recent years from 15 percent in 2000 to 20 percent in 2005. The youth unemployment rate is about three times higher than the adult unemployment.

Figure 1.3 shows the differences across a number of Organization for Economic Cooperation and Development (OECD) countries over the years 1984, 1995, 2000, and 2005 for the rate of unemployment of the young age fifteen to twenty-four. One sees that Belgium is in the same league as France, Italy, Spain, and Sweden—countries with very high youth unemployment.

A key feature of Belgian youth unemployment is that it concerns unskilled workers. Figure 1.4 gives the evolution of unemployment for three levels of education. One clearly sees that the rate of unemployment of unskilled has been increasing over the period 1992 to 2004 for both genders and is above the double of the rate of unemployment of young with medium or high levels of education.

Consider four standard explanations for youth unemployment in Belgium:

- Lack of professional training
- Mismatching
- Unemployment compensation combined with family arrangements
- Minimum wages and employment regulation

1. In Belgium, the transition from school to work is very abrupt. Full-time education is the norm, with dual apprenticeship schemes remaining marginal. Internship is not an integral part of a student's school or university career.

2. Mismatching is another important cause of unemployment. Mismatching can be due to the educational system that is not sufficiently aimed at the needs of the industrial world but also to the lack of geographical mobility.

3. As we have seen, the young are entitled to unemployment compensations even without working experience. For unskilled young, these compensations are not high. However, combined with the possibility of staying within the family, these compensations generate a rather high reservation wage.

4. Belgium has a minimum wage, which is often viewed as a cause of unemployment, particularly among young workers. There is not much difference between the wages earned by young people and by adults. These relatively high wages paid to young workers can act as a barrier to the recruitment of unskilled young. Another barrier is the relatively strict set of employment regulation protecting insiders, coupled with the rules restricting the temporary contracts that many young workers have.

Assume that forcing elderly workers out of the labor force through all sorts of routes such as early retirement, disability, and unemployment generates employment opportunities for the young. This assumption assumes that the labor market is a zero-sum game, which clearly is rejected by most economists. Making this assumption, we want to show that even under this implausible case, it is not even sure that exiting elderly workers from the labor market does imply employment for the unemployed.

With mismatching, insufficient training, and high reservation wages as explanatory factors of unemployment, it is unlikely that increasing the quantity of jobs will generate more employment of the young. In other words, to

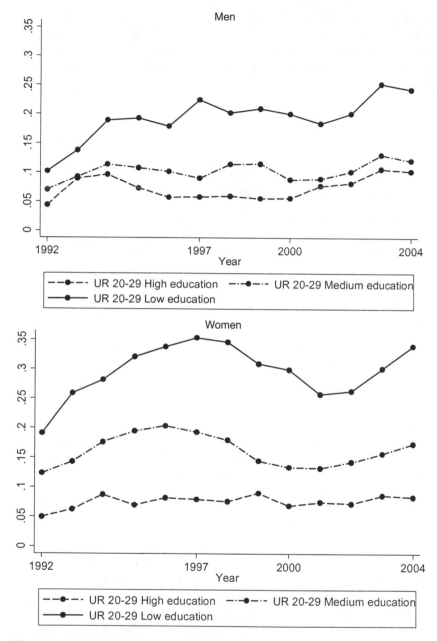

Fig. 1.4   Youth unemployment rates by education level and gender
Source: European Labor Force Surveys (1983–2004).

foster youth employment, the solution is not early retirement but a better integration of the entering workforce as well as a reform of the educational system, of the unemployment insurance, and of the minimum wage.[6] More importantly, a drastic change in values is crucial. But, as Kipling would say, "that is another story."

1.4   The Data

1.4.1   Labor Force Data

We subdivide the population into three subgroups: the older workers (fifty-five to sixty-four years of age), the prime aged workers (twenty-five to fifty-four) and the young (twenty to twenty-four). The precise cutoff points between these different groups are clearly of a key importance and mostly dictated by the institutional setting. Since in Belgium education is compulsory until the age of eighteen and data is generally available in five-year age brackets, we do not consider any five-year age bracket, including people subject to compulsory schooling. Therefore, the lowest age considered is the age of twenty.[7]

Our analysis draws heavily on the European Labor Force Survey (LFS) for the time period 1983 to 2004. The data are used to derive labor force measures such as employment rate (ER), unemployment rate (UR), and labor force participation rate (LFP). Similarly, other demographic indicators are also computed for the individuals studied using the LFS data. For deriving the labor force indicators, we relied on the internationally recognized definitions as proposed by the International Labor Organization (ILO) rather than relying on administrative classifications.[8]

Other data are derived from OECD databases. In particular, the gross domestic product (GDP) indicators come from the OECD national accounts database (2006b),

Figures 1.5 and 1.6 present some illustrative data to set the stage. They illustrate the weak link between the unemployment (UR) of the two younger age groups in Belgium as compared to the labor force participation rate of the older workers (LFP). There does not seem to be a uniform relation between the labor force participation of the elderly and the employment possibilities of the young. While during the earlier period, reduced labor

6. High Employment Council (2007) showed that a large part of the unemployment in Brussels and Flanders are of foreign origin.

7. Furthermore, Belgium has a high rate of school attendance even between ages eighteen and twenty. In 1997, 90 percent of the young age eighteen to twenty were still at school.

8. This means, for example, that people qualified as early retirees or aged unemployed according to the Belgian administrative classification would be classified as being out of the labor force under ILO standards.

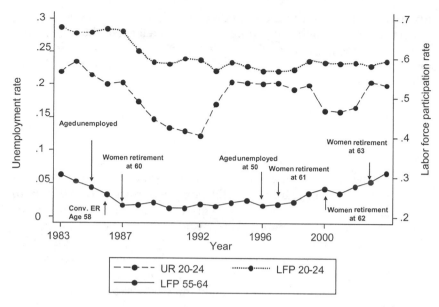

Fig. 1.5   Trends in unemployment and labor force participation of the young compared to the labor force participation of the old

Source: European Labor Force Surveys (1983–2004).

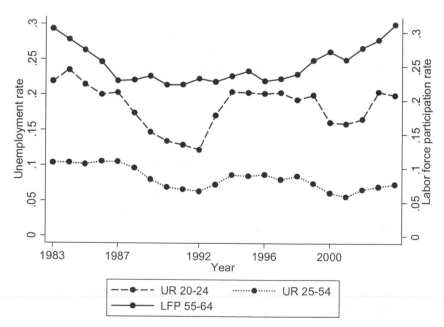

Fig. 1.6   Trends in unemployment of the young and prime aged workers compared to the labor force participation of the old

Source: European Labor Force Surveys (1983–2004).

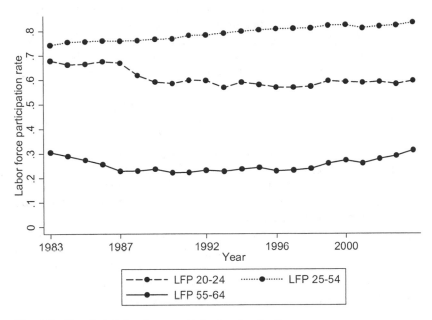

Fig. 1.7   **Trends in labor force participation for the three age groups**
Source: European Labor Force Surveys (1983–2004).

force participation of the elderly seemed to move in parallel with lower unemployment for the young, this relation does not hold anymore since the middle of the 1990s. These results are hard to match with any specific policy change described in section 1.2. While the most important policy change was undoubtedly the reform of the 5 percent rule in 1991, no major effect seems to be observable in the labor market outcomes. On the contrary, this reform has been followed by a large increase in youth unemployment rate.

Finally, it is interesting to compare the labor force participation of the old to that of the young and the prime age as in figure 1.7. The graph reveals that the young are the only age group with a constantly falling labor force partici-pation rate over the entire time period. Prime age workers have experienced a sustained growth in activity over the entire time period, whereas the same is also true for the older group since the middle of the 1990s.

1.4.2   The Inducement to Retire

Beyond these labor force data, we use another set of data on early retire-ment, namely indicators of incentive measures. The reason for constructing separate incentive measures instead of using the survey data is that we want to use a measure of the inducement to retire to explain labor force behavior. To avoid endogeneity problems in our ensuing empirical analysis, we need to develop a simulation approach by which we compute hypothetical benefit levels for a typical worker for all possible year and age cells covered by the labor force data that we described in the previous subsection.

To compute such aggregate incentive measures we perform benefit simulations akin to those presented by Jousten et al. (2005) for all cohorts under study. We then use the various benefit amounts derived for a hypothetical representative individual corresponding to the median of the income distribution. We compute these benefits profiles for the three main exit paths that this median individual may encounter: unemployment insurance, conventional early retirement, and normal retirement. Each of these paths yields different benefits. We then compute for each possible age and year as well as for each sex the present discounted value of these benefits using a 3 percent discount rate. We will continue to call the thus derived present discounted values Social Security Wealth (W) in accordance with the previous literature on individual retirement incentives.[9]

Once these W figures are obtained year by year for each individual exit path and possible retirement age, we aggregate those three incentives into one aggregate W incentive measure that represents the global incentive to retire according to year and to age. Expressed in symbols, this is equivalent to deriving

$$W = W_{pen} + p_{unem} \times \max[0, W_{unem} - W_{pen}] + p_{ear} \times \max[0, W_{ear} - W_{pens}],$$

where p_{unem} and p_{ear} represents the cohort and year-specific probabilities of exiting by the specified routes of unemployment or early retirement.[10] For pure reasons of simplicity, we assume that over the age span ranging from fifty to sixty-five the whole cohort leaves the labor market and goes into retirement—a rather reasonable assumption in the Belgian context given the quasi-compulsory nature of retirement at the latest when reaching the full retirement age.[11] The exit probabilities are calculated using the LFS for the period of 1983 to 2004, and the results are rescaled to obtain a total departure by the age of sixty-five. Finally we average over sex to obtain one W by cohort.

Figure 1.8 illustrates the trends in the incentive measure as experienced by successive cohorts of hypothetical Belgian median wage earners. It displays a secular upward trend in benefit levels for the successive cohorts, combined with a hump-shaped profile of benefit for each individual cohort. The only major benefit change over the period under study was the change in the

9. All these incentives are expressed in 2002 euros.

10. We use the empirically observed age- and cohort-specific cumulative hazard until the normal retirement as a proxy for the probabilities of departure through the early retirement and unemployment pathways.

11. Technically, an individual can continue to work but largely loses his protection against layoffs. Furthermore, the continuation of work is only possible with the explicit written agreement on the part of the employer.

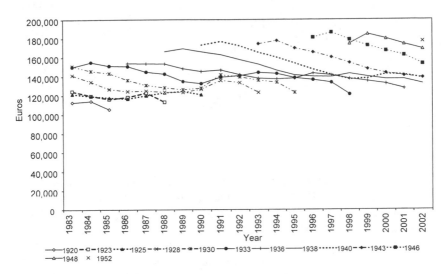

Fig. 1.8   SSW for selected cohorts by year
Source: Results from our own simulation.

actuarial adjustment rule in 1991. Unsurprisingly, it has the biggest impact on cohorts close to the early retirement age of sixty—which translates into an upward bump in the incentive variable for older cohorts in 1991. Other factors, such as the generalization of the exemption from job search in the middle of the 1990s, have a very limited effect, thus leading one to conjecture that even in the absence of a formal ruling unemployment beneficiaries were anyway already de facto exempted from job search. The impact of the expansion of the conventional early retirement provisions to the age of fifty-eight in 1986 was modest for retirement incentives, hence indicating that the prevalence of other routes must have been such that the importance of this legislative change was rather limited. Further aggregating up these year- and age-specific W, it is possible to compute a yearly index that takes into account the various incentives by age. We proceed to estimate two incentive indexes that are weighted sums of incentive indicators. The first one, denoted $\overline{W}$, is purely based on the age- and-year specific W thus derived. The second indicator—that we will call the "inducement to retire," denoted $\overline{I}$—is a mix of the concept of W and that of Peak Value (PV):

$$\overline{W}(y) = \sum_{a=50}^{a=65}\left[\frac{P(a, y)}{\sum_{a=50}^{a=65} P(a, y)} \right]$$

$$\times \left[\frac{\sum_{t=0}^{a-50} W(a-t, y-t) \times \text{LFP}(a-t, y-t-1)}{\sum_{t=0}^{a-50} \text{LFP}(a-t, y-t-1)} \right]$$

$$\bar{I}(y) = \sum_{a=50}^{a=65} \left[\frac{P(a, y)}{\sum_{a=50}^{a=65} P(a, y)} \right]$$

$$\times \left[\frac{\sum_{t=0}^{a-50} I(a - t, y - t) \times \text{LFP}(a - t, y - t - 1)}{\sum_{t=0}^{a-50} \text{LFP}(a - t, y - t - 1)} \right]$$

with

(1) $I(a, y) = W(a, y) + \alpha[W(a, y) - PV(a, y)].$

In the above expressions, W represents the Social Security Wealth, and PV, the Peak Value. The PV at age a is defined as the maximum W the individual can obtain by optimally choosing the time of retirement between the current moment y and the statutory retirement age. Variable LFP is the labor force participation and P is the proportion of retired persons of that age in that year, and both variables are derived using the LFS.

In equation (1) the concept I summarizes two broad pieces of information. The first element on the right-hand side expresses the idea that the larger W, the larger the wealth a person has at his avail, and thus the easier it is for him to retire early. The second term expresses the idea that by waiting till the optimal time—as summarized by the gain in present discounted value between immediate retirement and the optimal retirement maximizing the present discounted value—the individual faces an incentive to stay at work. Finally, α is a coefficient that reflects the notion of discounting future revenue gains with respect to present wealth—beyond the pure effect of financial discounting as captured by the 3 percent discount rate.[12] The idea behind this parameterization is to capture the individual's possible impatience, making them less willing or incapable ($\alpha = 0$) to consider future revenue or wealth gains before they become available.

We endogenously estimate the parameter value for α using two different procedures. The results of these estimations are displayed in table 1.1. The equation we estimate is given by

(2) $\text{LFP}_{old,t} = \gamma \overline{W}_t + \varphi(\overline{W_t - PV_t}) + \phi X_t + \varepsilon_t.$

The first two terms on the right-hand side of equation (2) correspond to the components of the incentive indicator I, and X is a vector of control variables. The implied value of α thus corresponds to the ratio of φ over γ.

Then, we validate the previous results using an iteration process on φ and γ that attempts to maximize R^2 as an objective function—a process one could qualify as a simplified maximum likelihood approach.

In table 1.1, the value of α given by both iteration and regression pro-

---

12. Setting the financial discount rate to infinity is equivalent to assuming the individual is perfectly liquidity constrained.

Table 1.1   **Estimating the parameters of I**

	γ	φ	α	R^2	Implied $\bar{I}$ weighting
1. Iterating over γ and φ with 0.25 intervals and regressing LFP of old on $\bar{I}$ and covariates	0.5	−1.25	−2.5	0.924	$0.5 \times \overline{W} - 1.25 \times \overline{W-PV}$
2. Iterating over φ with $\gamma = 1$ with 0.25 intervals and regressing LFP of old on $\bar{I}$ and covariates	1	−2.25	−2.25	0.924	$1 \times \overline{W} - 2.25 \times \overline{W-PV}$
3. Time series regression of LFP of old on $\overline{W}$ and $\overline{W-PV}$	0.748*	−1.745***	−2.4	0.924	$0.748 \times \overline{W} - 1.745 \times \overline{W-PV}$

Notes: Reported is the coefficient on the inducement to retire in thousands. Covariates include GDP per capita, the growth in GDP per capita, and the share of GDP coming from manufacturing sector, α corresponds to the ratio of φ over γ.

***Significant at the 1 percent level.
**Significant at the 5 percent level.
*Significant at the 10 percent level.

cedures is negative, which is inconsistent with the methodology proposed. The reason for such a result can be found in the methodology itself. The computation of this indicator of the inducement to retire likely results in an overly aggregated and averaged indicator, especially in the context of the multitude of early retirement pathways as present in Belgium. In the next section, we will only use $\overline{W}$ as an incentive since the negative value of α leads us to assume that it is nil in the econometric estimations. If $\alpha = 0$, $\bar{I}$ is equal to $\overline{W}$. We will come back to the estimation of $\bar{I}$ in section 1.6 where we study women and men separately.

1.5   Regression Analysis

Moving beyond the purely descriptive analysis of the previous section, we now turn to ordinary least squares (OLS) regression analysis. It proceeds in two steps. The first step is an econometric study of the direct relationship between the employment of the old and the employment of the young. The second step is an analysis of how the incentives faced by the old directly influence the employment outcomes of the young.

For the first type of analysis, we estimate both regressions in levels and in differences. We settle on four specifications: in levels, with a three-year lag and also with five-year difference and five-year log difference. The levels regression links the labor force performance measures of the young and middle-aged to those of the old:

$$A_t = \theta + \beta B_t + \delta X_t + \varepsilon_t$$

$$A_t = \theta + \beta B_{t-3} + \delta X_t + \varepsilon_t$$

where A_t is the UR or the ER for either youth or prime age population. Similarly, by extension, we consider a regression of the percent of young still in an educational program (SCH). Variable B_t is either the labor force participation rate of the old workers, and X_t is a set of covariates that includes GDP per capita, the growth in GDP per capita, and the share of GDP coming from manufacturing sector.

The difference specification takes the following form:

$$A_{t+5} - A_t = \theta + \beta[B_{t+5} - B_t] + \delta[X_{t+5} - X_t] + \varepsilon_{t+5} - \varepsilon_t$$

$$\ln A_{t+5} - \ln A_t = \theta + \beta[\ln B_{t+5} - \ln B_t] + \delta[\ln X_{t+5} - \ln X_t] + \varepsilon_{t+5} - \varepsilon_t.$$

Results are reported in table 1.2. We run the regressions with and without control variables. As exposed previously, table 1.2 presents four alternative specifications in order to identify clearly the likely effects of elderly labor force participation on younger labor outcomes. The table also shows the estimated effect of the activity of elderly on the proportion of youth in school. One immediate observation is that elderly participation seems to play a more important role when controlling for other effects. Thus, we will pay more attention to these results.

Whatever one of the first three specifications, when they are significant, the coefficients are of the same sign and magnitude. Concerning the youth regressions, the results are contradictory. The labor force participation of the old appears to have a positive impact on youth unemployment rate and also a positive impact on the youth employment rate.[13] On the contrary, it has, when significant, a negative effect on the rate of schooling. As explained before, the rate of employment is much more relevant to account for activity in youth than one minus the rate of unemployment. We may thus conclude that the elderly participation has a positive effect on youth employment and schooling.

The five-year log difference specification contrasts with these results. The effect on youth unemployment disappears but we still have the same kind of effects on the employment and schooling. The regressions between older and prime age workers seem to display a slight substitution between those workers. Yet for the five-year log difference specification, we do not find any effect on youth employment but a negative effect on unemployment.

We now turn to the second exercise that tries to relate the incentives faced

---

13. It might be useful to remember that unemployment rate is not one minus employment rate. If we denote P total population, L active population, and U unemployed population, the unemployment rate is U/L and the employment rate is $(L - U)/P$.

Table 1.2   **Direct effect of elderly labor outcomes on the young (women and men combined)**

	Youth 20 to 24			Prime age 25 to 54	
Specification	UR	ER	SCH	UR	ER
	No controls				
Levels	0.539**	0.067	0.081	0.056	0.094
	(0.217)	(0.219)	(0.278)	(0.124)	(0.262)
3-year lag	0.328	0.589**	−0.627*	0.337**	−0.589**
	(0.278)	(0.235)	(0.297)	(0.116)	(0.248)
5-year difference	0.591	0.292	−0.092	0.116	−0.089
	(0.357)	(0.208)	(0.171)	(0.136)	(0.089)
5-year log	0.883	0.152	−0.075	0.296	−0.039
difference	(0.549)	(0.111)	(0.132)	(0.448)	(0.032)
	With controls				
Levels	0.619***	0.185	−0.118	0.151**	−0.116**
	(0.180)	(0.157)	(0.129)	(0.068)	(0.054)
3-year lag	0.534**	0.372*	−0.259	0.273***	−0.262***
	(0.221)	(0.211)	(0.173)	(0.076)	(0.048)
5-year difference	0.683***	0.351**	−0.099	0.198***	−0.166**
	(0.139)	(0.125)	(0.153)	(0.038)	(0.056)
5-year log	0.093	0.408***	−0.330*	0.092	0.408***
difference	(0.294)	(0.108)	(0.169)	(0.294)	(0.107)

Notes: Reported is the coefficient on elderly participation rate. Covariates include GDP per capita, the growth in GDP per capita, and the share of GDP coming from manufacturing sector.
***Significant at the 1 percent level.
**Significant at the 5 percent level.
*Significant at the 10 percent level.

by the elderly to the labor market outcomes of the younger cohorts. As discussed in section 1.4, this approach has the advantage of being less prone to endogeneity problems than the approach just presented.

Table 1.3 presents only the results for $\overline{W}$ (and not for $\overline{I}$) since the estimations of section 1.4 lead us to consider a value of α equal to zero. The variable $\overline{W}$ explains very well the fall in labor force participation of older persons, which is a prerequisite for using it as an instrumental variable in the following estimations. The regression coefficients when considering younger cohorts outcomes are hardly significant in levels but we observe higher significance with the five-years' difference specification. The estimates confirm results obtained with labor outcomes regressions. It is difficult to observe any clear result concerning the younger people, especially if we have some doubt about youth unemployment rate as a suitable indicator. The effect, if any, on the prime age workers indicates some substitution between elderly and prime age workers.

Table 1.3   Direct effect of the inducement to retire (women and men combined)

Using $\overline{W}$ as an explanatory variable	In level			In 5-years difference		
	Coefficient	Standard error	R^2	Coefficient	Standard error	R^2
LFP of old	−0.820***	0.101	0.823	−0.806***	0.132	0.819
Unemployment of young	−0.487**	0.226	0.493	−0.799***	0.078	0.978
Employment of young	−0.148	0.183	0.547	−0.125	0.169	0.688
School of young	−0.069	0.135	0.849	−0.237*	0.108	0.735
Unemployment of prime age	−0.059	0.084	0.720	−0.179***	0.051	0.929
Employment of prime age	0.040	0.061	0.963	0.081	0.066	0.698

Notes: Reported is the coefficient on the inducement to retire in thousands. Covariates include GDP per capita, the growth in GDP per capita, and the share of GDP coming from manufacturing sector.
***Significant at the 1 percent level.
**Significant at the 5 percent level.
*Significant at the 10 percent level.

1.6   Alternative Specification: Women and Men Separated

Until now we have considered the aggregate labor market performance. Realities change when we differentiate according to sex. Indeed, the labor outcomes of men and women have been largely different in the past decades. The growing participation of women, for example, has clearly changed the situation of the labor market. Figures 1.9, 1.10, and 1.11 present these different patterns. On figure 1.9, we observe that if both activity of young men and women has slightly decreased during the period, the unemployment rates of the two groups have evolved in a different direction. The young men unemployment rate has increased while the young women unemployment rate has decreased. On figure 1.10, the unemployment rate of prime-age men and women is displayed. Here we also see that the women unemployment rate has decreased during the period considered, which is not the case for men. Finally, figure 1.11 presents the labor force participation of the three age groups. Both older and prime age women's activity has been increasing.

While the earlier regressions only took into account the average behavior of labor outcomes in Belgium, we propose to run the same regressions when differentiating by sex the left-hand side. In other words, we still consider the effect of labor force participation of all elderly workers but we account for differences between young men and women. The previous figures show that in Belgium, the labor market performances of men and women are different. The idea is to explore whether the diverging labor outcomes of younger age

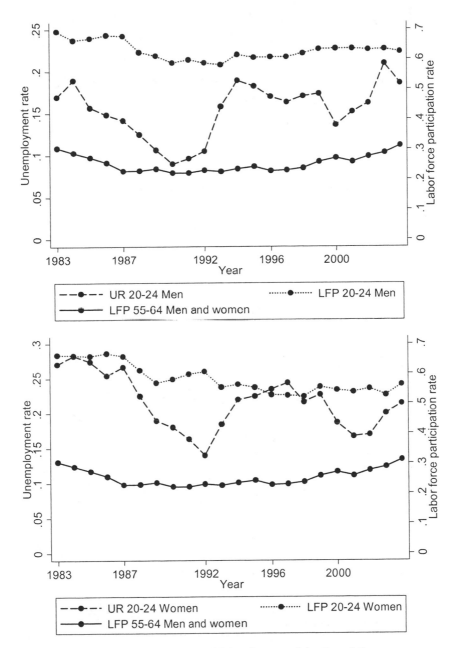

Fig. 1.9   Trends in unemployment and labor force participation of the young compared to the labor force participation of the old by sex

Source: European Labor Force Surveys (1983–2004).

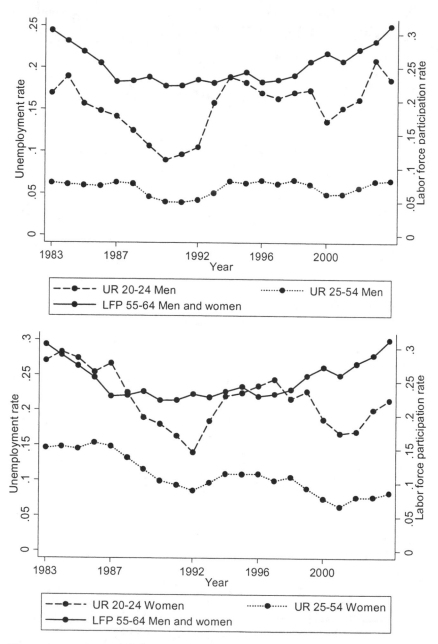

Fig. 1.10 Trends in unemployment of the young and prime aged workers compared to the labor force participation of the old by sex

Source: European Labor Force Surveys (1983–2004).

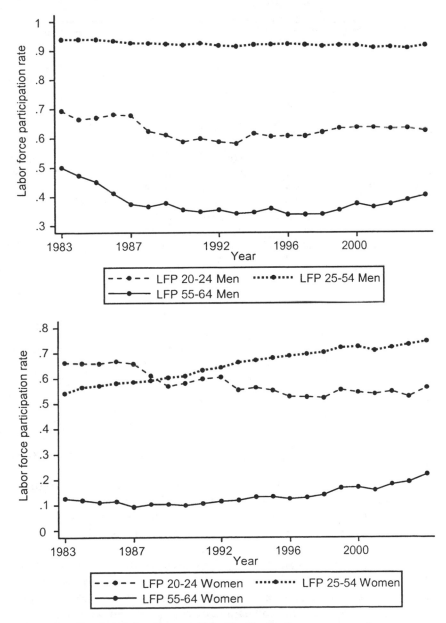

Fig. 1.11   Trends in labor force participation for the three age groups by sex
Source: European Labor Force Surveys (1983–2004).

Table 1.4   Direct effect of elderly labor outcomes on the young (women and men separated)

Specification	Youth 20–24				Prime age 25–54	
	UR	ER	SCH	"Ext."UR	UR	ER
	No controls					
Levels	0.536**	0.068	0.089	−0.157	0.053	0.104
	(0.252)	(0.272)	(0.205)	(0.214)	(0.181)	(0.858)
3-year lag	0.336	0.585*	−0.627***	0.042	0.341*	−0.597
	(0.301)	(0.327)	(0.227)	(0.267)	(0.197)	(1.001)
5-year	0.589**	0.293	−0.090	−0.202	0.115	−0.083
difference	(0.269)	(0.185)	(0.134)	(0.125)	(0.109)	(0.166)
5-year log	0.941**	0.154	−0.074	−0.305	0.331	−0.068
difference	(0.416)	(0.101)	(0.103)	(0.192)	(0.348)	(0.073)
	With controls					
Levels	0.619***	0.184	−0.117	−0.067	0.150	−0.111
	(0.164)	(0.131)	(0.109)	(0.102)	(0.090)	(0.247)
3-year lag	0.538**	0.369**	−0.258*	−0.111	0.274**	−0.261
	(0.203)	(0.177)	(0.148)	(0.137)	(0.105)	(0.278)
5-year	0.684***	0.349**	−0.098	−0.252*	0.198***	−0.159***
difference	(0.139)	(0.159)	(0.121)	(0.131)	(0.039)	(0.057)
5-year log	0.020	0.430***	−0.353**	−0.622**	−0.416**	−0.052
difference	(0.319)	(0.130)	(0.138)	(0.283)	(0.158)	(0.041)

Notes: Reporteds is the coefficient on elderly participation rate. Covariates include GDP per capita, the growth in GDP per capita, and the share of GDP coming from manufacturing sector.
***Significant at the 1 percent level.
**Significant at the 5 percent level.
*Significant at the 10 percent level.

groups have been differently influenced by the global labor force participation of older workers.

As presented in table 1.4, these new regressions do not give different results from those of table 1.2. Whatever the specification, the coefficients are of the same magnitude and display similar significance except for the level regression with controls. This is important since it shows that the results presented in table 1.2 are robust to taking into account differences between sexes. However, these estimates are still confusing for the youth. Table 1.4 displays also the effect of participation of older workers on a different indicator of youth outcome. We have seen in section 1.2 that the youth unemployment is very dependent on the institutional framework and for this reason it may not be a good indicator of the youth labor market performance. When dividing the youth population according to status, differentiating the unemployed, employed, and at school young people is not sufficient. There is still a proportion of individuals that do not belong to any of these categories. Think of the young people who are no longer attending schools but are also not looking for a job because of bad prospects of employment. The "extended"

Table 1.5   **Estimating the parameters of I (women and men separated)**

	γ	φ	α	R^2	Implied $\bar{I}$ weighting
1. Iterating over γ and φ with 0.25 intervals and regressing LFP of old on $\bar{I}$ and covariates	Any values when $\gamma = \varphi$		1	0.991	$1 \times \overline{W} + 1 \times \overline{W - PV}$
2. Iterating over φ with $\gamma = 1$ with 0.25 intervals and regressing LFP of old on $\bar{I}$ and covariates	1	1	1	0.991	$1 \times \overline{W} + 1 \times \overline{W - PV}$
3. Time series regression of LFP of old on $\overline{W}$ and $\overline{W - PV}$	−0.458***	−0.464***	1.01	0.991	$1 \times \overline{W} + 1.01 \times \overline{W - PV}$

Notes: Reported is the coefficient on the inducements to retire in thousands. Covariates include GDP per capita, the growth in GDP per capita, and the share of GDP coming from manufacturing sector and a sex dummy; α corresponds to the ratio of φ over γ.
***Significant at the 1 percent level.
**Significant at the 5 percent level.
*Significant at the 10 percent level.

unemployment indicator proposed in table 1.4 accounts for this group in addition to conventional unemployment. The coefficients are hardly significant, but they show that the activity of elderly has a negative effect on this indicator. With this result, one observes that the effect of the labor force participation of the old on the young seems to be running contrary to the boxed economy proposition.

As in section 1.5, we turn to models that links the incentives faced by the elderly to the labor market outcomes of the young. The new sample requires that we reestimate the parameter value for α as we did in section 1.4 for women and men together. In this case, we consider specific indicators of incentives for each sex since the inducement to retire has been different for women and men but we estimate the value of α pooling men and women together. Table 1.5 shows that the iteration and the regression procedures give the same result. Overall, α is equal to 1.

We perform levels regression and five-year difference regression using $\overline{W}$ and one construction of $\bar{I}$. We use $\alpha = 1.01$. Results of regressions are presented on table 1.6 and are very similar when we consider either $\overline{W}$ or $\bar{I}$. First, a larger inducement to retire leads to a negative effect on elderly labor force participation, both for levels and difference regressions. Second, levels regressions do not present any significant effect of the incentive to retire on either the unemployment or the employment of the young workers. The difference approach displays, on the contrary, a negative and significant effect on youth unemployment, which is in line with table 1.4 results. However, this should be read with a lot of caution. There does not

Table 1.6   Direct effect of the inducement to retire (women and men separated)

	Estimating inducement to retire on outcomes for the old and the young					
	In level			In 5-years difference		
	Coefficient	Standard error	R^2	Coefficient	Standard error	R^2
1. Using $\overline{W}$						
LFP of old	−0.720***	0.055	0.988	−0.699***	0.118	0.737
Unemployment of young	0.053	0.115	0.609	−0.757***	0.001	0.906
Employment of young	0.033	0.085	0.782	0.046	0.167	0.432
Extended unemployment of young	0.138**	0.056	0.855	0.221*	0.124	0.251
School of young	−0.172***	0.058	0.822	−0.268***	0.084	0.650
Unemployment of prime age	0.174***	0.046	0.866	−0.172***	0.038	0.908
Employment of prime age	−0.651***	0.090	0.977	0.045	0.055	0.917
2. Using implied $\overline{I}$ weighting from model 3 (see table 1.5): $1 \times W + 1.01 \times (W - PV)$						
LFP of old	−0.459***	0.029	0.991	−0.385***	0.047	0.829
Unemployment of young	−0.036	0.071	0.610	−0.381***	0.048	0.913
Employment of young	0.005	0.053	0.781	−0.022	0.082	0.432
Extended unemployment of young	0.088**	0.035	0.848	0.123**	0.060	0.387
School of young	−0.094**	0.037	0.812	−0.100**	0.045	0.588
Unemployment of prime age	0.077**	0.031	0.838	−0.086***	0.019	0.909
Employment of prime age	−0.329***	0.069	0.965	0.034	0.026	0.920

Notes: Reported is the coefficient on the inducement to retire in thousands. Covariates include GDP per capita, the growth in GDP per capita, and the share of GDP coming from manufacturing sector and a sex dummy.

***Significant at the 1 percent level.

**Significant at the 5 percent level.

*Significant at the 10 percent level.

seem to be any effect on the employment rate of the young, which is the key labor market outcome in our view. When we consider the "extended" unemployment indicator, the sign of the coefficient is reversed but still significant.

The results obtained for the prime age group, twenty-five- to fifty-four-years-old, are contradictory across levels and five-years' differences model specifications, both in table 1.4 and in table 1.5. Overall, we cannot draw any definitive conclusion with respect to the link between early retirement and activity rates among the prime age group.

1.7   Conclusions

Belgium is characterized by a relatively high rate of unemployment of the young and a low rate of activity of the elderly workers. The latter is the consequence of high incentives to exit the labor force and these incentives are generally justified in the name of fostering youth employment.

In this chapter we have tested the validity of such a belief. At the outset, we were not expecting too much from these tests for two reasons. First, theoretically one knows that there is no foundation for the idea that there would be such a thing as a fixed lump of labor, implying that less elderly workers means more young workers. Second, the nature of youth unemployment in Belgium is such that it is pretty insensitive to variations in labor demand, but rather is the result of structural weaknesses in the areas of education, unemployment insurance, and wage formation.

In order to proceed with this test, we have constructed average indicators of incentive toward early retirement and we have shown that these incentives explain well variations in activity rates among elderly workers. But when we relate either participation rate of the elderly or the incentive indicators to unemployment or employment of the young, the results are mixed and have to be taken with caution.

First it seems important to know which variable of youth labor market performance is relevant. We have seen that youth unemployment rate is largely influenced by the employment policies toward the young. In this respect it seems preferable to use the employment rate.

Second, we emphasize the sharp contrast between men and women. The results are, however, not different if we consider the aggregate labor market or if we make the distinction between men and women. We have shown that labor outcomes by gender have been slightly different over the period but they do not turn into different results than those obtained with aggregate labor market outcomes.

With these warnings in mind, we do not observe any clear positive link between the fall of labor force participation of elderly and youth employment. The lump of labor conjecture must be rejected for Belgium at least in the private sector to which this chapter is restricted.

References

Blondal, S., and S. Scarpetta. 1999. The retirement decision in OECD countries. Organization for Economic Cooperation and Development (OECD) Economics Department Working Paper no. 202. Paris: OECD Economics Department.

Boldrin, M., J. Dolado, J. Jimeno, and F. Perrachi. 1999. The future of pension in Europe. *Economic Policy* 29:289–320.

European Labour Force Surveys 1983–2004. Luxembourg: Eurostat.

Gruber, J., and D. Wise. 1999. *Social Security and retirement around the world.* Chicago: University of Chicago Press.

———. 2003. Social Security and retirement around the world: Micro-estimation. Chicago: University of Chicago Press.

High Employment Council. 2007. Rapport Annuel, Bruxelles. Available at: www .emploi.belgique.be.

Jousten, A., M. Lefèbvre, S. Perelman, and P. Pestieau. 2005. Social Security in Belgium: Distributive outcomes. Institute for the Study of Labor (IZA) Discussion Paper no. 1486.

Layard, R., S. Nickell, and R. Jackman. 1991. *Unemployment: Macroeconomic performance and the labour market.* Oxford: Oxford University Press.

Organization for Economic Cooperation and Development (OECD). 2006a. OECD Labour Force Indicators Database. Paris: OECD.

———. 2006b. OECD National Accounts Database. Paris: OECD.

Office national de l'Emploi (ONEM). 2001. Les bénéficiares d'allocations d'attente et de transition. Direction Etudes et direction Statistiques et Publications. Bruxelles: ONEM.

The Interaction of Youth and Elderly Labor Markets in Canada

Michael Baker, Jonathan Gruber, and Kevin Milligan

2.1 Introduction

The composition of the Canadian labor force has changed dramatically over the past few generations. One of the most important changes has been in the age composition. This change has been driven partially by demographics as the baby boom generation pushed its way through youth and middle-age; and now approaches traditional retirement ages. However, in addition to demographic thrusts there have also been behavioral changes as Canadians react both to macroeconomic and fiscal incentives to work. Seeing these large composition changes, the potential impact of labor market trends in one age segment on other age segments becomes an important question.

On the production side of the economy, younger and older workers can in theory be either substitutes or complements. For example, if there are important gains from sharing knowledge, training, or combining experience levels to produce output, then older and younger workers may be complements. On the other hand, if there is little substantive difference between workers of different ages, then older and younger workers may be substitutes. It is important to keep in mind, however, that a large change in the supply of older workers can also have an impact on the demand for output, meaning

Michael Baker is professor of economics and public policy at the University of Toronto and a research associate of the National Bureau of Economic Research. Jonathan Gruber is professor of economics and associate head of the Department of Economics at the Massachusetts Institute of Technology and a research associate of the National Bureau of Economic Research. Kevin Milligan is associate professor of economics at the University of British Columbia and a faculty research fellow of the National Bureau of Economic Research.

This chapter was prepared as part of the NBER International Social Security project. We thank Kelvin Chan for excellent research assistance.

that the number of jobs in the economy will change as well, not just the identity of who fills them.

In previous work, we have investigated the strength of the fiscal incentives to retire (Gruber 1999), estimated their impact on retirement decisions (Baker, Gruber, and Milligan 2004), and simulated the impact of reforms on elderly labor force behavior (Baker, Gruber, and Milligan 2007). In this chapter, we build on this existing work by examining the impact of the previously-studied long-run trends in elderly labor market behavior on younger workers.

We begin by providing a history of public pensions in Canada, viewed in the context of the political pressures coming from both older and younger workers. We then present some time series graphs of labor market behavior from the 1970s to the 2000s by age group and sex, looking for evidence of substitution between older and younger workers. Finally, we present some regression results to check how well the inferences from the graphs hold up to a more rigorous analysis.

2.2   History of Public Pension Reforms in Canada

The development of public pensions in Canada can be divided into five distinct eras, each with its own social concerns, policy debates, and policy actions. In this section we review each of these eras in order to provide historical context for the debate about the relationship between older and younger workers. Our historical research consisted of reviewing articles published in *The Globe and Mail* from 1950 to the present. We do not focus here on the parametric details of the different reforms and pensions, but instead on the politics surrounding each reform.

2.2.1   1940s/1950s: Introduction of the Old Age Security (OAS)

Before the Second World War, the Royal Commission on Dominion-Provincial Relations (commonly called the Rowell-Sirois Commission) laid the groundwork for major changes to the Canadian federation in response to the economic crises of the Great Depression. Included in the recommendations of the Commission were several proposals to enhance the ability of the federal government to provide national social insurance, such as unemployment insurance and pensions, which had been provided provincially until that point. After the war, progress on some of the recommendations was made by the Liberal (centrist) government of Louis St. Laurent with the introduction of a family allowance, a national health insurance program, and public pensions. These were meant to create a "comprehensive social security program" that was "based on increasing acceptance of the principles of social justice" (*Globe and Mail,* October 26, 1951). The concern that generated the policy moves, therefore, was one of social justice and a desire to reduce misery and want.

The public pension component of the post-war policy development was called the Old Age Security (OAS) pension. This pension was a universal demogrant paid to those age seventy and over and was funded on a pay-as-you-go basis from dedicated taxes. The predominant issues in the debate were the nature of funding and the base for taxation. No fewer than six editorials in the *Globe and Mail* between 1950 and 1953 criticized the OAS system for its lack of prefunding and the nonrelationship at an individual level between taxes paid and benefits received. Notable for its absence was any discussion of the impact of pensions on labor market behavior.

2.2.2   1960s: Introduction of the Canada Pension Plan (CPP)

In the 1960s, continued concern about the well-being of the elderly led to pressure for an expansion of the public pension system. The Liberals, now led by Prime Minister Lester B. Pearson, argued that 70 percent of Canadians were not covered by workplace pensions and that an employment-based public pension plan could improve the incomes of the elderly. The opposition Conservatives preferred to enhance the existing OAS system with an addition of ten dollars per month. Extra-parliamentary opposition came from the insurance industry, which argued that private pensions were a prime source of investment capital that would disappear with the introduction of a public plan. There was also some debate about prefunding the pension, which was one of the primary issues leading to Quebec's decision to form its own plan so that Quebec could pursue its social investing goals. In the end, the Canada Pension Plan became law and began collecting contributions in 1966 and paying benefits in 1967 as a pay-as-you-go plan. The Quebec Pension Plan (QPP) was introduced at the same time and was in many ways similar to the CPP.

While labor market concerns were not pivotal in the discussion, one argument raised during the debates was the benefit of a portable public pension to workers, in contrast to employment-based pensions that tended to tie an employee to an employer.

2.2.3   1980s: Early Retirement in the CPP/QPP

The next era of pension reform arrived in the early 1980s. Two social concerns led to pressure for reform. First, high unemployment—especially among the youth—led to demands that older workers be forced out of the labor force to "make room" for younger workers. There was also a desire to allow the elderly more time in retirement; more leisure and less work.

In 1984, the Parti Quebecois (social democratic) government in Quebec introduced an early retirement option to the Quebec Pension Plan that allowed for actuarially-adjusted retirement with benefits as early as age sixty. According to the *Globe and Mail* on December 20, 1986, the intent of the change was to lower unemployment. A federal election in 1984 delayed the response of the Canada Pension Plan, but by 1987 the new Progressive

Conservative government had implemented a similar early retirement package in the rest of the country for the CPP.

In contrast to the earlier eras, the early retirement reform in 1984 to 1987 was directly motivated by concerns emanating from the labor market. This was the stated motivation of the government and also appeared in arguments by organizations outside government.

2.2.4   1990s: Reforming the CPP

The next era of change in public pensions in Canada focused on the Canada Pension Plan in the mid-1990s. The motivation for reform was the long-term financial health of the program. Projections from the Chief Actuary suggested that contribution rates would have to rise dramatically if promised benefits were to be paid.

Several possibilities for reform were contemplated. Higher payroll taxes were discussed both as affecting intergenerational burdens and as affecting labor markets. There was a fear that higher payroll taxes would increase unemployment. In addition, proposals to increase the retirement age were met with the charge that this would "clog up job opportunities" (*Globe and Mail*, June 5, 1996).

2.2.5   2000s: Labor Market Shortages

The final era to be considered is the boom period starting in the middle part of the 2000s decade. With Canadian unemployment rates reaching generational lows, discussion shifted from unemployment to worker shortages in many industries. The policy actions under consideration were changes to public pensions to encourage more work (see Milligan 2005) and also changes to mandatory retirement regulations. Several provinces changed their labor laws to make them less amenable to mandatory retirement in union contracts. An interesting feature of this debate has been the lack of vigor among those supporting mandatory retirement. Because of labor market tightness, there has been little concern about the impact of these changes on the work opportunities of the young.

2.2.6   Summary

To conclude, the importance of labor market considerations in the public debate about public pensions has varied tremendously through time. In the first post-war reforms, the welfare of the elderly was of utmost concern. However, as unemployment became a dominant social issue in the early 1980s, the impact of elderly work on younger workers gained in political importance. Reforms in the 1990s that aimed to restore long-run financial stability to public pensions were evaluated in part by considering their impact on labor markets. Finally, the labor market boom of the 2000s has seemingly removed concerns about the impact of elderly work on the young from the political consciousness.

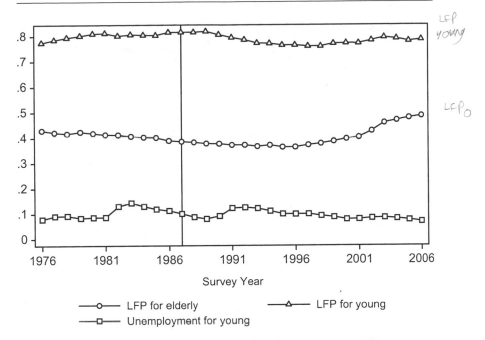

Fig. 2.1 **Evolution of elderly labor force participation for elderly and the young, both sexes**

Figure 2.1 shows the development of elderly labor force participation over the 1976 to 2006 time period for males and females pooled together. There is a line drawn in 1987 when the early retirement provisions of the CPP were introduced. Elderly in this graph is defined as the age range fifty-five to sixty-four. (We explain the data source in detail in the next section.) Also on the graph is the labor force participation (LFP) rate for the young and the unemployment rate for the young, where young is defined as ages twenty to twenty-four. Elderly labor force participation moves quite smoothly and slowly down from 1976 to 1996, dropping from 42.9 percent down to 36.3 percent. After 1996, elderly LFP increases over the next ten years up to 48.5 percent. This phenomenon is studied in Schirle (2008), who finds that a substantial source of the trend is joint retirement—married males are increasingly likely to have a still-working wife, and do not want to retire alone. The unemployment rate and LFP rate for the young show more signs of cyclicality than evident for the elderly. However, in the late 1990s as elderly LFP rose, the LFP of the young appears to have risen as well, providing some preliminary evidence against a "crowd out" effect of elderly LFP on the labor market behavior of the young.

Looking at males and females separately in figures 2.2 and 2.3, subtle differences emerge. First, elderly LFP for males declines by about 15 percentage points from 1976 to 1996, before rebounding over the last decade.

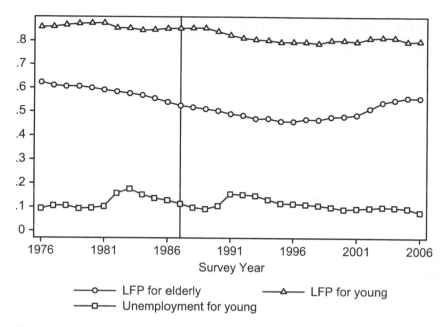

Fig. 2.2   Evolution of elderly labor force participation for elderly and the young, males

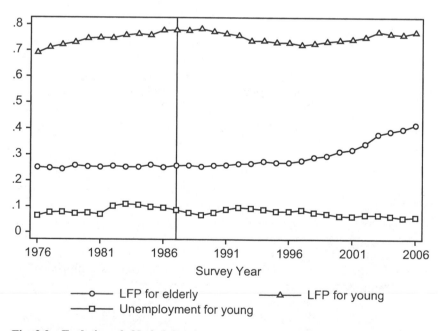

Fig. 2.3   Evolution of elderly labor force participation for elderly and the young, females

In contrast, elderly female LFP grows gently until the mid-1990s, and more sharply thereafter. For the young, the lines for males show higher cyclicality. Unemployment rates (in particular for males) rise more sharply in the recessions of the early 1980s and early 1990s, whereas female unemployment changes are more muted. As with the pooled sex graphs, however, there is little evidence here that the labor supply changes of the elderly are having impact on the young.

2.3   Time Trends

To examine the impact of the labor market behavior of the old on the work of the young, we now turn to the data. The best data source available to us is the monthly Labor Force Survey (LFS) conducted by Statistics Canada. The Labor Force Survey is a monthly survey into which a nationally representative sample is chosen. Households stay in the survey for six months. The microdata are available from January 1976 to 2006. Sample sizes are typically about 50,000 per month. This survey gives us the best combination of long time frame, detailed and consistent questions, and large sample. Alternatives such as the Survey of Consumer Finances or the Census do not give annual coverage and are not available much earlier than the LFS.

The first step in preparing our analysis is to divide the LFS sample into age groups. We do this by designating individuals age twenty to twenty-four as "young," twenty-five to fifty-four as "prime age" and fifty-five to sixty-four as "elderly." We then form variables indicating the labor market activity of each individual, with variables for labor force participation, employment, unemployment, and in school. To form the annual time series that we use for this analysis we simply pool together the twelve months within each calendar year.

We plot both sexes pooled together, followed by separate graphs for males and females in each case. Because the substitution between older and younger workers could happen between males and females, the overall pooled graphs are most relevant for the study of elderly-young labor market interactions. However, the pooled graphs obscure some of the long-run trends affecting each sex, so we also provide separate graphs by sex.

The time series graph shown in figure 2.4 plots the labor force participation (LFP) of the elderly against unemployment rates for the young and prime age groups. The motivation for this graph is to see whether movements in elderly LFP have translated into impacts on the work opportunities of the rest of the labor market. The overwhelming impression of elderly LFP over the first twenty years of the sample is its flatness up to 1996. Over this time period, the ebbs and flows of the business cycle are evident on the unemployment rates of the young and prime age samples. Over the last ten years of the series, the LFP of the elderly increased by more than 10 percentage points. However, over this same time period, the unemployment rates of the

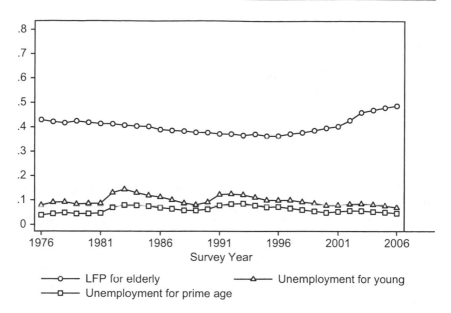

Fig. 2.4   Elderly labor force participation versus unemployment for the young and prime age, both sexes

young and prime aged dropped. Overall, this first look at the data gives no indication that trends in elderly LFP have any influence on the unemployment rates of the young and prime aged.

Figures 2.5 and 2.6 repeat the same analysis for males and females. As with figures 2.1 through 2.3, male elderly employment shows a U-shaped pattern while for females a gentle upward trend becomes steeper in the mid-1990s. The milder cyclicality of female youth unemployment compared to males carries forward to the prime-age females and males. However, for both males and females the prime age unemployment rates show less cyclicality than for the youth.

The next set of time series graphs show the LFP of the elderly against employment rates for the young and prime aged. This provides a slightly different view on the matter, since it is possible that elderly LFP does not affect unemployment if those displaced by elderly LFP move from employment to being out of the labor market entirely. Figure 2.7 shows both sexes together. Elderly LFP is repeated in figure 2.7 the same as was seen in figure 2.4. Employment rates for the young show strong business cycle effects, with drops in 1982 and in the early 1990s. Employment of the prime aged shows a similar pattern, but with muted amplitudes relative to the young. Again, in the post-1996 era the labor market of all three age groups is improving, with no sign of any crowding out of the employment of the young and prime aged from the increasing LFP of the elderly. Figures 2.8 and 2.9 repeat the

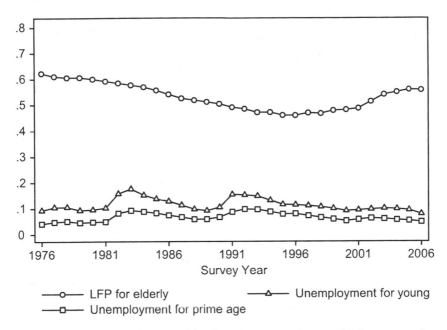

Fig. 2.5 Elderly labor force participation versus unemployment for the young and prime age, males

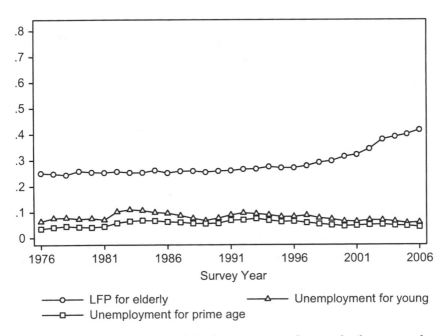

Fig. 2.6 Elderly labor force participation versus unemployment for the young and prime age, females

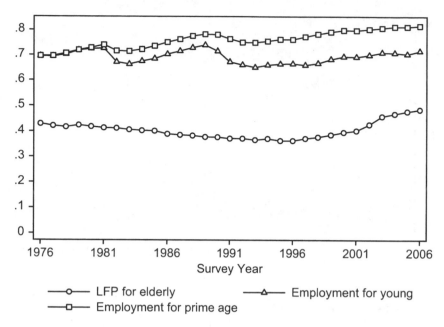

Fig. 2.7 **Elderly labor force participation versus employment for the young and prime age, both sexes**

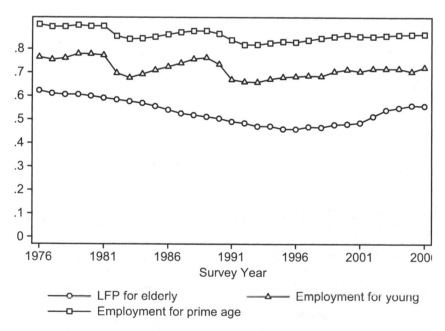

Fig. 2.8 **Elderly labor force participation versus employment for the young and prime age, males**

Fig. 2.9   Elderly labor force participation versus employment for the young and prime age, females

exercise for males and females separately. The previously noted trends are present here as well, with more cyclicality present for younger and male lines. The most striking trend is the sharp, consistent upward march of prime aged female employment over this time period. Overall, there does not appear to be much visual evidence of any crowding out of the employment of younger workers by the elderly.

2.4   Regression Results

In the next stage of our analysis, we turn to regression evidence to see if the inferences drawn from the graphs stand up to more rigorous tests. We estimate time series regressions of the form:

$$Y_t = \beta_0 + \beta_1 \, \text{ELDERLYEMP}_t + X_t \beta_2 + e_t.$$

The dependent variable Y_t is a measure of labor force participation, ELDERLYEMP_t is the employment rate for the elderly age group, X_t is a vector of national-level control variables, and e_t is the usual error term. We use several different dependent variables, including the rate of unemployment, employment, and school attendance for the young, and unemployment and employment for the prime aged. The key independent variable in each regression is the rate of elderly employment. We try specifications with and without additional control variables. The additional control variables include the percent share of gross domestic product (GDP) in manufacturing, the level of GDP per capita, and the growth rate of GDP per capita.

We also try some transformations of the data. First, we try lagging the elderly employment variable by three years to see if there might be a delay in the timing of the response to changes in elderly employment. Second, we difference the data across five years in order to look at changes rather than levels. We chose five years in order to try to difference out fluctuations in the business cycle. Finally, we tried a five year difference of the log of elderly employment and the log of the dependent variables.

2.4.1   Direct Effect of Elderly Employment on Young and Prime-Age Outcomes

We first look for a direct effect of the employment of the elderly on younger labor market participants. The results appear in table 2.1. The result shown in the upper left cell reports that a one point increase in elderly employment predicts a –0.334 point drop in the unemployment rate for the young. This result is in the opposite direction of what would be expected if increased elderly employment cost younger participants work opportunities. The results for employment in the second column are consistent with the first column. Prime age results are also similar. These results in the top panel of the table, however, are from a specification without any control variables. In the bottom panel of the table we show that the coefficients are slightly attenuated when we control for manufacturing share, GDP, and GDP growth.

In the second row of the table, we use a three-year lag of elderly employment. The impact on young unemployment is now slightly positive, but not even close to statistically significant. The youth employment effect is still positive, however. Neither of the effects on prime aged behavior is statistically significant.

In the third and fourth rows of the table, we investigate differenced specifications. Using both the fifth difference and the fifth log difference, the inferences remain unchanged. There is no evidence of crowding out of labor market activity of the young when the elderly increase their labor force participation.

The bottom panel of table 2.1 repeats the same set of analyses, but includes several controls variables for GDP, GDP growth, and share of manufacturing in GDP. With the control variables included, the signs on almost all of the estimates are unchanged, but the magnitudes and statistical significance becomes more muted. This suggests that the results in the top half of the panel were driven in part by strong economic growth—in a strong growth environment both young and elderly employment improves.

Focusing on the prime aged results, some confusion arises. Elderly employment appears to have a negative impact on both unemployment and employ-

Table 2.1   **Direct regressions of labor market crowd-out: Both sexes**

	Youth			Prime age	
	UE	EMP	SCH	UE	EMP
No controls					
Levels	−0.334	0.413	−0.048	−0.287	0.251
	(0.082)	(0.107)	(0.157)	(0.048)	(0.188)
3-year lag on elderly	0.031	0.371	−0.571	−0.125	−0.288
employment	(0.146)	(0.175)	(0.178)	(0.090)	(0.225)
5-year difference	−0.347	0.638	−0.275	−0.299	0.220
	(0.136)	(0.175)	(0.061)	(0.081)	(0.117)
5-year log difference	−1.790	0.458	−1.274	−2.445	0.139
	(0.604)	(0.120)	(0.238)	(0.594)	(0.075)
With controls					
Levels	−0.224	0.407	−0.349	−0.276	−0.136
	(0.060)	(0.103)	(0.068)	(0.032)	(0.049)
3-year lag on elderly	−0.149	0.558	−0.539	−0.246	−0.132
employment	(0.081)	(0.141)	(0.076)	(0.050)	(0.061)
5-year difference	−0.187	−0.078	0.001	−0.246	−0.318
	(0.136)	(0.131)	(0.069)	(0.072)	(0.081)
5-year log difference	−1.034	0.039	−0.427	−2.355	−0.117
	(0.605)	(0.069)	(0.301)	(0.585)	(0.046)

Notes: Reported in each cell is the coefficient on elderly employment in separate regressions with the dependent variable listed in the column headings. The standard error is beneath each estimate in parentheses. The different specifications appear in each row of the table. The specifications are explained in the main text.

ment of prime aged men and women. This is not impossible, however, since employment and unemployment rates do not need to sum to one. Instead, being out of the labor force must rise. This provides some suggestive evidence of a degree of crowding out between elderly and prime aged individuals. We investigate this further following in our men-only sample.

We repeat the analysis in table 2.2, but for males only. Through this time period, the graphical analysis tells us that there is more variation in unemployment and employment among males, and that male employment is higher. For this reason, we seek to find out if an analysis focused on males only reveals different results. The impact of elderly male employment rates on youth male unemployment rates is more muted than for the pooled sexes results, but still the signs are mostly negative. Similarly, the positive effect on youth employment persists in the male sample.

The prime aged results seen in the pooled men and women sample are strongly overturned here in the men-only sample. Again, the unemployment rate responds negatively to more elderly employment. However, in contrast to the pooled analysis, here with males only we find a positive response of prime aged employment to increasing elderly employment. This suggests that the negative relationship uncovered in table 2.1 might be driven by the

Table 2.2   Direct regressions of labor market crowd-out: Males only

	Youth			Prime age	
	UE	EMP	SCH	UE	EMP
No controls					
Levels	−0.070	0.465	−0.325	−0.152	0.352
	(0.075)	(0.071)	(0.044)	(0.042)	(0.038)
3-year lag on elderly	0.145	0.253	−0.354	0.010	0.178
employment	(0.074)	(0.096)	(0.027)	(0.049)	(0.058)
5-year difference	−0.349	0.651	−0.223	−0.308	0.451
	(0.148)	(0.176)	(0.051)	(0.084)	(0.097)
5-year log difference	−1.791	0.553	−1.246	−2.677	0.318
	(0.706)	(0.148)	(0.245)	(0.715)	(0.069)
With controls					
Levels	−0.139	0.435	−0.241	−0.190	0.335
	(0.051)	(0.067)	(0.037)	(0.026)	(0.032)
3-year lag on elderly	−0.103	0.478	−0.316	−0.170	0.347
employment	(0.063)	(0.087)	(0.033)	(0.037)	(0.047)
5-year difference	−0.106	0.135	−0.021	−0.169	0.180
	(0.141)	(0.140)	(0.052)	(0.074)	(0.077)
5-year log difference	−0.591	0.151	−0.469	−2.010	0.183
	(0.766)	(0.125)	(0.263)	(0.809)	(0.061)

Notes: Reported in each cell is the coefficient on elderly employment in separate regressions with the dependent variable listed in the column headings. The standard error is beneath each estimate in parentheses. The different specifications appear in each row of the table. The specifications are explained in the main text.

secular and strong upward trend in female labor force participation seen in figure 2.9.

The largest impression from the evidence in table 2.1 and table 2.2 is the absence of any consistent indication that the labor market behavior of the elderly had a negative impact on the employment of the young. For the prime aged there was some evidence in favor of crowd-out in the pooled sample, but this was reversed in the men-only sample. What's more, if anything, the evidence suggests that employment of the different age groups tends to move together rather than in opposite directions.

2.4.2   Effect of Retirement Incentives on Employment Patterns

A concern with the evidence presented in tables 2.1 and 2.2 is that both elderly employment and young employment are driven by common but unmeasured factors. To try to improve the inferences on the causal nature of the relationship, we turn to an approach that exploits changes in policy through time. We develop an annual index of the incentives for elderly workers to retire, based on the parameters of Canada's public pension system. When the incentive index is larger, there is a greater incentive to exit the

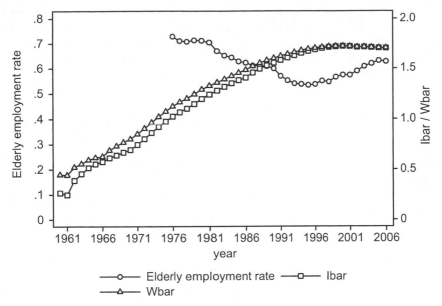

Fig. 2.10   Elderly employment rate, $\bar{I}(y)$ and $\bar{W}(y)$

labor market. We provide further detail on the construction of this index in the appendix.

We graph the incentive measures in figure 2.10. There are two indexes we use: Wbar and Ibar. Both are described in detail in the appendix. The Wbar represents the average Income Security Wealth among labor market participants. The Wbar includes both Income Security Wealth and a dynamic incentive measure called "peak value" that captures the pension accrual from continued work. For the case of Canada, the difference between current and peak wealth is typically quite flat, so there is little difference between Ibar and Wbar. Both of these incentive measures show strong, consistent growth until the mid-1990s when they level out. The figure also graphs the employment rate among the elderly. It is only available from 1976 when the LFS data start. Elderly employment declines through the mid-1990s when it begins to rebound.

This graph suggests there may be a relationship between incentives and employment of the elderly. However, given that we have only two time series to conduct the inference, it is far from certain that the relationship observed is causal. Other factors could be influencing each of these trends.

Another view on this relationship is provided in figure 2.11, which plots the fifth difference of the Ibar measure and elderly employment. There appears to be a tight negative relationship between them. However, upon closer inspection, the serial pattern of the data points cautions us to consider that this relationship may be spurious.

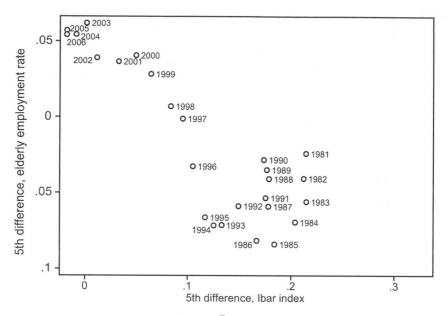

Fig. 2.11   Elderly employment rate and $\bar{I}(y)$ index in fifth differences

The regression results are displayed in table 2.3 for both sexes pooled together. To begin, we look at the results for the elderly. These results are in some sense the "first stage," as we expect the incentives to have an impact on the work behavior of the elderly as a precursor to their impact on the younger workers. The results without control variables in the top half of table 2.3 are mixed. However, when the control variables are included in the bottom half of the table, the results become more consistent. As the policy incentives to retire increase, the employment of the elderly decreases. There is also a small increase in the measured unemployment rate of the elderly. These results hold across all four specifications in the table.

When looking at the results for the young and the prime aged, the specification can be thought of as a "reduced form" estimate. That is, we are estimating the effect of a higher incentive for the elderly to retire on the work behavior of the young and middle aged. The presumed path through which the changes in incentives affect the younger workers is through their impact on the labor market behavior of the elderly. For the young, the results for employment are in some places small and insignificant but are almost all negative. This suggests that, if anything, a decrease in elderly employment is associated with a decrease in young employment. This does not support the crowd-out story. The results for the prime aged individuals, however, are more mixed. The positive coefficients on employment suggest that greater incentives for the elderly to retire are associated with more work by middle-aged workers, which is consistent with the idea that induced retirement of the

Table 2.3 Impact of retirement incentives on the employment of the elderly, prime aged, and young (both sexes)

	Elderly		Youth			Prime age	
	UE	EMP	UE	EMP	SCH	UE	EMP
No controls							
Levels	0.011	−0.021	−0.013	−0.027	0.119	0.016	0.140
	(0.005)	(0.028)	(0.015)	(0.019)	(0.009)	(0.010)	(0.014)
3-year lag on elderly employment	0.008	−0.006	−0.014	−0.019	0.097	0.010	0.116
	(0.004)	(0.023)	(0.012)	(0.016)	(0.007)	(0.009)	(0.010)
5-year difference	0.041	−0.449	0.131	−0.171	0.071	0.121	−0.005
	(0.026)	(0.045)	(0.072)	(0.103)	(0.039)	(0.044)	(0.063)
5-year log difference	1.808	−1.022	2.006	−0.276	0.526	2.843	0.019
	(0.848)	(0.145)	(0.777)	(0.180)	(0.426)	(0.772)	(0.100)
With controls							
Levels	0.029	−0.285	0.054	−0.135	0.121	0.074	0.038
	(0.006)	(0.014)	(0.018)	(0.030)	(0.018)	(0.010)	(0.015)
3-year lag on elderly employment	0.029	−0.269	0.056	−0.139	0.120	0.072	0.030
	(0.006)	(0.015)	(0.016)	(0.027)	(0.016)	(0.009)	(0.015)
5-year difference	0.018	−0.361	0.054	0.056	−0.010	0.078	0.148
	(0.020)	(0.032)	(0.055)	(0.049)	(0.024)	(0.031)	(0.024)
5-year log difference	1.767	−0.973	1.197	−0.043	0.369	2.486	0.123
	(0.743)	(0.121)	(0.654)	(0.079)	(0.305)	(0.647)	(0.045)

Notes: Reported in each cell is the coefficient on the retirement incentive index in separate regressions with the dependent variable listed in the column headings. The standard error is beneath each estimate in parentheses. The different specifications appear in each row of the table. The specifications are explained in the main text.

elderly creates more employment for the middle aged. However, the unemployment results for the prime aged are also positive, which is contradictory to the employment results. This leads us again to look at males only.

In table 2.4 we explore the results in the subsample of males. To begin, the "first-stage" effect of the incentive measure on elderly employment is very strong here. For example, in the levels regression with controls, the coefficient in table 2.4 is –0.443, versus –0.285 with both sexes pooled in table 2.3. The estimates for youth unemployment and employment are for the most part consistent in both magnitude and sign with the estimates from table 2.3. For the prime aged males, however, we now find a negative relationship for employment. That is, we no longer have evidence of crowd-out. As with the previous analysis in tables 2.1 and 2.2, this difference may be driven by a secular upward trend in female employment as seen in figure 2.9.

In sum, the results using the incentive to retire index suggest that the incentives may have an impact on the elderly, but it is not clear if it is causal. The changes in elderly employment have a mixed and mostly small impact on the working behavior of the young and prime aged. There is some evidence in favor of a positive relationship between elderly and the employment of younger individuals, but no consistent evidence of any crowding out.

2.5   Conclusions

In this chapter we have studied the relationship between the work of the elderly and the work of Canadians in other age groups. Historically, the political concern about the impact of elderly employment on younger workers seems to be strongly related to the business cycle and especially the unemployment rates of younger workers. In the graphs, we find little visual evidence that trends in elderly labor force participation have had an impact on the labor markets of the younger. Finally, our regression evidence has shown that—if anything—the employment of the young and prime aged tends to move in the same direction as the elderly.

Several important caveats limit the conclusions that may be drawn from our results. First, the movements in elderly labor force participation over the 1976 to 2006 period have not been sharp, so there simply may not be enough variation to identify any effects on other labor markets. Second, the results we find here for Canada may not hold in other countries with different labor market institutions, practices, and histories. Finally, the time series regressions we run are in some ways quite crude and rely on very few observations to describe the behavior of millions of workers. With these caveats in mind, however, it is possible for us to conclude that we find no strong evidence of elderly employment crowding out the work of the young.

Table 2.4   Impact of retirement incentives on the employment of the elderly, prime aged, and young (just males)

	Elderly		Youth			Prime age	
	UE	EMP	UE	EMP	SCH	UE	EMP
No controls							
Levels	0.004	-0.226	-0.012	-0.097	0.092	0.018	-0.074
	(0.007)	(0.023)	(0.019)	(0.022)	(0.009)	(0.013)	(0.014)
3-year lag on elderly employment	0.002	-0.179	-0.014	-0.076	0.077	0.012	-0.058
	(0.006)	(0.022)	(0.016)	(0.019)	(0.007)	(0.011)	(0.012)
5-year difference	0.065	-0.535	0.174	-0.266	0.062	0.150	-0.203
	(0.036)	(0.064)	(0.096)	(0.125)	(0.041)	(0.057)	(0.072)
5-year log difference	2.036	-0.960	2.076	-0.454	0.374	3.079	-0.290
	(0.899)	(0.167)	(0.907)	(0.215)	(0.439)	(0.943)	(0.103)
With controls							
Levels	0.034	-0.443	0.067	-0.193	0.103	0.087	-0.151
	(0.009)	(0.019)	(0.023)	(0.031)	(0.018)	(0.012)	(0.015)
3-year lag on elderly employment	0.034	-0.429	0.067	-0.196	0.105	0.085	-0.150
	(0.008)	(0.018)	(0.021)	(0.028)	(0.016)	(0.011)	(0.013)
5-year difference	0.038	-0.442	0.084	-0.068	-0.019	0.086	-0.084
	(0.029)	(0.052)	(0.069)	(0.070)	(0.026)	(0.037)	(0.039)
5-year log difference	1.966	-0.902	1.193	-0.223	0.167	2.493	-0.209
	(0.807)	(0.152)	(0.744)	(0.122)	(0.305)	(0.750)	(0.058)

Notes: Reported in each cell is the coefficient on the retirement incentive index in separate regressions with the dependent variable listed in the column headings. The standard error is beneath each estimate in parentheses. The different specifications appear in each row of the table. The specifications are explained in the main text.

Appendix

Calculating the Incentive Measure

The goal of the exercise is to arrive at a single incentive number for each calendar year to be used in the time series regressions. We begin with a single birth cohort born in 1920 and build a lifetime earnings profile for them. Data are drawn from the Survey of Consumer Finances for available years and then extrapolated forward and backward using indexes of wage growth. This earnings profile is then shifted for inflation forward and backward to generate equivalent real wage profiles for all birth cohorts. We repeat this exercise for each decile of the earnings distribution, separately for males and females. This method ensures that the only difference in incentive measures across years will be in changes in benefit formulas and not cross-cohort differences in wages.

These cohort age-earnings profiles are next pushed through our Canadian income security benefits calculator developed in Baker, Gruber, and Milligan (2004, 2007). At each age from fifty-five to sixty-nine, we calculate the capitalized value of future benefits (Income Security Wealth or ISW) and also the "peak value" concept found in Baker, Gruber, and Milligan (2004). The peak value represents the difference between current ISW and its highest value in the future, given current information for a forward-looking individual.

To collapse this down to an annual time series, we start by recognizing that an individual viewed at age a has faced retirement incentives at age $a, a - 1$, $a - 2, \ldots$ back to the first age of eligibility. We therefore average the incentives within a cohort across ages (from the current age back to age fifty-five), using the aggregate age-year-sex-specific labor force participation as weights. We generate the age-year-sex labor force participation rates from the Survey of Consumer Finances. Since this survey only goes back to 1971 and is also missing some years, we fill in missing years and extrapolate backwards using an assumption of constant age-sex labor force participation rates. This calculation gives us an average exposure to retirement incentives for each cohort in each year of interest.

The final step involves collapsing the average incentive measures to a single number for each year. This means we must average the incentive measures faced by each cohort in a given year. To do this, we weight by the proportion of the population represented by each age in a given year.

To enrich the measurement of incentives, we assign a weight to the ISW component and the peak value component. We determined these weights using an iterative technique, finding weights that maximized the fit of a regression of elderly LFP on the incentive measure.

The foregoing can be expressed mathematically as follows. The incentive measure I at age a and year y can be expressed as:

$$I(a, y) = \{\gamma W(a, y) + \alpha[W(a, y) - PV \times (a, y)]\},$$

where $W(a,y)$ is the ISW at age a and year y, $PV \times (a,y)$ is the peak value of ISW, and α and γ are the weighting parameters for the wealth level and peak value difference, respectively. These $I(a,y)$ terms are then summed across all previous ages, within cohort:

$$\bar{I}(a, y) = \sum_{a=55}^{a=69} \left(\left\{ P(a,y) \times \left[\frac{\sum_{t=0}^{a-55} I(a,y) \times \mathrm{LFP}(a-t, y-t-1)}{\sum_{t=0}^{a-55} \mathrm{LFP}(a-t, y-t-1)} \right] \right\} / \sum_{a=55}^{a=69} P(a,y) \right),$$

where $LFP(a - t, y - t - 1)$ is the labor force participation rate for a member of the cohort in a previous year. The extra minus one accounts for the fact that we want the labor force participation rate at the beginning of the year, not during the year. Finally, we average across all cohorts in a particular year, where $P(a,y)$ is the population of the cohort in a given year. This $\bar{I}(y)$ term is the incentives index used for the regressions appearing in tables 2.3 and 2.4.

We also make use of $\overline{W}(y)$, which is calculated by substituting the ISW of the individual at age a and year y, $W(a,y)$, in for $I(a,y)$. This $\overline{W}(y)$ term calculates the average pension wealth across individuals in a given year.

References

Baker, M., J. Gruber, and K. Milligan. 2004. Income security programs and retirement in Canada. In *Social security programs and retirement around the world: Micro-estimation,* ed. J. Gruber and D. A. Wise, 99–152. Chicago: University of Chicago Press.

———. 2007. Simulating the response to reforms of Canada's income security programs. In *Social Security programs and retirement around the world: Fiscal implications of reform,* ed. J. Gruber and D. A. Wise, 83–118. Chicago: University of Chicago Press.

Gruber, J. 1999. Social Security and retirement in Canada. In *Social Security Programs and retirement around the world,* ed. J. Gruber and D. A. Wise, 73–100. Chicago: University of Chicago Press.

Milligan, K. 2005. Making it pay to work: Improving the incentives in Canada's public pension system. Commentary 218. C. D. Howe Institute: Toronto, Ontario.

Schirle, T. 2008. Why have the labor force participation rates of older men increased since the mid-1990s? *Journal of Labor Economics* 26 (4): 549–94.

Social Security, Retirement, and Employment of the Young in Denmark

Paul Bingley, Nabanita Datta Gupta, and Peder J. Pedersen

3.1 Introduction

The demographic prospects in Denmark are, like those in most other rich Organization for Economic Cooperation and Development (OECD) countries, characterized by an increasing share of elderly people, that is, until the middle of the century. A decline in fertility, a trend until recently toward earlier retirement, and longer expected lifetimes interact to increase the share of elderly people in the population with derived impacts on the economy in many different ways; that is, on the public sector budget and on the relative as well as the absolute size of the labor force, unless policy changes are enacted.

A major part of the trend toward earlier retirement is, apart from the impact from higher incomes and wealth, explained by the introduction of programs for early retirement, either directly or by expanding other retirement programs with an early retirement option, intended to reduce youth unemployment and increase welfare for eligible older workers retiring through these programs. In this chapter we concentrate on the question of whether older workers retiring earlier from the labor force create job openings for young workers. If the number of jobs in the economy were of a given magnitude, there would exist a substitution of jobs between older and younger workers, which some might invoke as an argument in support of early retirement programs.

Paul Bingley is a professor at the Danish National Centre for Social Research. Nabanita Datta Gupta is a professor at the Aarhus School of Business and a guest researcher at the Danish National Centre for Social Research. Peder J. Pedersen is a professor at the School of Economics and Management of Aarhus University.

The purpose of the present chapter is to study the eventual evidence for or against this substitution hypothesis over the thirty years up to the turn of the century, using microdata for employment, unemployment, and enrollment in education for different age groups in the Danish economy. In section 3.2 we describe briefly the demographic perspectives in Denmark along with the main elements of social security retirement programs. There are a number of important and potentially very informative policy reforms—performing as natural experiments—during this period that are exploited to provide variation identifying our estimated models. Next, section 3.3 contains a number of descriptive indicators of employment and unemployment for the young, the prime aged, and the older group organized around the policy changes that occurred between 1971 and 2001. Section 3.4 contains a number of regression results with the aim of getting a measure of the simple correlations between employment, unemployment, and labor force participation across age groups. This is followed by analyses in section 3.5 introducing incentive measures for the old as the structural factor creating the basis for an eventual substitution of old for young jobs. Section 3.6 concludes the chapter.

3.2   Demographic Perspectives and Social Security Programs

The official retirement age in Denmark defined as the time from which you become eligible for National Old Age Pension (OAP) is sixty-five years from 2004, reduced from sixty-seven years.[1] The actual average retirement age is lower, at around sixty-one to sixty-two years. Due to this, the ratio shown in figure 3.1 underestimates the impact from the coming demographic shift by depicting the conventional calculation of the sixty-five years and older relative to the whole population and to the sixteen to sixty-four years old based on the most recent population forecast from Statistics Denmark.

With unchanged policies in the area of social security retirement programs, a forecast of more than a 20 percentage point increase in the dependency ratio shown in figure 3.1 will have quite strong implications for public expenditures with derived implication for taxes and/or public expenditures. Assuming unchanged labor force participation rates implies that the number of people in the labor force will go down and the consequence is a shrinking tax base at the same time as the increasing pressure on the expenditure side occurs. An obvious policy reaction is to consider changes in the rules regarding social security retirement with the double effect of reducing future

1. This is in contrast to the increase in eligibility ages enacted in most countries. The rational explanation of this change of rules is the fact that most people sixty-five and sixty-six years old were in an early retirement program—the PEW, compare following—with higher benefits than the OAP.

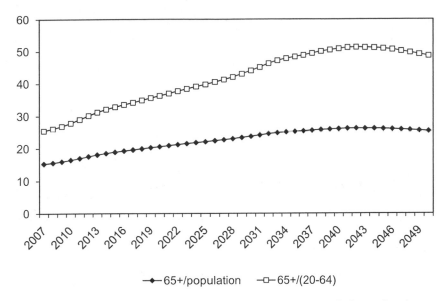

Fig. 3.1   The population sixty-five and older relative to the population and to the number of people sixteen to sixty-four years old

expenditures and increasing the future tax base.[2] The projected composition on age groups of the twenty- to sixty-four-years-old is shown in figure 3.2. The share of young workers twenty to twenty-four years old is very stable for the whole forecast period up to 2050. It is seen that the main change in the first twenty years is a 5 percentage point decline in the share of the prime age group, twenty-five to fifty-four, followed by a nearly 5 percentage point decline in the share of workers fifty-five to sixty-four years old in the last twenty years of the forecast period.

As a background for the analyses in the subsequent sections, we present a brief survey of the Danish social security retirement programs. Regarding the eventual substitution of young for old jobs, a number of important program innovations have occurred in the last quarter of a century. Until 1979, National Old Age Pension (OAP) and social disability pension (SDP) were the only elements in the Social Security part of provision for retirement, along with unemployment or sickness benefits as a pathway to retirement. In 1977 a law-preparing committee was appointed to make an outline for an early retirement program where eligibility, in contrast to social disability pension, should depend on objective criteria and not on a visitation

2. Based on the work in a Government committee on Welfare, policy changes have been enacted to adjust the earliest ages of eligibility for both PEW and OAP programs to the average life expectancy. However, these changes become only effective as from 2019.

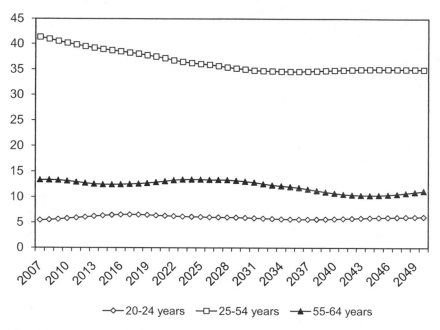

Fig. 3.2   Relative population shares twenty- to sixty-four-year-olds

on medical and/or social criteria. In the years before this committee was appointed, the union for unskilled workers had argued for the introduction of a program for early retirement where the target group was intended to be people with a long history of work in physically demanding jobs. The program was intended to be a more attractive option than disability pension. Based on this, the so-called Post Employment Wage (PEW) was introduced in 1979 as an early retirement program with eligibility based solely on being at least sixty years old and having sufficient tenure as member of an unemployment insurance fund.[3]

When the law introducing PEW was passed in parliament, one of the main arguments was that the program was supposed to be an element in labor market policy where a presumed fairly constant number of jobs should be redistributed from older workers (retiring early on the new program) to younger workers (among whom unemployment was high at the time). The secondary motive was to function as an alternative to disability pension for workers with a long record of physically demanding jobs. The main line of argument is expressed in a 1978 quote from the Minister of Labor, Svend Auken: "Unemployment among the youth is perhaps the most serious

3. Unemployment insurance is not mandatory in Denmark. Membership of so-called Ghent-type unemployment insurance funds is voluntary. The funds are administered by unions with revenues from membership fees and with the state as the actor carrying the residual financial burden under recessions.

problem of today, because we cannot hide from the fact that we risk losing a whole generation of young persons from the labor market and from society as a whole . . ." (Proceedings of Parliament, 1978). In the policy debate at the time of introduction of the program, counterarguments regarding the basic idea; that is, a more or less given number of jobs, was nearly absent. However, one member of parliament (chairman of a tax protest party at the time, called the Progress Party) named Mogens Glistrup in very colorful language expressed a deep skepticism regarding this argument: "This is a shimmering blue, lifelong-lying illusion used to trick the people into thinking that this legislation will reduce the ranks of the unemployed . . . with so much as even one single individual . . . the laws of economics don't work that way . . ." (Proceedings of Parliament, 1978).

The same basic motivation, a given number of jobs, was also used in the early 1980s to motivate other, smaller policy changes. This was the case regarding some of the elements in a pension reform of 1984, containing the following.

- Stricter means testing of old age pension relative to earnings from work.
- Cancellation of a—modest—actuarial element in the old age pension program where the motive was to increase economic incentives for older workers to leave the labor force at the first eligible age.

Entry to the PEW program was very high compared to initial estimates in the policy preparation phase. Significantly more men than women in the affected age groups of sixty and above fulfilled the membership demands in the unemployment insurance funds. The very strong impact from the PEW program is illustrated in figure 3.3, which shows the labor force participation rate for men in the age group sixty to sixty-four years from before the introduction of PEW to the most recent period. The data for the long period covered by figure 3.3 are from different sources. Due to this, the decline in labor force participation at the time of introduction of PEW as shown in figure 3.3 may be biased somewhat upwards. The data for the years before PEW are either census data, 1960, 1965, and 1970, or survey-based (while they are based on the Register-based Labour Force Statistics [RAS] register since 1980 where all persons are classified relative to the labor market based on their main activity in the first week of November in the preceding year). An alternative illustration of the impact on the employment rate for men sixty to sixty-four years old is shown following, using consistent data for the period 1971 to 2001 based on mandatory contributions to a universal labor market pension program called ATP (Danish Labor Market Supplementary Pension Fund).

Although other factors, including SDP and occupational pensions with early retirement options also influence the participation rates, the timing of the changes depicted in figure 3.3 is narrowly related to characteristics of the

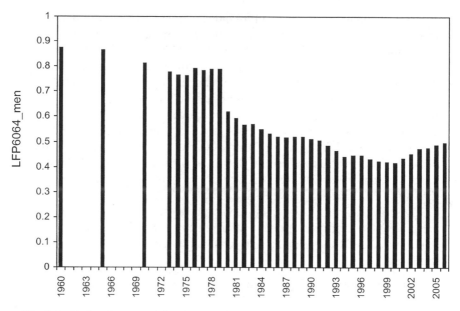

Fig. 3.3   Labor force participation rate for men, sixty to sixty-four years old, 1960 to 2006

PEW program. Immediately after the introduction of the program in 1979 the participation rate for the sixty- to sixty-four-year-old men goes down steeply from around 80 percent. Over the following twenty years participation declines further, with about 20 percentage points to close to half the pre-PEW level. In 1999 a policy reform was enacted with the purpose of reducing the economic incentives for entry into the program. In figure 3.3, we notice a fairly strong increase in participation rates in the most recent years, which most probably is due to the reform in 1999 and a shift of the statistical criteria for drawing the line between retirement and in the labor force, implying that a number of individuals receiving the PEW benefits at the same time had earnings from work high enough to shift them into the employed category of workers. More liberal rules for combining PEW with earnings from some work was part of the 1999 reform. In section 3.3 we treat the labor market reactions to PEW in more detail.

Besides the PEW program, a more restricted early retirement program in the Social Security area, called the Transitional Benefits Program (TBP), was opened for long term unemployed people fifty to fifty-four years old in 1992. In 1994 eligibility was extended to fifty-five to fifty-nine years old long term unemployed people. Entry was closed again in 1996. Benefits were set at 80 percent of PEW benefits and those admitted to the program remained in it and were transferred to the PEW program by the age of sixty.

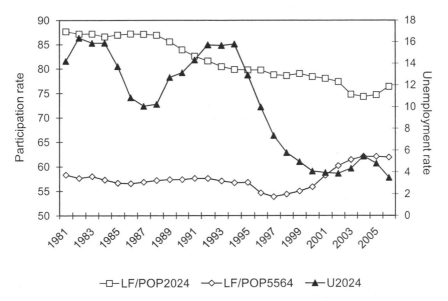

Fig. 3.4   Labor force participation twenty to twenty-four and fifty-five to sixty-four years old (unemployment twenty to twenty-four years old, 1981 to 2006)

3.3   Description of Changes in Unemployment and Employment for Age Groups

A first summary impression of the development in some relevant age-related labor market indicators is given in figure 3.4 for women and men together. Figure 3.4 is based on the RAS data, which are consistent for the period 1981 to 2006. The labor force participation rate for the old, defined as the fifty-five- to sixty-four-year-old group, shows a moderate decline from 1981 to the mid-1980s. The RAS data has 1981 as the first year, making it difficult to illustrate the impact from the PEW that was shown for sixty- to sixty-four-year-old men in figure 3.3.[4] Based on alternative data we illustrate the change before and after the introduction of PEW. Further, the impact from the TBP on the labor force participation among people in their fifties is clearly visible in figure 3.4.

For the young, figure 3.4 contains two indicators. The labor force participation rate is nearly constant until the late 1980s, followed by a decline of 10 percentage points until the turn of the century. Unemployment shows big cyclical movements until the mid-1990s around a high level, followed by a steep decline to a very low level at the end of the period. Based on figure

4. By convention, the RAS data for a given year *t* indicates the state relative to the labor market for all individuals in November of year *t* − 1.

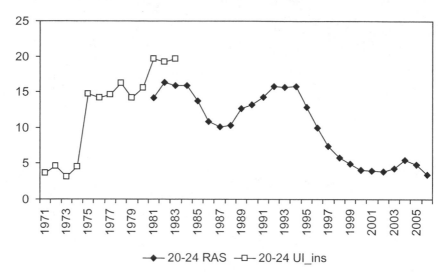

Fig. 3.5   Unemployment, twenty to twenty-four years old (1971 to 1983, no. of full-time insured unemployed/no. of insured, 1981 to 2006, based on the RAS register)

3.4, there is no indication of any impact from PEW on youth unemployment. A fundamental policy change regarding unemployed younger than twenty-five enacted in 1994 seems, on the other hand, to have had a strong effect on youth unemployment—supported by a general cyclical upturn beginning in 1994.

It is obviously interesting, considering the natural experiment nature of the introduction of PEW to go back beyond 1981. The problem with this approach is that we have to link different series. This is illustrated in figures 3.5 and 3.6, including the whole period from 1971. The RAS data as mentioned starts off in 1981. Before that, insurance-based data are available reporting unemployment by age for full time insured workers twice a year, respectively, for January and July. The average values are shown in figure 3.5, which includes, for illustration, three overlapping years.

Finally, figure 3.6 shows the profile for youth unemployment 1971 to 2006 with the two series linked in 1981. The very strong increase, beginning at the time of the first oil price shock, was part of the motivation for PEW (compare to the previous discussion). On the other hand, just comparing trends in aggregate series, no impact is seen from PEW on youth unemployment.

In figure 3.7, covering the period 1981 to 2006, labor force participation for the young in figure 3.4 has been replaced with unemployment in the prime age group. It can be seen that unemployment for the two age groups correlate in the first part of the period and practically become equal to each other since the late 1990s.

Finally, figure 3.8 collects labor force participation rates for the young, the

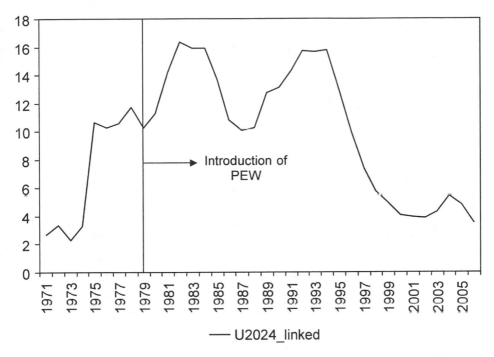

Fig. 3.6   Linked unemployment rate, twenty to twenty-four years old, 1971 to 2006

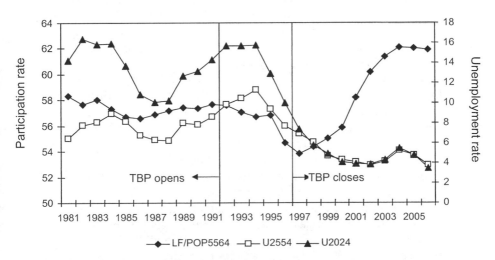

Fig. 3.7   Labor force participation fifty-five to sixty-four years old and unemployment rates for the young, twenty to twenty-four years, and the prime age group, twenty-five to fifty-four years old

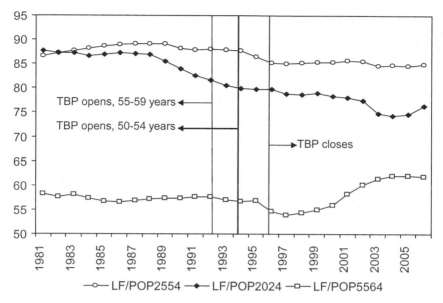

Fig. 3.8   Labor force participation rates, twenty to twenty-four, twenty-five to fifty-four and fifty-five to sixty-four years old, 1981 to 2006

prime age group, and older workers fifty-five- to sixty-four-years-old in one graph. The most spectacular change is the decline in labor force participation among the young beginning in the late 1980s. The big changes for the group of older workers are not captured in figure 3.8 due to the series in the graph beginning after the PEW introduction and due to the aggregation of two groups below and above sixty years of age.

In figure 3.9 to 3.11 we extend the time scale to begin in 1971; that is, before the first oil price shocks and before the enactment of PEW. Figure 3.9 shows the employment share for men and women combined and disaggregating to two age groups in their fifties and the PEW relevant sixty- to sixty-four-year-old group. The employment data are from the microdata set and are complete for the age groups included here. Looking first at the oldest group, the falling employment rate until introduction of PEW is affected by the cyclical downturn after the oil price shock, where older workers who became unemployed subsequently had great difficulties entering a new job. The impact from PEW is clearly visible until the leveling-off in the employment rate as the economy moves up strongly in the mid-1990s.

Figures 3.10 and 3.11 show the profiles over time for men and women separately. It has been mentioned before that a higher proportion of men fulfilled the conditions for entering PEW. As a consequence of that, the impact from PEW is much more pronounced and concentrated in time for men. For women the cohort effect implies that employment rates for women

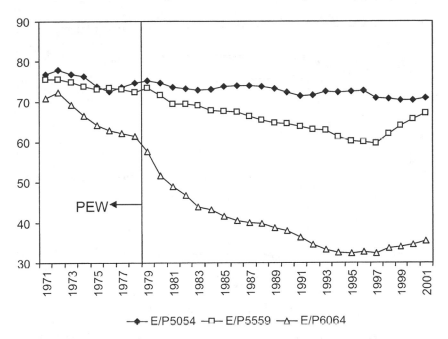

Fig. 3.9 Employment rates, fifty to sixty-four years old, 1971 to 2001 (based on microdata)

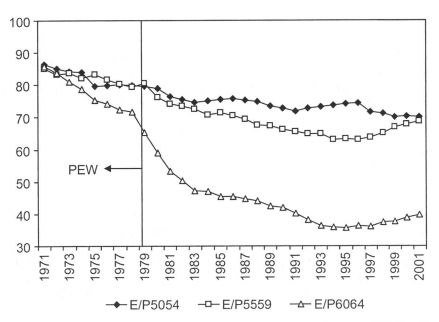

Fig. 3.10 Employment rates, fifty to sixty-four years old, men, 1971 to 2001 (based on microdata)

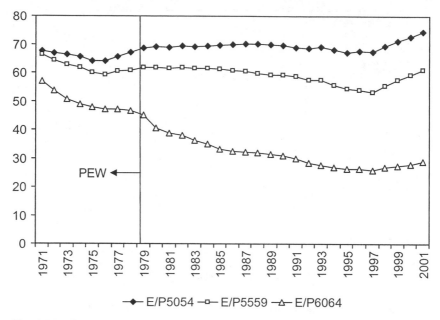

Fig. 3.11   Employment rates, fifty to sixty-four years old, women, 1971 to 2001 (based on microdata)

in their fifties are stable or slightly increasing up to the same level to which the rates for men are decreasing.

The data covering the longer period are based on microdata where employment is derived from payment of contributions to a mandatory pension called ATP. To evaluate the validity of the ATP-based data relative to the RAS data, we have looked into the difference between male employment in different age groups using the two data sources for an overlapping period. The overall impression is that the two employment series are highly correlated and can substitute for each other in regressions with a level difference only.

Finally, figure 3.12 extends figure 3.7 by including the years 1971 to 1980. In the recession years 1974 to 1983, the employment rate for older workers declines at the same time as unemployment goes up, most pronounced for the young, but also for the prime age group. From the mid-1980s to the mid-1990s unemployment moves cyclically around a high level for both age groups, while employment for the older workers continues the downward trend. Finally, from the mid-1990s a cyclical upturn begins with unemployment rates going down steeply while employment stabilizes among the older workers. Comparing these trends does not lend support to a substitution going on between jobs for the old and the young or the prime age group. In the next two sections we go on to examine this question in a regression setting.

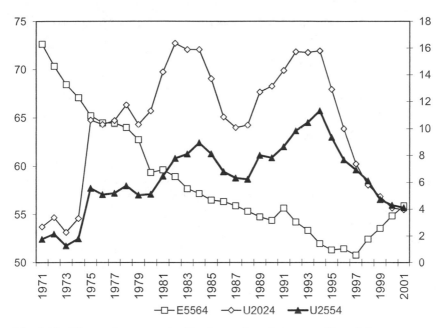

Fig. 3.12   The employment rate, fifty-five to sixty-four years old, and the unemployment rates for young, twenty to twenty-four, and prime age group, twenty-five to fifty-four, 1971 to 2001

3.4   Elderly Employment and Youth and Prime Age Activity

In this section we move from graphical evidence in the previous section to presenting descriptive ordinary least squares (OLS) time series regressions of youth and prime age activity explained by elderly employment. This allows a more careful description by controlling for a number of factors by covariates or transformations of the data. Coefficients on elderly employments from these various transformations with and without controls are presented in table 3.1.

The upper panel reports coefficients from regressions without additional covariates. The lower panel controls for gross national product (GNP), GNP growth, and manufacturing employment share. Dependent variables are *rates* throughout, and within each panel the four lines represent different transformations of the data. First, we regress on untransformed levels (of rates) on levels; second, we regress levels on three-year lags to allow for a time lag in the response; third, we regress five-year differences on five-year differences; and fourth, we regress log of five-year differences on log of five-year differences where the transformations rid the data of nonstationarities.

The first three columns show youth behavior and the last two columns

Table 3.1   Direct relationship between elderly employment and youth and prime age activity

Specification	Sample Youth UE	Youth EMP	Youth SCH	Prime UE	Prime EMP
No controls					
Levels	−0.407	−0.044	−4.180	−0.164	−0.175
	0.210	0.055	0.187	0.031	0.020
3-year lag	0.109	0.023	−3.412	−0.086	−0.143
	0.213	0.058	0.219	0.034	0.022
5-year	−2.600	−0.049	−2.466	−0.376	−0.159
difference	0.509	0.243	0.638	0.117	0.081
5-year log	−4.981	0.034	−0.659	−3.147	−0.086
difference	1.516	0.151	0.169	1.187	0.056
With controls					
Levels	−2.691	−0.088	−2.764	−0.391	−0.212
	0.255	0.153	0.348	0.070	0.055
3-year lag	−1.845	0.004	−1.747	−0.0261	−0.223
	0.396	0.163	0.478	0.085	0.058
5-year	−3.254	−0.390	−3.182	−0.433	−0.279
difference	0.652	0.362	0.937	0.177	0.124
5-year log	−3.774	0.020	−0.241	−1.374	−0.158
difference	4.039	0.363	0.447	3.145	0.112

prime age work. Focusing on the results for the youth (with no controls added), an increase in elderly employment in the differenced specifications has a statistically significant and negative impact on youth unemployment but no effect in the levels or three-year lag specification. This finding does not carry over to effects on youth employment, however, which are insignificant no matter which transformation of the data is being considered. On the other hand, in both levels and differences, youth enrollment is significantly reduced when elderly employment increases. Thus, the evidence suggests either complementarity or no relationship at all between elderly and young labor. For prime aged workers, we find again that unemployment is significantly reduced when elderly employment increases but that no clear statistical relationship between elderly employment and prime age employment can be discerned.

Adding controls for GNP, GNP growth, and manufacturing share reinforces the patterns found previously in the case of the first three transformations: that is, youth unemployment is significantly reduced, no significant effect is found for youth employment, and youth enrollment decreases significantly. For prime aged workers, adding controls results in both unemployment and employment being significantly reduced when elderly employment increases, which on the face of it appears somewhat puzzling. In the case of the last transformation—the five-year log difference—effects on both youth and the prime aged become imprecise and all statistical significance vanishes.

To summarize, the results from table 3.1 in which we seek to establish a direct relationship between elderly employment and youth (and prime age) activity turn up no evidence that an increase in elderly employment crowds out youth employment. Rather, in the instances where we can discern a clear relationship, youth unemployment and youth enrollment tend to decrease as elderly employment increases, suggesting complementarity between these worker groups.

3.5 Retirement Incentives and Employment

One concern with the correlations presented in the previous section is that the time series might have common but unobserved determinants. To make a more credible claim about measuring the effect of elderly employment on youth and prime age workers we use variation in social security provision for the elderly. Our previous work has shown that, based on individual microdata, more generous social security provision for the elderly induces earlier retirement. The challenge now is to aggregate up from an individual-based incentive to a *summary index* of the annual incentives to retire for the elderly together. A higher value of this index should reduce total elderly employment, consistent with micro evidence. Assuming that retirement incentives affect younger workers only through their effect on elderly employment, the correlation between the summary index and youth and prime age activity indicates a direct effect of elderly employment on younger workers.

A summary index of retirement incentives needs to incorporate social security eligibility conditions and levels and trajectories of potential entitlements for retiring now and later. Concepts of social security wealth (SSW) and peak value (PV) developed in Gruber and Wise (1999) and used in our previous work have been found to capture incentives well at the individual level. The SSW is the discounted present value of social security benefits received from the present until death, if retiring this year. It is assumed that individuals discount the future at 3 percent per year, use age-gender life tables (1980 life table is used 1980 to 1989, 1990 life table for 1990 to 1999, and so forth, but assuming no chance of survival beyond age 100) and believe that current social security rules will remain in force indefinitely. At the current age an individual can calculate SSW for retiring this year and for staying in work until retirement at any future age (assumed latest age eighty). For future retirement, intervening net earnings predictions are assumed calculated from age-specific means in the current year. Comparing SSW for retiring in this and all future years we can obtain PV, which is the maximum.

In order to capture variation in incentives across the population and over time we create a simulated data set of combinations of: ten levels of earnings (the midpoints of deciles of the earnings distribution) $\times$ 2 genders $\times$ 2 marital states $\times$ 3 pension program eligibilities (post employment wage, or public employees pension, or neither) $\times$ 2 disability states (eligible for social and disability pension or not) $\times$ 31 years (1971 to 2001). Our aim is to collapse incentive measures from these 7,440 simulated individuals into thirty-one annual summary indexes to be used in time series regressions. The index should reflect the retirement incentives faced by currently retired individuals when they were still in the labor force.

In order to explain construction of the index, consider a simplified example for the sake of illustration where we want to construct the index for 1990. Assume first age of social security eligibility is sixty. Those currently retired and aged sixty in 1990 must have retired in 1990 and the relevant incentive measure is obviously the mean incentive measure (a function of SSW and PV) for sixty-year-olds in 1990. Those currently retired and aged sixty-one in 1990 could have retired aged sixty in 1989 or aged sixty-one in 1990. A mean incentive measure for these currently retired sixty-one-year-olds needs to weight them according to their chance of being exposed to these incentives at these ages: employment rate of fifty-nine-year-olds in 1988 and sixty-year-olds in 1989, respectively. This can be extended until, say, those currently retired and aged sixty-six in 1990—who could have retired at sixty in 1984, sixty-one in 1985, sixty-six in 1990—and combined with relative exposure weights: employment rates of fifty-nine-year-olds in 1983, sixty in 1984, sixty-five in 1989, respectively. Hence, for the stock of current retirees aged sixty to sixty-six in 1990 we have seven incentive measures. Together these are weighted by the proportion of retirees of each age to form a single measure.

Consider the following function of SSW and PV, which should be aggregated

$$I(a, y, \alpha) = \mathrm{SSW}(a, y) + \alpha\,[\mathrm{SSW}(a, y) - \mathrm{PV}(a, y)],$$

where an individual at age a in year y is giving the gains delaying retirement (within square brackets) weight α. This weighting allows discounting of future gains beyond the 3 percent already accounted for in SSW and PV calculation: $\alpha = 0$ implies myopia and disregarding future gains, $\alpha = 1$ implies no departure from standard discounting. Variable α is determined by comparing goodness-of-fit from OLS regressions explaining elderly employment by GNP, GNP growth, manufacturing employment share, and $I(\alpha)$ calculated using different values for α. We tried α in the range 0 through 1.50 in steps of 0.25 and found 1.25 yielded the highest R-squared.

Simulated individuals are first assumed to be at risk of retirement at age fifty and must retire at (the latest) age eighty. In order to calculate weights it is necessary to back-cast earnings trajectories and employment probabilities. We observe the distribution of earnings in microdata back to 1977 and simulate earnings trajectories for decile midpoints before that date by

Table 3.2   **Retirement incentives and elderly, youth and prime age activity**

Specification	Sample elderly UE	Elderly EMP	Youth UE	Youth EMP	Youth SCH	Prime UE	Prime EMP
No controls							
Levels	0.037	−0.189	0.058	0.003	0.788	0.029	0.033
	0.007	0.009	0.042	0.011	0.053	0.007	0.004
3-year lag	0.029	−0.145	−0.050	−0.008	0.647	0.014	0.026
	0.008	0.013	0.041	0.011	0.059	0.007	0.005
5-year	0.009	−0.105	0.215	−0.051	0.089	0.029	0.017
difference	0.025	0.022	0.103	0.036	0.122	0.020	0.013
5-year log	−0.028	−0.238	0.759	−0.042	0.076	0.304	0.032
difference	0.360	0.038	0.531	0.045	0.064	0.404	0.016
With controls							
Levels	0.023	−0.147	0.345	−0.015	0.346	0.049	0.034
	0.018	0.019	0.078	0.027	0.091	0.016	0.010
3-year lag	0.017	−0.093	0.150	−0.022	0.150	0.032	0.026
	0.021	0.029	0.100	0.030	0.109	0.018	0.013
5-year	−0.010	−0.061	0.028	−0.048	−0.033	−0.004	0.028
difference	0.037	0.030	0.146	0.055	0.176	0.030	0.020
5-year log	−0.489	−0.186	−0.369	−0.089	−0.063	−0.576	0.023
difference	0.584	0.042	0.968	0.080	0.103	0.716	0.027

deflating with wage inflation. Employment microdata is observed back to 1964 and before that date we assume employment by age and gender to be constant at the 1964 level.

Different potential routes to retirement are captured by simulated individuals with eligibilities for social and disability pension, post employment wage, public employee pension, or combinations of these. Combining these routes into a single SSW and PV for each individual involves a straightforward comparison of alternative routes to find the relevant maximum path. Further to the procedure previously described for aggregating over individuals, different exit routes require scaling according to the proportion of those retiring by program. We observe different exit routes back to 1977 and assume the different exit route weighting before 1977 is constant at the 1977 level.

Having constructed the annual retirement incentive index, we can now run a time series OLS regression explaining labor market activity. Estimates of the coefficient on retirement incentive index for various specifications are presented in table 3.2. The upper panel reports coefficients from regressions without additional covariates. The lower panel controls for GNP, GNP growth, and manufacturing employment share. Dependent variables are *rates* throughout and within each panel the four lines represent different transformations of the data. First, we regress on untransformed levels (of rates) on levels; second, we regress levels on three-year lags, third, we regress

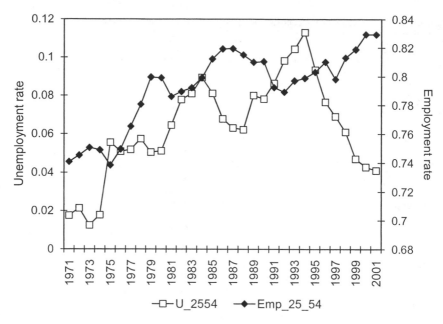

Fig. 3.13   The employment and unemployment rate, prime age group, twenty-five to fifty-four, 1971 to 2001

five-year differences on five year differences; and fourth, we regress log of five-year differences on log of five-year differences.

The first two columns show the impact of incentives on work behavior of the elderly. These show consistently negative (positive) significant effects of retirement incentives on elderly employment (unemployment). Columns (3) through (5) show youth behavior and the last two columns prime age work. To the extent that signs for elderly and younger groups are the same (opposite) we can think of them as being complements (substitutes) for each other in the labor market. With the exception of prime age employment, these younger workers are, if anything, found to be complements for the elderly in that they move together.

Prime age employment and unemployment have the same sign, which is somewhat counterintuitive. This was also the case in the previous section, where elderly employment directly explained prime age activity—prime age unemployment had an anomalous sign. A similar explanation is in order here, too. Consider again figure 3.13, where it can be seen that prime age employment and unemployment trend together for most of the observation period until the cyclical upturn starting in the mid-1990s, largely reflecting secular trends in labor force participation, especially among women, which explains why the share outside the labor force for the prime age group has gone down.

3.6 Conclusions

The purpose of this chapter has been to describe and investigate the relationship between elderly employment and the employment, unemployment, and educational enrollment of young and prime aged workers in the Danish economy. In particular, we studied whether older workers leaving the labor force by way of early retirement programs freed up job opportunities for younger workers. Denmark presented a good test case for this substitution hypothesis because of the sharp drop in labor force participation of the elderly, which occurred following the introduction of the PEW. This key reform and other policy reforms occurring over the period were largely fueled by a concern over rising youth unemployment at the time and provided the variation used to identify effects of elderly labor force participation on other segments of the labor market.

Examining linked microdata spanning a long time period, we find no observable relationship between trends in employment of the older and younger age groups. Similarly, the statistical evidence does not indicate that older workers and younger workers are substitutes. On the contrary, our regression results suggest that if anything, young workers are complements for the elderly in Denmark because youth employment tends to rise and fall together with elderly employment. For prime age workers, on the other hand, both employment and unemployment tend to rise with elderly employment, but this is most likely driven by the secular increase in female labor force participation over the period, bringing more prime aged workers into the labor market.

Reference

Gruber, J., and D. Wise, eds. 1999. *Social Security and retirement around the world.* Chicago: University of Chicago Press.

4

Labor Force Participation by the Elderly and Employment of the Young
The Case of France

Melika Ben Salem, Didier Blanchet, Antoine Bozio, and Muriel Roger

4.1 Introduction

One of the justifications that has been provided for early retirement policies in developed countries is the idea that such policies can facilitate access to the labor market for younger people and help lower global unemployment. Such a belief has undoubtedly played a role in France, where early retirement policies started to expand during the 1970s in response to rising unemployment.

Three decades later, France not only ends up with one of the lowest employment rates for the elderly among the Organization for Economic Cooperation and Development countries but also with one of the highest youth unemployment rates. Given such an outcome, beliefs about the efficiency of early retirement policies have considerably lost ground. Even if the idea of making room for new generations remains a frequent self-justification for individuals who choose to retire early, few economists or policymakers would now argue that early retirement policies are a miracle tool for fighting unemployment. The political agenda has rather shifted

Melika Ben Salem is a professor at the Université Paris-Est Marne-la-Vallée and a lecturer at the Paris School of Economics (INRA). Didier Blanchet is head of the department of General Economic Studies at the French National Statistical Institute (INSEE). Antoine Bozio is a senior research economist at the Institute for Fiscal Studies. Muriel Roger is a research economist at the Paris School of Economics (INRA) and a member of the department of General Economic Studies at the French National Statistical Institute (INSEE).

This chapter forms part of the International Social Security Project at the NBER. The authors are grateful to the other participants of that project. Material from the Enquete Emploi was made available by the Centre Quetelet. Any errors are the responsibility of the authors alone.

toward increasing activity and employment rates for older workers, especially since the 2003 pension reform.

But some questions remain. One is retrospective: how far must we push the idea that these policies have been ineffective or counterproductive? Can we definitely be confident that such policies have been of no help, even for the short run? To put it in another way, would our labor market situation have been better or worse without these early retirement policies?

The other question is symmetrical and prospective: are we sure that returning to higher retirement ages will have no adverse effects on unemployment rates? This remains a key political issue in France (Blanchet and Legros 2002). There are some advocates of the supply-side view that a strong positive shock on incentives to remain in the labor force for older workers could be sufficient to increase the employment rate for older workers while causing no harm to younger ones (D'Autume, Betbeze, and Hairault 2005). But detractors of such a policy argue that at least in the short run, it will only make unemployment worse for all age groups, with no net financial gains for social insurance. They believe that measures aimed at increasing the retirement age should not be pursued before any significant decline of the unemployment rate or even before the downturn of the labor force leads us to situations of labor shortage. In short, even if there is an increasing consensus on the fact that increasing the retirement age is more or less unavoidable in front of expected demographic trends, views continue to diverge concerning the optimal timing, intensity, and modalities of such an increase.

In this context, any empirical element on the articulation between retirement policies and general equilibrium on the labor market is welcome. The present chapter will try to contribute to this debate by concentrating on the retrospective issue. Its objective is to study the long-term relationship between labor force participation (LFP) of the old and unemployment of the young. The chapter will be organized as follows. Section 4.2 will be devoted to a presentation of the main reforms of social security and early retirement schemes since the beginning of the 1970s. We will pay particular attention to the role played by labor market considerations in justifying these reforms. Section 4.3 will then present one assessment of the incidence of these changes on labor market outcomes for younger workers. This first approach will correlate LFP for older workers with employment or unemployment rates for young or middle-age workers. One limit of this approach is that changes in LFP rates for senior workers do not only reflect the impact of retirement policies. Employment rates for all age groups are influenced by general labor market conditions, and this might lead to spurious correlation due to a simultaneity issue. Controlling for the economic cycle is one way to minimize this bias, but this comes at a cost—namely, that of abandoning the search for an unconditional relationship between young and old employment. The main criticism of economists regarding early retirement policies is that they don't take into account the knock-on effect on output.

Testing substitution conditional on output would therefore not be sufficient to establish the long-term efficiency or inefficiency of these policies. Even when controlling for the economic cycle, one may want to look for more direct effects of pension reforms on employment of the youth.

Therefore, the rest of the chapter tries to adopt another strategy, which assesses directly the impact of incentives to early retirement on youth unemployment. This strategy involves two steps. The first one is to build indicators that measure the intensity of these incentives. This step is presented in section 4.4.1. Once this has been done, these indicators are used as explanatory variables for labor market outcomes of the different age groups in section 4.4.2. This second strategy is not without flaws, either. In the case of France, we show that the incentives are themselves endogenous; that is, they have been put in place at times of rising unemployment. This means that a causal interpretation of our results remains problematic. The conclusion will come back to the general interpretation of our results.

4.2 Background: Debates and Policies

The aim of this section is to present a brief history of the development of early retirement in France, with specific attention to the role played by labor market considerations in debates that have accompanied this trend.

Several factors have converged in favor of these policies. The aspiration of workers or labor unions to early retirement has naturally played a strong role; it was the continuation of the fight against "work alienation." In the 1970s, a campaign slogan of the CGT (*Confédération Générale du Travail*), a communist-inspired union, was thus "Better Retired than Unemployed" (Guillemard 1983). In 1997, four years after the first reform that tried to increase the normal retirement age, the CGT union still officially favored the fifty-five-year-old retirement age for everyone, in particular with the goal to lower unemployment. According to a poll released at the time in the daily newspaper *Le Monde,* 61 percent of French people were in favor of "the 55 retirement age in order to lower unemployment."[1] Surveys on the perception of early retirement by employees also showed that if the first reason for accepting early retirement was the wish to stop working, many employees stated the need to leave jobs for the young as a clear motivation for their choice (Caussat and Roth 1997). The attraction for early retirement still remains relatively high in France compared to other countries, according to some results from the Survey of Health, Ageing, and Retirement in Europe (SHARE; Blanchet and Debrand 2008).

But employers and governments have also played a large role in the development of this "culture of early exit," to use an expression coined by Guillemard (2003). Employers saw these early exits as a way to facilitate

1. *Le Monde,* January 9, 1997.

the restructuring of old industries or to solve their problems of excess labor capacity. As far as governments are concerned, these early retirement policies have been one dimension of a global Malthusian answer to labor market problems, based on the idea that the total amount of work is constrained, so unemployment is just the result of an unequal distribution of work. In this context, work sharing appeared to be a good way to lower unemployment, either within cohorts (working-time reduction) or between cohorts (early retirement or longer studies). The idea that work sharing was a solution to unemployment problems was also supported by books like *The End of Work* (Rifkin 1996), which topped the best seller list in France in the 1990s. This general orientation has been common to right-wing and left-leaning governments, the only difference concerning the choice of instruments: conservative governments favored policies excluding women or immigrants from the labor force and subsidizing employers for early retirement; left-leaning governments favored lowering hours of work or lowering the age of normal retirement.

We shall examine how all these policies have been implemented, with a specific focus on policies that have applied to wage earners in the private sector, who represent the majority of the population. These workers traditionally benefit from a basic pension delivered by the *"general regime"* and from one or two complementary benefits delivered by two complementary schemes—ARRCO (*Association pour le Régime de Retraite Complémentaire des Salariés*) and AGIRC (*Association Générale des Institutions de Retraite des Cadres*)—the second one being specific to highly skilled white-collar workers. Besides these two or three forms of "normal" benefits, many of these workers have benefited during the same period from the emergence and consolidation of various forms of early or pre-retirement schemes.

To make the presentation easier to follow, we shall distinguish three main phases, identified on figure 4.1, which gives the evolution of global stocks of retired or pre-retired people for the fifty-five to sixty-four age group by broad categories:

- The first phase is a phase of increased generosity of normal pension benefits, with a normal age of retirement that remained equal to sixty-five, but accompanied by the progressive development of pre-retirement schemes for the sixty to sixty-four age group. This period lasted until the end of the 1970s.
- The second period is a period of acceleration of these early exits: first through the expansion of pre-retirement between sixty and sixty-four, then through the lowering of the normal retirement age to sixty (1983 reform), and last by the development of new pre-retirement routes that have extended the phenomenon to the fifty-five to fifty-nine age bracket.

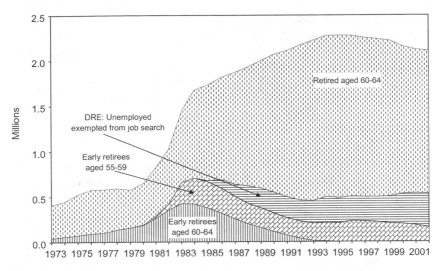

Fig. 4.1   Social security and early retirement programs (1973 to 2002)

- The third phase is one of relative stabilization, with a combination of closure or resorption of some schemes, partly compensated by the development of other ones, accompanied with two pension reforms that have started paving the way for future increases in the normal retirement age—the 1993 and 2003 reforms.

4.2.1   The Seventies: More Generous Pensions at Sixty-Five and Development of Pre-Retirement for the Sixty to Sixty-Four Age Group

Before 1971, the "general regime" offered a pension that at best was 40 percent of a reference wage, which was the average of past wages computed on the ten last years of one's career. This level was proposed at age sixty-five. A reduction/bonus of 10 percent per missing/additional year of age was applied to this pension level. For mortality conditions of the period, such an adjustment was not very far from actuarial neutrality.

The Boulin Law in 1971 has been the main change that has occurred over the period for this general regime; it increased the global generosity of the system. The normal replacement rate was raised from 40 percent to 50 percent, and the reference wage started to be computed over the ten best years of one's career rather than the ten last ones. At this stage, the motivation was not at all to encourage earlier exits. It was essentially to reduce the income gap between workers and retirees. No strong change occurred concerning retirement age; the normal age remained sixty-five, with the same bonuses/penalties for postponement/anticipation.

In this context, retirement before sixty-five took two routes. The first one was the opportunity to leave and get a normal retirement as soon as sixty in the general regime for specific categories of people, such as veterans, blue-collar working mothers, and so forth.

The second one has been the progressive development of pre-retirement schemes. It was in 1963 that such early retirement policies first appeared in France with the creation of the National Job Fund (*Fond National pour l'Emploi,* FNE) and with the associated benefit (ASFNE). This scheme provided a replacement rate of 80 percent to 90 percent of the previous net wage. It started as a very specific program but became more massive in the seventies when the steel industry underwent massive restructuring, affecting entire areas in the north of France. The fund was completely financed by the government. It must be mentioned that at the outset, this scheme did not really respond to workers' will to retire early. Early dismissal of workers belonging to declining industries was often seen by these workers as a form of denial of their social utility and therefore not welcomed by them. And the idea of using this policy to fight global unemployment was not dominant, either. The question was more sector specific, and this policy was considered transitory. The idea was just to lower the social cost of restructuring older industries. The scheme remained targeted to these regions and limited to collective layoffs.

The early retirement policy for the steel industry was further strengthened in 1972 with the creation of the CGPS (*Convention Générale de Protection de la Sidérurgie*), extending pre-retirement to wage earners as young as fifty. In the meantime, other sectors had started making large use of early exits, such as the automobile and textile industries, as a way to reduce their workforce and/or automate their production chains. A consensus was reached between unions and employers that led UNEDIC (*Union Nationale Interprofessionnelle pour l'Emploi dans l'Industrie et le Commerce,* the unemployment insurance[2]) to provide an early retirement scheme (*garantie de ressources,* GR) on a large scale. The program was first limited to layoffs (*Garantie de Ressources Licenciement,* GRL). It was targeted to the sixty to sixty-five age group. The replacement rate was 70 percent of the previous gross wage, thus higher than a full-rate pension.

It is over this period that the idea of using early exits to facilitate access to employment for younger workers took importance. As unemployment rose in the 1970s due to macroeconomic shocks, collective layoffs appeared more and more socially difficult to accept, and early retirement policies developed at a considerable rate. A consensus favored these policies as a good way to reduce unemployment. The evolution of the *garantie de ressources* is the best testimony of this change. Initially limited to layoffs in 1972, it was extended in 1977 to those people who voluntarily left their jobs (*Garantie de*

---

2. The unemployment insurance is financed and managed by unions and employers.

Ressources Démission, GRD), with the explicit ambition of reducing unemployment for the young. The preamble of the 1977 agreement clearly states, "All the parties signing this agreement expect the release of jobs allowing many unemployed to find jobs."

4.2.2   The Early 1980s: Lowering of the Normal Retirement Age and a New Phase of Expansion for Pre-Retirement

The development of these policies was also influenced by the desire to win votes in forthcoming elections.[3] For example, in 1980, just before the 1981 presidential election, the right-wing government in office reactivated the old ASFNE scheme, extending it to wage earners fifty-six years and two months old, and even fifty-five by derogation. This tendency was continued by the Socialist government that took over in 1981. Between June 1982 and December 1983, the CSPRD (*Contrat de Solidarité préretraite démission*) scheme offered a replacement rate of 70 percent of the gross wage to wage earners older than fifty-five with more than ten years of contribution who had resigned. The objective of a one-for-one substitution of senior workers by younger ones was explicitly stated, conditional on the firm maintaining its staff constant, hiring in priority young workers under twenty-six, lonely women, or unemployed people.[4] Announcing the scheme in Lille—the north of France that had been particularly hit by massive restructuring in manufacturing—the French prime minister of the time, Pierre Mauroy, asked the older workers to accept this scheme: "And I would like to speak to the elders, to those who have spent their lifetime working in this region, and well, I would like them to show the way, that life must change; when it is time to retire, leave the labor force in order to provide jobs for your sons and daughters. That is what I ask you. The Government makes it possible for you to retire at age 55. Then retire, with one's head held high, proud of your worker's life. This is what we are going to ask you. . . . This is the "contrat de solidarité." That those who are the oldest, those who have worked, leave the labor force, release jobs so that everyone can have a job."[5]

This CSPRD scheme has been the victim of its large success. In less than a year, more than 200,000 people retired through this scheme, which led to its closing (for cost reasons) one year later in December 1983, with intentions of returning to a more rigorous policy. But in the meantime, the government had decided to fulfill one of its electoral promises—retirement at age sixty. This measure was taken in a context that was temporarily favorable

---

3. Even if governments might have been convinced that early retirement was not effective in the long run, they might have used these schemes as way to secure a short-term reduction in the unemployment rate.

4. This scheme is very similar to the job release scheme implemented in the United Kingdom since 1977 (see chapter 11 in this volume), except that the level benefit—earnings related—was much more generous, particularly for high-wage earners.

5. Quoted in Gaullier (1982, 230).

for the general regime. The age group depleted by low birth rates during the First World War (i.e., born between 1915 and 1919) had started retiring in 1980. During a few years, the number of pensioners decreased, lowering the demographic ratio and generating surpluses in the pension system. The idea, therefore, was to seize this opportunity for a switch of the burden of early retirement from unemployment insurance (UNEDIC), which suffered from large deficits, to the pension system.

Formally, this 1983 reform did not change the minimum retirement age that was already equal to sixty before the reform.[6] The point was that leaving at this age initially implied a very high penalty, with a replacement rate of only 25 percent. The reform removed this penalty, allowing a 50 percent replacement rate at sixty, conditional on 37.5 years of contribution (with an unchanged penalty for those not fulfilling this condition). Contrary to early retirement schemes that were targeted, albeit imperfectly, toward the less-qualified workers, the 1983 reform was a general incentive to early retirement, given the fact that a large majority of people fulfilled this condition at sixty—at least among men.

The debate in 1983 around this lowering of the retirement age (from sixty-five to sixty) made clear once again that the goal of the reform was to release jobs for the young as well as to provide more leisure for the elderly. The best illustration of this is the fact that the reform not only increased the replacement rate but also discouraged the pursuit of work at older ages. In particular, increases in the pension rate were not possible once you had reached the "full rate."[7] The law stated that "the goal is to allow the grant of a full pension but not to encourage the pursuit of work after age 65."[8] The possibility to work while having a pension was also restricted in the hope that new pensioners would actually leave jobs for the young.[9] The Employment Ministry of the time presented the reform as a success: "The lowering of the retirement age strengthens the positive effects on employment that early retirement policies made possible. It even widens these positive effects as a large share of the population is concerned."[10]

These changes have been accompanied by changes in rules governing complementary pensions. These complementary pensions are computed according to a system that has some resemblance to the principle of notional accounts: contributions are used to buy "points," and the total number of

6. Technically, this reform was only for men, as women already had the opportunity to retire at age sixty, with full rate provided after 37.5 years of contribution. Women, however, were much less likely to fulfill this condition.

7. The only remaining way to increase its pension level was through an increase in the reference wage; that is, for employees with increasing wages after age sixty.

8. Preamble of the Ordonnance from March 26, 1982.

9. The Ordonnance from March 1982 restricted the work of pensioners. They were required to quit the firm where they were previously working and pay an additional tax to unemployment insurance. This tax was removed by the law of January 27, 1987.

10. "La retraite à 60 ans," *Droit Social,* no. 4 (April 1983).

points accumulated during one's career is converted into a pension level at retirement, with, until 1965, a quasi-actuarial adjustment according to retirement age. In 1965, the bonus for postponement had been suppressed for people retiring beyond sixty-five but the penalty maintained for retirement before sixty-five. In 1983, this penalty itself was fully removed for people retiring from the general regime with the full rate, reinforcing the incentive to retire at sixty for these people.

4.2.3   Since the mid-1980s: Changes and Continuity

The 1983 reform was expected to lead to the extinction of early retirement schemes for the sixty to sixty-four age bracket.[11] It was also expected that no further development of pre-retirement would take place. The government now wanted to avoid the development of similar amounts of early exits upstream the new retirement age of sixty (i.e., in the fifty-five to fifty-nine age bracket). Now that the normal retirement age had been lowered, pre-retirement was expected to play no more than a marginal role.

But this objective has not been fulfilled, given the continued pressure in favor of early retirement. The following story has been a story of permanent tension between the will to restrict early exits and the necessity to cope with employers' and employees' common interest in favor of early retirement. Evolutions that took place over this period can be classified according to whether they favored early exits or tried to limit them.

The main new evolution favoring early exits over this period has been the expansion of the unemployment insurance route. This essentially took place by the creation of the DRE (*Dispense de recherche d'emploi*) that was introduced in 1985.[12] The system exempts unemployed people from job seeking past a certain age (fifty-five at its creation) and offers them nondegressive benefits until they become entitled to a full-rate pension. One impact of this system has been to arithmetically lower the unemployment rate in the International Labor Organization (ILO) sense of the term, since the ILO definition considers job seeking as a necessary condition for being counted as unemployed, and this system is quasi-equivalent to pre-retirement, even if it offers replacement rates that are generally less generous than those provided by pre-retirement schemes *stricto sensu*. The unemployed who are exempted from job seeking can currently receive three different forms of benefits: the ASS (*allocation de solidarité spécifique*) provides an unemployment benefit 50 percent higher for those fifty-five and older who have at least ten years of contribution; the ACA (*allocation chômeurs âgés*) is targeted at the unemployed with forty years of contribution; and the AER (*allocation équivalent retraite*) is a means-tested additional benefit. In the 1990s, the

---

11. The switch was progressively done, because GR schemes were more generous than SS provisions, so most early retirees remained in the scheme until age sixty-five.

12. Again, this scheme was implemented just before the 1986 parliamentary elections.

DRE became numerically more important than early retirees. A regulation of this system through financial penalties on layoffs of older workers was attempted (the Delalande contributions) but with limited success (Behaghel, Crépon, and Sedillot 2005).

On the other side, we have seen the progressive closing of schemes that existed at the beginning of the period and their replacement by new schemes that have been increasingly short-lived and/or more targeted. We have already mentioned the complete closing of the CSPRD in 1983 and the progressive extinction of the *garantie de ressources*. A reduction of ASFNE benefits also took place. The initial replacement rate of the ASFNE, which was originally 70 percent, was reduced in 1982 to 65 percent under the social security (SS) ceiling[13] and to 50 percent between one and two ceilings. In 1994, this scheme was restricted to wage earners older than fifty-seven. It is now becoming progressively extinct.

The alternative pre-retirement schemes that have been created over the period to replace the former schemes have had much narrower targets. One example is the ARPE (*allocation de remplacement pour l'emploi*) scheme created in 1995, targeted at wage earners older than fifty-eight with at least forty years of contribution. The ARPE benefit provided a replacement rate of 65 percent of gross wage of the last twelve months.[14] The idea of encouraging youth employment was still present in this scheme; employers using the ARPE were compelled to replace early retirees by younger workers, especially under age twenty-six. In the case of no new hiring, firms had to reimburse the unemployment insurance. The ARPE itself was suppressed after five years of existence and replaced in 2000 by the still more focused CATS (*cessation d'activité de certains travailleurs salariés*) and CAATA (*cessation anticipée d'activité des travailleurs de l'amiante*). The CATS scheme is targeted at workers who had especially difficult working conditions (at least fifteen years on an assembly line or with night work). The minimum age is fifty-seven, although this condition can be lowered to fifty-five for certain sectors. The benefit is 65 percent of gross wage under the SS ceiling and 50 percent between one and two ceilings. The CAATA scheme targets workers exposed to asbestos; the benefit is computed as in the CATS scheme.

The other major change in the direction of later exits took place at the level of the pension scheme itself, with the two reforms enacted in 1993 and 2003.

The 1993 reform has affected incentives to retire in two ways. One way is by the reduction of pension levels at the full rate: instead of being computed on the ten best years of one's career, the reference wage is progressively

---

13. This threshold represents approximately the average wage in France.
14. Similarly, the CFA (*Congé de fin d'activite*) has also existed in the public sector, providing a replacement rate of 75 percent to civil servants older than fifty-eight with forty years of contribution.

computed on a longer period, up to twenty-five years for people born in 1948 or after. Coupled with less generous revalorization rules for these past wages, this is expected to have a strong long-run impact on pension levels. The second way is by the strengthening of the conditions required to get the full pension: it has progressively increased from 37.5 to forty years by one quarter each year.

As far as the retirement age is concerned, this 1993 reform remained symbolic, given that a large share of cohorts currently retiring go on fulfilling the new condition of forty years of past contributions. This led to the proposal of further strengthening this condition at the end of the 1990s (Charpin 1999), and this has been the main axis of the 2003 reform. For cohorts born between 1944 and 1948, the condition will temporarily remain fixed at forty years: this period has been used for organizing a convergence by public sector employees who are not concerned by the 1993 reform and for whom the condition has remained equal to 37.5. But starting in 2008, the progression of this condition starts again in the private sector: it is planned to be forty-one for the 1952 cohort and then to increase parallel with life expectancy, the progression now going at the same speed in the private and public sectors. Simultaneously, and still according to proposals from the Charpin report, the 2003 reform also changed the structure of incentives around the full rate: the penalty for early retirement has been reduced, and the bonus for postponement that had been suppressed in 1983 has been reintroduced, albeit at a lower level. After stabilization, the penalty should be 5 percent per year missing and the bonus equal to 3 percent per year of postponement. All this brings the rule closer but not strictly equivalent to actuarial neutrality.

4.2.4   Where Do We Stand? The Current State of
Ideas Concerning Early Retirement

Which preliminary conclusions can we draw from this rapid examination?

Concerning trends, the main message is that the "golden age" of early retirement expansion essentially lasted until the mid-1980s. We will use this period to test the impact of this policy on labor market outcomes. After this period, France has at best been able to stabilize the employment rate for its senior workers. Some steps in the direction of reincreasing the retirement age have been made by the 1993 reform (Bozio 2008), and more significantly by the 2003 reform, but the effects will be progressive at best and cannot be observed at this stage.

Concerning the evolution of opinions on the retirement/labor market relationship, the idea that Malthusian policies are an efficient answer to labor market disequilibrium has significantly lost ground. This applies both to early retirement policies and to other Malthusian policies such as working-time reduction. As far as retirement policy is concerned, the idea that raising the retirement age is the proper long-run solution to increased longevity has become widespread.

The point where dissensus remains more important concerns the facility of implementing such a policy in a context of high unemployment with especially low labor demand for senior workers.

At one extreme of the spectrum, the idea that it is nonsense to try to increase the age of retirement when unemployment is high remains pregnant. Just to quote one example, A. Lipietz, both a politician and economist, expressed in *Le Monde* in 1993 his opposition to proposals from a report (Commissariat Général du Plan 1991) that advised the increase of the required length of contribution: "The reduction of active life, which was an effective tool to reduce unemployment will be blocked. With a constant macroeconomic situation, each 'non out going' from the labor market will be immediately matched with a 'non in coming,' either an unemployed remaining unemployed or a young student becoming unemployed." This statement is now a bit dated but would probably continue to be shared by many observers or actors.

At the other extreme of the spectrum, some authors argue that this high unemployment rate is precisely the consequence of early retirement policies. A recent report from the Conseil d'Analyse Economique (D'Autume, Betbeze, and Hairault 2005) defends that view and argues that a stronger revision of incentives for early retirement could very well improve rather than deteriorate the employment situation of older workers: it would simply lengthen the horizon on which people plan the end of their active lives, restore their incitation to seek employment when they are unemployed, and contribute to restoring their employability from the point of view of employers. All this could take place without negative effects on other segments of the labor force, since there are little substitution effects between age groups on this labor market.

Somewhere in between, we can have the view that changes in the retirement age are indeed neutral for unemployment rates in the long run but not necessarily so in the short run. The long-run neutrality is warranted by the fact that changes in the retirement age only change the scale of the labor market, without impinging on its properties. But this does not necessarily warrant "superneutrality," (i.e., a complete absence of the impact of changes in the growth rate of labor supply). If we do not have such superneutrality, there is indeed a problem of appropriate timing for increasing the retirement age. Can we start this policy before having returned to full employment, or should we wait until full employment has been restored?

Current evolutions of the unemployment rate are not contradictory with this concern: the unemployment rate has been declining again in France since 2005, and many observers argue that this is partly the result of the fact that large cohorts of baby boomers have begun to retire. Increasing too rapidly the retirement age or being too restrictive on early retirement could slow down or even revert this process, at least for some time. This view is also consistent with quite a wide range of models of the labor market. This differentiation between short-run and long-run effects was already present in macroeconometric analysis of the impact of pre-retirement that had been performed during the 1990s (DARES 1996). It is confirmed by more recent explorations of alternative modelings of the consequences of demographic changes on unemployment (Ouvrard and Rathelot 2006).

At this stage, the question turns out to be an empirical one. We need to evaluate exactly what have been the consequences of these past policies, and this is what we shall try to do in the rest of this chapter.

4.3 Labor Force Participation for Older Workers and Labor Market Outcomes

We shall start our empirical examination with a simple visual examination of the links between these major policy changes and employment of older workers and a simple regression analysis of how these changes in older worker rates of employment did or did not affect labor market outcomes for other workers. One limit of this approach will be the fact that changes in LFP rates for senior workers do not only reflect the impact of retirement policies; they are also influenced by general labor market conditions. Controlling for the economic cycle will be one way to minimize this bias.

4.3.1 A Visual Examination

Time series of employment or unemployment rates have been provided by the Labor Force Survey (LFS) conducted by the French National Statistical Institute (INSEE) since 1950. We use the 1968 to 2005 waves of this LFS. From 1968 to 2002, the households included in the Labor Force Survey sample are interviewed in March of three consecutive years, with one-third of the households replaced each year. The French Labor Force Survey thus presents a break in the series in 2003 resulting from the transition from an annual to a continuous survey.[15] Since 2003, the households included in the French LFS have been interviewed in six consecutive quarters, with one-sixth of the households replaced each quarter. The survey samples are representative of the French population aged fifteen and up. Education and labor market status are completed for each interview.

Trends in labor force participation, employment, unemployment, and school attendance by age are given in figures 4.2 and 4.3. The rates are defined as the number of active, employed, unemployed, or in-school individuals in an age group divided by the total number of individuals in this age group. Age groups are the following: youth from twenty to twenty-four

---

15. The dummy variable introduced in the regressions to fix the problem was never significant.

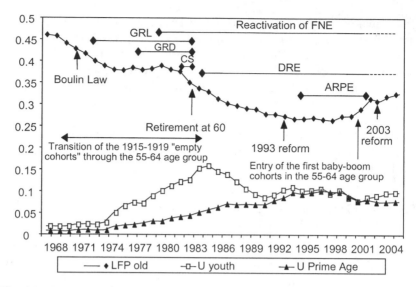

Fig. 4.2   Labor force participation of old workers and unemployment

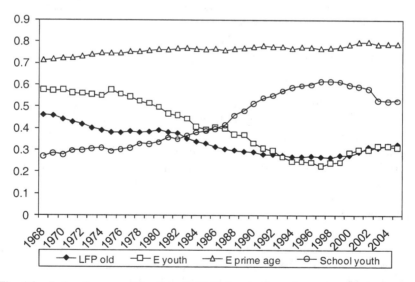

Fig. 4.3   Labor force participation of old workers and employment

years old, prime age from twenty-five to fifty-four, and seniors from fifty-five to sixty-five.

Participation rates of senior workers are quite low and are decreasing over the period, with a trend change at the end of the period due to the boom of the late 1990s. Until 1982, the decrease corresponds to a period of early retirement policies. The year 1982 marks a change in policy with the decrease in the retirement age.

The unemployment rate rose in France during the 1970s and 1980s in all age groups, and particularly for the young, with a peak in the beginning of the 1980s. The trend reverses after that. When considering figure 4.3, we see that the employment rate of the twenty to twenty-four age group is decreasing over nearly the whole period, except for a small increase in the beginning of the twenty-first century. The decrease in the youth unemployment rate is due to a massive increase in the school rate and not to a greater employment rate of young workers. The shape of the employment rate of young people is the exact opposite of the one of the school participation rate.

Concerning prime age workers, the employment rate has been quite stable over the period. The stability of the employment rate, despite massive unemployment, has to be linked with the increase of female labor participation.

4.3.2   Some Regression Results

To study the long-term relationship between labor force participation of the old and employment of the young, we will first present the results of simple ordinary least squares (OLS) regressions. The sample period for our yearly data goes from 1968 to 2005. We consider five dependent variables: the unemployment rate, the employment rate and the school attendance for young people, and the unemployment and employment rates for prime age workers. The parameter of interest is the coefficient of the labor force participation of old workers. Estimations are conducted in levels but also in three-year lags and five-year differences. Two sets of estimations have been made. In the first one, covariates included are gross domestic product (GDP) per capita, its growth rate, and the share of this GDP generated by manufacturing. In the second one, we add the mean school leaving age. Results are given in tables 4.1 and 4.2.

The first half of table 4.1 shows that direct estimation of the correlation, without controlling for general labor market conditions, suggests a negative link between senior LFP and youth unemployment and a positive link with youth employment. It also depresses the young's tendency to remain in school. All this goes more or less in the same direction of weakening the Malthusian view: a higher activity rate for senior workers stimulates the insertion of younger people into the labor market.

If we now turn to the case of prime age workers, we observe some differences. We still have a negative relationship between senior LFP and the unemployment rate of these prime age workers—once again an anti-Malthusian result. But the correlation with these prime age workers' employment rate is also negative. In other words, a lower senior LFP has the paradoxical effect of simultaneously increasing the probability to be employed and the probability to be unemployed for a prime age worker. The explanation of this paradox is probably in the increase of female labor force participation over the period.

In any event, once controls are included, many of these correlations van-

Table 4.1   **Direct relationship between the elderly labor force participation and the employment and unemployment of young and prime age persons**

	Youth, 20 to 24			Prime age, 25 to 54	
	Unemployment	Employment	School	Unemployment	Employment
	No controls				
Levels	−0.742	1.723	−1.486	−0.480	−0.250
	(0.062)	(0.165)	(0.170)	(0.030)	(0.034)
Three-year lag	−0.492	1.783	−1.683	−0.457	−0.185
on elderly	(0.090)	(0.136)	(0.141)	(0.024)	(0.031)
employment					
Five-year	−0.606	0.790	−0.208	−0.208	0.049
difference	(0.003)	(0.199)	(0.198)	(0.051)	(0.039)
Five-year log	−2.202	0.830	−0.502	−1.909	0.034
difference	(0.457)	(0.236)	(0.265)	(0.466)	(0.022)
	With controls				
Levels	−0.371	1.182	−1.080	−0.316	−0.080
	(0.246)	(0.566)	(0.677)	(0.108)	(0.097)
Three-year lag	0.161	1.433	−1.845	−0.345	−0.054
on elderly	(0.124)	(0.222)	(0.255)	(0.048)	(0.046)
employment					
Five-year	−0.455	0.116	0.348	−0.053	0.016
difference	(0.184)	(0.229)	(0.225)	(0.045)	(0.061)
Five-year log	−1.297	0.148	0.535	−0.152	0.011
difference	(1.119)	(0.227)	(0.370)	(0.714)	(0.038)

Notes: Reported is the coefficient of elderly labor force participation. Controls are GDP per capita, growth of GDP per capita, and the proportion of GDP generated by manufacturing. Three-year lag means that we regress the dependent variable on a three-year lag of elderly employment. Five-year difference means that we take fifth differences for the right- and left-hand sides. Five-year log difference means that we take the log of each X and Y variable, then take five-year differences.

ish, the coefficients of senior LFP becoming generally insignificant, as shown in the second half of table 4.1. Nevertheless, those coefficients that remain significant go on supporting the anti-Malthusian view that a high senior LFP is good news rather than bad new for other groups of workers. But controlling for output poses a number of problems. First, we are interested in the unconditional relationship between young and old employment, so any estimation controlling for GDP will remain unsatisfactory. Next, even if we were only interested in this conditional relationship, it is hard to pretend that our controls perfectly account for changes in labor demand. From these time series regressions, it is impossible to exclude the possibility that some simultaneity issue is not at play here.

There is a further issue when looking at youth employment rates, particularly striking in the case of France, and that is the role of education policies, which have dramatically affected the situation of people in the fifteen to twenty-four age group, as was shown in figure 4.3. To check whether this factor affects our results, we have made a second set of regressions, presented in table 4.2. This table is comparable to the second half of table 4.1 but

Table 4.2   **Direct relationship between the elderly labor force participation and the employment and unemployment of young and prime age persons, control by the mean school leaving age**

	Youth, 20 to 24		Prime age, 25 to 54	
	Unemployment	Employment	Unemployment	Employment
With controls				
Levels	−0.513	0.213	−0.103	−0.001
	(−0.274)	(0.399)	(0.057)	(0.104)
Three-year lag on	0.072	0.243	−0.120	0.070
elderly employment	(0.177)	(0.259)	(0.036)	(0.043)
Five-year difference	−0.381	0.338	−0.071	0.070
	(0.178)	(0.182)	(0.041)	(0.038)
Five-year log difference	−0.329	0.325	0.300	0.041
	(0.801)	(0.207)	(0.645)	(0.023)

Notes: Reported is the coefficient of elderly labor force participation. Controls are GDP per capita, growth of GDP per capita, the proportion of GDP generated by manufacturing, and the mean school leaving age. Three-year lag means that we regress the dependent variable on a three-year lag of elderly employment. Five-year difference means that we take fifth differ-ences for the right- and left-hand sides. Five-year log difference means that we take the log of each X and Y variable, then take five-year differ-ences.

with the mean age at leaving school used as an additional control variable. Results do not dramatically change compared to those of the first approach. Coefficients obtained after controlling for this school-leaving age are gener-ally less significant than before controls, but when they are, they generally go on supporting the non-Malthusian view that senior workers and workers from other age groups are complements rather than substitutes.

4.4   Measuring Changes in Retirement Incentives

Even when controlling for various determinants of general unemploy-ment, the approach followed in the previous section is difficult to interpret in terms of a causal impact of early retirement policies on employment rates of younger workers. Let's assume that some unobserved factors can have simultaneous impacts on the unemployment of younger workers and on labor force participation of older workers, these impacts being a priori of opposite signs. In principle, this will imply that periods of low labor force participation for older workers will also tend to be periods of high unemployment for younger ones. Let's also assume that a causal impact of retirement policies on youth unemployment actually exists and is of positive sign—that is, accelerating exits from the labor force by senior workers helps in lowering unemployment for younger workers. In such a context, the two relationships will offset each other, and the true benefits of early retirement policies on youth unemployment will be underestimated.

The ideal way to deal with these problems would be by instrumenting LFP rates of older workers with a variable that explains this labor force participation but that cannot be suspected of being endogenous to the global situation of the labor market. If policies had been decided completely independently from this labor market situation, an index summarizing the intensity of such policies would do the job. We shall actually look at the impact of such an index on labor market outcomes for the different age groups. But we know in advance that the exogeneity assumption is doubtful in the French case. Policies encouraging early exits have been at least partly motivated by the labor market situation, as seen in section 4.2. We shall therefore adopt a more agnostic strategy, looking at the possibility of reciprocal causation between policies and these labor market variables, relying on Granger causality tests.

The next subsection will present the method used for computing our indicator of the incentives to retire. Regression results and Granger causality tests will be presented in the subsequent one.

4.4.1   Incentive Measures

The purpose of this subsection is to translate the qualitative descriptions of section 4.2 into quantitative measures of the intensity of policies aimed at accelerating exits from the labor force by older workers. Among the many difficulties of such an exercise, one stems from the intrinsic complexity of the French system, which combines many different regulations applying to different categories of workers: wage earners in the private sector, civil servants, workers from large public firms (the so-called *régimes spéciaux*), or self-employed. As we did in section 4.2, we shall here bypass this element of complexity by concentrating on the case of wage earners in the private sector, for two reasons: these workers represent the large majority of the labor force (60 percent to 70 percent), and it is for this category of workers that the major changes occurred throughout the period.

As far as normal retirement is concerned, wage earners in the private sector are covered by one basic scheme (the *regime général*) and one or two complementary schemes—ARRCO and AGIRC—the latter being specific to highly qualified workers (*cadres*). Section 4.2 mentioned the major reforms that have been applied to the *régime général* during the period under review. Our analysis takes these reforms into account and also the associated changes in complementary schemes. Concerning access to pre-retirement, a one-by-one inclusion of all the possibilities that have existed over the period is beyond the scope of this chapter and would probably be of little interest, given the very aggregate nature of the index we are trying to build. The strategy has been instead to proxy all these routes by the dominant one for each period, giving to this route a global weight equal to the total flow of early retirees for each period.

Computations are made by gender, whatever the cohort, with a wage permanently equal to the current social security ceiling, and by deciles of length of services. Results are averaged over the subgroups. Assuming a career at the SS ceiling is close to assuming a "median" career, since the social security ceiling changed more or less in phase with the average wage.

Figure 4.4 presents results in terms of social security wealth (SSW), depending on age and time at retirement. It actually gives a good view of the main changes observed since the end of the 1960s. The SSW series has a general upward trend reflecting general economic growth. Under pre-1971 conditions, we have a strong progressivity of the pension level as a function of age. The 1971 reform leads to a strong jump. The jump is higher for people retiring around sixty, especially in 1972, due to transitory constraints on the maximum pension level that minimized the benefit of the reform for people retiring late. On the whole, the gap between pension levels reached between sixty and sixty-five remains rather large. The 1983 reform leads to an inversion of the relative position of the different curves: the reason is because offering the same replacement rate at sixty and sixty-five means offering a higher SSW at sixty than at sixty-five, due to the fact that the expected length of the retirement period is longer at sixty than at sixty-five. The opposite was true before 1983, due to the overactuarial magnitude of the penalty that applied before this date to people retiring before sixty-five.

The next step is to try combining this series into a single summary indicator. Let $W(a, y)$ represent the social security wealth of a person retiring at age a in year y. Let $q(a, y)$ represent the probability of facing such an incentive at this period and at this age; that is, the probability of still not being retired and of being entitled to such a benefit. Before the first eligibility age of sixty, this probability will be zero. After sixty, it will be 1 minus the share of people already retired; that is, $1 - p(a, y)$. Given these elements, the

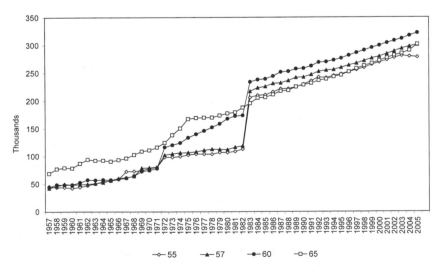

Fig. 4.4   **Social security wealth by date and age at retirement**

aggregation strategy averages past incentives $W(a, y)$ over the current stock of retirees, since what we want to measure is the cumulative effect of past incentives on current LFP rates of people over sixty. The global index that provides this aggregation is:

$$(1) \qquad \text{wbar}(y, r) = \sum_{55}^{65} \left[\frac{p(a, y)}{\sum_{55}^{65} p(a, y)} \right]$$

$$\times \left[\frac{\sum_{t=0}^{a-55} W(a - t, y - t, r) \times q(a - t, y - t)}{\sum_{t=0}^{a-55} q(a - t, y - t)} \right],$$

where the second bracket synthesizes past incentives faced by people currently retired at age a, which are then averaged over all groups of people currently retired, with ages comprised between fifty-five and sixty-five.

This aggregate indicator is provided in figure 4.5. It essentially captures the strong impact of the 1983 reform in favor of an earlier retirement.

We have also explored another version of the incentive measure, built not only on the expected social security wealth for retiring at a given age but also on the difference between the social security wealth derived for retiring now and the maximum possible value of this SSW for later ages at retirement. Let us call $PV(a, y)$ the "peak value"—that is, the maximum of the $W(a', y + a' - a)$ that can be attained for departures at ages higher than or equal to a and a^*, the corresponding age.

The aggregation of $W - PV$, using the same kind of formula as formula (1), is given by the bottom line of figure 4.5. The pattern of $W - PV$ unfortunately

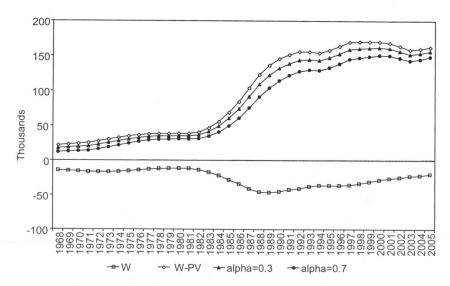

Fig. 4.5   Incentive measures

appears difficult to interpret. Previous results on microdata had underlined the importance of the peak value or of the distance to the peak value in the decision to retire. Following the microresults, an increase in $W - PV$ ($W - PV$ is negative) should induce a decrease in the labor force participation. An increase in $W - PV$ indeed means that individuals are approaching the optimal date to claim their pension. The 1983 pension reform in France induces a discontinuity in the age of the peak value. Before the reform, the optimal age to claim a pension was sixty-five; it moves to sixty in 1983. The discontinuity in $W - PV$ makes the aggregation difficult. Thus, figure 4.5 shows that $W - PV$ presents a decreasing pattern in 1983, even if we were expecting the reverse.

Nevertheless, we have attempted to build an index, mixing the incentives properties of both PV and ($W - PV$). The elementary formula is of the form:

(2) $$I(a, y, r) = W(a, y) + e^{-r(a^*-a)}[W(a, y) - PV \times (a, y)].$$

It can be interpreted as a weighted average between the gain from leaving immediately and the additional gain from postponing until the age that maximizes W, with a weighted factor for future gains equal to $e^{-r(a^*-a)}$, which will be proxied by a constant factor α. A global index ibar is computed as the global index wbar from formula (1). The conventional values $\alpha = 0.3$ and $\alpha = 0.7$ lead to the last two curves on figure 4.5. Given the relatively small difference between these curves and the initial one, we shall here concentrate on results based on W only. For comparison purposes with other countries, we give results based on the 'ibar' approach (equation [2]) in the appendix.

4.4.2   Measuring the Impact of Pension Policy Indices on Labor Market Outcomes

Tables 4.3 to 4.5 present the effects of aggregate social security wealth on different labor market outcomes: labor force participation of the old (denoted LFPold) and unemployment and employment rates of the young (denoted, respectively, Uyouth and Eyouth). Several specifications and sets of control variables are used to test the robustness of the results. In addition to the three control variables used in table 4.1 (GDP per capita, growth of GDP per capita—denoted DGDP—and the share of manufacturing in GDP—denoted MS), we have also used the mean age of the fifty-five to sixty-five age group (denoted MA_5565)[16] and the ratio of the minimum wage to the average wage (denoted MW). As in our previous analysis, the mean school leaving age (denoted MSLA) is used to measure the impact of

---

16. The labor force participation of the old is influenced by changes in the age structure. In particular, large changes in the mean age of the fifty-five to sixty-four age group were experienced in France between 1974 and 1985 as a result of the low fertility rates during World War I; that is, cohorts born between 1915 and 1918 are much smaller than previous and later cohorts.

education policies, which might have been fostered by concerns about youth unemployment and are essential in explaining the drop in youth labor force participation in France.[17]

All three tables have the same structure. In the top part, we present the coefficients of the wealth index according to various specifications. In the first specification (column [1]), we use the same set of control variables as in table 4.1 (GDP per capita, its growth rate, and the share of manufacturing in production). In the following columns, we add or remove control variables according to their relevance for the corresponding labor market outcome; that is, the mean age of the fifty-five to sixty-five age group in the LFPold regression or the minimum wage for Eyouth and Uyouth. The number of observations being relatively low (a maximum of thirty-eight observations to a minimum of thirty-two when taking the fifth differences of the variables), we test the robustness of these regressions by limiting the number of control variables, either for the business cycle (GDP per capita, its growth rate) or the productive structure of the economy (the share of manufacturing in production), in order to leave explaining power for the more specific variables (columns [3] and [4]). Endogeneity of the pension policy in the French political context, as discussed previously, is an issue that could not be put aside. We try to address this issue by implementing some Granger causality tests in a bivariate framework. We present these results in the bottom part of each table. Control variables are introduced as exogenous variables (we do not have enough degrees of freedom to deal with all variables as endogenous ones). We have two bivariate systems to estimate—youth unemployment and the pension wealth index and youth employment and the pension wealth index—and we test if past youth employment (or unemployment) could improve the prediction of the pension wealth index; that is, if youth unemployment (or employment) at date t helps to better predict the pension wealth index at date $t + 1$, whatever the exogenous variables.

Table 4.3 corresponds to the regressions with all the variables in levels. First, the effect of the wealth index on the labor force participation of the old has the expected negative sign. However, it is not significant in specification (2), which includes the largest set of controls, and in specification (3), for which the growth rate of GDP per capita has been omitted. When comparing specifications (1) and (4), the inclusion of the mean age of the fifty-five to sixty-five age group instead of the share of manufacturing in production increases the negative impact on the labor force participation of the old of the pension incentives index. For the other labor market outcomes, the effect of the wealth index is always significant, whatever the set of the control variables, and is with a similar size and the same sign: negative for both the

---

17. The share of the young in school (denoted Syouth) could be an alternative measure of these education policies. Yet, it is linked by an identity relationship to the unemployment and employment of the young.

Table 4.3   Regressions in level, wealth index estimated coefficient

	(1)	(2)	(3)	(4)
LFPold	**–0.022**	–0.000	–0.000	**–0.093**
	(0.012)	(0.011)	(0.011)	(0.008)
Uyouth	**–0.04**	**–0.076**	**–0.070**	**–0.057**
	(0.014)	(0.015)	(0.014)	(0.016)
Eyouth	**–0.191**	**–0.189**	**–0.196**	**–0.194**
	(0.018)	(0.022)	(0.020)	(0.023)
Syouth	**0.244**	**0.234**	**0.242**	**0.219**
	(0.015)	(0.020)	(0.019)	(0.019)
Causality tests				
Uyouth $\rightarrow W$	yes	yes	yes	yes
$W \rightarrow$ Uyouth	yes	yes	yes	yes
Eyouth $\rightarrow W$	no	no	no	no
$W \rightarrow$ Eyouth	no	no	no	no

Notes: (1): LFPold = GDP, DGDP, MS; Uyouth, Eyouth, Syouth = GDP, DGDP, MS. (2): LFPold = GDP, DGDP, MS, MA_5565; Uyouth, Eyouth, Syouth = GDP, DGDP, MS, MW. (3): LFPold = GDP, MS, MA_5565; Uyouth, Eyouth, Syouth = GDP, MS, MW. (4): LFPold = GDP, DGDP, MA_5565; Uyouth, Eyouth, Syouth = GDP, DGDP, MW. Parameters in bold are significant at the 5-percent threshold.

unemployment and employment of youth and positive for the schooling of youth. An increase in the social security wealth index is associated both with lower youth employment and lower youth unemployment. This result is not completely surprising, given that the pension wealth index is also associated positively with the share of the young in school. To rephrase this result in the light of our previous descriptive analysis (section 4.3), at a time of increased youth unemployment, both early retirement policies and expansion of schooling have taken place. Taking into account these education policies, which is done in table 4.5, may allow us to help shed light on the relationship between retirement policies and the labor market status of the young.

When looking at the results of the causality tests, we accept Granger causality between the unemployment of youth and the wealth index in both directions, whereas we reject it between the employment of youth and the wealth index. It is therefore more cautious to avoid causal interpretation of the effect of the wealth index on the youth labor market outcomes, given these endogeneity issues.

Results in table 4.4 correspond to regressions with all the variables in fifth differences. Differentiation is a way to address the endogeneity issue. By differencing, we lose control variables, such as the growth of GDP per capita, and we implement only two specifications. As we lose almost 10 percent of our observations, the coefficient of the wealth index is no longer significant in the regression on the labor force participation of the old. As a result, the regressions on the other outcomes cannot be interpreted in a causal way.

Surprisingly, the coefficient of the pension wealth index on the other labor market outcomes remains significant and of the same sign (the size is more volatile) as in the regressions in levels. The Granger causality tests confirm the results obtained in table 4.3. These results reinforce the need to control for education policies.

Table 4.5 is very similar to table 4.3, except that we systematically add the mean school leaving age in each set of control variables. There remain only two explained variables—employment and unemployment of youth—since the mean school leaving age is not relevant for the fifty-five to sixty-five age group (the coefficient for the LFPold regression is then the same as in table

Table 4.4   **Regressions in fifth differences, wealth index estimated coefficient**

	(1)	(2)
LFPold	−0.002	−0.002
	(0.026)	(0.014)
Uyouth	**−0.095**	**−0.211**
	(0.029)	(0.025)
Eyouth	**−0.078**	**−0.183**
	(0.030)	(0.039)
Syouth	**0.137**	**0.311**
	(0.027)	(0.032)
Causality tests		
Uyouth $\rightarrow W$	yes	yes
$W \rightarrow$ Uyouth	yes	yes
Eyouth $\rightarrow W$	no	no
$W \rightarrow$ Eyouth	no	no

Notes: (1): LFPold = GDP, MS; Uyouth, Eyouth, Syouth = GDP, MS. (2): LFPold = GDP, MS, MA_5565; Uyouth, Eyouth, Syouth = GDP, MS, MW. Parameters in bold are significant at the 5-percent threshold.

Table 4.5   **Regressions in levels, with the mean school leaving age added: Wealth index estimated coefficients**

	(1)	(2)	(3)	(4)	(5)
Uyouth	**−0.106**	**−0.052**	**−0.063**	0.024	−0.062
	(0.027)	(0.028)	(0.028)	(0.031)	(0.045)
Eyouth	**−0.140**	−0.047	**0.078**	**−0.124**	**−0.148**
	(0.033)	(0.039)	(0.039)	(0.048)	(0.038)
Causality tests					
Uyouth $\rightarrow W$	yes	yes	yes	yes	yes
$W \rightarrow$ Uyouth	yes	yes	yes	no	yes
Eyouth $\rightarrow W$	no	no	no	yes	no
$W \rightarrow$ Eyouth	no	no	no	no	no

Notes: (1): GDP, DGDP, MS. (2): GDP, DGDP, MS, MW. (3): GDP, MS, MW. (4): GDP, DGDP, MW. (5): GDP, DGDP. Parameters in bold are significant at the 5-percent threshold.

4.3), and it is certainly endogeneous in the Syouth regression. The effect of the wealth index on unemployment or employment of the youth and Granger causality between the wealth and the two outcomes of interest are the same as in table 4.3 when controlling for the mean school leaving age.

The causality tests lead us to confirm that these variables are indeed endogenous. Causal relationships are therefore impossible to establish, and we are left with the weak evidence of previous sections.

4.5   Conclusion

The main objective of this chapter has been to study the link between youth labor market status and older workers' labor force participation in the case of France. The main reforms favoring early retirement policies in the decade between 1975 and 1985 were based, at least in the political debate, on the argument that they would foster young workers' employment. Evidence of the correlation between youth labor market outcomes and old workers' labor force participation plead more in favor of a positive association between young and old workers in the labor market. An increase in the old workers' participation is indeed correlated with an increase in the employment rate of young workers and a decrease in their unemployment rate. Even when controlling for the economic cycle, this positive association remains—albeit less robustly. These correlations based on time series, however, are not evidence of a causal relationship between young and old employment. For a start, even if we had been able to properly measure substitution between these two age groups, controlling for total output in the economy, we would not be able to state that these policies have been effective in the long term, unconditional on output. In our case, we do not find evidence of substitution conditional on output. The second caveat of these time series correlations is that it is impossible to exclude the possibility that they are not faced with a simultaneity issue—that is, that general employment conditions, not taken into account in our controls, could explain both employment of the young and of the old.

To deal with this problem, we instead use the LFP rates of older workers in an index summarizing the intensity of policies aimed at removing older workers from the labor market, based on social security wealth. The effect of the wealth index on youth labor market outcomes is always significant, whatever the set of control variables we use, and is with a similar size and the same sign. The coefficient is negative for both the unemployment and employment of youth, with or without controlling for school attendance. Granger causality tests between unemployment of youth and the wealth index show a significant link in both directions, whereas nothing is significant between the employment of youth and the wealth index.

Establishing a causal relationship of the reduction of labor force participation of the old on employment prospects of the young is indeed challenging work. Given the general equilibrium element of their impact and the endogeneity of the policies at stake, one is constrained to look—within one country—at time series. If we do not find evidence that reducing the labor force participation of the old provides jobs for the young, we cannot exclude altogether the possibility that some general and unaccountable cause is hiding their true effect.

Appendix

Tables 4A.1 and 4A.2 are defined as table 4.3, and tables 4A.3 and 4A.4 are defined as table 4.5, except that the pension index here is a composite index, defined as:

$$I(a, y, r) = W(a, y) + e^{-r(a^*-a)}[W(a, y) - PV \times (a, y)].$$

The main issue with this pension index is to find a value for α, which is a kind of subjective preference for the present rate. According to the average values of different long-term and no-risk interest rates for the time period, it can range from 0.3 to 0.7. We thus replicate the same exercise as for the wealth index for two pension indices (denoted ibar), and tables 4A.1 and 4A.3 (respectively, tables 4A.2 and 4A.4) report the results for $\alpha = 0.3$ (respectively, $\alpha = 0.7$). Globally, the results are very similar to the results obtained with the wealth index. Indeed, we find that the paradoxal results remain; that is, the complementarity between youth employment and the

Table 4A.1   Regressions in level, $\alpha = 0.3$

	(1)	(2)	(3)	(4)
LFPold	–0.001	–0.021	–0.001	**–0.096**
	(0.011)	(0.012)	(0.011)	(0.009)
Uyouth	**–0.082**	**–0.040**	**–0.074**	**–0.067**
	(0.015)	(0.014)	(0.014)	(0.016)
Eyouth	**–0.202**	**–0.198**	**–0.198**	**–0.209**
	(0.023)	(0.019)	(0.019)	(0.024)
Syouth	**0.251**	**0.254**	**0.257**	**0.242**
	(0.019)	(0.013)	(0.013)	(0.018)
Causality tests				
Uyouth → ibar	yes	yes	yes	yes
Ibar → Uyouth	yes	yes	yes	yes
Eyouth → ibar	no	no	no	no
Ibar → Eyouth	no	no	no	no

Notes: (1): LFPold = GDP, DGDP, MS, MA_5565; Uyouth, Eyouth, Syouth = GDP, DGDP, MS, MW. (2): LFPold = GDP, DGDP, MS; Uyouth, Eyouth, Syouth = GDP, DGDP, MS. (3): LFPold = GDP, MS, MA_5565; Uyouth, Eyouth, Syouth = GDP, MS, MW. (4): LFPold = GDP, DGDP, MA_5565; Uyouth, Eyouth, Syouth = GDP, DGDP, MW. Parameters in bold are significant at the 5-percent threshold.

Table 4A.2   **Regressions in level, $\alpha = 0.7$**

	(1)	(2)	(3)	(4)
LFPold	–0.001	–0.021	**–0.101**	–0.001
	(0.011)	(0.012)	(0.010)	(0.011)
Uyouth	**–0.090**	**–0.040**	**–0.083**	**–0.080**
	(0.014)	(0.014)	(0.016)	(0.014)
Eyouth	**–0.221**	**–0.207**	**–0.226**	**–0.226**
	(0.024)	(0.020)	(0.027)	(0.022)
Syouth	**0.276**	**0.266**	**0.273**	**0.278**
	(0.017)	(0.011)	(0.016)	(0.015)
Causality tests				
Uyouth → ibar	yes	yes	yes	yes
Ibar → Uyouth	yes	yes	yes	yes
Eyouth → ibar	no	no	no	no
Ibar → Eyouth	no	no	no	no

Notes: (1): LFPold = GDP, DGDP, MS, MA_5565; Uyouth, Eyouth, Syouth = GDP, DGDP, MW. (2): LFPold = GDP, DGDP, MS; Uyouth, Eyouth, Syouth = GDP, DGDP, MW. (3): LFPold = GDP, MS, MA_5565; Uyouth, Eyouth, Syouth = GDP, MS, MW. (4): LFPold = GDP, DGDP, MA_5565; Uyouth, Eyouth, Syouth = GDP, DGDP, MW.

Table 4A.3   **Regressions in level with mean school leaving age, $\alpha = 0.3$**

	(1)	(2)	(3)	(4)	(5)
Uyouth	**–0.123**	**–0.065**	**–0.077**	0.018	*–0.093*
	(0.029)	(0.032)	(0.031)	(0.037)	(0.049)
Eyouth	**–0.160**	–0.056	**–0.091**	**–0.141**	**–0.167**
	(0.037)	(0.045)	(0.045)	(0.056)	(0.042)
Causality tests					
Uyouth → ibar	yes	yes	yes	yes	yes
Ibar → Uyouth	yes	yes	yes	no	yes
Eyouth → ibar	no	no	no	no	no
Ibar → Eyouth	no	no	no	yes	no

Notes: (1): GDP, DGDP, MS. (2): GDP, DGDP, MS, MW. (3): GDP, MS, MW. (4): GDP, DGDP, MW. (5): GDP, DGDP.

Table 4A.4   **Regressions in level with mean school leaving age, $\alpha = 0.7$**

	(1)	(2)	(3)	(4)	(5)
Uyouth	**–0.152**	**–0.091**	**–0.103**	–0.004	**–0.153**
	(0.031)	(0.038)	(0.036)	(0.049)	(0.052)
Eyouth	**–0.193**	–0.071	**–0.113**	**–0.165**	**–0.191**
	(0.044)	(0.055)	(0.054)	(0.071)	(0.048)
Causality tests					
Uyouth → ibar	yes	yes	yes	yes	yes
Ibar → Uyouth	yes	yes	no	no	yes
Eyouth → ibar	no	no	no	no	no
Ibar → Eyouth	no	no	no	yes	no

Notes: (1): GDP, DGDP, MS. (2): GDP, DGDP, MS, MW. (3): GDP, MS, MW. (4): GDP, DGDP, MW. (5): GDP, DGDP.

pension index in one hand and the substitutability with unemployment in the other hand.

References

Behaghel, L., B. Crépon, and B. Sédillot. 2005. Contribution Delalande et transitions sur le marché du travail. *Economie et Statistique,* no. 372:61–88.
Blanchet, D., and T. Debrand. 2008. The sooner the better: Analyzing preferences for early retirement in European countries. IRDES Working Paper no. 13. Paris: Institute for Research and Information in Health Economics.
Blanchet, D., and F. Legros. 2002. France: The difficult path to consensual reforms. In *Social security pension reform in Europe,* ed. M. Feldstein and H. Siebert, 109–35. Chicago: University of Chicago Press.
Bozio, A. 2008. How elastic is the response of the retirement-age labor supply? Evidence from the 1993 French pension reform. In *Pension strategies in Europe and the United States,* ed. R. Fenge, G. de Menil, and P. Pestieau, 37–85. Cambridge, MA: MIT Press.
Caussat, L., and N. Roth. 1997. De l'emploi à la retraite: Générations passées et générations futures. *Revue Française des Affaires Sociales* 51 (October): 177–205.
Charpin, J. M. 1999. *L'avenir de nos retraites, rapport au premier ministre.* Paris: La Documentation Française.
Commissariat Général du Plan. 1991. *Livre blanc sur les retraites: Garantir dans l'équité les retraites de demain.* Paris: La Documentation Française.
Direction de l'Animation de la Recherche, des Études et des Statistiques (DARES). 1996. *40 ans de politiques de l'emploi.* Paris: La Documentation Française.
D'Autume, A., J.-P. Betbeze, and J.-O. Hairault. 2005. *Les seniors et l'emploi en France.* Report for the Conseil d'Analyse Economique, no. 58. Paris: La Documentation Française.
Gaullier, X. 1982. *L'avenir à reculons: Chômage et retraite.* Paris: Les Éditions Ouvrières.
Guillemard, A.-M. 1983. La dynamique sociale des cessations d'activité. *Travail et Emploi* 15:15–31.
———. 2003. *L'âge de l'emploi: Les sociétés face au vieillissement.* Paris: Armand Colin.
Ouvrard, J.-F., and R. Rathelot. 2006. Demographic change and unemployment: What do macroeconometric models predict? INSEE Working Paper no. G2006-04. Paris: INSEE.
Rifkin, J. 1996. *The end of work.* New York: Tarcher.

Early Retirement and Employment of the Young in Germany

Axel Börsch-Supan and Reinhold Schnabel

5.1 Introduction

Early retirement in Germany is very costly and amplifies the burden that the German public pension system has to carry due to population aging. Benefits paid to individuals aged sixty-four years or younger are about one-quarter of total benefits paid. This corresponds to about 5 percentage points of the current contribution rate.

Our earlier analyses (Börsch-Supan and Schnabel 1998, 1999; Berkel and Börsch-Supan 2004; Börsch-Supan et al. 2004; Börsch-Supan, Schnabel, and Kohnz 2007) have shown that an important reason for the large and costly extent of early retirement in Germany is the force of early retirement incentives built into the German public pension system. The provisions driving workers into early retirement are not accidental side effects of the pension system design. They are still in place, with the explicit motivation to "make room for the young." Underlying this is the popular belief that employment of older individuals crowds out employment of younger individuals. Turned positively, many believe that for each individual sent into early retirement, a younger individual can take up a new job.

The belief is deeply rooted in the analogy of a small enterprise with a fixed

Axel Börsch-Supan is director of the Mannheim Institute for the Economics of Aging (MEA), professor of macroeconomics and economic policy at the University of Mannheim, and a research associate of the National Bureau of Economic Research. Reinhold Schnabel is professor of economics at the University of Duisburg-Essen.

Financial support was provided by the National Institute on Aging through the NBER and by the German Research Foundation (DFG) through Sonderforschungsbereich 504. We are also grateful for financial support by the State of Baden-Württemberg and the German Insurers Association (GDV).

and small number of clients who have a fixed demand for the product of the enterprise. Such an enterprise is boxed into a fixed amount of output and therefore can only employ a fixed lump of labor.

This chapter shows that this boxed-in enterprise is not at all a good analogy to an entire economy. In fact, our evidence shows that higher employment of older individuals is *positively* correlated with higher employment of the young. In contrast to the small enterprise just described, entire economies can grow, increasing the demand for all goods and services and therefore also the demand for labor. It is a fallacy to believe that there is a fixed lump of labor to be distributed among the young and the old: jobs for the old do *not* have to be taken away from the young. Moreover, costs for early retirement cannot be put on someone else's shoulders, as enterprises often can do it. In an entire economy, all social transfer expenses have to be borne by tax and contribution payers.

This insight might be unpopular. However, it is anything but new. Figure 5.1 shows data from a set of Organization for Economic Cooperation and Development (OECD) countries clearly indicating that countries with a high prevalence of early retirement generally have *higher* unemployment rates and *lower* employment of the young.

In spite of such suggestive evidence, the misconception of a fixed lump of labor that has to be shared between the old and the young (the "lump of labor fallacy" or the "boxed economy view") keeps dominating much of the policy debate on pension reform in Germany and elsewhere. The suggestive power of a small enterprise with a fixed and small number of clients as a model for the entire economy appears to be stronger than the suggestive power of figure 5.1.[1]

The topic is timely and relevant in Germany. A controversial 2007 reform ("Rente mit 67") will raise the statutory retirement age from sixty-five to sixty-seven in annual steps between 2012 and 2028. According to the original reform design, at the end of the transition phase in 2028, full benefits will be paid at age sixty-seven, and retirement at age sixty-five will lead to a 7.2 percent reduction (two years times 3.6 percent) of benefits.

This fundamental decision to adjust the length of working life to the increased total life span has been confronted with the argument that raising the retirement age would lead to higher unemployment among the young, and it continues to be watered down. First, already during the legislative process, the actuarial adjustments were limited to persons with an employment career of less than forty-five years—that is, there will be no actuarial adjustment for those with a "full" working life of forty-five years or more. Moreover, the duration of unemployment benefits has been extended for older workers, thereby reversing important decisions of the so-called Hartz

---

1. Figure 5.1 is only suggestive, as it depicts a positive correlation between two macrolevel variables but not a causal relationship; see the following discussion.

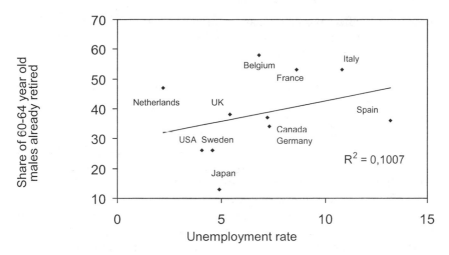

Fig. 5.1   Early retirement and unemployment in the OECD
Source: Own calculations based on OECD *Employment Outlook 2007.*

reforms of the German labor market. Finally, there is increasing pressure by the unions to extend subsidizing part-time retirement. Such subsidies were originally introduced to permit a flexible transition from full-time work via part-time work/part-time retirement to full retirement. However, almost all workers choose to divide the five-year transition period into one block of full-time work and another block of full retirement, effectively reducing the early retirement age by 2.5 years ("Blockaltersteilzeit").

Given the actual policy debate, it would be extremely helpful to know more about the relationship between retirement policy and employment of the young, specifically in Germany, and to provide a causal interpretation of figure 5.1. This is the aim of this chapter. It shows that the German data provide no evidence for the belief that older workers take jobs away from the young. In fact, if there is a link at all, higher employment of older individuals in Germany is positively correlated with higher employment of the young.

The chapter uses various pension design changes in Germany as instruments to identify how higher or lower employment of older individuals has affected the employment of the young. The central question of this chapter, therefore, is: how did pension reforms affect the labor market—in particular, employment and unemployment of the old versus the young?

Section 5.2 of the chapter summarizes important pension reform steps in Germany. Section 5.3 describes employment and unemployment over time by age group and attempts to draw first links between changes in employment patterns and pension reforms. Section 5.4 provides the analytical part of the chapter. We quantify the changes of early retirement incentives over time and measure their effect on older workers' employment. This follows our earlier work. We then answer the central and more difficult question:

how did this affect the labor market, in general, and employment of the young, in particular? Section 5.5 concludes.

Our methodology can be interpreted as a reduced-form analysis. We regress labor market outcomes for the young on employment of the old, using pension policy changes for a regression discontinuity design. We also regress labor market outcomes directly on changes in the policy instruments. The theoretical framework behind this reduced-form analysis is a macro-economic model of a pension system, labor markets for young and old, and product demand. Such a model is provided, for example, by Börsch-Supan and Ludwig (2008). It is noteworthy that such a model produces a *positive* correlation between retirement age and employment.

Quite clearly, we need "strong" reforms in order to empirically identify the effects of pension policies on labor market outcomes for the young, since there are many confounding factors operating at the same time. In Germany, we can identify several such important reforms that dramatically changed retirement incentives. In response, retirement behavior changed equally dramatically.

Moreover, we have to care about the potential endogeneity of pension policy changes. An endogeneity problem arises if the pension reform was triggered by higher youth unemployment. In this case, the reform cannot be used as an instrument in econometric analysis, and causal analysis will fail.[2]

Finally, pension reform may be just one element in a reform package, which also includes labor market reforms. In this case, it may be impossible to identify which reform element actually caused the results.

In order to take care of these concerns, we exploit what we know from the historical policy debate (section 5.2) and what we can learn from the labor market outcomes at that time (section 5.3). With respect to endogeneity, we will argue that at least two reforms were not motivated by employment concerns. The first reform came into effect in 1972 in a period of labor shortage, not youth unemployment. The second reform was drafted before reunification in 1989 in a situation of decreasing unemployment and was phased in between 1998 and 2004. This reform was motivated by concerns about the long-term solvency of the public pay-as-you-go (PAYG) pension system (Prognos 1995, 1998) in the face of population aging.

Potentially confounding factors were other reforms in Germany, among them being the extension of worker protection rules (layoff protection), the reductions in standard working hours through collective contracts, various changes in education policy (increasing educational attainment, prolonged education), and changes in immigration policy. Most of these other policy changes can be dated precisely. Hence, we focus on those pension reforms that did not concur with general labor market reforms. In addition, we will

2. A causal interpretation of figure 5.1 suffers from this critique.

investigate the time and lag patterns in order to minimize the contamination of the relation between retirement and employment of the young.

5.2 Regimes of Retirement Policies in Germany

The German pension system, designed by Bismarck almost 120 years ago, began as a funded system but was transformed into a pay-as-you-go system in 1957 after about half of the capital stock was lost in two world wars and a hyperinflation.

As opposed to other countries such as the United Kingdom and the Netherlands, which originally adopted a Beveridgian social security system that provided only a base pension, public pensions in Germany are designed to extend the standard of living that was achieved during working life also to the time after retirement: individual pension benefits are essentially proportional to individual labor income averaged over the entire life course and feature only few redistributive properties.

The following brief history of the German pension system distinguishes four phases:[3] (a) a relatively stable phase after the introduction of the pay-as-you-go system until 1972; (b) a phase of increasing generosity precipitated by the 1972 pension reform; (c) a phase of cost-cutting reforms after 1992, leading to a sustainable pension system by 2007; and (d) first signs that we may actually experience a phase of reform backlash. While this section focuses on pension reforms, we will at several instances refer to the following section 5.3 for concurring labor market outcomes.

5.2.1 Phase 1 (1957 to 1972): Stability

Initially, the pay-as-you-go system introduced in 1957 had a single eligibility age for old-age pension: age sixty-five for men and age sixty for women (conditioned on a minimum number of years of service). Earlier retirement was impossible unless one could prove a disability. Disability rates were very high after World War II and then declined; employment of elderly males was increasing until about 1967 and declined slightly after the recession of 1967 (see the employment history provided in section 5.3—in particular, figure 5.6).

5.2.2 Phase 2 (1972 to 1992): Increasing Generosity

The 1972 reform was a major change in policy. It introduced "flexible retirement" by providing old-age pension benefits at age sixty-three, given that workers had a minimum of thirty-five years of which they contributed to the system. These benefits were not actuarially adjusted. It is important to note that the 1972 reform was not motivated by labor market con-

---

3. For a detailed description of the evolution of the German pension system, see Börsch-Supan and Wilke (2006).

cerns. Rather, this very popular bipartisan reform decision was celebrated as a major achievement to provide more leisure to the workers. Indeed, the average retirement age dropped by more than two years, and employment rates of older individuals plummeted (see figure 5.6).

Between 1984 and 1987, early retirement was further extended by creating a "bridge to retirement." The government introduced more generous unemployment insurance benefits for older workers, which were especially attractive in the age range from fifty-five to fifty-nine years: up to thirty-two months of unemployment insurance benefits at 63 or 68 percent of former net wages. These benefits were not means tested, and job-search activities were not required for those unemployed who were aged fifty-five and older. In addition, severance pay became tax advantaged for the employees.

As opposed to the 1972 reform, these changes in the eligibility and duration of unemployment benefits were explicitly motivated by the increasing unemployment (see figure 5.2) and the desire to "make room for young workers." As a result of the "bridge to retirement," registered unemployment of the elderly (age fifty-five to fifty-nine) rose immediately, and the pathways to retirement changed dramatically. Disability benefits declined, while the uptake of unemployment insurance became the most important pathway to retirement by 1990 (see figure 5.5).

5.2.3   Phase 3 (1992 to 2007): Sustainability Reforms

Threatened by demographic change, Germany began in the early 1990s a fifteen-year-long process of reform steps. These reform steps were not masterminded; some "happened" due to budget crises and new political constellations. Seen from hindsight, however, the reform steps follow an astoundingly consistent red threat.

Step 1: Toward Actuarial Adjustments (1992)

The first step in the long German reform process was the 1992 reform. It anchored benefits to net rather than to gross wages. This removed an odd mechanism that would have created a vicious cycle of increasing pension benefits in response to increasing contribution rates. At the same time, credits for higher education were abolished and survivor benefits reduced.

The second important element in the 1992 reform was the introduction of "actuarial" adjustments to benefits to retirement age. "Actuarial" is set in quotation marks because the adjustment factors have been set discretionarily at 3.6 percent for each year of earlier retirement and are not directly linked to changes in life expectancy. They are about 1.5 percentage points lower than current life tables, and a 3 percent discount rate would imply.[4]

---

4. Actuarial computations depend on a discount or interest rate, which makes payments made or received at different points in time commensurable. Usually, a rate of 3 percent is assumed—sometimes 4 or 5 percent. The German computations rest on a discount rate of about 1 percent.

Nevertheless, their gradual introduction between 1998 and 2006 reduced incentives to retire early, and retirement age and labor force participation of older individuals has indeed increased since then, almost symmetrically to the decline after the 1972 reform (see figure 5.3 and Börsch-Supan (1992) for an early prediction of this effect).

Step 2: Toward a Genuine Multipillar System (2001)

The financial situation of the pension system worsened rather quickly after the 1998 elections that brought the Social Democrats to power in Germany. As a remarkable irony in politics, the former union leader, then secretary of labor Walter Riester, successfully passed a major reform bill through parliament in 2001.[5]

The Riester reform is a major change of the German public pension system. It changed the monolithic pay-as-you-go retirement insurance to a genuine multipillar system by partially substituting pay-as-you-go financed pensions with funded pensions. The reform aimed to achieve three main objectives. First, the reform was to stabilize contribution rates. The Riester reform law actually states that contribution rates to the public retirement insurance scheme must stay below 20 percent until 2020 and below 22 percent until 2030, while the net replacement rate must stay above 67 percent. Failure must precipitate further government action. Second, a new pillar of supplementary-funded pensions was introduced. Contributions to this pillar are subsidized, either by tax deferral and tax deduction or by direct subsidies. These supplementary pensions, however, are not mandatory. Third, benefits of the pay-as-you-go system were scheduled to be gradually reduced in proportion to the maximum subsidized contribution to the new supplementary pensions.

Step 3: Toward Sustainability (2004)

Although praised as a "century reform," it quickly became obvious that the cost-cutting measures of the Riester reform would not suffice to meet the contribution rate targets. A new reform commission, the Commission for Sustainability in Financing the German Social Insurance Systems, was established in November 2002.[6] Its twin objectives were those of the Riester reform: to stabilize contribution rates, while at the same time ensuring appropriate future benefit levels.

The commission met in 2003 under very different circumstances than Riester faced just a few years earlier. Unexpectedly high unemployment rates and the poor performance of the German economy with extremely low growth rates precipitated a short-run financial crisis of the pension system

5. The 2001 reform, therefore, is popularly referred to as the Riester reform.
6. This was popularly referred to as the Rürup commission after its chairman, Bert Rürup. The commission was in charge of making reform proposals for the pension system, health care, and long-term care insurance. We only refer to the proposals of the pension group, which was cochaired by one of the authors of this chapter.

and created a sense of urgency for reform. Moreover, the electorate became increasingly aware that stabilizing social security contributions and thus limiting the increase of total labor compensation would be essential for enhancing future growth. This paradigm shift away from thinking in pension claims toward thinking in financing possibilities had a noticeable impact on the commission's reform proposals.

The commission proposed an entire reform package (Kommission 2003). In addition to a gradual shift of the retirement age in proportion to the expected change of life length after retirement, the key element of the commission's reform proposal was a new pension benefit indexation formula, linking benefits to the system dependency ratio, called the "sustainability formula."[7] It would lead to further decreases in pension benefits vis-à-vis the path planned by the Riester reform. Most of the commission proposals, and most significantly the introduction of the sustainability formula, were quickly passed by the German Parliament in May 2004.

In parallel, the government also passed major changes to the unemployment insurance system, called the "Hartz reforms."[8] They dramatically shortened the duration of unemployment benefits, especially for older individuals, to eighteen months (rather than thirty-two months) and made unemployment insurance much less attractive as a substitute for early retirement benefits.

Step 4: Toward Later Retirement Ages (2007)

The commission also proposed an increase of the normal retirement age from sixty-five to sixty-seven years, according to a schedule from 2011 to 2035 reflecting expected future changes in life expectancy. The underlying rationale was to divide the life time gained in proportion to the current division between life time in work and in retirement—namely, two to one. In order to prevent substitution into early retirement and disability pensions as a result of the increase of the retirement age, the commission also proposed to increase the early retirement ages (to the same extent and on the same schedule as the normal retirement age) and to increase the actuarial adjustments for disabled and long-term insured workers.

The shift in the retirement age was deemed too politically dangerous and was excluded from the legislation package in March 2004. The unions heavily opposed this adaptation of retirement age to life expectancy, arguing that it would lead to higher unemployment and take jobs away from the young.

Nevertheless, in yet another ironic move, just two years later, with population aging high on the political agenda, the then labor secretary Müntefering unilaterally announced an accelerated increase of the retirement age, to be fully effective in 2028. It was legislated in March 2007.

---

7. Technical details are described in Börsch-Supan and Wilke (2006).
8. Peter Hartz, former chief personnel officer at Volkswagen, headed the commission.

5.2.4   Phase 4: Reform Backlash?

The increase of the retirement age angered the left wing and was watered down by exemptions for those workers who had forty-five years of service. This may have been the beginning of a period of reform backlash. Under increasing pressure from the newly founded "Left Party," the grand coalition government reverted the decision to shorten the duration of unemployment insurance benefits for older workers, which was part of the "Hartz-IV" labor market reform. Moreover, the government decided in the spring of 2008 to make a two-year exemption from the sustainability formula in order to increase pension benefits in 2008 and 2009 when federal elections would be held. Finally, the issue of "blockwise partial retirement"—essentially, an early retirement device—is back on the agenda. It is too early to judge whether these changes will end the phase of sustainability reform and begin a phase of reform rollbacks. It is important to note that the "make place for younger workers" argument is quoted almost always as a motivation to revert earlier reform steps.

5.3   Descriptive Analysis: Employment and Retirement Over Time

As noted, most pension reforms—those that increased generosity as well as those that cut costs to improve sustainability—had immediate consequences for employment and retirement. This section provides a more detailed depiction of employment and retirement patterns between 1960 and 2006. It is based on employment and labor force participation data taken from the German Bureau of the Census ("Mikrozensus"), unemployment figures from the Federal Labor Agency ("Bundesagentur für Arbeit"), and retirement patterns from the German Public Pension Administration ("Deutsche Rentenversicherung Bund").

We first give an extensive description of the employment, unemployment, and retirement patterns before and immediately after the 1972 reform. Subsection 5.3.2 then summarizes the main labor force trends between 1972 and 2006, with particular attention to two further reform steps—namely, the "bridge to retirement" in 1984 and the gradual phase in of actuarial adjustments after 1998. The third subsection is devoted to a detailed analysis of youth (un)employment. Subsection 5.3.4 draws first conclusions from our descriptive analyses.

5.3.1   Employment, Unemployment, and Retirement
Patterns before and after the 1972 Reform

The 1972 reform was introduced during a time of full employment—or better, even labor shortage. Unemployment rates, quickly declining during the German "economic miracle" in the 1950s, were very low in the 1960s and early 1970s before the first oil shock; see figure 5.2.

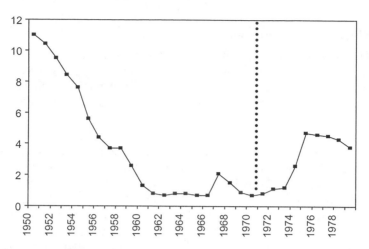

Fig. 5.2   Unemployment rate in West Germany, 1950 to 1979
Source: Statistisches Bundesamt.

Even in the recession year 1967, the aggregate unemployment rate barely exceeded 1 percent. As a matter of fact, companies were forced to hire millions of foreign workers from southern Europe and Turkey to overcome serious problems of labor shortage. Therefore, the pension reform of 1972 (indicated by the dotted line in figure 5.2 and drafted well before that year) was certainly not motivated by labor market problems of the young. The unemployment rate of young workers below age twenty-five was about the same as the average rate of 0.7 percent in the prereform year 1971; see table 5.1. During the sixties and early seventies, youth unemployment was consistently low and about the same level as unemployment of prime age workers (age twenty-five to fifty-four).

The unemployment rate of elderly workers was only slightly higher at 1.06 percent in the prereform year 1971. During the recession of 1967, the unemployment rate of the elderly jumped to 3.6 percent, which was twice the average rate. However, it is also unlikely that labor market problems of the elderly motivated the pension reform of 1972, given that unemployment of the elderly normalized to levels around 1 percent immediately after the recession of 1967 (figure 5.2).

The 1972 reform had an immediate effect on the labor force participation of older men.[9] Figure 5.3 shows the dramatic decline of the mean retirement age from about age sixty-five years in the years preceding the reform to about age 62.5 after the reform. The subsequent stability of the retirement age during the eighties and nineties is remarkable; a significant change occurred only after the year 2000.

The effect of the 1972 reform is particularly pronounced as a change in

---

9. The law did not change the much earlier retirement age for women.

the most frequently chosen retirement age; see figure 5.4. Before the 1972 reform, the most frequent retirement age was sixty-five—the statutory retirement age—with retirement before that date only due to disability. In 1975, two peaks emerged: age sixty-five—the statutory retirement age—and age sixty-three—the new early eligibility age. In 1980, age sixty became

Table 5.1   **Unemployment rates by demographic groups in year 1971 (%)**

All	Males	Females	Age < 25	Age 25 to 54	Age 55+
0.70	0.6	0.9	0.76	0.59	1.06

Source: Statistisches Bundesamt.

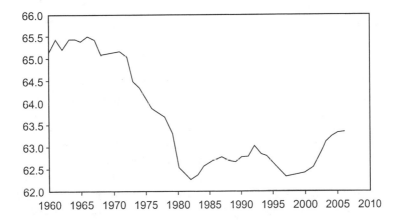

Fig. 5.3   Mean retirement age, old-age pensions, males
Source: Deutsche Rentenversicherung Bund, Rentenzugangsstatistik.

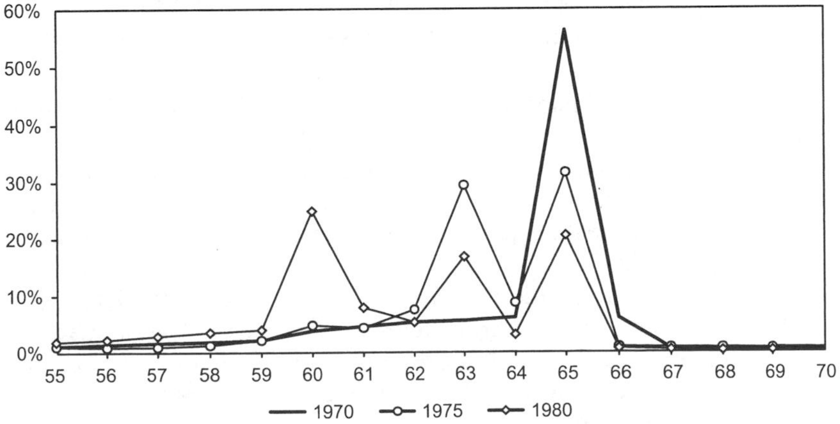

Fig. 5.4   Distribution of retirement ages: Males
Source: Deutsche Rentenversicherung Bund, Rentenzugangsstatistik.

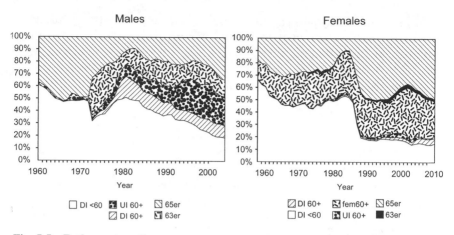

Fig. 5.5   **Pathways to retirement**
Source: Deutsche Rentenversicherung Bund, Rentenzugangsstatistik.

the most frequent actual retirement age, reflecting the various exemptions from the early eligibility age of sixty-three that were due to unemployment, among other things.

The 1972 reform law also dramatically changed the pathways to retirement for men; see figure 5.5. The new "flexible retirement" at age sixty-three became very popular and replaced a substantial portion of disability pensions. After a short while, however, people discovered that the newly introduced old-age pensions for the disabled and/or unemployed were even more attractive, creating the spike at age sixty that is visible in figure 5.4. Note that there was no corresponding change in retirement pathways of women, who were not affected by the 1972 reform.

5.3.2   Employment and Unemployment after the 1972 Reform

Labor force participation of the elderly dropped immediately after 1972—see figure 5.6—reflecting the earlier exit from the labor force (the first vertical bar indicates the 1972 reform). By the end of the eighties, only 30 percent of the age group sixty to sixty-four were employed.

However, this did not seem to help the young, whose labor force participation actually fell in parallel to labor force participation of the old. The youth unemployment rate actually jumped to 5.6 percent in 1975 and remained at that level until 1978; see figure 5.7.

The cause for the dramatic change in labor market conditions after 1973 was the first oil shock. Unemployment rose to new levels in Germany, reaching 4 percent in 1975. The youth workforce was hit most by that recession. Youth unemployment became a major political concern at the end of the seventies. This was also connected to the concern that the large size of the baby boom generations might cause additional problems.

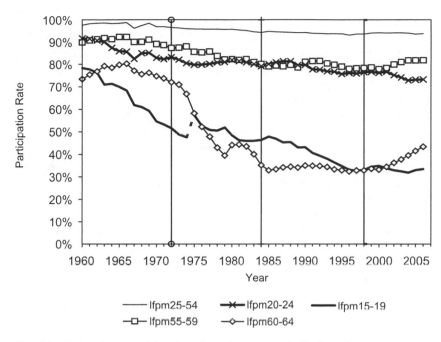

Fig. 5.6   Labor force participation of youth, young and elderly males
Source: German Mikrozensus.

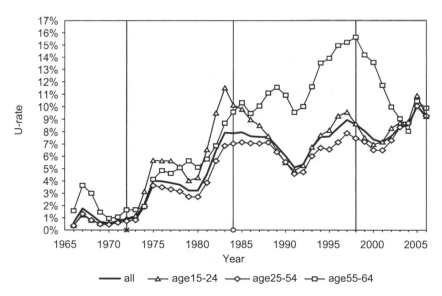

Fig. 5.7   Unemployment rates, 1966 to 2006, by age groups (West Germany)
Source: Bundesagentur für Arbeit.

A new problem evolved in the 1980s: unemployment did not return to prerecession levels after the first oil shock. Instead, it remained high and exhibited the pattern of a hysteresis problem. This pattern was repeated in each of the following business cycles. Unemployment rates hit a high in the winter of 2004/2005.

In 1984, the "bridge to retirement" (see section 5.2) was introduced (indicated by the second vertical bar in figures 5.6 and 5.7). It decreased employment of individuals aged fifty-five to fifty-nine (see figure 5.6). At the same time, their unemployment rate went up dramatically, indicating the popularity of using unemployment insurance as an early retirement pathway (figure 5.7). The employment effects on the young, however, did not go up in response (figure 5.6), as those who believe in the "boxed economy view" would have predicted.

Another reform step is indicated by the third vertical bar in figures 5.6 and 5.7. It represents the phasing in of "actuarial" adjustments after 1998. Figures 5.3 and 5.6 show the trend reversal of employment of the elderly: labor force participation increases from 30 percent to 40 percent in the age group from sixty to sixty-four years.

5.3.3   Employment and Unemployment of the Young

Labor force participation of the young (ages fifteen to nineteen) was as high as 80 percent in 1960. It dropped below 50 percent due to extended schooling (introduction of tenth grade in middle school) and rising participation in higher education (gymnasium, college) well before the 1973 recession; see figure 5.8.

The main expansion of education took place in the years from 1960 to 1974—that is, during times of full employment: the number of the young in education doubled from 20 percent to 40 percent in the years between 1960 and 1974. Extended general schooling was not a device to take youth from the unemployment rolls; if anything, it aggravated labor shortages.

Unemployment rose quickly after 1974. If extended education had been a substitute for unemployment in those years, we would expect increasing education during times of rising unemployment (i.e., 1974 to 1977, 1980 to 1983). Education rates, however, stayed fairly constant around 40 percent from 1974 to 1990.

College enrollment increased linearly from 1960 to 2003, very independently from economic booms and busts. Enrollment as a fraction of the population at ages nineteen to twenty-nine was 3 percent in 1960, 8.5 percent in 1974, 12.8 percent in 1988, and 18.5 percent in 2002.

5.3.4   Conclusions from the Descriptive Analysis

Combining the insights from sections 5.2 and 5.3, the following four conclusions can be drawn:

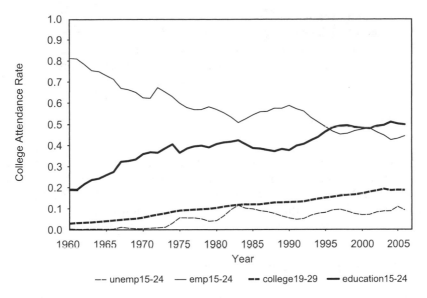

Fig. 5.8   Youth employment, unemployment, education, and college

Source: Own calculations based on the German Mikrozensus (Statistisches Bundesamt 2007) and unemployment statistics (Bundesagentur für Arbeit 2008).

- The 1972 reform was not driven by labor market considerations. It dramatically reduced retirement age, labor force participation, and employment of older individuals. In spite of the dramatic reduction of old-age employment in the aftermath of the 1972 reform, youth employment did not increase.
- The "bridge to retirement" introduced in 1984 further decreased employment of individuals aged fifty-five to fifty-nine. Their unemployment rate went up dramatically, indicating the popularity of using unemployment insurance as an early retirement pathway. Employment of the young, however, did not go up in response.
- The phasing in of "actuarial" adjustments after 1998 reversed the trend of early retirement. Employment increased from 30 percent to 40 percent in the age group from sixty to sixty-four years. There is a very slight concurrent decrease in employment of the young.
- Increasing education from 1960 to 1974 was not driven by labor market problems of the young. Over the entire period (1960 to 2006), there is no correlation between the uptake of education and youth unemployment.

Hence, the "boxed economy view" is not supported by the employment trends from 1960 to 2006. In almost all cases, employment of the young and the old moved in tandem up or down. The only exception is the time after 1998. We claim, however, that the slight decrease in employment of the young is a reflection of the business cycle and not a response to the introduction of actuarial adjustments. In order to show this claim, we proceed to a more analytical approach in the following section.

5.4   Regression Analysis: Effects on the Young

Our regression analysis is based on the assumption that an exogenous policy $Z(t)$ changes the labor supply of the elderly—for example, by raising the implicit tax on labor for the elderly. In our earlier work, we have shown that such a change in the incentives to retire significantly affects the employment of the *elderly.* In this section, we focus on the empirical effects of early retirement policies on the employment of the *young,* focusing on three labor market outcomes:

- EMP(a, y) = employment rate (employment in age group a in year y/population in age group a in year y)
- UE(a, y) = unemployment rate (unemployed persons in age group a in year y/labor force participation in age group a in year y)
- SCH(y) = educational participation of the young (persons in education in age group fifteen to twenty-four in year y/population aged fifteen to twenty-four in year y)

We use age group fifteen to twenty-four to indicate young individuals because of the specific German system of schooling and training. The regular school leaving age used to be fifteen (after ninth grade). This was followed by an apprenticeship, which counts as employment, and combined on-the-job training and work on four days with formal schooling on one day per week. Prime aged individuals are defined as aged between twenty-five and fifty-four.

5.4.1   Labor Outcome for the Young as Function of Elderly Employment

We first regress the labor outcome variables of young and prime aged individuals on the elderly employment variable. Results are shown in table 5.2. The first panel shows the coefficients of elderly employment without controls, the second panel with controls. These controls should account for general macroeconomic effects and include gross domestic product (GDP) per capita and the growth rate of GDP per capita, plus the average wage and the effective minimum wage (social assistance benefits on an hourly basis).

Each panel of table 5.2 includes four different specifications: a regression in levels, a regression in levels with a three-year lagged dependent variable, a regression in differences (five years), and a regression in log differences.

Table 5.2   **Labor market outcomes of young and prime aged persons as a function of elderly employment**

	Youth, 15 to 24			Prime age, 25 to 54	
	Unemployment	Employment	School	Unemployment	Employment
	No controls				
Levels	−.5069**	1.3025**	−63.9830**	−.4003**	*−.3557**
	(.0545)	(.1825)	(8.7886)	(.0511)	*(.0732)*
Three-year lag on	−.4768**	1.1500**	−67.6406**	−.4265**	*−.4167**
elderly employment	(.0533)	(.1457)	(6.6038)	(.0409)	*(.0582)*
Five-year difference	*.0107*	*−.4804**	*.4896*	*.0710*	.3426**
	(.0911)	*(.2184)*	*(3.2134)*	*(.0630)*	(.0940)
Five-year difference	−1.5536	*−.2452*	−.0310	−1.036	.2075**
in logs	(1.6741)	*(.1632)*	(.0881)	(1.8496)	(.0578)
	With controls				
Levels	−.2535**	*−.3641*	−9.7485**	−.1267	*−.0879*
	(.1374)	*(.2335)*	(4.1037)	(.0930)	*(.0689)*
Three-year lag on	−.1666**	*−.3680**	*1.2367*	−.1285**	*−.0058*
elderly employment	(.0848)	*(.1311)*	*(2.4476)*	(.06315)	*(.0502)*
Five-year difference	−.0024	*−.4709**	−.1026	*.0692*	.3509**
	(.0963)	*(.2361)*	(3.3805)	*(.0657)*	(.0980)
Five-year difference	−1.5023	*−.2389*	−.0415	−.9751	.2156**
in logs	(1.7613)	*(.1760)*	(.0931)	(1.9131)	(.0614)

Notes: Reported is the coefficient of elderly employment. Standard errors in parentheses. Significant effects in bold and marked with asterisks. Estimates in accordance with the boxed economy view are italicized. Controls include GDP per capita, growth rate of GDP per capita, minimum wage equivalent, and average wage. Data from 1960 to 2006, men and women.
**Significant at the 5 percent level.

Results are very sensitive to the specification chosen. However, there are very few specifications that support the "lump of labor" view (marked in bold italics). In many more specifications, higher employment of the elderly goes hand in hand with higher employment and lower unemployment of the young (marked in bold). The "effect" of elderly employment on unemployment of the young is either significantly negative, or it is insignificant. The same holds for the relation between elderly employment and unemployment of prime age persons, once controls are active.

The relation between employment of younger and elderly persons seems to be a bit more complicated. Most of the coefficients indicate a positive relationship. Only for the employment of prime age persons do we get a significant negative relationship.

Adding controls to the specification reduces the effects of elderly employment in general. A notable exception is the five-year difference effect on prime age employment. Here, we see that the strong positive effect of elderly employment on prime age employment remains strongly positive.

5.4.2 Labor Outcome for the Young as Function of Incentives to Retire Early

We first calculate the incentives to retire. We do this separately for men and women. We use two incentive variables used in our earlier work—namely, social security wealth (SSW) and peak value (PV). We compute these values considering two pathways to retirement: disability retirement and old-age retirement. We weight the two incentive measures using the probability to retire through disability.

We then combine the two incentive variables as follows. Let social security wealth at age a in year y be denoted by SSW(a, y) and peak value by PV$^*(a, y)$. Then, our comprehensive incentive measure is defined as

$$I(a, y) = \{SSW(a, y) + \alpha[SSW(a, y) - PV^*(a, y)]\}$$

with weight

$$\alpha = (1 - r)^{(a^* - a)}.$$

We set r equal to 3 percent; a^* denotes the age at which SSW is maximized. If pension benefits are unavailable at age a, then the pension in the given year is set to zero.

Finally, we combine values for men and women using weights of the labor force participation of males and females by age and year.

The results for the regressions on the incentives variable are presented in table 5.3. Again, we report the results for two age groups, with and without controls, for level and first differences and for various outcome measures.

Table 5.3 Labor market outcomes of young and prime aged persons as a function of incentives to retire early

	Youth, 15 to 24			Prime age, 25 to 54		Elderly
	Unemployment	Employment	School	Unemployment	Employment	Employment
			No controls			
Levels	.1547**	−.4888**	23.939**	.1377**	.1571**	−.2189**
	(.0171)	(.0379)	(1.803)	(.0128)	(.0151)	(.0323)
First difference	−.3775	.0742	−.8753	−.2503	.0287	.0366
	(.5855)	(.0581)	(.4957)	(.5968)	(.0194)	(.0259)
			With controls			
Levels	.1015**	−.0717	.3597	.0708**	−.0374**	.0163
	(.0250)	(.0530)	(.8262)	(.0184)	(.0149)	(.0362)
First difference	−.0107	−.0081	−.4632	.3506	.0091	.0168
	(.0172)	(.0358)	(.5107)	(.5222)	(.0159)	(.0569)

Notes: Reported is the coefficient of the comprehensive incentive variable. Standard errors in parentheses. Significant effects in bold and marked with asterisks. Estimates in accordance with the boxed economy view are italicized. Controls include GDP per capita, growth rate of GDP per capita, minimum wage equivalent, and average wage. Data from 1960 to 2006, men and women.

**Significant at the 5 percent level.

In addition, we report the effect of incentives on elderly employment in the last column of table 5.2.

Looking at the first row of results (in levels), we see that stronger incentives to retire early reduce employment of the younger age groups and increase their unemployment. The last column shows the expected negative impact on old-age employment. However, switching to a first-difference specification renders the results insignificant. (A similar result is obtained with a five-year difference specification.)

Adding controls mitigates the statistical relationship between incentives and employment measures in the level specification. The signs remain unchanged. We do not display in the table the relationship between elderly employment and young employment. Adding controls in the difference specification does not change results, either; the first-difference results remain insignificant, with or without controls.

5.5   Conclusions

The provisions driving workers into early retirement are often motivated by "making room for the young." Underlying this is the popular belief that employment of older individuals crowds out employment of younger individuals. Such beliefs play a strong role in the current German discussion about increasing the retirement age from sixty-five to sixty-seven.

This chapter shows that there is no empirical evidence for this belief. In fact, if there is a link at all, the German data reveal that higher employment of older individuals is positively correlated with higher employment of the young. We first looked at employment trends between 1960 and 2006. In almost all cases, employment of the young and the old moved in tandem up or down.

We gave particular attention to those time periods after pension reforms when those pension reforms were prima facie not motivated by labor market concerns. This avoids potential endogeneity issues. Good cases are the 1972 reform—which dramatically expanded the German public pension system—and the 1992 reform—which started a cost-cutting reform process. Again, employment of the young and employment of the old were positively correlated in the aftermath of these reforms.

Finally, we used various regression approaches to purge this correlation from business cycle effects and to study the direct effect of early retirement incentives on youth and prime age employment. The results vary considerably across specifications; many remain insignificant. Of the significant ones, few specifications follow the "boxed economy view," while many more support the positive correlation visible in the time series data.

Hence, the suggestive power of the often invoked analogy of a small enterprise with a fixed and small number of clients as a model for the entire economy is grossly misleading. In contrast to a small enterprise, entire economies can grow, increasing the demand for all goods and services and therefore also the demand for labor. Moreover, costs for early retirement cannot be put on someone else's shoulders, as enterprises often can do it. In an entire economy, all social transfer expenses have to be borne by tax and contribution payers. Since costs for early retirement increase total labor compensation of the young, thus making their labor more expensive, it should not come as a surprise that early retirement for the old causes less employment of the young.

References

Berkel, B., and A. Börsch-Supan. 2004. Pension reform in Germany: The impact on retirement decisions. *Finanzarchiv* 60 (3): 393–421.

Börsch-Supan, A. 1992. Population aging, social security design, and early retirement. *Journal of Institutional and Theoretical Economics* 148 (4): 533–57.

Börsch-Supan, A., S. Kohnz, and R. Schnabel. 2007. Budget effects of pension reform in Germany. In *Social security programs and retirement around the world: Fiscal implications,* ed. J. Gruber and D. Wise, 201–52. Chicago: University of Chicago Press.

Börsch-Supan, A., and A. Ludwig. 2008. Old Europe ages: Reform chances and reform backlash. Paper presented at the National Bureau of Economic Research conference, Demography and the Economy. 11–12 April, Napa, California.

Börsch-Supan, A., and R. Schnabel. 1998. Social security and declining labor force participation in Germany. *American Economic Review* 88 (2): 173–8.

———. 1999. Social security and retirement in Germany. In *Social security and retirement around the world,* ed. J. Gruber and D. A. Wise, 135–81. Chicago: University of Chicago Press.

Börsch-Supan, A., R. Schnabel, S. Kohnz, and G. Mastrobuoni. 2004. Micro-modeling of retirement decisions in Germany. In *Social security programs and retirement around the world: Micro-estimation,* ed. J. Gruber and D. Wise, 285–343. Chicago: University of Chicago Press.

Börsch-Supan, A., and C. B. Wilke. 2006. The German public pension system: How it will become an NDC system look-alike. In *Pension reform: Issues and prospects for non-financial defined contribution (NDC) schemes,* ed. R. Holzmann and E. Palmer, 573–610. Washington, DC: World Bank.

Kommission für die Nachhaltigkeit in der Finanzierung der Sozialen Sicherungssysteme. 2003. *Abschlußbericht.* Berlin: Bundesministerium für Gesundheit und Soziale Sicherheit. Available at: http://www.bmg.bund.de.

Prognos. 1995. *Perspektiven der gesetzlichen Rentenversicherung für Gesamtdeutschland vor dem Hintergrund politischer und ökonomischer Rahmenbedingungen.* Basel: Prognos.

———. 1998. *Auswirkung veränderter ökonomischer und rechtlicher Rahmenbedingungen auf die gesetzliche Rentenversicherung in Deutschland.* Basel: Prognos.

Youth Unemployment and Retirement of the Elderly
The Case of Italy

Agar Brugiavini and Franco Peracchi

6.1 Introduction

The dramatic increase in life expectancy at older ages and the trend toward earlier withdrawal from the labor force are changing the age composition of the labor force in many European countries, but especially in Italy. The Lisbon declaration (2000) by the European Union (EU) has emphasized the importance of increasing labor supply by setting an ambitious target participation rate of 70 percent for the working-age population. Besides women, the segments of the Italian population that are furthest away from this target are the youth and the elderly. As for the elderly, the financial incentives of the Italian social security system have encouraged retirement at relatively young ages throughout the 1980s and most of the 1990s (Brugiavini and Peracchi 2003, 2007), and only recently have these trends shown some sign of reversal.

We have shown in previous work (Brugiavini and Peracchi 2007) that the welfare gains of the elderly are large both in absolute and in relative terms; that is, relative to other demographic groups, particularly the young. The issue that we address in this chapter is whether early exit prompted reductions in the youth unemployment rate, as is often claimed by union leaders, thus partly compensating for the welfare redistribution operated in favor of the elderly. This question necessarily relates to the labor market policies enacted during the last decades and the impact that these had on the participation rate of younger workers. The aim of this chapter is to analyze

Agar Brugiavini is professor of economics at the University Ca' Foscari of Venice and a research associate of the IFS and SSAV. Franco Peracchi is professor of econometrics at the University of Rome "Tor Vergata."

the interaction of these policies and the social security legislation in shaping the age profile of the labor market and the trends in labor force participation.

6.2   Unemployment Trends in Italy

The Italian labor market is characterized by relatively high unemployment rates, particularly for the young. The two main characteristics of the youth unemployment rate in Italy are (a) an extraordinary regional variability and (b) a high percentage of first-job seekers among the unemployed young, particularly in the southern regions.

Figure 6.1 shows the trend in unemployment rates of young people (aged twenty to twenty-four) between 1977 and 2004, both in aggregate terms and separately for males and females. The vertical bars indicate the years of the main reforms in the social security system. The youth unemployment rate shows a clear upward trend with a strong cyclical component and reaches a first peak of 28.6 percent in 1987 and a second peak of 32.5 percent in 1998. It is clear that Italy is a country with a serious youth unemployment problem.

The large variability across regions is documented in figure 6.2, which distinguishes five regions: northeast (NE), northwest (NW), center (C), southeast (SE), and southwest (SW). While in the southern regions, the unemployment rate for the age group twenty to twenty-four can be as high

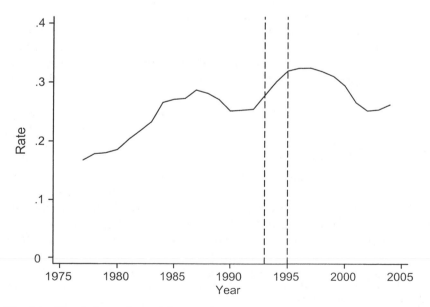

Fig. 6.1   Trends in youth unemployment rate

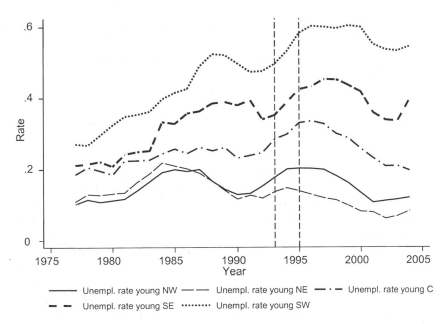

Fig. 6.2   Trends in the regional youth unemployment rate

as 50 percent, northern regions witness youth unemployment rates below 20 percent, and for the regions in the northeast, even below 10 percent.

Several explanations have been put forward to interpret these figures. One strand of the literature looks at the issue of labor mismatch. In particular, some authors have explored the hypothesis that the unbalanced evolution of labor demand and supply across different geographical areas (i.e., regional mismatch) is partly responsible for the increase in aggregate and youth unemployment, particularly in the southern regions.[1] According to this view, the determinants of the regional unemployment differential can be seen in the following elements: employment performance in the south has worsened in the presence of a sustained labor force growth; labor force mobility from the south to the northern and central areas has sensibly declined with the reduction of earnings differentials and with the increase in social transfers per head; and real wages in the south are not affected by local unemployment conditions but depend on the unemployment rate prevailing in the leading areas—that is, northern regions (Brunello, Lupi, and Ordine 2001). In other words, despite the increasing unemployment in the south, labor mobility from the south to the north has been low, and relative wages have not adjusted to reflect worsened local labor market conditions.

---

1. See Attanasio and Padoa-Schioppa (1991), Bodo and Sestito (1991), and Manacorda and Petrongolo (2006).

Together with the regional mismatch and the lack of geographical mobility, the skill mismatch also plays a role in determining high youth unemployment rates in Italy. Some authors (see, for example, Caroleo [1999]) stress the fact that despite the higher educational attainments of the new entrants into the labor market, the educational mix does not match well to the trends in labor demand.

Figure 6.3 shows the time trend in the percentage of people with high school diplomas and university degrees among people aged twenty to twenty-nine. This percentage has increased sharply over the last thirty years. The percentage of people with high school degrees has nearly doubled, from less than 30 percent in 1977 to almost 60 percent in 2004. During the same period, the percentage of people with university degrees has increased by nearly three times, from about 7 percent to almost 20 percent. The increase in the educational attainments of the younger cohorts implies a delayed entry into the labor market (Contini 2005). It also gives rise to problems of mismatch between skills supplied and skills demanded. The relevance of these problems differs across regions (Caroleo and Mazzotta 1999). In the southern regions, the mismatch between skills supplied—often generic and of low qualification—and skills demanded is just one of the explanations of youth unemployment. On the other hand, in the northern and central regions, skill mismatch seems to represent the main problem. In this case, employers ask for specialized manual workers, whereas young suppliers offer a medium-high, but generic, educational level.

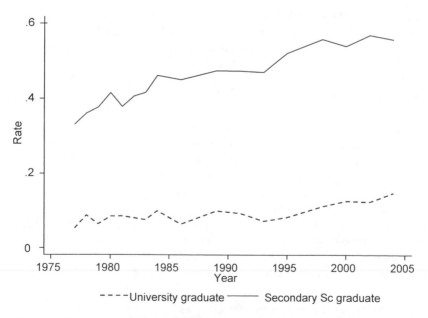

Fig. 6.3   Trend of educational attainments: Rate of high school diploma and university degrees, workers age 20 to 29

Another element that has been often considered in explaining the high level of youth unemployment in Italy is the high reservation wage of the young, particularly in the south. This high reservation wage—combined with the fact that particularly in the south, the majority of the unemployed young are first-job seekers—is surely a relevant determinant of the high youth unemployment. It is generally agreed that the absence of welfare support for first-job seekers (i.e., the absence of minimum income provisions and unemployment benefits) and the strengthening of the role of the family have contributed to increasing the level of the reservation wage of young job seekers. Moreover, particularly in the south, the public sector has represented for a long time the only access to a "regular" job, and young people have built their own human capital and their own aspirations on this type of job. Consequently, their reservation wage is built on the level of wages in the public sector (Caroleo and Mazzotta 1999).

The existence of a legal minimum wage is usually regarded as a barrier to the recruitment of young workers. The situation in Italy represents somewhat of a paradox. In fact, Italy has no legal minimum wage. On the other hand, wage increases, especially in the public sector, depend mainly on seniority. The combination of these two features is often viewed as an important cause of the dramatic increase in the wage differential between younger and older workers observed during the last two decades. Instead of inducing a natural substitution between older and younger workers, the existence of this wage differential is often taken as a justification for early retirement policies, especially in the case of industries affected by negative sectoral shocks, which have only caused a dramatic exit of older workers, with little incentives for new entry of younger workers (Contini 2005).

A very popular explanation for the rigidity of the Italian labor market is its institutional features, especially the strictness of the Italian Employment Protection Legislation (EPL). The available empirical evidence about the effects of the EPL on aggregate labor dynamics[2] indicates that the EPL affects the composition of employment. In particular, countries like Italy where the EPL is stricter tend to display higher youth unemployment.[3] Figure 6.4 shows the relationship between youth unemployment and an index of EPL strictness for some European countries in 2003. The index we use is Version 2 of the overall EPL strictness index computed by the Organization for Economic Cooperation and Development (OECD) in its 2004 *Employment Outlook*. Although Italy had been scoring at the highest level until the late 1990s, the changes to the temporary employment legislation introduced in the last two decades have somewhat lowered its EPL index. Table 6A.1 in the appendix shows the EPL index and its components as computed by the OECD in its 1999 and 2004 *Employment Outlook*. We report data for

---

2. See, for example, Bentolila and Bertola (1990) and Bertola (1999).
3. See OECD (1999) for a survey on the main empirical evidence about the effects of the Employment Protection Legislation on the aggregate labor market.

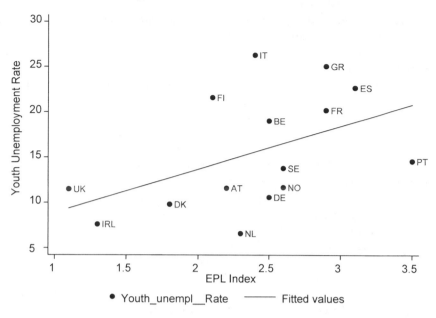

Fig. 6.4 EPL index and youth unemployment rate in Europe

Italy and a few other European countries (France, Germany, Spain, and the United Kingdom). It is clear that the Italian EPL is particularly restrictive on two dimensions: namely, "temporary employment" (although things improved substantially between the late 1980s and 2003) and "collective dismissal."

The "*young in, old out*" paradigm has been advocated in Italy mainly by trade unions and left-wing parties. With reference to the social security reforms of the 1990s and the more recent enactment of these reforms, one leading Italian trade union has argued that "one should not forget that raising the retirement age implies, not only that workers will be forced to work longer, but that two million jobs for the young will be lost."[4] Furthermore, the left-wing party "Rifondazione Comunista" claims that "the intergenerational exchange can be interpreted as the 50-years-old generation leaving their good jobs for the young. Would that be so dramatic for the social security administration? We do not think so."[5]

Although Boldrin et al. (1999) clearly argue that the "lump of labor" story is not operating in Europe, one could get the impression that a "young in, old out" policy was pursued in Italy in the years between 1985 and 1990 as a result of the incentives for firms to hire younger workers (Contini and Rapiti 1999) and the incentives for workers to retire at very young ages (before age

4. Circolare Cobas, October 2003.
5. From the Web site of "Rifondazione Comunista," available at: http://www.rifondazione.it.

fifty-five) due to the lack of any actuarial penalty on pension benefits. The overall effect on total labor force participation was basically close to zero, as the inflow of new workers balanced out with the outflow into retirement. However, this substitutability between workers of different age groups seems only temporary and in any case not "endogenous" but driven by separate determinants and partly by the business cycle. Indeed, the explanations for the changes in labor force participation, and particularly its composition, have been less straightforward after the year 1990.

One interpretation starts from the observation that two contrasting trends have taken place: after a period of "jobless growth" during the 1980s and mid-1990s, a total reversal occurred, such that labor markets appeared fairly lively in contrast with a stagnant economy and an output growth close to zero.

Some authors (Boeri and Garibaldi 2007) have referred to a "honeymoon effect" of labor market policies in creating such discrepancies in observed patterns of employment and unemployment data on the one hand and output data on the other hand, taking effect well after the onset of the labor market reforms.

The claim of Boeri and Garibaldi is that there is a link between growthless job creation and the asymmetric labor market reforms in EPL carried out in several European countries in the 1990s. In fact, such reforms introduced in Italy a two-tier system, as the labor market became more flexible mainly through a series of marginal reforms that liberalized the use of temporary (fixed term) contracts while leaving unchanged the legislation applying to the stock of workers employed under permanent (open-end) contracts. These authors emphasize that the changes of EPL and their impact on labor demand do not produce any sizeable, permanent employment effects.[6] The mechanism is that the reduction in EPL is bound to increase employment variability over the business cycle while not having any permanent effect on average labor demand. This is because EPL affects the incentives to both hire and to dismiss workers, and there is no reason to expect a priori that one effect could dominate the other.

Finally, some attention has to be devoted to reforms to the educational system, which have fostered the growth in school attendance—particularly at the university level. In 1969, a reform was passed that allowed access to the university from any secondary school; previously, only students coming from a "lyceum" could access. In the appendix, we present evidence[7] for two groups of people: the "treatment group" is comprised of people who could benefit from the reform, as they were around age twelve at the time of the reform (young cohorts), while the "control group" is comprised of people

---

6. See also Bentolila and Bertola (1990) and Bertola (1990).

7. The data set used is the Survey of Income and Wealth, conducted on behalf of the Bank of Italy for several years.

who could not benefit, as they were much older. In figures 6A.1 to 6A.3, we look at the status of these people well after the university age. In particular, we are interested in the difference in the prevalence of people by educational attainments. It is clear that the educational reform of 1969 has encouraged people to obtain a secondary school "diploma" and also a university degree (laurea). This is particularly evident for women.

6.3   Main Features of the Social Security System

The Italian social security system is based on a variety of institutions administering public pension programs for different types of workers (private-sector employees, public-sector employees, self-employed, and professional workers).[8] All programs are of the unfunded pay-as-you-go (PAYG) type. Despite a process toward convergence during the 1990s, the various programs maintain quite different rules.

Currently, about two-thirds of the labor force is insured with the National Social Security Institute (INPS). The institute is responsible for a number of separate funds, of which the most important covers the private-sector nonagricultural employees (Fondo Pensioni Lavoratori Dipendenti or FPLD). Because the basic aspects of the system are well documented elsewhere (see Brugiavini [1999], Franco [2002], and Brugiavini and Peracchi [2004]), we describe very briefly its main rules (eligibility, pensionable earnings, benefit computation, indexation, and taxation of benefits).

Starting in 1992, a sequence of legislated changes thoroughly modified the social security system, originally designed in 1969. The main reforms took place in 1992, 1995, and 1997. They are known, respectively, as the Amato, Dini, and Prodi reforms, from the names of the prime ministers at the time. In addition, smaller changes to the system have been made nearly every year since 1992. Of the three main reforms of the 1990s, the Dini reform appears as the most radical, because it completely redesigns the system by modifying the eligibility rules and by changing the benefit formula back from defined benefits to defined contributions, which was the type of formula in place prior to 1969. However, because it will only be introduced gradually through a very long transitional period, the direct effects of the Dini reform may be considered small compared to the less radical Amato reform.

Overall, because of the long transitional periods, the cohorts that reached the retirement age during the 1990s and those currently retiring remained largely unaffected by the reforms of the 1990s, as most of the burden of

---

8. "Social security system" and "pension system" in this chapter are used as synonyms. In fact, in Italy, social security is the main source of publicly provided income in old age. Contributions are compulsory for employers and employees, and benefits are earnings related. There is only a minor flat component granted to very old people (over sixty-five) under means testing if the beneficiary has no other income.

the adjustment fell on the younger cohorts (Franco 2002; Brugiavini and Galasso 2003). More precisely, the *1992 (Amato) reform* explicitly distinguished between workers with at least fifteen years of contribution at the end of 1992 and all other workers. The old system (introduced in 1969) applied, with some changes, to the former, whereas the new system only applied to the latter. The adoption of different rules for older and younger workers was maintained in the subsequent *1995 (Dini) reform* and *1997 (Prodi) reform.* In particular, with the exception of the new eligibility rules, very few changes applied to workers with eighteen or more years of contribution at the end of 1995 beyond those already introduced in 1992.

The following list of legislative changes highlights the exogenous variations in benefits envisaged by the reforms that are potentially relevant to our study and that in an ideal data set could be identified. We limit ourselves to the years 1976 to 2004, corresponding to the sample period, and focus particularly on changes that affect the decision to retire—hence, particularly on changes to eligibility rules.

- In 1992 (Amato reform), the age requirement for an old-age pension gradually increased by one year of age every two years, starting from 1994, until reaching age sixty-five for men and age sixty for women in 2002.
- The new requirements for an old-age pension (age sixty-five for men and age sixty for women) applied starting in 1994 to managers and self-employed workers. Also in 1994, the requirement was set at age sixty-five for central government employees (irrespective of gender) and age sixty for local government employees (again, irrespective of gender). The old requirements remained unchanged for a few special categories (army and police personnel, flight personnel, traveling personnel of public transportation services, firemen, and employees of the entertainment industry).
- The number of years of contribution required for an old-age pension gradually increased by one every two years, starting from 1993, until reaching twenty years of contribution in 2000.
- For workers with less than fifteen years of contribution at the end of 1992, the reference period for computing pensionable earnings gradually increased until it included the whole working life, with past wages adjusted to inflation on the basis of the annual rate of change of the cost-of-living index increased by 1 percent.
- New rules for combining pensions and earned income applied to pension granted after 1992: seniority pensions now could not be combined with earned income, whereas disability and old-age pensions could be combined, but only partially. The possibility of combining seniority pensions with income from self-employment was subsequently reintroduced in 1993.

- Pensions were automatically adjusted only to the changes in the cost of living.
- In 1995 (Dini reform), the payroll tax rate increased from 27 percent to 32 percent.
- There was a gradual introduction of an age limit for seniority pensions, equal to age fifty-seven for both men and women in the year 2008.
- A new defined contribution (DC) system based on notional accumulated contributions applied to workers who started their career after 1995.
- A "proquota" system applied to workers with less than eighteen years of contribution at the end of 1995.
- After 1995, the main changes were an acceleration in the introduction of the age limit for seniority pensions and further harmonization of the pension rules for public-sector and private-sector employees.

6.4   Labor Market Legislation and Reforms

The rigidity of labor market rules in Italy goes back to 1966 when legislation on unfair dismissals established that employers had either to reemploy the worker or pay him or her a generous severance lump sum. The payment was higher for firms with more than sixty employees. An important change took place in 1970 (Statuto dei Lavoratori) establishing that firms with fifteen employees or more had to hire back workers undergoing unfair dismissal and also pay them the foregone wages, while firms below fifteen employees were totally exempted from this rule.

The changes to the labor market legislation between 1970 and 2004 can be divided into four main periods (Boeri and Garibaldi 2007): pre-1985, between 1985 and 1997, between 1997 and 2003, and post-2003.

As for the first period, an important change occurred in 1985 when special hiring conditions were granted to firms for contracts that envisaged on-the-job training ("contratti formazione lavoro"). These were clearly aimed at reducing youth unemployment, and indeed, hiring of younger workers (age twenty-five or less) became sizeable, particularly in the industrial sector.

The second period goes from 1985 to 1997. This is characterized by a wider use of fixed term contracts (if allowed by industry-level collective agreements) and a reorganization of public employment agencies (Law 28/2/1987, number 56), which in principle should guarantee a more efficient matching process.

The first important landmark was the 1997 reform known as the "*Treu Package*." This included a reduction of the penalties occurring in the case of violation of the fixed term contracts' discipline (conversion of fixed term contract into an open-ended one). It allowed for temporary work agencies to operate in the labor market. Nonpermanent labor contracts were encouraged by reducing social security contributions and pension provisions into open-ended ones. The package also made it easier to rely on apprenticeship and work-training contracts and set further incentives for on-the-job training.

A fourth period started with the *"Biagi Law"* of 2003. New types of labor contracts came into life: job on-call, job sharing, supplementary work, and "lavoro a progetto," which slightly tightened the regime for the already existing short-term contracts (known as "Co.co.co").

Overall, the Treu Package and the Biagi Law regulated in a less restrictive way the labor market and opened the way to temporary contracts.

6.5   Descriptive Evidence on the Italian Labor Market

This section briefly describes the data sources used in the chapter and the way we constructed the key variables for the analysis. It then presents some descriptive evidence on the Italian labor market.

Our main data sources are the Labor Force Survey (Indagine sulle Forze di Lavoro) or LFS, conducted by the Italian National Statistical Institute (ISTAT), and the Survey of Household Income and Wealth (I Bilanci delle Famiglie Italiane) or SHIW, conducted on behalf of the Bank of Italy.

6.5.1   The LFS Data Set

The Labor Force Survey is a quarterly longitudinal survey that was first conducted in 1959. It was carried out every second working week of each quarter (i.e., January, April, July, and October) until 2004. From 2005, it is carried out continuously during the year. The Labor Force Survey covers 300 thousand households and 800,000 individuals distributed in 1,351 Italian municipalities. In this chapter, we use the quarterly Labor Force Survey data from 1977 to 2004.

The statistical units are *de facto households,* and the questionnaire is administered to all household members who are more than fifteen years of age. The classification of the individuals by employment status is based on the status that individuals self-report and on a series of answers regarding the job activity of the respondent during the week before the interview. Moreover, the classification of the respondent is constructed following a hierarchical process: first, the employed are identified; second, among all the nonemployed, the job seekers/unemployed (both previously employed and first-time seekers) are identified; finally, all the remaining individuals are classified as out of the labor force.

The definitions and classifications used in the Labor Force Survey are based on the principles stated by the International Labour Office in 1982, and are the result of the harmonization process that makes them comparable with the ones adopted by the European Union. In particular, the definition of "unemployed" has changed during the years. First, in 1984, the definition of "job seeker" was changed to capture the criterion of self-reported "willingness to work." In 1986, the definition was restricted to those individuals who self-reported to have actively searched for work. Finally, in 1992, the job-search period of the unemployed was limited to thirty days before the interview date.

6.5.2   Trends in the Labor Force

By making use of the different waves of the LFS, we can trace out the trends of the activity rates and of the employment/unemployment rates for different age groups in the population. In particular, these groups are as follows:

- *Young:* people aged twenty to twenty-four
- *Prime age:* people aged twenty-five to fifty-four
- *Old:* people aged fifty-five to sixty-four

However, we can look at finer disaggregations by age group, which may be relevant for certain aspects of the labor market (e.g., distinguish the group aged fifteen to nineteen from the group aged twenty to twenty-four). One advantage of our data sets is that we can also exploit, both for the LFS and the SHIW sample, important regional variations in the Italian labor market. In particular, we distinguish five geographical areas: northwest, northeast, center, southwest, and southeast.

The most intuitive description of the labor force trends by age group is provided by the time series presented in levels. One point to be stressed is that the labor force series have a break in 1993 due to the recording methods: the Italian Statistical Office has revised the series before 1993 so that the break is no longer visible in the labor force partipation rate and in the unemployment rate.[9]

Figure 6.5 shows the labor force participation rate for young workers and older workers and the unemployment rate for the young for the period from 1977 to 2004. The vertical bars refer to the years of the social security reforms. The unemployment rate is defined in the usual way as the ratio between the unemployed and the active people. Hence, this rate is more sensitive to business cycle fluctuations than the employment rate, particularly for young people.

The descriptive evidence suggests that there is no simple relationship between the labor force participation rate of the old and the unemployment rate of the young. In the 1970s and 1980s, the labor force participation of the old declined steadily, while the unemployment rate of the young increased. It is only in recent years that the effect of the social security reforms are

9. We are grateful to the Italian Statistical Office (ISTAT) for allowing us access to the Modello di Analisi Regionale della Spesa Sociale (MARSS) database.

Fig. 6.5   Trends of labor force participation of young and old workers compared to the unemployment rate of the young

felt: a reversal of the declining trend in labor force participation is observed for the age group fifty-five to sixty-four (i.e., workers for which the age limits to access early retirement have gradually become binding) around the year 2000.[10]

Overall, these trends suggest that the reforms had some impact: the youth unemployment rates decreased after 1997, while social security reforms increased labor force participation amongst the older workers.

There is no evidence of substitutability between older workers and younger workers. If anything, the two time series seem to be positively correlated: when the unemployment rate of the young increases, there are also more older workers leaving the labor market. The evidence of procyclical behavior is also confirmed by the time series of youth labor force participation.

The aggregate figures, however, conceal important gender differences. Figures 6.6 and 6.7 present times series evidence that distinguishes between male workers (figure 6.6) and female workers (figure 6.7). The unemployment rate of the young shows the same trends and cycles for males and females, with higher levels of unemployment for females in each year. The labor force participation of older workers also shows marked gender differences: male workers in the age group fifty-five to sixty-four exit the labor force at an increasing rate over time, apart from the reversal in the trend after

10. In the appendix, the same rates are presented in index form, where 1977 is the base year (set at one hundred).

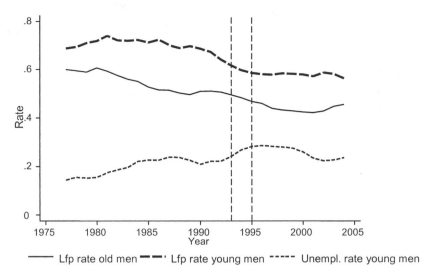

Fig. 6.6   **Trends of labor force participation of young and old workers compared to the unemployment rate of the young: Males**

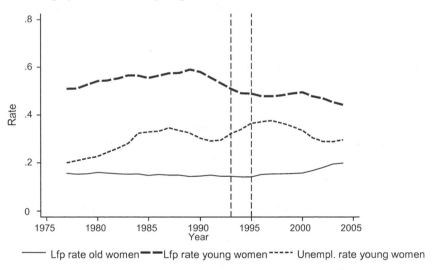

Fig. 6.7   **Trends of labor force participation of young and old workers compared to the unemployment rate of the young: Females**

the year 2000; for female workers of the same age group, the time series is flat or even increasing due to relevant cohort effects.

Figure 6.8 shows the same patterns, but the emphasis is on the trend in the unemployment rate of prime age workers (age twenty-five to fifty-four). For this age group, the unemployment rate is at a much lower level, hence confirming that youth unemployment is the main determinant of total unemployment (see also figures 6.9 and 6.10).

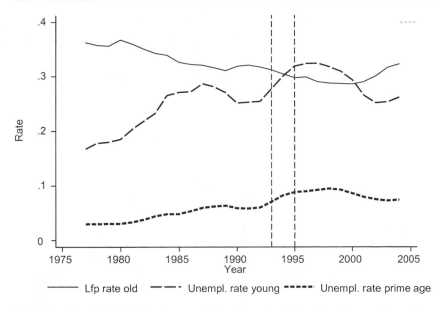

Fig. 6.8   Trends in the labor force participation rate of the old and unemployment rate of the young and prime age

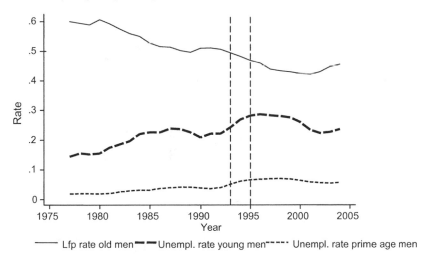

Fig. 6.9   Trends in the labor force participation rate of the old and unemployment rate of the young and prime age: Males

Figure 6.11 stresses once more that the labor force participation of the younger group and of the older group are procyclical. The decline in labor force participation of the young occurring in the late 1980s and early 1990s is largely due to increasing participation in schooling and to the rigidity of the labor market in those years. Only in recent years is the labor force participation rate of the elderly reversing the trend thanks to the pension reforms.

Fig. 6.10   Trends in the labor force participation rate of the old and unemployment rate of the young and prime age: Females

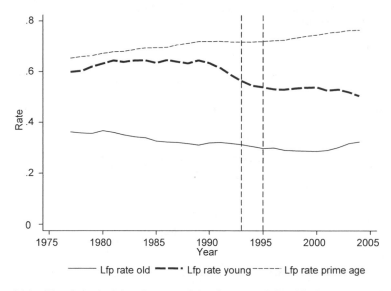

Fig. 6.11   Trends in the labor force participation rate of the old, the young, and the prime age group

For these trends, too, there is a clear gender difference: due to cohort effects, there is a growth in older female workers after the year 1997. For younger females, the pattern is similar to that observed for younger males, as schooling also plays an important role in this case (see figures 6.12 and 6.13).

As for the exits from the labor force, Italy has two main routes: old-age

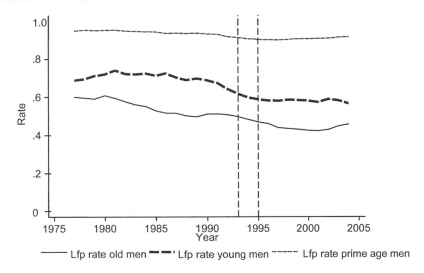

Fig. 6.12   Trends in the labor force participation rate of the old, the young, and the prime age group: Males

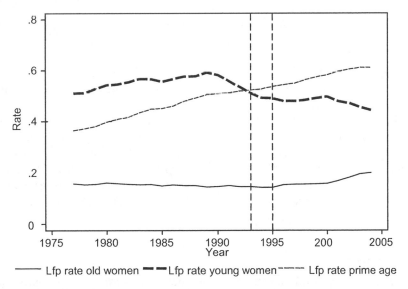

Fig. 6.13   Trends in the labor force participation rate of the old, the young, and the prime age group: Females

and early retirement. Invalidity pensions were relevant until the beginning of the 1980s, but regulation on access to invalidity benefits became much stricter in those years, and the inflow of such benefits was driven down to very small numbers within a ten-year period.

Figure 6.14 shows the composition of the stock of outstanding benefits

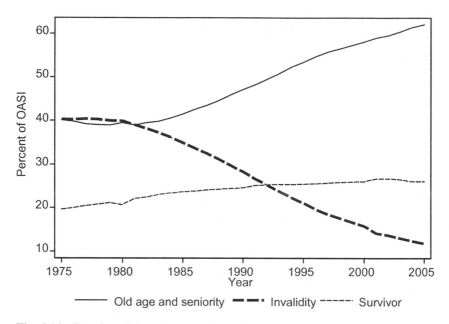

Fig. 6.14   Benefit recipients by type of benefit and year

by type of benefit and year.[11] The stock of disability (invalidity) pensions is very high until 1984, but it goes down slowly over time as beneficiaries age and eventually die.

Figures 6.15 and 6.16 show the evolution of the stock of early retirement/old-age benefits. From the year 2000, we can distinguish by age class. Under the assumption that in the age brackets fifty to fifty-four and fifty-five to fifty-nine we find early retirement benefits and that in some cases these are also claimed between the ages sixty and sixty-four, one can draw the conclusion that the restrictions on eligibility rules for early retirement have indeed been biting in recent years.

6.6   Incentives to Retire

In order to capture the effects of changes in legislation, particularly the effects of pension reforms, we compare the time series behavior of the incentives with that of the labor force.

We develop a simulation method to construct our incentive measures: this way, we can embed, in each year, legislated changes in the social security system (i.e., changes to benefit calculation and eligibility rules) while at

11. ISTAT, Casellario delle Pensioni.

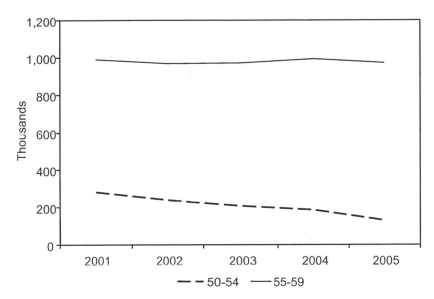

Fig. 6.15   Number of recipients of early retirement/old-age social security

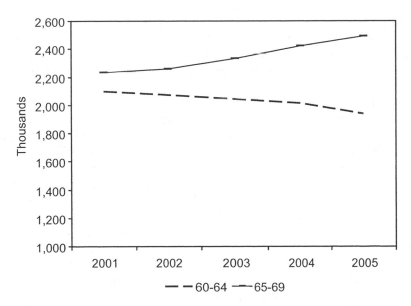

Fig. 6.16   Number of recipients of early retirement/old-age social security

the same time avoiding the endogeneity problems contaminating the actual social security data series.

In order to carry out this simulation (based on Brugiavini and Peracchi [2005]), we make use of the SHIW data, which contains detailed information on the personal characteristics that are needed to compute or approximate pension benefits under the various regimes.

6.6.1   The SHIW Data

The SHIW is a repeated cross-sectional survey that was first conducted in 1965. It was carried out annually until 1987 (except for 1985), then every two years until 1995, and then again in 1998, 2000, and 2002, the last used in this chapter. The 2002 survey covers about 8,000 households and 21,000 people. From 1989, the survey also contains a panel component. Currently, about half of the sample (4,000 households in all) is included in the panel. In this chapter, we use the historical database (Bank of Italy 2004), which contains the harmonized microlevel data for the whole period from 1977 to 2002.

The survey units are de facto households. All household members (including those aged less than fifteen) are asked to indicate their income in the year before the survey. Questions about the household are submitted to the head of the household (see also the appendix for details). Because of oversampling of certain population strata in some years (especially in 1987) and differential nonresponse and attrition rates, it is crucial to use the survey weights when estimating population features such as means, variances, and percentiles.

The quantity and quality of the information collected by the survey increased over time. For example, until 1983, age was only recorded in broadly defined brackets. From 1984, age has been recorded in years, so one can study the behavior of birth cohorts defined by single years of age. Until 1989, little information was available for those who did not receive any income. Basically, only gender, age, relationship to the head, and main activity (housewife, student, etc.) were recorded, but there was no information on, for example, educational attainments and marital status. The frequent changes in the definitions complicate the task of constructing time-consistent measures. This is particularly true for variables such as the schooling level, the sector of employment, and the type of job. However, the "historical archive" of the Bank of Italy provides harmonized measures that mostly overcome these problems for the purpose of this study.

6.6.2   Incentive Measures

Before turning to the simulation methodology, we look at a simple measure capturing changes in eligibility rules: this is the sum of minimum age requirements and the number of years of seniority necessary to apply for an early retirement benefit. In fact, workers could retire in Italy either when they reached a certain age (the legal retirement age for old-age benefits, which is now sixty-five for men) or a certain number of years of contribution (for example, any age if forty years of contribution had been completed) or a combination of the two (for example, fifty-seven years of age and thirty-five years of contribution). We call this sum the "*quota*": before 1995, the quota was not defined, as individuals could retire at any age. It was introduced in 1995 at level eighty-three and increased gradually thereafter.

Figure 6.17 shows the relationship between the unemployment rate of the young, the employment rate of the old, and the "quota" variable. The quota "index" keeps growing until the most recent years, while the unemployment rate of the young shows a relevant swing. The jump in the "quota" indicator anticipates by a few years the rise in employment of the old group.

Because the "quota" variable is a rather rough measure of the complex financial incentives of the social security system, we construct a set of incentive measures that capture different dynamic features of the social security system.

6.6.3   Social Security Wealth and Incentives

The SHIW sample offers considerable variation, which reflects both the differences in individual characteristics and the different rules of the pension system for different categories of workers: private-sector employees, public-

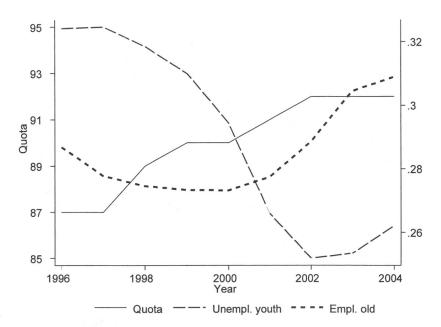

Fig. 6.17   Trends in the unemployment rate of the young, the employment rate of the old, and the "quota" variable

sector employees, and the self-employed (in this chapter, we refer to these as "employment types" or simply "jobs").

To compute the simulated benefits, we start from the profile of median earnings for a given cohort. As in Brugiavini and Peracchi (2004), we focus on cohorts born before the Second World War; in particular, individuals born in 1938 and 1939. We estimate their earnings profiles by gender and by employment type (private employee, public employee, and self-employed). We then smooth the earnings profiles by means of age polynomials and also by nonparametric smoothers. The same estimated earnings profile is then imputed (taking account of the relevant job-gender group) for all members of that group. Productivity growth of the different cohorts is attributed by shifting the age profile.[12]

Simulated benefits are obtained by applying the prevailing legislation for each employment type, taking account also of eligibility rules. For example, we model the reform of 1992 (implemented in 1993) known as the "Amato" reform as follows. Changes affected both currently retired people (through a reduced indexation based on inflation only) and future retirees through changes in the benefit calculation, eligibility rules, and indexation of future benefits (see Brugiavini and Peracchi [2004] for details). Hence, effects on current variables, such as social security benefits, are immediately captured after 1992, both because of the effects on pensioners and because of the changes (gradually less and less generous) to newly awarded benefits during the transitional period. It should be noted that there are differences both in the way rules changed for different types of employees and in the way these changes impacted individual behavior (e.g., consumption), because these groups of the population started from different conditions (public-sector employees had more generous pensions to start with). All monetary amounts are measured in euros at constant 2005 prices.

Although several changes have been made to the benefit computation rules, eligibility rules remained almost unchanged in the relevant years until the 1992 reform. Also, the existence of a generous early retirement option allowed retirees to have plenty of flexibility on the timing of retirement, so the introductions of more restrictive eligibility rules in the early 1990s had little impact on the current cohorts of retirees. The effects of the minimum requirements have been felt more recently, especially for the younger old.

Figure 6.18 provides a graphical representation of social security wealth by year and cohort for a hypothetical "median wage earner" of that cohort. The cohort-specific time series are obtained as weighted averages of the social security wealth of men and women of different employment type.

---

12. Growth rates in earnings for the different cohorts are computed on the basis of two sources: Rossi, Sorgato, and Toniolo (1993) for the data before 1990 and the SHIW data set for the more recent years.

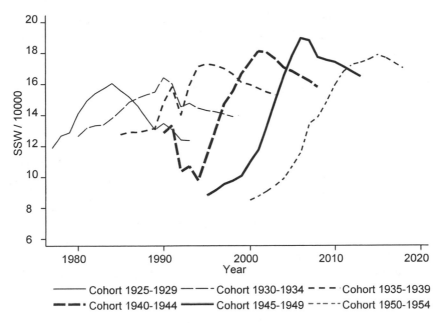

Fig. 6.18   Social security wealth (W) by cohort and year (pooled data)

For each cohort, the pattern is generally hump-shaped; that is, social security wealth (W) reaches a peak at some eligible age, and it then declines thereafter. Besides a secular increasing trend in the level of W, one can observe
also a corresponding trend toward larger dispersion: after the reforms of the
1990s, W starts at a lower level and reaches a peak at a much older age. Part
of this variability across cohorts is also due to changes in productivity and
in mortality.[13] It is clear that changes in eligibility conditions, particularly the
minimum age requirement for access to early retirement, play an important
role in shaping the SSW profile. Changes in the benefit computation rules
occurring after 1992 explain why retirees who claim early retirement would
have low benefits due to lower average "pensionable earnings," despite the
lack of an actuarial penalty for early retirement in Italy.

When aggregating the age-year values of social security wealth, one
obtains a yearly index of the incentives faced by different cohorts in that
particular year. We make use of two incentive measures, both weighted averages: the first one is called $\overline{W}$ and is the weighted sum of W; the second
is called $\overline{I}$ and combines both the level of social security wealth and its

---

13. We experimented by fixing both the productivity and the mortality probabilities so that
the only variability is in the age-earnings profile and in legislation. Important variability across
cohorts is still observed due to the reforms.

peak value. The first measure $\overline{W}$ is a synthetic incentive measure that reflects the mean expected social security benefit faced by each cohort a in year y:

(1) $$\overline{W}(a, y) = \sum_{t=0}^{a-50} \frac{\text{LFP}(a-t, y-t-1)}{\sum_{t=0}^{a-50}\text{LFP}(a-t, y-t-1)} W(a-t, y-t).$$

This is the average value of $W(a, y)$, the social security benefit, between the year when cohort a becomes eligible for benefits and year y. Weights are based on labor force participation rates by year and cohort (data source: ISTAT). This formula is implicitly assuming that before age fifty (i.e., before eligibility), the social security benefit of cohort a is zero. The rationale is that $W(a, y)$ takes into account the forgone benefit by a member of cohort a if he or she decides not to retire in year y. Hence, if cohort a is not eligible in year y, individuals of that cohort have no choice of whether to retire and therefore have no forgone benefits.

The next step is to build an aggregate measure of expected social security benefits across cohorts for a given year. This is done by averaging $\overline{W}(a, y)$ over the cohorts' population in a given year:

(2) $$\overline{W}(y) = \sum_{a=50}^{64} \left[\frac{P(a, y)}{\sum_{a=50}^{64}P(a, y)} \right] \overline{W}(a, y)$$

$$= \sum_{a=50}^{64} \left[\frac{P(a, y)}{\sum_{a=50}^{64}P(a, y)} \right] \left[\sum_{t=0}^{a-50} W(a-t, y-t) \frac{\text{LFP}(a-t, y-t-1)}{\sum_{t=0}^{a-50}\text{LFP}(a-t, y-t-1)} \right],$$

where $P(a, y)$ is the proportion of retired persons in the given year, estimated from the SHIW, and LFP is the labor force participation rate by year and age, taken from the Labor Force Survey. We regard age fifty as the first eligibility age. Because we exploit both gender and regional variation, this measure has been computed conditional on gender and macroregion and then aggregated at the national level.

Our second index is based on the peak value $PV^*(a, y)$. The peak value is defined as the maximum present value of $W(a, y)$ for ages greater than a. This may vary with y, and it may also vary with age in a given year because of different earnings histories for the different cohorts. The index $I(a, y)$ takes into account both expected social security benefits and the peak value using a discount factor α and weights q, which represent the proportion of individuals in the labor force of a given age and in a given year (LFP):

(3) $I(a, y) = \{W(a, y) + \alpha[W(a, y) - PV^*(a, y)]\} q(a, y).$

The peak value $PV^*(a, y)$, consistently with the underlying measure $W(a, y)$, is set to zero if the current age is below the eligibility age. The value of the discount factor α will be chosen optimally, as discussed next. By averaging over the different cohorts, we obtain an annual time series $\bar{I}(y)$, defined as:

$$(4) \quad \bar{I}(y) = \sum_{a=50}^{64} \left[\frac{P(a,y)}{\sum_{a=50}^{a=64} P(a,y)} \right] \left[\sum_{t=0}^{a-50} I(a-t,y-t) \frac{\text{LFP}(a-t,y-t-1)}{\sum_{t=0}^{a-50} \text{LFP}(a-t,y-t-1)} \right].$$

The intuition behind the index I is to combine both the wealth effect generated by the social security wealth variable and the dynamic gains from waiting to retire. It captures the trade-off between a higher social security wealth W, which may induce the worker to retire early, and the gains from postponing retirement ($W - \text{PV}$), which represent the advantage of staying at work. The latter is discounted by the appropriate discount factor that depends on the impatience of the individual. If $\alpha = 0$, we have the extreme case where individuals are so impatient that they do not take future gains or losses into account.

In order to obtain endogenously an optimal discount factor, we make use of two methodologies called, respectively, the *iteration procedure* and the *regression approach*. Both build on the simple relationship:

$$(5) \qquad \text{LFP}_{\text{old},t} = \gamma \overline{W}_t + \theta(\overline{W}_t - \text{PV}_t) + \beta X_t + \varepsilon_t,$$

where W and $(W - \text{PV})$ are the two terms in the index I, X is a matrix of controls, and ε is a random error. The iteration procedure is implemented by setting $\gamma = 1$ and letting θ vary on a given grid in order to maximize the R^2 associated with equation (5). The value of θ that gives the highest R^2 is chosen as the optimal α. In the regression approach, we instead let both parameters γ and θ vary freely and compute α as the ratio between the two.

Both indexes, W and I, are computed by taking as benchmark the earnings of the median worker, estimated from the SHIW.

Table 6.1 shows the estimates of these parameters obtained from the two methodologies. We also distinguish the case where workers are "liquidity constrained"—that is, they cannot access their benefits before the eligibility age, and therefore both W and $(W - \text{PV})$ are set to zero.

As it emerges from table 6.1, our preferred specification (the one delivering the highest R^2) according to the iteration method sets $\alpha = 1.50$ both in the unconstrained and the constrained case.[14] As for the regression method, we obtain opposite signs, which is counterintuitive, but these estimates are hardly significant. Hence, in the remainder of this chapter, we focus on estimates of the incentive effect on labor force participation obtained by setting α equal to 1.50.

Figure 6.19 and 6.20 show the time series of our incentive indexes. The

14. It should be noted that in this chapter, α is exactly the discount factor presented in equation (3).

I-index is more hump-shaped, as it reflects the dynamic in the peak value that emerges from figure 6.18. It is interesting to note that when liquidity constraints are introduced, the *I*-index is rather sensitive to this change, because for Italian workers, such constraints are binding by effectively reducing the access to early retirement benefits.

Figure 6A.4 in the appendix shows the effect of the different parameter configurations on the index *I*: the higher is α, the more pronounced is the

Table 6.1   **Italy: Estimates of the parameters of the *I*-index**

		LFP old			
	Gamma	Alpha	Ratio	R^2	Ibar weighting
Iterating over alpha with gamma = 1, with 0.25 intervals and regressing LFP of old on ibar					
Unconstrained	1	1.50	1.50	0.8134	$1*W + 1.50*(W-PV)$
Liquidity constrained	1	1.50	1.50	0.8038	$1*W + 1.50*(W-PV)$
Time series regression of LFP old on W and (W − PV)					
Unconstrained	0.2991315	−0.2480815	−0.83	0.8201	$0.299*W - 0.248*(W-PV)$
Liquidity constrained	0.7126528	−0.5474849	−0.77	0.7809	$0.713*W - 0.547*(W-PV)$

Note: *I* is divided by 100,000. The estimates of alpha and gamma for the regression method, though being of different sign, are not significant. Covariates have been used to estimate the best alpha, both in the regression method and in the iteration method. Covariates include: year, GDP per head, GDP per capita growth, median wage of the age group under study, percentage of people in school in the age group under study, and share of added value by industry on the GDP.

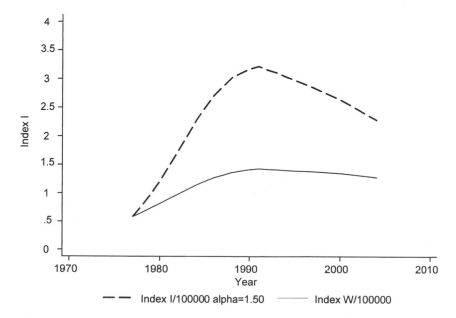

Fig. 6.19   Incentives to retire by year (*W* and *I*), no constraints

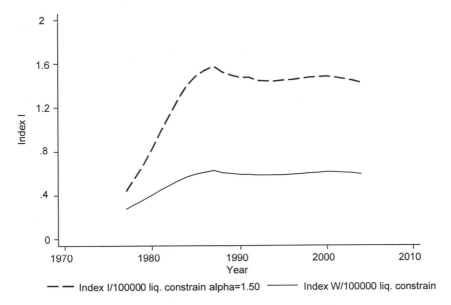

Fig. 6.20   **Incentives to retire by year (*W* and *I*), with constraints**

hump. The index W is dominated by the growth of the generosity of the system in the early years and by the fact that older cohorts started collecting benefits having completed full careers in the 1970s. The index W peters out at the end of the 1990s, both as an effect of the reduced generosity and as a result of the demographic changes.

Figures 6.21 and 6.22 show the relationship between the index W of equation (2), the index I, and the unemployment rate of the young and of the prime age group. Although there seems to be some correlation between the secular trends in the time series, this correlation vanishes after the reforms, when the unemployment rates fluctuate while the indexes decline steadily.

A similar picture emerges from figures 6.23 and 6.24, which relate the incentive measures to the employment rates of the young and of the prime age group.

6.7   Regression Analysis

Our descriptive evidence shows evidence of a negative correlation between the unemployment rate of the young and the labor force participation of the old. We argued, however, that this correlation may just be due to the underlying business cycle. Incentive variables, which represent our "instrumental variables" in capturing the possible nexus between pension policies and labor market trends, also seem to play a role in explaining the behavior of older workers (but presumably not of younger people).

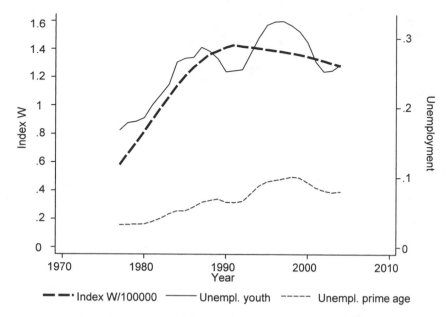

Fig. 6.21 Unemployment rate of the young and of the prime age group and the incentive variable *W*, no constraints

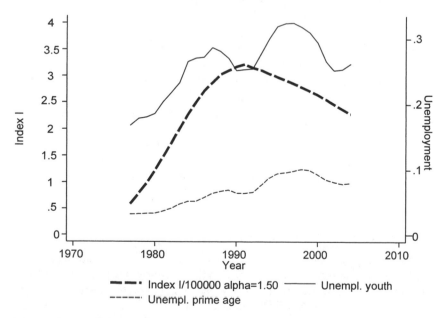

Fig. 6.22 Unemployment rate of the young and of the prime age group and the index *I*, no constraints

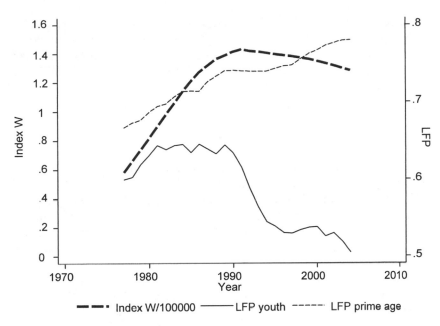

Fig. 6.23   Employment rate of the young and of the prime age group and the incentive variable *W*, no constraints

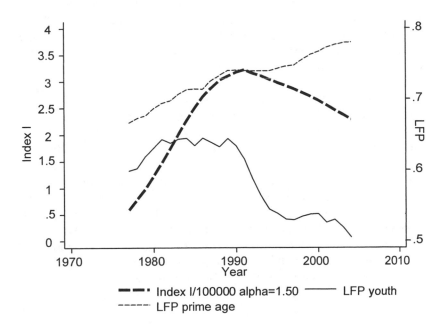

Fig. 6.24   Employment rate of the young and of the prime age group and the incentive variable *I*, no constraints

These questions are better addressed in a more structured fashion by resorting to regression analysis. In a first set of regressions (referred to as "ordinary least squares [OLS] regressions"), we investigate a simple linear relationship between the labor market trends for the young (prime age) and that of the old. The estimated relationship is of the type

$$(7) \qquad Y_t = \gamma + \theta V_t + \beta X_t + \varepsilon_t,$$

where Y_t represents either the unemployment rate or the employment rate of the young, and V_t represents either the labor force participation or the employment rate of the old. In a different specification, we also model the percentage of young individuals in education.

The covariates are GDP, a dummy for the change in compulsory education age, the median wage, the contractual wage (variation only over time), and the percentage of people in school. Apart from GDP, which is derived from the ISTAT Yearly Statistical Bulletin, all other series are derived from the SHIW data.

Results are shown in tables 6.2, 6.3, and 6.4. Table 6A.2 in the appendix also shows the results with the full set of covariates. We consider both a specification with the pooled data (table 6.2) and one where we allow for gender variation and make use of a "male" dummy. This is quite relevant for Italy, as the graphs on unemployment and labor force participation rates show substantial welfare variation. There are four specifications for each regression: one is in levels, while the others experiment with different lag structures. We also consider one specification with no other covariates besides the labor force participation, one with a full set of covariates (including median wage, contractual wage, GDP per capita, etc.), and one where we select only a subset of covariates (GDP per capita, GDP growth, and the share of GDP produced by the industrial sector).[15]

All specifications that relate the unemployment rate (or the employment rate) of the young to the labor force participation of the older workers confirm the descriptive evidence that they tend to move in a procyclical fashion; that is, when the labor force participation of the old goes up, the employment rate of the young also increases (unemployment decreases). These estimates are also significant and robust to the inclusion of covariates. As for the young people in school, we find mixed evidence: for the level specification, an increase in labor force participation of the old is negatively related to the trend in school attendance. However, this result is usually reversed in the regression with five-year differences, suggesting that there might be a long wave in this relationship. Our view is that this result is dominated by the underlying increasing trend in schooling, which is little sensitive to business

---

15. It should be noted that in Italy, there is no such thing as a "minimum wage" going back for the entire time period. This is mainly because contracts envisage only a minimum contractual wage at industry level.

Table 6.2 Direct effect of LFP old on unemployment or employment of young and prime age groups and on schooling participation of the younger age group. Pooled genders: National level data

| | Young (20 to 24), pooled | | | | | | Prime age (25 to 54), pooled | | | |
| | Unemployment rate | | Employment rate | | School | | Unemployment rate | | Employment rate | |
	Coefficient	Standard error	Coefficient	Standard error	Coefficient	Standard error	Coefficient	Standard error	Coefficient	Standard error
					No covariates					
Levels (28 observations)	-1.624	0.157	1.955	0.204	-1.253	0.264	-0.823	0.047	-0.380	0.125
Three-year lag on elderly LFP (25 observations)	-0.712	0.247	1.709	0.234	-1.013	0.164	-0.608	0.087	-0.464	0.090
Five-year difference (23 observations)	-2.177	0.377	1.104	0.415	0.657	0.334	-0.684	0.105	0.593	0.176
Five-year log difference (23 observations)	-2.564	0.502	0.848	0.322	0.551	0.387	-3.443	0.476	0.285	0.082
					All covariates					
Levels (27 observations)	-2.706	0.458	0.477	0.363	1.176	0.619	-0.619	0.072	0.559	0.115
Three-year lag on elderly LFP (25 observations)	0.355	0.974	-0.633	0.827	-0.388	0.627	0.407	0.371	-0.355	0.354
Five-year difference (23 observations)	-2.794	0.308	0.935	0.260	0.837	0.496	-0.527	0.065	0.451	0.109
Five-year log difference (23 observations)	-4.993	0.695	1.488	0.349	1.589	0.317	-3.380	0.321	0.337	0.022

(continued)

Table 6.2 (continued)

| | Young (20 to 24), pooled | | | | | | Prime age (25 to 54), pooled | | | |
| | Unemployment rate | | Employment rate | | School | | Unemployment rate | | Employment rate | |
	Coefficient	Standard error	Coefficient	Standard error	Coefficient	Standard error	Coefficient	Standard error	Coefficient	Standard error
All covariates, without school leaving age dummy and contractual wage										
Levels (27 observations)	-2.758	0.201	1.071	0.177	0.501	0.309	-0.653	0.056	0.597	0.108
Three-year lag on elderly LFP (25 observations)	0.144	1.404	0.028	0.989	0.671	0.656	0.233	0.360	-0.105	0.318
Five-year difference (23 observations)	-2.769	0.179	0.997	0.150	0.389	0.312	-0.613	0.040	0.527	0.077
Five-year log difference (23 observations)	-4.583	0.641	1.165	0.346	1.483	0.339	-2.736	1.057	0.343	0.084
Selected covariates										
Levels (27 observations)	-2.250	0.333	1.058	0.410	0.540	0.319	-0.662	0.096	0.585	0.119
Three-year lag on elderly LFP (25 observations)	0.947	1.460	-2.842	1.216	1.897	0.561	0.641	0.472	-0.623	0.488
Five-year difference (23 observations)	-2.276	0.277	1.099	0.182	0.388	0.285	-0.628	0.044	0.525	0.073
Five-year log difference (23 observations)	-2.893	0.544	1.013	0.175	0.254	0.415	-3.515	0.517	0.297	0.041

Notes: Dependent variables: unemployment and employment of young and prime age; percentage of people in school of young people. All covariates: year (not in the five-year difference case); GDP per capita/1,000; GDP growth (not in the difference case); percentage of people in school; share of industry in the GDP; median wage/1,000; contractual wage/1,000; dummy for changes in the compulsory school leaving age (dropped in the five-year log difference case). Selected covariates: GDP per capita/1,000; GDP growth (not in the difference case); share of industry in the GDP. Specification of regressions: levels: $Y =$ employment of old $+$ year $+$ GDP per capita $+ \ldots$; three-year lag on elderly employment: $Y =$ employment of old $[n-3] +$ year $+$ GDP per capita $+ \ldots$; five-year difference: $Y - Y[n-5] =$ (employment of old $-$ employment of old $[n-5]$) $+$ (GDP per capita $-$ GDP per capita $[n-5]$) $+ \ldots$; five-year log difference: $Y - Y[n-5] = [\log$ (employment of old) $- \log$(employment of old $[n-5]$)] $+ [\log$(GDP per capita) $- \log$(GDP per capita $[n-5]$)] $+ \ldots$.

Table 6.3   Direct effect of LFP of the old. Gender variability: National level data

| | Youth (20 to 24) | | | | | | Prime age (25 to 54) | | | |
| | Unemployment rate | | Employment rate | | School | | Unemployment rate | | Employment rate | |
	Coefficient	Standard error	Coefficient	Standard error	Coefficient	Standard error	Coefficient	Standard error	Coefficient	Standard error
					No covariates					
Levels (56 observations)	−0.251	0.030	0.447	0.034	−0.101	0.038	−0.159	0.014	1.222	0.036
Three-year lag on elderly LFP (50 observations)	−0.236	0.026	0.417	0.034	−0.118	0.031	−0.157	0.013	1.134	0.037
Five-year difference (46 observations)	−0.735	0.243	0.562	0.193	0.518	0.113	−0.236	0.077	0.840	0.111
Five-year log difference (46 observations)	−1.148	0.293	0.390	0.165	0.441	0.145	−1.903	0.312	0.407	0.084
					All covariates					
Levels (54 observations)	−0.201	0.137	0.614	0.082	0.476	0.067	−0.003	0.032	1.225	0.060
Three-year lag on elderly LFP (50 observations)	−0.055	0.101	0.644	0.104	0.392	0.066	0.007	0.036	1.379	0.071
Five-year difference (46 observations)	−0.629	0.301	0.460	0.189	0.475	0.183	−0.198	0.075	0.288	0.082
Five-year log difference (46 observations)	−1.858	0.356	0.610	0.144	0.394	0.208	−1.808	0.333	0.149	0.045

(continued)

Table 6.3 (continued)

No covariates	Youth (20 to 24)						Prime age (25 to 54)			
	Unemployment rate		Employment rate		School		Unemployment rate		Employment rate	
	Coefficient	Standard error	Coefficient	Standard error	Coefficient	Standard error	Coefficient	Standard error	Coefficient	Standard error
	All covariates, without school leaving age dummy and contractual wage									
Levels (54 observations)	−0.306	0.208	0.597	0.098	0.467	0.065	−0.052	0.030	1.224	0.053
Three-year lag on elderly LFP (50 observations)	0.310	0.168	0.395	0.135	0.372	0.070	−0.056	0.036	1.366	0.060
Five-year difference (46 observations)	−1.410	0.301	0.615	0.164	0.478	0.141	−0.383	0.069	0.364	0.069
Five-year log difference (46 observations)	−1.975	0.370	0.595	0.141	0.370	0.207	−2.268	0.417	0.081	0.042
	Selected covariates									
Levels (54 observations)	−0.283	0.131	0.508	0.102	0.443	0.069	−0.032	0.044	1.240	0.062
Three-year lag on elderly LFP (50 observations)	−0.103	0.141	0.381	0.138	0.386	0.075	0.037	0.050	1.241	0.085
Five-year difference (46 observations)	−1.372	0.266	0.681	0.146	0.474	0.147	−0.413	0.072	0.377	0.068
Five-year log difference (46 observations)	−1.735	0.364	0.627	0.131	0.341	0.194	−2.247	0.387	0.126	0.044

Notes: Dependent variables: unemployment and employment of young and prime age; percentage of people in school of young people. All covariates: year (not in the five-year difference case); gender (not in the no covariates case); GDP per capita/1,000; GDP growth (not in the difference case); percentage of people in school; share of industry in the GDP; median wage/1,000; contractual wage/1,000; dummy for changes in the compulsory school leaving age (dropped in the five-year log difference case). Selected covariates: GDP per capita/1,000; GDP growth (not in the difference case); share of industry in the GDP; gender. Specification of regressions: levels: Y = employment of old + year + GDP per capita + . . . + gender; three-year lag on elderly employment: Y = employment of old $[n − 3]$ + year + GDP per capita + . . . + gender; five-year difference: $Y − Y[n − 5]$ = (employment of old − employment of old $[n − 5]$) + (GDP per capita − GDP per capita $[n − 5]$) + . . . + gender; five-year log difference: $Y − Y[n − 5]$ = [log (employment of old) − log(employment of old $[n − 5]$)] + [log(GDP per capita) − log(GDP per capita $[n − 5]$)] + . . . + gender.

Table 6.4 Direct effect of LFP of the old. Pooled genders: Regional variation (northwest of Italy as benchmark)

| | Youth (20 to 24) | | | | | | Prime age (25 to 54) | | | |
| | Unemployment rate | | Employment rate | | School | | Unemployment rate | | Employment rate | |
	Coefficient	Standard error	Coefficient	Standard error	Coefficient	Standard error	Coefficient	Standard error	Coefficient	Standard error
					No covariates					
Levels (140 observations)	−0.783	0.201	1.334	0.129	−0.531	0.096	−0.490	0.088	−0.539	0.087
Three-year lag on elderly LFP (125 observations)	−0.042	0.189	1.153	0.133	−0.662	0.098	−0.352	0.086	−0.600	0.072
Five-year difference (115 observations)	−1.625	0.235	0.774	0.194	−0.007	0.178	−0.477	0.071	0.452	0.081
Five-year log difference (115 observations)	−2.295	0.346	0.657	0.168	−0.025	0.129	−2.521	0.321	0.219	0.041
					All covariates					
Levels (135 observations)	−0.800	0.171	0.423	0.135	−0.076	0.194	−0.192	0.055	0.261	0.073
Three-year lag on elderly LFP (125 observations)	0.236	0.218	−0.332	0.184	0.303	0.244	0.042	0.077	−0.218	0.099
Five-year difference (115 observations)	−0.873	0.203	0.424	0.171	0.089	0.219	−0.286	0.060	0.255	0.070
Five-year log difference (115 observations)	−2.461	0.345	0.918	0.137	0.134	0.206	−2.737	0.328	0.279	0.036

(continued)

Table 6.4   (continued)

| | Youth (20 to 24) | | | | | | Prime age (25 to 54) | | | |
| | Unemployment rate | | Employment rate | | School | | Unemployment rate | | Employment rate | |
	Coefficient	Standard error	Coefficient	Standard error	Coefficient	Standard error	Coefficient	Standard error	Coefficient	Standard error
All covariates, without school leaving age dummy and contractual wage										
Levels (135 observations)	-1.632	0.199	0.866	0.134	-0.010	0.165	-0.330	0.064	0.361	0.074
Three-year lag on elderly LFP (125 observations)	0.049	0.339	-0.255	0.240	0.311	0.240	0.095	0.104	-0.268	0.116
Five-year difference (115 observations)	-1.821	0.208	0.036	0.007	0.094	0.175	-0.513	0.067	0.501	0.073
Five-year log difference (115 observations)	-2.495	0.347	0.890	0.144	0.131	0.205	-2.785	0.336	0.262	0.037
Selected covariates										
Levels (135 observations)	-1.374	0.333	0.669	0.205	-0.024	0.169	-0.311	0.147	0.334	0.134
Three-year lag on elderly LFP (125 observations)	-0.119	0.464	-0.442	0.307	0.378	0.242	-0.032	0.210	-0.166	0.190
Five-year difference (115 observations)	-1.845	0.210	0.916	0.172	0.098	0.177	-0.523	0.065	0.498	0.073
Five-year log difference (115 observations)	-2.548	0.353	0.915	0.148	0.098	0.205	-2.760	0.327	0.278	0.038

Notes: Dependent variables: unemployment and employment of young and prime age; percentage of people in school of young people. All covariates: year (not in the five-year difference case); regional dummies; GDP per capita/1,000; GDP growth (not in the difference case); percentage of people in school; share of industry in the GDP; median wage/1,000; contractual wage/1,000; dummy for changes in the compulsory school leaving age (dropped in the five-year log difference case). Selected covariates: GDP per capita/1,000; GDP growth (not in the difference case): share of industry in the GDP; regional dummies. Specification of regressions: levels: $Y = $ LFP of old $+$ year $+$ GDP per capita $+ \ldots +$ gender; three-year lag on elderly employment: $Y = $ LFP of old $[n-3] +$ year $+$ GDP per capita $+ \ldots +$ gender; five-year difference: $Y - Y[n-5] = $ (LFP $-$ LFP of old $[n-5]$) $+$ (GDP per capita $-$ GDP per capita $[n-5]$) $+ \ldots +$ gender; five-year log difference: $Y - Y[n-5] = $ [log (LFP) $-$ log(LFP of old $[n-5]$)] $+$ [log(GDP per capita) $-$ log(GDP per capita $[n-5]$)] $+ \ldots +$ gender.

cycle variations. Interestingly enough, when we consider the employment (unemployment) of prime age workers, we find a mostly procyclical pattern: employment of prime age workers and labor force participation of the old move together. We run a simple "causality" test by looking at the impulse response functions of the unemployment rate of the young and the activity rate of the old in response to a one-time change in GDP per capita. Results are shown in the appendix (figures 6A.5 and 6A.6): the unemployment rate of the young is much more reactive to GDP changes, but this effect is not precisely estimated. One can see that both series respond to GDP in a procyclical fashion. In particular, the response of the unemployment rate is leading that of the activity rate, but the impulse response function clearly suggests that GDP is the main driver. These results are also robust to the introduction of gender variability (table 6.3) and regional variability (table 6.4). Overall, the time series of employment and unemployment of the young do not seem to be directly affected by the labor force participation rate of the old; the "young in, old out" paradigm is contradicted by the data.

As we argued, there are potential endogeneity problems in relating the unemployment rate of the young directly to the labor force participation of the old. In order to overcome these problems, we also consider a set of specifications where the main explanatory variables are the incentive variables. Results are presented in table 6.5.

Table 6.5 contains different cases:

1. The first case is obtained by choosing different levels of the α parameter in (3). This can take value zero (effectively focusing on the incentive variable W only) or value 1.5, which is our preferred specification. Finally, it can take the value emerging from the regression methodology (albeit with the wrong sign and not significant).

2. The second case is obtained by including liquidity constraints in the estimation of the index I.

3. The third case varies with the use of covariates.

4. The fourth case depends on the lag/differencing structure, starting, as usual, from the specification in levels.

Results are very robust to the different variants just described. By focusing attention on the case where $\alpha = 1.5$ and where there are no liquidity constraints, one can see that a larger inducement to retire has a positive and significant effect on the unemployment rate of the young (negative on the employment rate). Hence, incentives directed to the elderly have no beneficial effect on the unemployment rate of the younger generations. A similar lesson is drawn when the dependent variable is the schooling rate of the young. The only cases where some of the effect is lost is when we resort to five-year differences (which reduces the sample size). On the other hand, incentives to retire have a strong and positive effect on exits from the labor

Table 6.5 Effect of incentives on LFP of the old and on employment, unemployment, and in-school population of the young. Pooled genders: **Different values of alpha and gamma ($N = 28$)**

| | Youth (20 to 24) | | | | | | Old (50 to 64) | |
| | Unemployment rate | | Employment rate | | School | | Labor force participation | |
	Coefficient	Standard error	Coefficient	Standard error	Coefficient	Standard error	Coefficient	Standard error
Alpha = 1.50, no liquidity constraints								
No covariates								
Levels	0.050	0.006	-0.042	0.011	0.037	0.009	-0.021	0.003
Three-year lag of incentive	0.034	0.006	-0.052	0.008	0.021	0.007	-0.017	0.003
Five-year difference	0.041	0.014	-0.001	0.013	0.005	0.010	-0.021	0.006
Five-year log difference	0.335	0.084	0.014	0.055	0.134	0.052	-0.075	0.028
All covariates, without school leaving age dummy and contractual wage								
Levels	0.082	0.015	-0.025	0.015	0.001	0.011	-0.036	0.010
Three-year lag of incentive	0.075	0.020	-0.042	0.015	0.004	0.012	-0.042	0.011
Five-year difference	0.067	0.009	-0.027	0.004	0.010	0.008	-0.058	0.009
Five-year log difference	0.691	0.083	-0.231	0.033	0.207	0.066	-0.091	0.024
Selected covariates								
Levels	0.040	0.009	-0.002	0.010	-0.001	0.007	-0.022	0.004
Three-year lag of incentives	0.036	0.009	-0.014	0.011	-0.012	0.005	-0.025	0.004
Five-year difference	0.054	0.010	-0.015	0.008	0.010	0.008	-0.026	0.005
Five-year log difference	0.513	0.074	-0.120	0.038	0.214	0.047	-0.121	0.026
Alpha = 1.50, liquidity constraints (SSW = 0 before eligibility; W – PV = 0 before eligibility)								
No covariates								
Levels	0.123	0.015	-0.106	0.028	0.111	0.019	-0.045	0.009
Three-year lag of incentives	0.078	0.016	-0.111	0.025	0.054	0.018	-0.036	0.009
Five-year difference	0.110	0.030	0.001	0.030	0.046	0.021	-0.041	0.016
Five-year log difference	0.432	0.105	0.025	0.070	0.230	0.057	-0.077	0.038

	(1)	(2)	(3)	(4)	(5)	(6)	(7)	(8)
All covariates, without school leaving age dummy and contractual wage								
Levels	0.151	0.028	−0.020	0.030	0.006	0.021	−0.053	0.022
Three-year lag of incentives	0.146	0.057	−0.051	0.043	0.010	0.029	−0.086	0.032
Five-year difference	0.180	0.008	−0.061	0.011	0.038	0.017	−0.053	0.018
Five-year log difference	0.975	0.098	−0.230	0.070	0.296	0.072	−0.067	0.036
Selected covariates								
Levels	0.118	0.022	0.0005	0.027	0.020	0.019	−0.056	0.013
Three-year lag of incentives	0.066	0.027	−0.001	0.029	−0.037	0.012	−0.050	0.014
Five-year difference	0.137	0.019	−0.021	0.019	0.039	0.016	−0.055	0.012
Five-year log difference	0.587	0.095	−0.104	0.051	0.276	0.050	−0.120	0.036
Alpha = −0.248, gamma = 0.299, no liquidity constraints								
No covariates								
Levels	0.528	0.058	−0.516	0.104	0.454	0.081	−0.208	0.033
Three-year lag of incentives	0.345	0.063	−0.565	0.078	0.260	0.070	−0.160	0.036
Five-year difference	0.523	0.168	−0.005	0.161	0.087	0.120	−0.256	0.080
Five-year log difference	0.691	0.173	0.028	0.113	0.250	0.111	−0.159	0.058
All covariates, without school leaving age dummy and contractual wage								
Levels	1.017	0.176	−0.282	0.190	0.012	0.137	−0.437	0.127
Three-year lag of incentives	0.935	0.236	−0.501	0.179	−0.007	0.140	−0.533	0.133
Five-year difference	0.840	0.102	−0.333	0.047	0.150	0.098	−0.659	0.114
Five-year log difference	1.364	0.159	−0.465	0.060	0.385	0.143	−0.196	0.048
Selected covariates								
Levels	0.521	0.104	−0.030	0.122	0.005	0.088	−0.285	0.051
Three-year lag of incentives	0.455	0.112	−0.188	0.134	−0.150	0.064	−0.313	0.052
Five-year difference	0.671	0.119	−0.163	0.095	0.150	0.092	−0.316	0.059
Five-year log difference	1.110	0.146	−0.273	0.077	0.426	0.105	−0.267	0.052

(continued)

Table 6.5 (continued)

| | Youth (20 to 24) | | | | | | Old (50 to 64) | |
| | Unemployment rate | | Employment rate | | School | | Labor force participation | |
	Coefficient	Standard error	Coefficient	Standard error	Coefficient	Standard error	Coefficient	Standard error
Alpha = −0.547, gamma = 0.713, liquidity constraints (SSW = 0 before eligibility; W − PV = 0 before eligibility)								
No covariates								
Levels	0.438	0.047	−0.434	0.084	0.398	0.062	−0.166	0.028
Three-year lag of incentives	0.282	0.054	−0.460	0.069	0.221	0.057	−0.128	0.031
Five-year difference	0.470	0.138	0.005	0.136	0.125	0.099	−0.208	0.069
Five-year log difference	2.098	0.491	0.069	0.331	0.636	0.334	−0.483	0.167
All covariates, without school leaving age dummy and contractual wage								
Levels	0.798	0.137	−0.167	0.152	0.022	0.107	−0.312	0.104
Three-year lag of incentives	0.736	0.215	−0.351	0.164	0.020	0.120	−0.424	0.120
Five-year difference	0.758	0.062	−0.284	0.040	0.148	0.079	−0.402	0.095
Five-year log difference	3.871	0.319	−1.261	0.160	0.842	0.454	−0.599	0.141
Selected covariates								
Levels	0.474	0.089	−0.019	0.108	0.003	0.088	−0.247	0.047
Three-year lag of incentives	0.359	0.101	−0.114	0.117	−0.135	0.054	−0.251	0.049
Five-year difference	0.594	0.091	−0.123	0.081	0.149	0.075	−0.263	0.050
Five-year log difference	3.531	0.335	−0.908	0.212	1.105	0.345	−0.860	0.137
Alpha = 0.0, no liquidity constraints								
No covariates								
Levels	0.156	0.017	−0.152	0.031	0.134	0.024	−0.061	0.010
Three-year lag of incentives	0.102	0.019	−0.167	0.023	0.077	0.021	−0.047	0.011
Five-year difference	0.154	0.050	−0.001	0.048	0.025	0.035	−0.076	0.023
Five-year log difference	0.685	0.172	0.028	0.112	0.248	0.110	−0.158	0.057

All covariates, without school leaving age dummy and contractual wage

Levels	0.300	0.052	-0.083	0.056	0.004	0.040	-0.129	0.037
Three-year lag of incentives	0.275	0.070	-0.148	0.053	-0.002	0.041	-0.157	0.039
Five-year difference	0.247	0.030	-0.098	0.014	0.044	0.029	-0.195	0.033
Five-year log difference	1.350	0.158	-0.460	0.059	0.379	0.142	-0.194	0.048

Selected covariates

Levels	0.153	0.031	-0.009	0.036	0.001	0.026	-0.084	0.015
Three-year lag of incentives	0.134	0.033	-0.055	0.040	-0.044	0.019	-0.092	0.015
Five-year difference	0.198	0.035	-0.048	0.028	0.044	0.027	-0.093	0.017
Five-year log difference	1.100	0.145	-0.270	0.077	0.421	0.104	-0.265	0.052

Alpha = 0.0, liquidity constraints (SSW = 0 before eligibility; W − PV = 0 before eligibility)

No covariates

Levels	0.402	0.049	-0.363	0.089	0.381	0.058	-0.143	0.030
Three-year lag of incentives	0.251	0.055	-0.371	0.081	0.190	0.058	-1.112	0.031
Five-year difference	0.361	0.105	0.018	0.104	0.161	0.070	-0.130	0.056
Five-year log difference	0.693	0.168	0.046	0.111	0.355	0.094	-0.121	0.061

All covariates, without school leaving age dummy and contractual wage

Levels	0.514	0.099	-0.060	0.105	0.016	0.072	-0.175	0.075
Three-year lag of incentives	0.438	0.202	-0.120	0.148	0.058	0.097	-0.264	0.112
Five-year difference	0.624	0.031	-0.205	0.039	0.139	0.057	-0.161	0.062
Five-year log difference	1.464	0.164	-0.325	0.111	0.447	0.123	-0.098	0.060

Selected covariates

Levels	0.410	0.082	0.012	0.096	0.001	0.026	-0.191	0.047
Three-year lag of incentives	0.219	0.096	0.007	0.100	-0.124	0.043	-0.166	0.050
Five-year difference	0.461	0.070	-0.063	0.065	0.140	0.055	-0.181	0.044
Five-year log difference	0.967	0.148	-0.172	0.081	0.429	0.085	-0.198	0.057

Notes: I bar is divided by 100,000. All covariates: year (not in the five-year difference case); GDP per capita/1,000; GDP per capita growth (not in the difference case); percentage of people in school; share of industry in the GDP; median wage/1,000; contractual wage/1,000; dummy for changes in the compulsory school leaving age (dropped in the five-year log difference case). Selected covariates: GDP per capita; GDP per capita growth (not in the difference case); share of industry in the GDP. Specification of regressions: levels: $Y = 1 + year + GDP$ per capita $+ \ldots$. Three-year lag of incentives: $Y = I[n-3] + year + GDP$ per capita $+ \ldots$. Five-year difference: $Y - Y[n-5] = I[n-5] + (GDP$ per capita $- GDP$ per capita $[n-5]) + \ldots$. Five-year log difference: $Y - Y[n-5] = [\log I - \log(I[n-5])] + [\log(GDP$ per capita$) - \log(GDP$ per capita $[n-5])] + \ldots 0$

force of the elderly, as the labor force participation of the older groups shows a negative and significant coefficient.

6.8   Conclusions

Italy is a country characterized by high rates of unemployment, particularly for the younger generations. The generosity of the pension system prior to the reforms of the 1990s has encouraged many workers to retire early, and some policymakers, particularly unions, have supported the "young in, old out" paradigm. We show that for Italy, the "lump of labor" assumption fails, and we do this through two main routes.

First we show that the direct relationship between the unemployment rate of the young (age twenty to twenty-four) and the labor force participation of the old (fifty-five to sixty-four) is procyclical; that is, higher labor force participation of the old is associated with a lower unemployment rate of the young. This correlation occurs because both are driven by the business cycle. This result is very robust to the lag structure that we impose, so it is not just an artifact of the timing of the business cycle. It does not change when we distinguish groups by gender, given the important gender differences in labor market behavior.

The second route recognizes that the previous approach may suffer from endogeneity problems. Hence, we resort to a simulated variable, "the inducement to retire," which is constructed by simulating the social security benefits accruing to the median worker, taking into account the relevant social security legislation. There are two versions of this incentive variable: one is simply the average social security wealth, and the other is an index that also includes the potential gains (losses) from postponing retirement; the latter captures elements of forward-looking behavior.

We relate the unemployment rate of the young to these incentive measures and find that a higher inducement to retire is associated with a higher unemployment rate—quite the opposite of the "young in, old out" story. The variables capturing the inducement to retire have a significant effect on the labor force participation of older workers. This effect has the expected sign (the higher the incentive, the lower labor force participation) and is very robust to different specifications, suggesting that Italian workers responded to social security incentives.

Appendix

Table 6A.1   Employment Protection Legislation Index

A OECD Employment Outlook 1999

| | Regular employment | | Temporary employment | | Collective dismissals | Overall EPL Strictness[a] | | |
| | | | | | | Version 1 | | Version 2 |
	Late 1980s	Late 1990s	Late 1980s	Late 1990s	Late 1990s	Late 1980s	Late 1990s	Late 1990s
France	2.3	2.3	3.1	3.6	2.1	2.7	3.0	2.8
Germany	2.7	2.8	3.8	2.3	3.1	3.2	2.5	2.6
Italy[b]	2.8	2.8	5.4	3.8	4.1	4.1 (1)	3.3 (3)	3.4 (3)
Spain	3.9	2.6	3.5	3.5	3.1	3.7	3.1	0.1
United Kingdom	0.8	0.8	0.3	0.3	2.9	0.5	0.5	0.9

B OECD Employment Outlook 2004

| | Regular employment | | | Temporary employment | | | Collective dismissals | | | Overall EPL strictness | | | |
| | | | | | | | | | | Version 1 | | Version 2 | |
	Late 1980s	Late 1990s	2003	Late 1980s	Late 1990s	2003	Late 1980s	Late 1990s	2003	Late 1990s	2003	Late 1990s	2003
France	2.3	2.3	2.5	3.1	3.6	3.6	2.7	2.1	2.1	3.0	3.0	2.8	2.9
Germany	2.6	2.7	2.7	3.8	2.3	1.8	3.2	3.5	3.8	2.5	2.2	2.6	2.5
Italy	1.8	1.8	1.8	5.4	3.6	2.1	3.6 (3)	4.9	4.9	2.7 (4)	1.9 (11)	3.1 (3)	2.4 (9)
Spain	3.9	2.6	2.6	3.8	3.3	3.5	3.8	3.1	3.1	2.9	3.1	3.0	3.1
United Kingdom	0.9	0.9	1.1	0.3	0.3	0.4	0.6	2.9	2.9	0.6	0.7	1.0	1.1

Notes: In the *Employment Outlook 1999* (panel A), the regular employment index for Italy is based also on the TFR (severance payment), which is regarded as "employment protection." In panel B, the TFR is excluded.

[a]Version 1 excludes *collective dismissal*.

[b]In the overall index for Italy, the ranking vis-à-vis the other EU12 countries is in parentheses. Position 1 is the highest level of workers' protection.

Table 6A.2 Direct effect of elderly LFP on unemployment or employment of young and prime age groups and on schooling participation of younger age group. Pooled genders: National level data

| | Youth (20 to 24) | | | | | | Prime age (25 to 54) | | | |
| | Unemployment rate | | Employment rate | | School | | Unemployment rate | | Employment rate | |
	Coefficient	Standard error	Coefficient	Standard error	Coefficient	Standard error	Coefficient	Standard error	Coefficient	Standard error
				All covariates						
Levels (27 observations)										
LFP old	-2.706	0.458	0.477	0.363	1.176	0.619	-0.619	0.072	0.559	0.115
Year	0.021	0.007	-0.022	0.006	-0.002	0.011	0.007	0.001	-0.006	0.002
GDP per capita/1,000	-0.075	0.023	0.041	0.019	0.030	0.034	-0.017	0.003	0.024	0.005
GDP per capita growth	-0.079	0.310	-0.429	0.246	-0.182	0.456	-0.031	0.076	-0.042	0.121
People in school	0.638	0.159	0.282	0.126	—	—	-0.053	0.254	-0.482	0.405
Age at end of compulsory education	0.001	0.020	-0.027	0.016	0.042	0.028	0.003	0.004	-0.005	0.006
Median wage/1,000	0.018	0.009	0.014	0.007	-0.009	0.013	0.001	0.002	-0.005	0.003
Contractual wage/1,000	0.002	0.003	-0.002	0.002	-0.007	0.004	0.0005	0.0005	-0.002	0.001
Share of industry on GDP	2.761	1.332	-0.956	1.056	-2.071	1.910	1.083	0.258	-0.999	0.412
R^2	0.9555		0.9834		0.8923		0.9928		0.9744	
Five-year difference (23 observations)										
LFP old	-2.794	0.308	0.935	0.260	0.837	0.496	-0.527	0.066	0.451	0.109
GDP per capita/1,000	-0.116	0.022	0.100	0.018	-0.004	0.038	-0.016	0.003	0.028	0.005
People in school	0.510	0.143	0.429	0.121	—	—	-0.259	0.174	0.052	0.289
Age at end of compulsory education	-0.002	0.014	-0.004	0.012	0.028	0.024	0.007	0.004	-0.011	0.007
Median wage/1,000	0.035	0.008	-0.004	0.007	-0.002	0.014	0.0004	0.002	0.006	0.003
Contractual wage/1,000	-0.002	0.003	-0.001	0.002	-0.005	0.005	-0.0002	0.001	-0.003	0.001
Share of industry on GDP	4.398	0.951	-3.126	0.804	-1.493	1.624	1.220	0.237	-1.105	0.393
R^2	0.9512		0.9444		0.5550		0.9714		0.9453	

All covariates

Levels (27 observations)

LFP old	-2.758	0.201	1.071	0.177	0.501	0.309	-0.653	0.056	0.597	0.108
Year	0.022	0.005	-0.030	0.004	0.009	0.008	0.008	0.001	-0.006	0.001
GDP per capita/1,000	-0.077	0.014	0.067	0.012	-0.009	0.023	-0.018	0.002	0.024	0.004
GDP per capita growth	-0.178	0.204	-0.044	0.180	-0.004	0.333	-0.059	0.073	-0.025	0.139
People in school	0.604	0.137	0.259	0.121	—	—	0.034	0.253	-0.585	0.485
Median wage/1,000	0.020	0.005	0.003	0.005	-0.003	0.009	0.002	0.001	-0.0005	0.002
Share of industry on GDP	3.102	0.676	-2.805	0.596	-0.667	1.094	1.276	0.194	-1.434	0.372
R^2	0.9540		0.9788		0.8653		0.9919		0.9587	

Five-year difference (23 observations)

LFP old	-2.769	0.179	0.997	0.150	0.389	0.312	-0.613	0.040	0.527	0.077
GDP per capita/1,000	-0.113	0.017	0.104	0.014	-0.029	0.030	-0.020	0.002	0.028	0.004
People in school	0.526	0.129	0.432	0.109	—	—	-0.147	0.162	-0.116	0.316
Median wage/1,000	0.031	0.007	-0.007	0.005	-0.0002	0.012	0.002	0.001	-0.0002	0.002
Share of industry on GDP	3.999	0.623	-3.487	0.522	-0.955	1.111	1.447	0.160	-1.862	0.311
R^2	0.9489		0.9426		0.4995		0.9664		0.9110	

Selected covariates

Levels (27 observations)

LFP old	-2.250	0.333	1.058	0.410	0.540	0.319	-0.662	0.096	0.585	0.119
GDP per capita/1,000	-0.007	0.003	-0.010	0.004	0.014	0.003	0.002	0.001	0.008	0.001
GDP per capita growth	-0.332	0.364	0.227	0.448	-0.102	0.349	-0.163	0.105	0.170	0.131
Share of industry on GDP	0.190	0.904	-0.257	1.112	-1.552	0.866	0.517	0.261	-1.146	0.324
R^2	0.8269		0.8447		0.8344		0.9407		0.8726	

Five-year difference (23 observations)

LFP old	-2.276	0.277	1.099	0.182	0.388	0.285	-0.628	0.044	0.525	0.073
GDP per capita/1,000	-0.056	0.011	0.075	0.007	-0.029	0.012	-0.016	0.002	0.029	0.003
Share of industry on GDP	1.743	0.840	-3.499	0.551	-0.944	0.864	1.245	0.132	-1.944	0.221
R^2	0.8305		0.8836		0.4995		0.9536		0.9102	

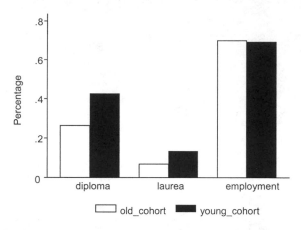

Fig. 6A.1   Prevalence of a secondary degree (diploma), university degree (laurea), or work for different cohorts

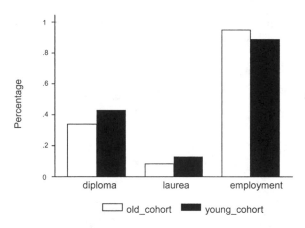

Fig. 6A.2   Prevalence of a secondary degree (diploma), university degree (laurea), or work for different cohorts: Males

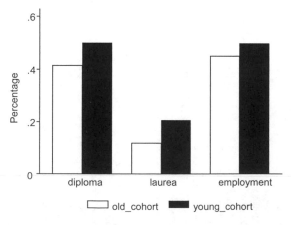

Fig. 6A.3   Prevalence of a secondary degree (diploma), university degree (laurea), or work for different cohorts: Females

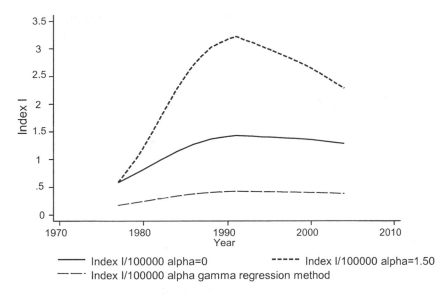

Fig. 6A.4 Index _I_ for different values of alpha

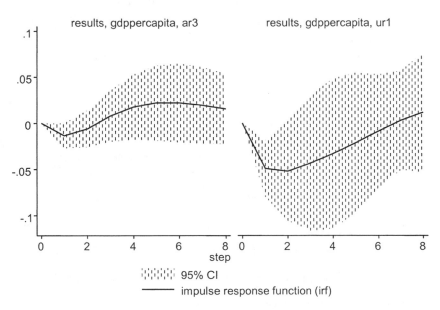

Fig. 6A.5 Impulse response function of the activity rate of the old (AR3) and the unemployment rate of the young (UR1) in response to GDP per capita

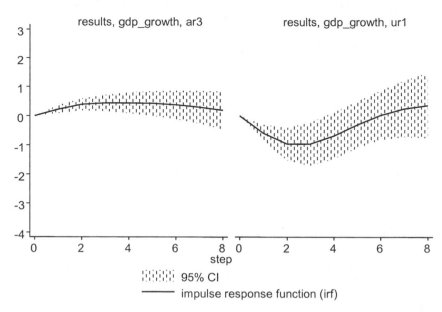

Fig. 6A.6   Impulse response function of the activity rate of the old (AR3) and un-employment rate of the young (UR1) in response to GDP growth

Notes: The impulse response function, computed after running a vector autoregression (VAR), shows the change over time of the variables UR1 (unemployment young) or AR3 (activity old) in response to a one-time impulse of the variables GDP per capita or GDP growth. This is done keeping all the other variables of the VAR constant.

References

Attanasio, O., and F. Padoa-Schioppa. 1991. Regional inequalities, migration and mismatch in Italy, 1960–1986. In *Mismatch and labour mobility,* ed. F. Padoa-Schioppa, 237–32. Cambridge: Cambridge University Press.

Bank of Italy. 2004. *Historical Database of the Survey of Italian Household Budgets, 1977–2002: Version 3.0.* Rome: Bank of Italy.

Bentolila, S., and G. Bertola. 1990. How bad is eurosclerosis? *Review of Economic Studies* 57 (3): 381–402.

Bertola, G. 1990. Job security, employment and wages. *European Economic Review* 34 (4): 851–66.

———. 1999. Microeconomic perspectives on aggregate labour markets. In *Handbook of labour economics,* vol. 3B, ed. O. Ashenfelter and D. Card, 2985–3028. Amsterdam: North-Holland.

Bodo, G., and P. Sestito. 1991. *Le vie dello sviluppo.* Bologna: Il Mulino.

Boeri, T., and P. Garibaldi. 2007. Two tier reforms of employment protection: A honeymoon effect? *Economic Journal* 117 (521): 357–85.

Boldrin, M., J. Dolado, J. Jimeno, and F. Peracchi. 1999. The future of pensions in Europe. *Economic Policy* 29:289–320.

Brugiavini, A. 1999. Social security and retirement in Italy. In *Social security and retirement around the world,* ed. J. Gruber and D. A. Wise, 181–237. Chicago: University of Chicago Press.

Brugiavini, A., and V. Galasso. 2004. The social security reform process in Italy: Where do we stand? *Journal of Pension Economics and Finance* 3:165–95.

Brugiavini, A., and F. Peracchi. 2003. Social security wealth and retirement decisions in Italy. *Labour* 17 (special issue): 79–114.

———. 2004. Micro-modeling of retirement behavior in Italy. In *Social security programs and retirement around the world: Micro-estimation,* ed. J. Gruber and D. A. Wise, 345–98. Chicago: University of Chicago Press.

———. 2005. The length of working lives in Europe. *Journal of the European Economic Association* 3:477–86.

———. 2007. Fiscal implications of pension reforms in Italy. In *Social security programs and retirement around the world: Fiscal implication of reforms,* ed. J. Gruber and D. A. Wise, 253–94. Chicago: University of Chicago Press.

Brunello, G., C. Lupi, and P. Ordine. 2001. Widening differences in Italian regional unemployment. *Labour Economics* 8 (1): 103–29.

Caroleo, F. E., and F. Mazzotta. 1999. Youth unemployment and youth employment policies in Italy. ILO Employment and Training Paper no. 42. Geneva: International Labor Organization.

Contini, B. 2005. Invecchiamento e precarizzazione giovanile nell'occupazione italiana: È possibile una chiave di lettura unificata? *Rivista di Politica Economica* (March–April): 323–35.

Contini, B., and F. M. Rapiti. 1999. "Young in, Old Out" revisited: New patterns of employment replacement in the Italian economy. *International Review of Applied Economics* 13:395–415.

Franco, D. 2002. Italy: A never-ending pension reform. In *Social Security pension reform in Europe,* ed. M. Feldstein and H. Siebert, 211–62. Chicago: University of Chicago Press.

Manacorda, M., and B. Petrongolo. 2006. Regional mismatch and unemployment: Theory and evidence from Italy, 1977–1998. *Journal of Population Economies* 19:137–62.

Organization for Economic Cooperation and Development (OECD). 1999. *Employment outlook.* Paris: OECD.

Rossi, N., A. Sorgato, and G. Toniolo. 1993. I conti economici italiani: Una ricostruzione statistica, 1890–1990. *Rivista di Storia Economica,* 2nd ser., 10 (1993):1–47.

7

Does Social Security Induce Withdrawal of the Old from the Labor Force and Create Jobs for the Young? The Case of Japan

Takashi Oshio, Satoshi Shimizutani, and
Akiko Sato Oishi

7.1 Introduction

The current speed of aging in Japan is unprecedented and is far more rapid than in other developed countries. The proportion of the old, defined as those aged sixty-five and over, was 4.9 percent of the total population in 1950, increased to 12.5 percent in 1990, and further reached 22.1 percent in 2008, implying that one-fifth of the population is currently occupied by the old (National Institute of Population and Social Security Research [NIPSSR]).[1] Population aging will continue into the future and even accelerate. According to the latest population projection released by the NIPSSR in December 2006, the share of those aged sixty-five years and above is expected to reach 30.5 percent of the total population in 2025 and further increase to 39.6 percent in 2050.

The rapid pace of population aging has raised concerns about the sustainability of the current programs and stimulated a series of major pension reforms since the mid-1980s, which called for a rise of eligibility ages, a reduction of benefit levels, and a rise of contribution rates. The latest reform in 2004 is to extend the eligibility age from sixty to sixty-five by 2025 and has introduced an automatic adjustment of benefit levels due to demographic

Takashi Oshio is a professor at the Institute of Economic Research at Hitotsubashi University. Satoshi Shimizutani is a senior research fellow at the Institute for International Policy Studies. Akiko Sato Oishi is associate professor of law and economics at Chiba University.

The original version of this chapter was presented at the conference on the International Social Security Project (phase 5) organized by the National Bureau of Economic Research (NBER) in Lisbon, Portugal, on May 23 and 24, 2008.

1. The United Nations defines a society in which people aged sixty-five and above account for more than 7 percent as one that is aging and a society in which this age group shares more than 14 percent as one that is aged. It took only twenty-four years for Japan to move from being an aging society to an aged one, while it took more than fifty years for most Western countries.

and macroeconomic factors in order to cope with the expected increase of benefits and the deteriorating fiscal balances.

Naturally, these reforms are likely to have affected the labor supply of the elderly and possibly of the nonelderly. Thus, an interesting question is to quantify the effects of social security programs on labor market outcomes for both the old and the young: does a generous social security program provide jobs for the young by encouraging the old to exit the labor market? Does a rise in the eligibility age make the old stay longer in the workplace and crowd out the young? When addressing these issues, we have to keep in mind the possibility of the endogeneity of changes in social security programs with respect to the employment or unemployment of the young. Fortunately, it is unlikely that endogeneity is an issue in Japan, because the timings of reforms are exogenously determined, regardless of economic and demographic circumstances.

This chapter examines whether social security programs in Japan induce withdrawal of the elderly from the labor force and create jobs for the young. Our discussions proceed as follows. Section 7.2 provides a historical overview of social security reforms and employment policies toward the elderly. Section 7.3 presents the long-term employment and unemployment trends of both the old and the young and performs a regression analysis to examine the direct relationship between the employment of the young and that of the old. Section 7.4 examines whether changes in social security programs are associated with the employment of the young or the old, using measures for the inducement to retire. Section 7.5 concludes. The two appendices provide a detailed description of data construction and sources of the main variables used in this study.

7.2 Background

7.2.1 Social Security Reforms

This section provides historical information on social security reforms and employment policies for the elderly. We focus on what their main purposes have been and whether the prospect of creating jobs for the young has played a large role in the policy debate.

Table 7.1 overviews the directions of past social security reforms in terms of the benefits of the Employees' Pension Insurance (EPI, *Kosei Nenkin*) and National Pension Insurance (NPI, *Kokumin Nenkin*), which are at the core of the public pension scheme in Japan (see section 7.4 for more details).[2] Both EPI and NPI laws require benefit and contribution schemes to be reviewed

---

2. See Komamura (2007) for more details. The EPI and NPI cover 48.0 and 45.5 percent of the population insured by public pension programs. The Mutual Aid Insurance (*Kyosai Nenkin*) covers the remaining 6.5 percent, most of whom are employees in the public sector and private schools.

Table 7.1   **Changes in social security benefits in key reforms**

Social security reform	Employees' Pension Insurance			National Pension Insurance	
	Wage-proportional benefit	Flat-rate benefit (annual, yen)		Flat-rate benefit (annual, yen)	
	Benefit multiplier (/1,000)	Nominal	2005 prices	Nominal	2005 prices
1954	5	24,000	[127,292]	—	—
1959	6	24,000	[127,620]	42,000	[223,336]
1965	10	120,000	[473,412]	96,000	[378,730]
1969	10	192,000	[624,086]	153,600	[499,269]
1973	10	480,000	[1,185,185]	384,000	[948,148]
1976	10	624,000	[1,022,951]	624,000	[1,022,951]
1980	10	984,000	[1,279,584]	806,400	[1,048,635]
1985	7.5	600,000	[681,044]	600,000	[681,044]
1989	7.5	666,000	[729,463]	666,000	[729,463]
1994	7.5	780,000	[773,810]	780,000	[773,810]
2000	7.125	804,200	[786,888]	804,200	[786,888]
2004	7.125	804,200	[801,795]	804,200	[801,795]

Note: Flat-rate benefits have been applied to beneficiaries with forty-year contributions in the 1965 reform and after, while they were fixed regardless of years of contributions in the 1954 and 1959 reforms. National Pension Insurance started in 1959.

every five years (at least) from the viewpoint of financial balances and their sustainability, so the timing of social security reform is exogenously determined, regardless of economic, demographic, and other conditions.

Until the early 1970s, the main purpose of the major social security reforms had been consistently to raise benefits levels, aiming to improve income levels of elderly persons in line with the rising average standard of living under rapid economic growth. The government had continued to raise the benefit multiplier for the wage-proportional benefit and/or the benefit unit for its flat-rate benefit, and it also introduced wage and price indexation to the benefits in 1973.

However, slower economic growth from the mid-1970s and a rapid and continuous drop in the fertility rate raised concerns about the financial sustainability of social security programs. The 1985 reform was revolutionary in that it incorporated a reduction in the benefit multiplier and flat-rate benefit for the first time, aiming to hold down an increase in total pension benefits. Under rising concerns about demographic pressures, subsequent reforms have continued to seek to improve the financial balances of the programs by reducing the benefit multiplier, scaling down benefit indexations, and extending eligibility ages, as well as raising the premium rate.

Figures 7.1 and 7.2 depict the eligibility ages for EPI benefits: figure 7.1 applies to male beneficiaries and figure 7.2 to female beneficiaries. In the case of male pensioners, the eligibility age for both flat-rate and wage-proportional benefits was raised to sixty in 1973 from the previous fifty-five

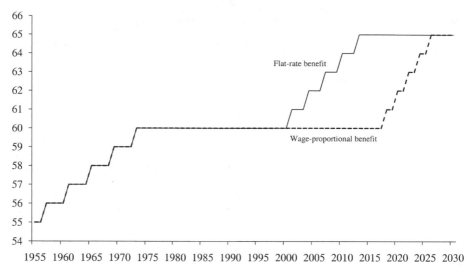

Fig. 7.1   Eligibility ages for EPI benefits: Males

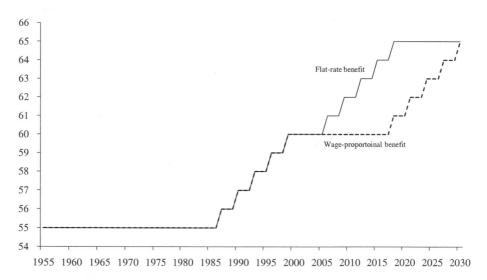

Fig. 7.2   Eligibility ages for EPI benefits: Females

and then stayed there until 2000. Since 2001, the eligibility age for the flat-rate component has been scheduled to increase by one year for every three years to sixty-five in 2013, while the eligibility age for the wage-proportional component will remain at sixty. In addition, the eligibility age for the wage-proportional component is scheduled to rise by one year every three years from 2013, reaching sixty-five in 2025. For female beneficiaries, the eligibility age had been fifty-five until 1985 and then was gradually raised to sixty in 1999 to catch up with men. Their eligibility ages are set to increase, albeit with a five-year lag for men: from 2006 for the flat-rate benefit and from 2018 for the wage-proportional benefit.

In Japan, there has been no eligibility age that is exactly equivalent to a so-called "early retirement" age widely observed in other advanced countries, and there has been no attempt to lower the eligibility age. However, there is a means-tested *Zaishoku* pension scheme for the EPI program, which is applied to those who stay in the labor force after the eligibility age. Some preceding research studies find disincentive effects of this scheme on the willingness of the elderly to work, but its impact on the overall labor force of the elderly remains mixed and is yet to be examined in detail.

7.2.2 Employment Policies for the Elderly

The employment policies for the elderly have been reformed in accordance with social security reforms, especially aiming to expand job opportunities for the elderly whose eligibility ages were extended. For example, the government revised the Employment Measures Law in 1973 to include a declaration clause on raising the mandatory retirement age and to introduce a subsidy paid to employers who extend the mandatory retirement age to sixty. In 1986, the Law Concerning Stabilization of Employment of Older Persons introduced a new endeavor clause on extending the mandatory retirement age to sixty or over and changed it as the obligatory target.

This trend of extending the mandatory retirement age continued. In response to a scheduled rise in the eligibility age for EPI benefits in the 1994 pension reform, the government established a new type of wage subsidy—the Continued Employment Benefit for Older Workers—to compensate for the reduced wages of older workers who continue to be employed after the mandatory retirement age. This wage subsidy is intended to encourage the old to continue working after retiring from their primary jobs rather than extending the mandatory retirement age. The government also revised the Employment Measures Law in 2000 and 2004, which includes an obligatory clause that requires firms to raise the mandatory retirement age to sixty-five or above by 2013 or to completely abolish it.

As a result, the distribution of mandatory retirement ages has been changing substantially over the past decades, as demonstrated in figure 7.3, which is based on the Survey on Employment Management (*Koyo Kanri Chosa*) compiled by the Ministry of Health, Labor, and Welfare (MHLW). The share of firms that had a mandatory retirement scheme was less than 50 percent until around 1980, and a significant portion of those firms set the retirement age at fifty-five. After that, the proportion of firms with mandatory retirement steadily increased to above 90 percent in the mid-1990s. The most dominant retirement age is now sixty, and some firms have started extending it further to sixty-five.[3]

---

3. It should be noted that this survey covers only firms employing thirty and more workers, and many smaller firms have no mandatory retirement age.

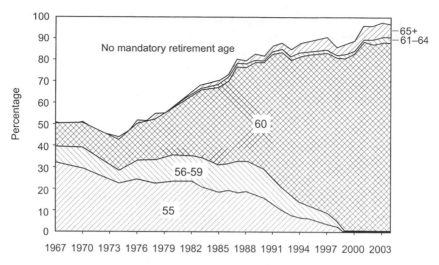

Fig. 7.3   Distribution of mandatory retirement ages set by firms
Source: Surveys on Employment Management, MHLW.
Notes: The "55" category includes a small number of firms with mandatory retirement age of fifty-four and younger. Figures are for firms with thirty or more employees.

7.2.3   Current Issues

As suggested by our brief overview on social security reforms and employment policies for the elderly, there has been virtually no policy intention among Japanese policymakers to link the employment of the old and young. Their main concern has consistently been how to encourage the old to stay longer in the labor market in accordance with a rise in the eligibility age for pension benefits. Contrary to some European countries, which observe active policy debates to use social security provisions to create jobs for the young, there seem to have been virtually no such arguments in Japan, both in the policy arena and in academia. This observation supports the view that changes to social security programs in Japan have not been endogenous with respect to the employment of the young and that any change in specific provisions has not been correlated with job creation for the young.

To be sure, unemployment among the young has been rising sharply since the early 1990s, reflecting the sluggish economy, which made firms more cautious about recruiting new graduates under strong cost-cutting pressures. The unemployment rate for those aged fifteen to twenty-four was around 5 percent in the early 1990s and tracked an upward trend during the decade, reaching 10.3 percent in 2003.[4] Similar to some European countries that suffer from a high unemployment rate among the young, the historically

---

4. The unemployment rate for those aged fifteen to twenty-four resumed its fall in 2004 but remained at around 8 percent, well above the average during the early 1990s.

high level of unemployment among the young captured a lot of political and social attention in Japan. Indeed, several policy measures have been proposed to increase job opportunities for the young, such as provision of job skills, expansion of temporary workers, and strengthening job matching for the young. However, the deteriorated labor market conditions for the young has not front-loaded social security reforms or induced the government to provide job opportunities through legislative changes on plan provisions.

We speculate that one of the important reasons for the absence of debate in Japan is that employment of the old and that of the young are not substitutes. The Japanese labor market is characterized by the prevalence of a long-term employment practice (called "lifetime employment"). A large volume of previous studies discusses how Japanese firms, especially larger ones, hire new school graduates, and most workers stay with the same firm for decades to gain firm-specific human capital that contributes to the productivity of the firm (see Aoki, Patrick, and Sheard [1994]). Shimizutani and Yokoyama (2009) show that the average years of tenure of Japanese workers became even longer after 1990 under the long recession. These arguments suggest that there is a large productivity gap between young and older workers and thus that they are not substitutes.

7.3   Long-Term Employment Trends

7.3.1   Three Age Groups

This section graphically overviews the long-term trends of employment and unemployment by age bracket in Japan since 1960. We present the employment trends of three age groups in terms of three employment measures (labor force participation [LFP], employment, and unemployment), pooling genders. The data construction and data sources of the main variables in this section are explained in appendix A.

In what follows, to examine if employment of the old "crowds out" employment of younger persons, we define three age groups: "young" (aged twenty to twenty-four), "prime age" (aged twenty-five to fifty-four), and "old" (aged fifty-five to sixty-nine).

- "Young" refers to people aged twenty to twenty-four. Of those graduating from high school, about half continue on to junior colleges and universities (51 percent in 2007). Most students complete undergraduate programs by the age of twenty-four. Unfortunately, there are no official data on the number of people enrolled in schools by age, so we tentatively assume that those who are out of the labor force at ages twenty to twenty-four are in school (colleges, graduate, and vocational schools).
- "Prime age" refers those aged twenty-five to fifty-four. They form the

core of the labor force in Japan. The mandatory retirement age had been fifty-five for 20 percent or more of total employed workers until the mid-1980s (see later).

- "Old" refers to those aged fifty-five to sixty-nine. The mandatory retirement age was extended from fifty-five to sixty in the 1990s and now is in a transition process to sixty-five, although adoption of the mandatory retirement age of sixty-five is optional, and the adoption rate varies by industry and firm size. We should also keep in mind that the mandatory retirement age means the age at which a person leaves his or her "prime work" in Japan. Retired workers are sometimes provided an opportunity to be employed by the same or affiliated firms with lower incomes but flexible working conditions.[5]

7.3.2   Long-Term Trends of Employment and Unemployment

Figure 7.4 presents long-term trends of the LFP of the old, as well as the LFP and unemployment of the young between 1965 and 2005, pooling genders. The LFP and unemployment are expressed as a percentage of the total population for each age group. The figure also shows the dates of key social security reforms with dotted lines for reference, which correspond to those in table 7.1.

We confirm the following facts. First, there is no relationship between the LFP or unemployment of the young and the dates of social security reforms, which have been exogenously determined by laws. This is also the case for the 1985 reform, which was the largest revision to the social security programs in Japan. Second, the LFP of the old and the LFP of the young have been moving in parallel over the medium term, although over the long term, the former shows an upward trend (probably due to extended mandatory retirement ages), and the latter shows a downward trend (probably due to increasing demand for higher educational attainment). Third, we find no clear correlation in the short-term movements of the old LFP and the unemployment of the young, while both of them have long-term upward trends.

Figure 7.5 compares the LFP of the old, the unemployment of the young, and the unemployment of the prime age group. If the LFP of the old and that of the younger age groups are substitutes, the LFP of the old and the unemployment of the younger age groups would have moved in the same directions. To be sure, such movements are observed around 1980 and during the 1990s. During the mid-1960s and the mid-1970s, however, a reduction in the LFP of the old was not accompanied by a fall in the unemployment of

---

5. Unfortunately, we cannot distinguish changes in the routes to retirement due to a lack of information available from published statistics. OECD (2004) shows that the effective retirement age, which is defined as the average age at which workers aged forty or above retire, is seventy and sixty-six years old for Japanese males and females, respectively, for 1997 to 2002. Shimizutani and Oshio (2009) discuss the transition from prime work to retirement in more detail.

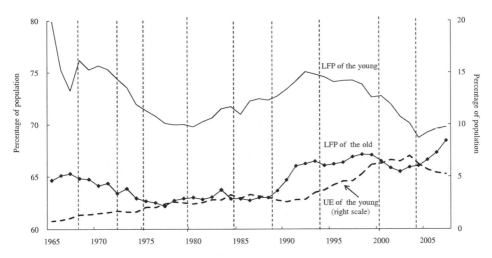

Fig. 7.4   LFP of the old and LFP and unemployment of the young

Note: Dotted lines indicate the dates of key social security reforms.

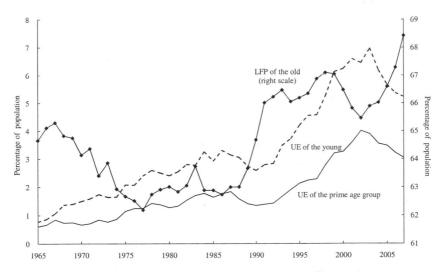

Fig. 7.5   LFP of the old and unemployment of the young and prime age groups

the younger age groups. Moreover, the LFP of the old and unemployment in the younger age groups have been moving clearly in opposite directions since around 2000. Such observations confirm that unemployment in the younger age groups has been uncorrelated with the LFP of the old.

Figure 7.6 compares long-term trends in the LFP of the old, young, and prime age groups. The LFP of the prime age group shows a moderate upward trend, while the LFP curves of the young and old show cyclical

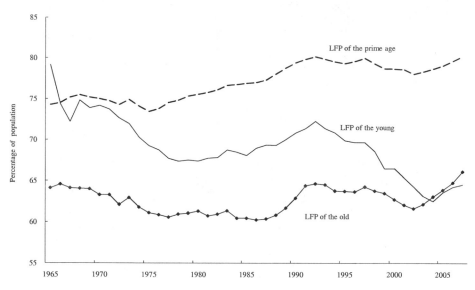

Fig. 7.6   LFP of the old, young, and prime age groups

movements. This fact suggests that employment adjustments by Japanese firms tend to concentrate on employment of the young and old, keeping the core labor force of the prime age group intact against cyclical fluctuations of business conditions.

In all, figures 7.4 to 7.6 do not support the view that jobs for the old crowd out jobs for the young. Rather, employment of the old and employment of the young tend to move in the same direction. This is presumably the main reason why Japanese policymakers have never considered early retirement policies to promote employment of the young.

7.3.4   Ordinary Least Squares (OLS) Regressions for the Direct Relationship

Next, we run several regressions to reveal the direct relationship between the LFP of the old and the employment/unemployment of the younger age groups. There are five dependent variables: unemployment (UE), employment (EMP), and in school (SCH) for the young, and unemployment (UE) and employment (EMP) for the prime age group. The key independent variable is the LFP or employment of the old. When using the LFP of the old in a regression, all labor force variables are measured as a rate of the total population of each age group, and men and women are combined. First, we use only the LFP or employment of the old as an explanatory variable with no controls; then, we add real gross domestic product (GDP) per capita, its growth, and the share of manufacturing in GDP as controls.

We consider four specifications for OLS regressions:

- Regress levels on levels.
- Regress the dependent variables on a three-year lag of elderly LFP or employment.
- Take the five-year differences for all the right- and left-hand-side variables.
- Take the log of all variables, and take five-year differences.

Table 7.2 summarizes the regression results when we take the LFP of the old as the key independent variable. Reported are the estimated coefficients on the LFP of the old. The upper and lower panels present the results with no controls and with controls, respectively. The following facts are noteworthy.

Regarding the unemployment of the young, the results are mixed: three of eight specifications show significant and positive coefficients, while others have all insignificant ones. Mixed results are also observed for un-

Table 7.2   **Direct relationship between the elderly LFP and the employment and unemployment of young and prime age persons, men and women combined: 1965 to 2007**

	Youth, 20 to 24			Prime age, 25 to 54	
Specification	Unemployment	Employment	School	Unemployment	Employment
	No controls				
Levels	0.638***	−0.406	−0.232	0.353***	0.958***
	(0.128)	(0.318)	(0.215)	(0.074)	(0.134)
Three-year lag on	0.535***	−0.178	−0.357	0.313***	0.411***
elderly employment	(0.150)	(0.343)	(0.224)	(0.085)	(0.203)
Five-year difference	−0.057	0.431	−0.374	−0.054	0.593***
	(0.072)	(0.281)	(0.261)	(0.045)	(0.078)
Five-year log	−2.136	0.425	−1.051	−2.254	0.508***
difference	(1.392)	(0.254)	(0.716)	(1.397)	(0.066)
	With controls				
Levels	0.108	0.887***	−0.996***	0.065	0.336***
	(0.066)	(0.207)	(0.193)	(0.044)	(0.072)
Three-year lag on	0.194***	0.656***	−0.850***	0.114***	0.200***
elderly employment	(0.052)	(0.199)	(0.178)	(0.036)	(0.074)
Five-year difference	−0.017	0.429*	−0.412	−0.026	0.541***
	(0.052)	(0.258)	(0.252)	(0.023)	(0.063)
Five-year log	−2.011	0.610**	−1.076	−4.517***	0.540***
difference	(1.389)	(0.261)	(0.764)	(1.026)	(0.064)

Notes: Reported is the coefficient on elderly LFP. Controls include real GDP per capita, growth in real GDP per capita, and the share of manufacturing in GDP. Levels regression means that we regress levels on levels. Three-year difference means that we regress the dependent variables on a three-year lag of elderly LFP. Five-year difference means that we take five-year differences for the right- and left-hand-side variables. Five-year log difference means that we take the log of each X and Y variable, then take five-year differences.

***Significant at the 1 percent level.

**Significant at the 5 percent level.

*Significant at the 10 percent level.

employment in the prime age group. In addition to the three specifications, a significant *negative* coefficient is observed in the five-year log difference model. Hence, we cannot obtain definite results on the relationship between the LFP of the old and the unemployment of the younger age groups.

Turning to the employment of the young, we do not find any significant correlation with the LFP of the old if we include no controls. With controls, however, all specifications produce significant and positive coefficients. In the case of the employment of the prime age group, in all specifications, the coefficients are positive and significant, both with and without controls. These results indicate that the LFP of the old and employment of the younger age groups move in the same direction and contradict the view that employment of the old and employment of the younger age groups are substitutes. If we take the in-school rate as a dependent variable, we do not obtain any significant coefficients if we include no controls, but we have significant and negative coefficients in two specifications with controls. This negative correlation could be spurious, because a long-term uptrend of the in-school rate probably reflects a long-term increase of demand for higher education. In fact, there is no significant correlation within the difference specifications.

Table 7.3 reports the estimated coefficients when we replace the LFP of the old with their employment. While the basic picture remains the same as that shown in table 7.2, we find the following facts. First, the UE models tend to have negative and even significant coefficients for both the young and the prime age groups in more cases. This implies little possibility that the LFP of the old caused unemployment in the younger age groups. Second, when we regress the EMP of the young on the LFP of the old, we observe three significant, positive coefficients. These results also support the view that employment of the old and that of the younger age groups tend to move in the same direction.

7.4   Inducements to Retire and Labor Market Outcomes

7.4.1   Incentive Measures: Social Security Wealth (SSW) and Peak Value (PV)

In this section, we investigate the relationship between inducements for the old to exit the labor force and the employment and unemployment of the young. To facilitate this analysis, we construct a simple summary indicator of the inducement of the old to leave the labor force. The indicator should capture key aspects of inducements such as eligibility age, benefit level given eligibility, and change in the benefit if the receipt of benefits is delayed (essentially an actuarial adjustment when retirement is delayed).

The core for constructing the inducement indicator is EPI benefits. Most

Table 7.3   **Direct relationship between the elderly employment and the employment and unemployment of young and prime age persons, men and women combined: 1965 to 2007**

Specification	Youth, 20 to 24			Prime age, 25 to 54	
	Unemployment	Employment	School	Unemployment	Employment
	No controls				
Levels	0.129	0.566	−0.695***	0.069	0.599***
	(0.174)	(0.339)	(0.208)	(0.099)	(0.195)
Three-year lag on	−0.059	0.832***	−0.773***	−0.031	−0.175
elderly employment	(0.162)	(0.298)	(0.181)	(0.092)	(0.199)
Five-year difference	−0.159***	0.519**	−0.360	−0.110***	0.540***
	(0.057)	(0.234)	(0.222)	(0.036)	(0.060)
Five-year log	−3.385***	0.490**	−0.979	−3.813***	0.443***
difference	(1.064)	(0.204)	(0.590)	(1.036)	(0.051)
	With controls				
Levels	0.025	0.778***	−0.803***	0.018	0.275***
	(0.060)	(0.185)	(0.181)	(0.040)	(0.066)
Three-year lag on	0.115**	0.740***	−0.855***	0.053	0.210***
elderly employment	(0.052)	(0.166)	(0.150)	(0.035)	(0.065)
Five-year difference	−0.072	0.435*	−0.362	−0.046**	0.473***
	(0.046)	(0.230)	(0.228)	(0.020)	(0.060)
Five-year log	−2.976***	0.558***	−0.973	−4.566***	0.425***
difference	(1.027)	(0.203)	(0.603)	(0.677)	(0.052)

Notes: Reported is the coefficient on elderly employment. Controls include real GDP per capita, growth in real GDP per capita, and the share of manufacturing in GDP. Levels regression means that we regress levels on levels. Three-year difference means that we regress the dependent variables on a three-year lag of elderly LFP. Five-year difference means that we take five-year differences for the right- and left-hand-side variables. Five-year log difference means that we take the log of each *X* and *Y* variable, then take five-year differences.

***Significant at the 1 percent level.
**Significant at the 5 percent level.
*Significant at the 10 percent level.

NPI members are self-employed, and their retirement decisions are not closely linked to social security benefits; flat-rate NPI benefits are not means tested and adjusted actuarially fairly if claimed at ages other than the normal eligibility age of sixty-five. Moreover, the Mutual Aid Insurance (MAI, *Kyosai Nenkin*) which covers employees in the public sector, has almost the same benefit scheme as the EPI, so we can reasonably treat MAI pensioners as if they were EPI members.[6]

The basic strategy for constructing inducement measures is as follows. First, we construct social security wealth, SSW (see appendix B, which explains in detail how to construct it). If one retires at age a and the eligibility age is a^*, social security benefit received at age a, $B(a)$, is calculated as:

6. Meanwhile, we are forced to ignore the impact of the means-tested *Zaishoku* benefits and wage subsidies on the elderly's decisions to retire due to a lack of data available from official statistics. A more comprehensive analysis, which takes into account multiple benefit schemes, should be an important topic for future research.

$$B(a) = C + k \times \text{CAMI}(a, m) \text{ if } a \geq a^*; = 0 \text{ if } a < a^*,$$

where C is a constant term corresponding to the basic pension benefit, k is a benefit multiplier, and $\text{CAMI}(a, m)$ is the career average monthly income at age a and with months of service m. The values of a and m are estimated from published data. Then, (gross) SSW at age a, $W(a)$, is calculated as:

$$W(a) = \sum_{i=a}^{D} \pi(i)B(i),$$

where $\pi(a)$ is a cumulative discount factor that reflects both interest rate (which is assumed to be 3 percent) and mortality (which is available from official statistics). The variable D is the maximum age, which we set at one hundred.

At age a, one can expect social security benefit and SSW if he or she retires at age $a + j$ as

$$B(a + j) = C + k[m \times \text{CAMI}(a, m) + \text{wage}(a + j)]/(m + 12j),$$

$$W(a+j) = \sum_{i=a+j}^{D} \pi(i)B(i),$$

where wage is the projected wage based on cross-sectional data at the year when one is aged a. We then calculate the peak value for each age, $\text{PV}(a)$, defined as

$$\text{PV}(a) = \max[W(a), W(a + 1), \ldots, W(D)].$$

That is, $\text{PV}(a)$ is the maximum value of SSW, which is obtained by adjusting the timing of retirement. We take into account a change in C and k reflecting each social security reform when calculating SSW and PV. In actual estimations, we choose the cohort born in 1935 as the base cohort and use its fixed earnings trajectories to address possible endogeneity of earnings in response to social security reforms.

7.4.2   Inducement Measure

The next task is to construct the inducement measure utilizing SSW, PV, and labor force participation. Assume that at given age a and year y, SSW per capita, the proportion of people in the labor force, and the number of retirees are given as $W(a, y)$, $\text{LFP}(a, y)$, and $P(a, y)$, respectively. Then, averaging $W(a, y)$ over different age groups—specifically, over fifty-five and sixty-nine—we have the annual average SSW, which is denoted by $\overline{W}(y)$, such that

$$(1) \quad \overline{W}(y) = \sum_{a=55}^{69} \left[\frac{P(a,y)}{\sum_{a=55}^{69} P(a,y)} \right] \left[\frac{\sum_{t=0}^{a-55} W(a,y) \times \text{LFP}(a-t, y-t-1)}{\sum_{t=0}^{a-55} \text{LFP}(a-t, y-t-1)} \right],$$

which gauges the overall generosity of social security benefits at each year.

It is reasonable to assume that an individual considers not only the level of SSW by itself but also potential gains from postponing retirement when deciding to continue working or to retire. Hence, we additionally consider $W(a, y) - PV(a, y)$, which is the difference between the SSW an individual obtains by retiring at age a and the maximum SSW he or she can obtain by postponing retirement from that age. In Japan, the value of $W(a, y) - PV(a, y)$ is expected to be negative before the eligibility age and zero beyond that. As in the case of SSW, we obtain the annual average of $W(a, y) - PV(a, y)$:

$$(2) \quad \overline{[W - PV]}(y) = \sum_{a=55}^{69} \left[\frac{P(a,y)}{\sum_{a=55}^{69} P(a,y)} \right]$$
$$\times \left[\frac{\sum_{t=0}^{a-55}[W(a,y) - PV(a,y)] \times LFP(a-t, y-t-1)}{\sum_{t=0}^{a-55} LFP(a-t, y-t-1)} \right].$$

Finally, we combine SSW and its potential gain from postponing retirement to construct the inclusive incentive measure, which is defined as:

$$I(a, y) \equiv W(a, y) + \alpha[W(a, y) - PV(a, y)],$$

where α is a nonnegative parameter. In addition, averaging $I(a, y)$ over age, we calculate its annual average as

$$(3) \qquad \overline{I}(y) = \overline{W}(y) + \alpha \overline{[W - PV]}(y).$$

A higher value of SSW itself makes an individual more inclined to retire, but its disincentive effect is partly offset by potential gains from postponing retirement. Putting these two factors together, the inclusive incentive indicator captures the net effect of social security benefits. The value of the weight on $\overline{W - PV}$, α, should be estimated empirically, as discussed in the next subsection.

It is useful to examine whether annual average incentives are consistent with the expected effects of past reforms. Figure 7.7 depicts the LFP-weighted averages of $\overline{W}$ at 2005 prices for males and females of the 1935 cohort. Because $\overline{W - PV}$ is almost flat compared to $\overline{W}$, it suffices to look at $\overline{W}$ to capture the long-term trend of the inducement of retire.

The figure shows that the level of $\overline{W}$ continued to rise until the mid-1980s, then started to decline gradually, and has remained roughly stable since the late 1980s. This trend is consistent with the history of social security reforms, which is summarized in table 7.1. Until the mid-1980s, the government had continued to increase the generosity of the programs by increasing

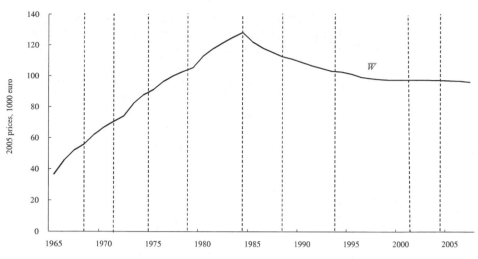

Fig. 7.7   Annual average SSW ($\overline{W}$)

Note: Weighted average of male and female figures. Dotted lines indicate the dates of key social security reforms.

the flat-rate benefit as well as the benefit multiplier for the wage-proportional benefit. The 1985 reform, however, decisively changed the policy direction by reducing the generosity of the benefit formulae. Since the 1985 reform, the government has been raising the flat-rate benefit but subduing the overall generosity of the program by reducing the benefit multiplier, postponing the eligibility age, and reducing the benefit indexation.

7.4.3   Estimation Methodologies

We now move to the relationship between the measure for inducement to retire and the employment and unemployment of younger age groups. Figure 7.8 compares the trends of unemployment and $\overline{W}$. There seems to have been a negative correlation between the two since the late 1980s, but a clear upward trend in the unemployment rate makes it difficult to interpret the relationship. Figure 7.9 replaces unemployment with employment and compares it with $\overline{W}$. We find that until the 1990s, employment of the young and $\overline{W}$ moved in opposite directions, while there seems to be no clear relationship between employment of the prime age group and $\overline{W}$. We have to control other factors that are likely to affect labor market outcomes, however, to precisely capture the impact of the inducement to retire on labor outcomes of the younger age groups.

In addition, we have to estimate the weight on $\overline{W} - \mathrm{PV}$, α, in equation (2). We use two methods. The first method is the iteration procedure. The estimation model here is given by

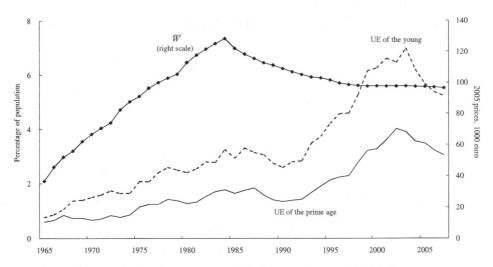

Fig. 7.8   Unemployment of the young and prime age groups and the inducement to retire

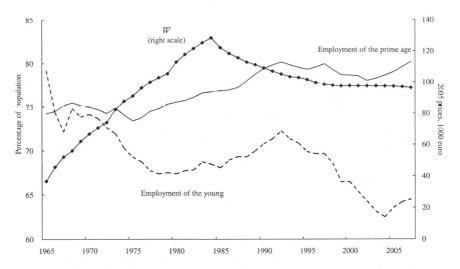

Fig. 7.9   Employment of young and prime age groups and the inducement to retire

$$(4) \qquad \mathrm{LFP}_{\mathrm{OLD}}(y) = \delta \bar{I}(y) + X_y\beta + e_y$$
$$= \delta\{\overline{W}(y) + \alpha[\overline{W - \mathrm{PV}}](y)\} + X_y\beta + e_y,$$

where X_y is a vector of covariates. We iterate over α with 0.25 intervals, starting at zero, and regress LFP of the old on $\bar{I}$ and on covariates to search the value of α that gives the highest R^2; δ is expected to be negative.

The second is the regression procedure. The estimation model in this case is given by

$$(5) \qquad \mathrm{LFP}_{\mathrm{OLD}}(y) = \delta_1 \overline{W}(y) + \delta_2 [\overline{W - \mathrm{PV}}](y) + X_y \beta + e_y.$$

We regress LFP of the old on $\overline{W}$ and $\overline{W - \mathrm{PV}}$ as well as covariates to estimate coefficients on $\overline{W}$ and $\overline{W - \mathrm{PV}}$ separately—that is, δ_1 and δ_2. Then, we obtain the implied weight, α, by calculating δ_2 / δ_1.

After estimating α based on either of these two methods, we regress labor market outcomes on the estimated $\overline{I}$—which is based on either of the two methods—and on the covariates. We conduct these two procedures using not only the levels for all variables in equations (4) and (5) but also their five-year differences, because most of the variables have strong time trends. In all estimation models, we use real GDP per capita, its growth rate, share of manufacturing in GDP, and one-year difference in the share of the elderly of total population. The estimation period is between 1975 and 2007 due to data limitations. As already implied by figures 7.8 and 7.9, regressions based on the levels might lead to a spurious relationship between the inducement measure and labor market outcomes.

7.4.4   Estimation Results

Table 7.4 presents estimation results using the level of each variable. The upper panel summarizes the estimated parameters of $\overline{I}$. The first method obtains 8.75 for the estimated value of α. The second method obtains -0.512 and -4.419 for the estimated values of δ_1 and δ_2, respectively, implying that α is equal to 8.63, which is very close to 8.75. These high estimated values of α suggest that a change in $\overline{W - \mathrm{PV}}$ affects the elderly's retirement decisions much more than a change in $\overline{W}$ per se.[7] This means that the elderly are much more sensitive to potential gains from postponing retirement than to the level of social security wealth obtained by retiring at each age.

The lower panel shows the effects of the inducement to retire on outcomes for the old and the young. We regress the LFP of the old and unemployment, employment, and in-school of the young at the level of estimated $\overline{I}$ (based on estimated α) and covariates. In addition, we consider three cases: (a) using implied $\overline{I}$ weighing from the iteration procedure ($\overline{I} = \overline{W} + 8.75\,[\overline{W - \mathrm{PV}}]$); (b) using implied $\overline{I}$ weighing from the regression procedure ($\overline{I} = \overline{W} + 8.63\,[\overline{W - \mathrm{PV}}]$); and (c) using the estimated regression coefficients directly ($\overline{I} = 0.512\overline{W} + 4.419\,[\overline{W - \mathrm{PV}}]$), which is expected to obtain -1 as the coefficient on $\overline{I}$.

The following findings are noteworthy. First, using the weights on $\overline{W}$

---

7. Actually, we compare two cases: the first assuming that each individual is completely liquidity constrained so that $W(a, y)$ is treated as zero before the (first) eligibility age and the second assuming that there is no liquidity constraint so that $W(a, y)$ is not treated as zero. We focus on the latter case, which makes a much better fit in the model and obtains reasonable coefficients.

Table 7.4 Effect of inducement to retire on labor market outcomes (levels): 1975 to 2007

Estimating the parameters of $\bar{I}$

	γ	α	α/γ	R^2	Implied $\bar{I}$ weighting
(1) Iterating over α with 0.25 intervals and regressing LFP of old on $\bar{I}$ and covariates	1	8.75	8.75	0.9410	$\bar{W} + 8.75(\bar{W}-\mathrm{PV})$
(2) Time series regression of LFP of old on $\bar{W}$ and $(\bar{W}-\mathrm{PV})$	−0.512*** (0.158)	−4.419** (2.113)	8.63	0.9410	$-0.512\,\bar{W}-4.419(\bar{W}-\mathrm{PV})$ or $\bar{W}+8.63(\bar{W}-\mathrm{PV})$

Estimating inducement to retire on outcomes for the old and the young, using $\bar{I}$ and covariates

	$\bar{I}$		
	Coefficient	Standard error	R^2
(1) Using implied $\bar{I}$ weighting from (1) above			
LFP of old	−0.511***	(0.143)	0.9410
Unemployment of young	0.324**	(0.143)	0.9385
Employment of young	0.855*	(0.437)	0.8006
In-school of young	−1.179***	(0.358)	0.7624
(2) Using implied $\bar{I}$ weighting from (2) above $\bar{W} + 8.63(\bar{W}-\mathrm{PV})$			
LFP of old	−0.512***	(0.144)	0.9410
Unemployment of young	0.326**	(0.144)	0.9387
Employment of young	0.842*	(0.441)	0.7994
In-school of young	−1.168***	(0.362)	0.7596
(3) Using implied $\bar{I}$ weighting from (2) above $-0.512\,\bar{W} - 4.419(\bar{W}-\mathrm{PV})$			
LFP of old	−1.000***	(0.282)	0.9410
Unemployment of young	0.637**	(0.280)	0.9387
Employment of young	1.646*	(0.863)	0.7994
In-school of young	−2.283***	(0.708)	0.7596

Notes: Covariates include real GDP per capita, growth in real GDP per capita, the share of manufactu-ing in GDP, and the one-year difference in the share of the elderly. All dependent variables are percent rates. Inducement measures are at 2005 prices in million euros.

***Significant at the 1 percent level.

**Significant at the 5 percent level.

*Significant at the 10 percent level.

and $\overline{W - PV}$ determined by the iteration procedure ($\alpha = 8.75$) or by the regression procedure (converted by the ratio translation to 1 and 8.75) yields essentially the same results. This fact is confirmed by comparing the results reported in the first two sections of the lower panel. Second, the implied $\bar{I}$ is very strongly related to the LFP of the old. The coefficient of implied $\bar{I}$ is very significant and stable across specifications, indicating that our measure of the inducement to retire successfully captures the impact on the elderly's decisions on retirement. Third, the coefficients on the implied $\bar{I}$ are significantly positive in the unemployment models. At the same time, however, we obtain positive and significant coefficients in the LFP models, suggesting that these level-on-level regressions capture spurious correlations between the inducement to retire for the elderly and the labor market outcome for the young. Finally, the coefficients on the old LFP in the in-school models are negative and significant, which is difficult to understand.

The estimation results based on five-year differences of all variables, which are summarized in table 7.5, help us to check the robustness of the results based on the levels. We again obtain a relatively high value of α, which is 9.5 in the iteration procedure and 9.51 in the regression procedure. This confirms that the elderly are more sensitive to potential gains from postponing retirement than to social security wealth. Regarding the impact on labor market outcomes, we obtain very significant and negative coefficients on the LFP of the old across models, as reported in table 7.4.

However, all the coefficients in the models of young unemployment, employment, and in-school turn insignificant in sharp contrast to the results reported in table 7.4. There is no coefficient on the inducement measure that is statistically significant except for the LFP of the old. This result indicates that the results from the level-on-level regressions are misleading and that inducements to retire for the elderly do not significantly affect the labor market outcome for the young.

7.5   Conclusion

In this chapter, we examined whether social security programs in Japan induce withdrawal of the elderly from the labor force and create jobs for the young. First, we provided a historical overview of past social security reforms and employment policies for the elderly. Following this overview, we investigated the direct relationship between employment/unemployment of the young and employment of the old. Second, we explored whether social security induces withdrawal of the old from the labor force and creates jobs for the young.

The key messages are summarized as follows. First, our historical overview suggests that young unemployment issues have not motivated social security reforms and that changes in provisions are not endogenous with respect to young employment/unemployment. Second, the employment of the young

Table 7.5 Effect of inducement to retire on labor market outcomes (five-year differences): 1975 to 2007

	Estimating the parameters of $\bar{I}$				
	γ	α	α/γ	R^2	Implied $\bar{I}$ weighting
(1) Iterating over α with 0.25 intervals and regressing LFP of old on $\bar{I}$ and covariates	—	9.5	9.5	0.5956	$\bar{W} + 9.5(\bar{W}-\mathrm{PV})$
(2) Time series regression of LFP of old on $\bar{W}$ and $(\bar{W}-\mathrm{PV})$	-0.608*** (0.174)	-5.781* (3.241)	9.51	0.5956	$-0.608\bar{W} - 5.781(\bar{W}-\mathrm{PV})$ or $\bar{W} + 9.51(\bar{W}-\mathrm{PV})$

Estimating inducement to retire on outcomes for the old and the young, using $\bar{I}$ and covariates

	$\bar{I}$		
	Coefficient	Standard error	R^2
(1) Using implied $\bar{I}$ weighting from (1) above			
LFP of old	-0.608***	(0.175)	0.5956
Unemployment of young	0.020	(0.100)	0.7606
Employment of young	0.169	(0.250)	0.7537
In-school of young	-0.189	(0.307)	0.5471
(2) Using implied $\bar{I}$ weighting from (2) above $\bar{W} + 9.51(\bar{W}-\mathrm{PV})$			
LFP of old	-0.608***	(0.175)	0.5956
Unemployment of young	0.020	(0.100)	0.7606
Employment of young	0.170	(0.250)	0.7538
In-school of young	-0.190	(0.307)	0.5471
(3) Using implied $\bar{I}$ weighting from (3) above $-0.608\bar{W} - 5.781(\bar{W}-\mathrm{PV})$			
LFP of old	-1.000***	(0.288)	0.5956
Unemployment of young	0.033	(0.164)	0.7606
Employment of young	0.280	(0.412)	0.7538
In-school of young	-0.313	(0.505)	0.5471

Notes: Covariates include real GDP per capita, growth in real GDP per capita, the share of manufacturing in GDP, and the one-year difference in the share of the elderly. All dependent variables are percent rates. Inducement measures are at 2005 prices in million euros.

***Significant at the 1 percent level.

*Significant at the 10 percent level.

tends to be positively, not negatively, associated with the LFP of the old. Third, the inducement to retire for the elderly does not significantly affect the labor market outcome for the young. These findings confirm that there is no serious trade-off between the old and the young in the labor force.

Appendix A
Data Description

This appendix summarizes the data construction and data sources for the main variables used in the figures and tables.

Labor Force, Employment, and Unemployment

The data on labor force, employment, and unemployment are available from the Labor Force Survey (*Rodoryoku Chosa*) compiled by the Ministry of Internal Affairs and Communications. This survey has the LFP and other employment data by five-year age brackets. We sum up the figures in published tables to make those data for the young, prime age, and old groups in each year.

GDP Per Capita

The annual GDP data in 2005 constant prices is available from the *Annual Report on National Accounts* (*Kokumin Keizai Keisan Nenpo*) published by the Economic and Social Research Institute, Cabinet Office. The population data for each year are available from the *Annual Report on Population Estimates* (*Jinko Suikei Nenpo*) compiled by the Ministry of Internal Affairs and Communications.

Real Wages (Monthly Salary in Real Terms)

The data on nominal regular monthly wage are taken from the Basic Survey on Wage Structure (*Chingin Kozo Kihon Tokei Chosa*), which is compiled by the Ministry of Health, Labor, and Welfare (MHLW). The survey contains the most comprehensive wage data in Japan and provides tabulations on the average and population weights by (mostly) five-year age brackets. Nominal wage is converted into real terms by the consumer price index.

Appendix B

Construction of Social Security Wealth (SSW)

This appendix provides a detailed description of data used to construct SSW, as well as the limitations of the data and calculations.

Data Descriptions and Sources

Eligibility Ages

First, we define the eligibility ages for receiving pension benefits. Information on eligibility age for each cohort is available from the MHLW. We consider the eligibility ages for both the flat-rate and wage-proportional pension benefits for the Employees' Pension Insurance program. See figures 7.1 and 7.2.

Months of Premium Contributions

Second, we collect the months of premium contributions. The *Annual Report of the Social Insurance Agency* (*Shakai Hoken Cho Jigyo Nenpo*) provides the average months of contributions for the retired who initially claim benefits. For simplicity, we assume that these figures are entirely for those who retired at the eligibility age, because most beneficiaries start to receive benefits at the eligibility age. Indeed, 79.3 percent of EPI beneficiaries initially claimed their benefit at age sixty (which was the first eligibility age) in 2005, according to the latest annual report.

There were no data before 1988 except averages of pooled genders for 1981 to 1985 and for 1971 (from the *Annual Report on Health and Welfare* published by the MHLW). Hence, we first interpolate data for pooled genders for 1986 and 1987 using the figures in 1985 and 1988. Second, we interpolate data for 1972 to 1980 and for 1960 to 1970 using the trend after 1971. Third, we estimate the data for males and females using information on the proportion of those for males to the total for 1988 to 1992 and then calculate the corresponding figures for females.

Career Average Monthly Income (CAMI)

Third, we compute the career average monthly income (CAMI) for males and females. The data are available from the *Annual Report of the Social Insurance Agency*. Similar to the months of contributions, there were no data before 1988 except averages of pooled genders for 1981 to 1985. Because the proportion of the CAMI for workers before retirement to that for those who began to receive pension benefits was stable, we estimate the CAMI for retirees for 1960 to 1980 by multiplying the CAMI for workers (taken from the annual report) by the proportion between the two for the 1988 to 1993 period for males and females.

Pension Benefit Formula and Insurance Premiums

The "Recalculation of Fiscal Conditions" provides a formula to compute benefit levels. We assume that each change in the formula is effective in the following calendar year and that the insurance premium rate is common for all generations in a given year. See table 7.1.

Wage Rates for the Old

We calculate wage rates (excluding bonus payments) for those aged fifty-five to sixty-nine in each age bracket by gender in each year. *The Basic Survey on Wage Structure* contains monthly nominal regular wages for five-year age brackets by gender but not a more disaggregated level for those aged sixty-five and over. To estimate the average wage for each age, we assume that (a) the regular wages for each age between fifty-five and fifty-nine is identical to the average of the age bracket; (b) the average for age sixty is equal to the average for the sixty to sixty-four bracket; and (c) the average for those aged sixty-eight and over is equal to the average for the sixty-five and over bracket. We obtain data for those aged sixty-one to sixty-seven from a linear interpolation using data on those aged sixty and sixty-eight. Further, we assume that nominal wage for each age corresponds to that paid one year from birthday, because most of the elderly are in the secondary labor market.

Mortality Rates

The mortality rate by each age and gender has been available annually since 1996 from the MHLW. Before 1996, published data were available for five-year age brackets only. We interpolate the death rate for each age using the age pattern in 1996. We assume that all persons die at age one hundred.

Computation of SSW

We next compute SSW by following the steps below. Unfortunately, we cannot create the incentive measure separately by marital status or deciles of earnings distribution due to data limitations. Moreover, we cannot consider the weight for each route to retirement due to data availability.

Estimation of Wages Received When Not Retired

We use the *Basic Survey on Wage Structure* to construct data on the monthly regular wages for each age fifty-five to eighty in a given year (ignoring bonus payments). We estimate earnings trajectories for the cohort born in 1935 and apply their earnings trajectories to other cohorts.

Estimation of Pension Benefits

We obtain the average months of contributions and the average CAMI in a given year for those who reach the eligible age in each year from the

Annual Report of the Social Insurance Agency. Hence, it is straightforward to estimate pension benefits if they start to receive them at the eligible age. Otherwise, we recalculate the months of contributions (for example, if a person extends a year to receive benefits, we add twelve months to months of contributions) and the CAMI (based on estimated wages; see the preceding subsection to obtain the pension benefits for each retired age.

Discount Rates

We compute cumulative discount rates based on the mortality and the interest rates. First, we calculate the probability of survival after fifty-five for each age by (1 – mortality rate) in a given year (assuming that the person survives at fifty-five) for males and females using data on the mortality rate for each age bracket in a given year. Second, we add a 3 percent interest rate to this probability of survival to obtain the aggregate discount rates.

Social Security Wealth (SSW)

Assuming that all pensioners continue to receive the same benefit as that initially claimed at retirement until age one hundred, we compute the gross SSW by multiplying benefits and cumulative discount rates obtained from the preceding subsection. No one is entitled to receive any benefits before the eligibility age. To compute net SSW, we consider insurance premiums to be paid during work until age sixty-five. The current value of premiums is calculated by multiplying monthly regular wages by half of the premium rate and discounted by the discount factor. We then compute the cumulative amount of present value of the premiums until retirement.

References

Aoki, M., H. Patrick, and P. Sheard. 1994. The Japanese main bank system: An introductory overview. In *The Japanese main bank system: Its relevance for developing and transforming economies,* ed. M. Aoki and H. Patrick, 3–51. Oxford: Clarendon Press.

Komamura, K. 2007. The 2004 pension reform and the impact of rapid aging in Japan. *Japanese Journal of Social Security Policy* 6 (1): 144–56.

National Institute of Population and Social Security Research. Selected demographic indicators for Japan. Available at: http://www.ipss.go.jp/index-e.html.

Organization for Economic Cooperation and Development (OECD). 2004. *Ageing and employment policies: Japan.* Paris: OECD.

Shimizutani, S., and T. Oshio. 2009. New evidence on initial transition from career job to retirement in Japan. Institute of Economic Research working paper, 430. Tokyo: Institute of Economic Research, Hitotsubashi University.

Shimizutani, S., and I. Yokoyama. 2009. Has Japan's long-term employment practice survived? New evidence emerging since the 1990s. *Industrial and Labor Relations Review* 62 (3): art. 3.

Early Retirement and Employment of the Young in the Netherlands

Arie Kapteyn, Klaas de Vos, and Adriaan Kalwij

8.1 Introduction

Previous papers on the National Bureau of Economic Research International Social Security Project focused on the incentives to retire, the effects of possible reforms, and the well-being of the elderly. In this chapter, we return to one of the factors underlying the emergence of widespread early retirement opportunities: the desire to create or preserve jobs for the young. When early retirement was first proposed in the late seventies in the Netherlands, unemployment soared, and the idea was that by sending elderly workers into early retirement, younger workers would be able to keep their jobs. Early retirement was considered to be a win-win solution: the elderly who had worked hard during the reconstruction period after World War II could take up a well-deserved early retirement pension, while the young who were at risk of becoming a "lost generation" could take their places in the labor market. The first trade union plan (1975) proposing early retirement was in fact called "Jong voor Oud" ("Young for Old"). Next to the introduction of early retirement programs for elderly workers in most sectors in the late seventies and early eighties, employers and trade unions also colluded to send older workers into disability or unemployment, with employers often supplementing the already generous statutory benefits until the social security eligibility age (and mandatory retirement age) of sixty-five was reached.

All in all, the labor force participation (LFP) of the (male) elderly shows a considerable decrease between the late seventies and late nineties, after which most early retirement programs were scaled down because they were fast

Arie Kapteyn is a senior economist at RAND and director of RAND Labor and Population. Klaas de Vos is a senior researcher in the Quantitative Analysis department of CentERdata at Tilburg University. Adriaan Kalwij is a researcher at the Utrecht School of Economics.

becoming financially unsustainable, and the government finally appeared to succeed in effectively restricting access to unemployment and disability benefits.

In this chapter, we try to answer the question, did early retirement of the elderly from the labor force (be it via early retirement programs or alternative routes such as disability and unemployment benefits) indeed create jobs for the young? We start by providing a brief history of the main benefit schemes related to retirement: early retirement, disability, social security, and occupational pensions. Next, we present some graphical evidence on the relationship between employment and unemployment of the young and labor force participation of the old. After that, we present regressions explaining labor market status of the young as a function employment of elderly. Next, we investigate the time series properties of these variables and of a few indicators of retirement incentives. We will find that the incentive indicators we have constructed are plausibly caused by the employment of the young, confirming the view that these incentives were indeed introduced to alleviate the youth unemployment problem. It also implies that these variables cannot be used as instruments in regressions to explain youth employment as a function of employment of the elderly. However, we will find variables that do seem to be predetermined for labor force participation of the elderly. This allows us to estimate the effect of labor force participation of the elderly on employment of younger age groups in the labor markets, using instrumental variables. Generally, the relations we obtain suggest complementarity between labor force participation of the elderly and employment of the younger age groups. Thus, if anything, attempts to reduce unemployment via strong incentives for retirement most likely have aggravated the problem rather than alleviating it.

8.2   The Early Retirement Debate and Other Exit Routes from the Labor Market in the Netherlands

The first plan for the introduction of early retirement was proposed by a board member of the Netherlands Catholic Trade Union, Toon Riemen, in 1975. Mr. Riemen's plan was called "Young for Old" and had as its primary purpose to reduce youth unemployment.[1] The plan aimed to kill two birds with one stone. As he put it in a recent interview: "Since the 1973 oil crisis, there was a big problem with youth unemployment. At the same time you saw elderly employees who were at the end of their tether. Then you start brainstorming, can't we think of a plan to solve that." The essence of the plan was an old person out and a young person in (VPRO 2004).

The Minister of Social Affairs decided to set up a commission that was

---

1. The information about the history of the early retirement debate is partly taken from VPRO (2004). See also Van Oorschot (2007).

to advise on the merits of the early retirement (ER) plan. The commission, headed by a board member of the Unilever pension fund, Van Tets, advised against the idea. The commission felt that the plan's potential for solving the youth unemployment problem was illusory. Nevertheless, the Minister of Social Affairs, Boersma, decided to start an experiment in two sectors: education and construction. As of December 1, 1976, and April 1, 1977, respectively, employees in these sectors had the possibility to retire at the age of sixty-three or sixty-four, instead of the statutory retirement age of sixty-five.

Soon, the ER plans were extended to other sectors. In February 1975, the Minister of Social Affairs avoided an impending strike in Rotterdam harbor by offering employees an ER plan at the government's expense.

The ER plans proved to be very popular with both employees and employers. The ER was financially very attractive to employees. The before-tax replacement rate usually was on the order of 80 or 90 percent, and since no payroll taxes were levied on the retired, the net replacement rate could be very close to 100 percent. Moreover, one kept accumulating pension rights as if one was still employed.

Employers liked the ER plans because it made it easy to reduce the labor force during the economic downturn. Typically, employees would be eligible if they had worked for the same company for at least ten years.

In 1980, the ER experiment was codified into law and in the following years was incorporated in many collective agreements.

The financing of ER was pay-as-you-go. As such, it provided a classic example of a transfer between generations. The employed paid for the ER of the older generation by means of a special payroll tax, while the retired only reaped the benefits.

Not surprisingly, the take-up of ER was very large. For instance, in the first year more than 50 percent of the age-eligible construction workers decided to retire early, twice as many as anticipated by the government. In later years, take-up got close to 100 percent.

There is some debate about whether the spread of ER has contributed to the goal of reducing youth unemployment. The originator of the "Young for Old," Toon Riemen, does not think so: "Nothing is left of the original goal" (VPRO 2004).

8.2.1   Disability Insurance

Even before ER schemes were introduced, employees could retire before the standard retirement age of sixty-five. The most frequently used exit route was Disability Insurance (DI). Although various work disability laws had been in existence since the early twentieth century, a comprehensive DI law was introduced in 1967, covering all employees (but not self-employed). Interestingly, the law passed parliament without any nay vote. Any person with a whole of partial work disability was entitled to a benefit equal to 80 percent of previous earnings. In after-tax terms, this might be equivalent to 90 percent. There was no time limit to the benefit period, so in principle, one could expect to receive benefits until the statutory retirement age of sixty-five. Moreover, while drawing DI benefits, one often also kept accumulating pension rights, while one no longer had to pay the pension premium that workers pay.

The number of beneficiaries showed an explosive growth, as illustrated in figure 8.1. As with the later ER schemes, take-up was much higher than anticipated. The government had estimated that the maximum number of DI beneficiaries would be 200,000, but in 1976 the number of beneficiaries had already reached 500,000. As with ER, the scheme was popular among both employees and employers. For employees, it was an attractive exit route, as may be clear from the description of the financial aspects of the scheme. For employers, the scheme had the advantage of a relatively easy way to terminate employees, which under Dutch law would be complicated and costly otherwise.

The dramatic increase in the number of DI beneficiaries led to obvious budgetary problems, which triggered a number of reforms, all aimed at a reduction of the DI rolls. In 1985, despite massive protests, the benefit was reduced from 80 percent of previous earnings to 70 percent. In 1987, DI was no longer possible for individuals who were previously (fully or partially) unemployed. One can see from figure 8.1 that these changes did not have much of a visible effect on the growth of the DI rolls. In 1991, the length of the benefit period was reduced for persons who at that time were less than fifty years of age. Figure 8.1 suggests that this may have had some effect on the number of DI recipients in later years. In 1998, partial experience rating was introduced. In 2004, DI beneficiaries younger than fifty had to undergo strict medical reexaminations. Finally, in 2006, a new DI law replaced the old one. Under the new law, during the first two years after one becomes disabled, wages continue to be paid. After two years a determination takes place of whether one is permanently disabled for at least 80 percent. In that case DI benefits are 75 percent of a worker's previous wages until the age of sixty-five. Work limitations that are deemed to be less than 35 percent do not entitle a worker to DI benefits. Between 35 percent and 80 percent one receives a DI benefit equal to 70 percent of the earnings loss for a maximum period of thirty-eight months. After that, the benefit depends on earnings loss and the extent to which one uses the remaining earnings capacity; see, for instance, Van Oorschot (2007).

8.2.2   Social Security

The social security (SS) act was passed in 1957.[2] The system was extremely simple. Any man or unmarried woman was entitled to a fixed amount, in-

2. The information in this section has been derived from SVB (2007).

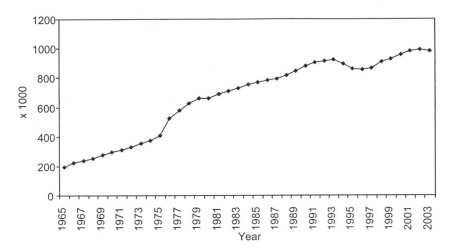

Fig. 8.1   Number of disability insurance benefits

dependent of work history. Married women were not entitled to their own benefit. Only in the eighties did the unequal treatment of men and women come to an end so that also women had their own independent entitlement to an SS benefit. As of 1979, the level of benefits is linked to the after-tax minimum wage. In later changes, benefits for younger partners of SS recipients were introduced. This will now be abolished by 2015. There is no earnings test for SS, so one can receive SS while being gainfully employed. Figure 8.2 shows the evolution of the level of SS benefits for both married and unmarried individuals since 1975. The figure shows steady growth of the benefit level until about 1979. The fact that after 1979 the benefit level falls in real terms is due to the linkage with after-tax minimum wages. The after-tax minimum wage also determines the level of welfare benefits. When in the early eighties the economy entered into a recession and government deficits ballooned, the government reacted by cutting the minimum wage, welfare benefits, and as a result, also SS benefits. Later fluctuations in the level of SS benefits mainly reflect economic conditions and the state of the government budget, which influenced minimum wages, welfare benefits, and through the linkage, also SS benefits. Changes in the tax system were another important determinant.

8.2.3   Private Pensions

The bulk of private pensions in the Netherlands consist of occupational pensions. Typically, employment for a certain company or in a certain sector implies mandatory participation in a pension plan. Pensions tend to be of the defined benefit type with benefits depending on final pay or average pay. Usually, a full pension will amount to 70 percent of either full or average

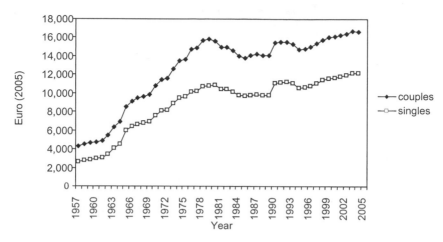

Fig. 8.2   **Social security benefits before taxes**

pay if one has contributed for forty years. For each year less, one loses 1.75 percentage points. Benefits are usually indexed by the wage index. Since the early 2000s, many pension schemes have moved from final pay to average pay and wage indexation has become less automatic. In principle pensions are portable if one changes jobs. The associated pension liabilities are moved from one pension fund to the next.

8.3   Measures of Employment

Based on the Organization for Economic Cooperation and Development (OECD) employment data, we consider the following measures of employment:

- LFP and employment (old, fifty-five to sixty-four) as fraction of total population
- LFP and employment (old fifty-five to sixty-four, male), as fraction of total population
- LFP and employment (old, fifty-five to sixty-four, female), as fraction of total population
- Unemployment (young, twenty to twenty-four), as fraction of total population
- Unemployment (prime age, twenty-five to fifty-four), as fraction of total population
- LFP and employment (young, twenty to twenty-four), as fraction of total population
- LFP and employment (prime age, twenty-five to fifty-four), as fraction of total population

From Statistics Netherlands, we obtain the percentage of persons twenty to twenty-four that are in school. Also from Statistics Netherlands, we use data on gross domestic product (GDP), GDP per capita, share of manufacturing in the economy, and the statutory minimum wage. Finally, we construct two measures of incentives to retire. One is a macroindicator of social security wealth and the other one is an indicator of peak value. The construction of these two variables is described in the appendix.

For elderly males and females, employment and labor force participation are very close. For most of the period under consideration, elderly unemployed were receiving benefits without having the obligation to seek a job. This effectively removed them from the labor market.

8.4 Graphical Evidence

Figures 8.3 through 8.5 show the evolution of the main variables of interest between 1971 and 2005. Figure 8.3 shows the LFP of older persons fifty-five to sixty-four, the LFP of young persons twenty to twenty-four, and the unemployment rate of young persons twenty to twenty-four. Figure 8.3 presents time series for the LFP of the elderly and the unemployment of the two younger age groups (twenty to twenty-four and twenty-five to fifty-four) and figure 8.4 presents time series for the LFP of the elderly and

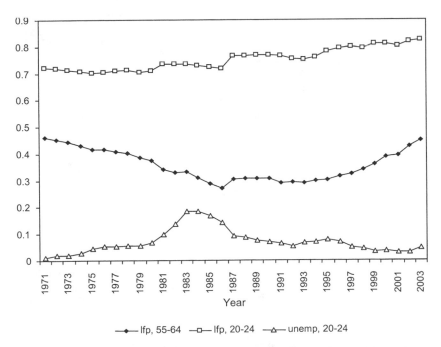

Fig. 8.3   **Labor force participation (old and young) and unemployment (young)**

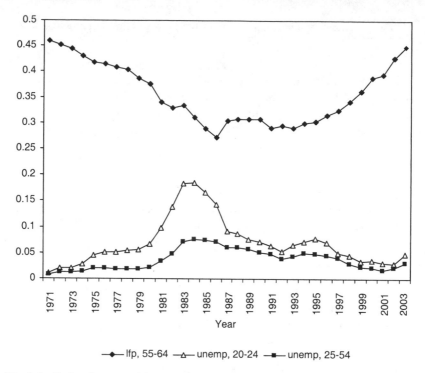

Fig. 8.4   Labor force participation (old) and unemployment (young and prime age)

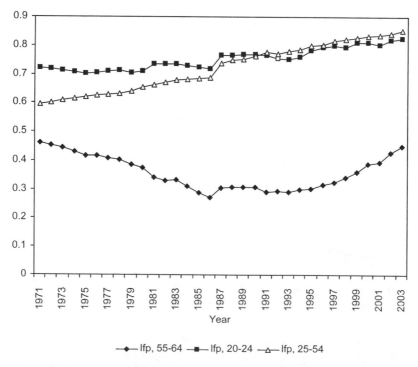

Fig. 8.5   Labor force participation (old, young, and prime age)

the two younger age groups. Taken on face value, the graphs do not provide much support for the idea that reducing employment of the elderly reduces unemployment for the younger age groups. If anything, unemployment of the younger age groups seems to go up while the employment of the elderly is low. Apart from obvious economic reasons why this may be so (such as complementarity of employment of different age groups), this may also simply be an artifact. If unemployment of all three age groups is correlated, and if the elderly unemployed leave the labor market, then we expect the pattern shown in figure 8.4.

A complicating factor in studying the relationship between the LFP of the elderly and employment and unemployment of the young is the fact that the LFP of the elderly males and females shows different trends during the first half of the period (1971 to 1987). See figure 8.6. Most likely this reflects a cohort effect whereby younger cohorts of females exhibit a higher LFP than older cohorts. The flat curve for female LFP during the first half of the period may therefore be the net result of an increase in the retirement hazard (just as for males) and at the same time a larger proportion working of younger cohorts. During the second half of the period, both female and male LFP are growing, but of course it still remains impossible to say how

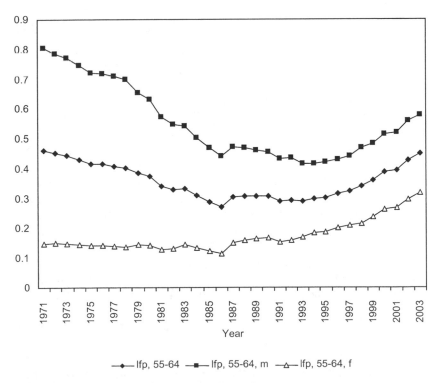

Fig. 8.6   **Labor force participation (old) by gender**

much of the growth in female LFP is a cohort effect and how much reflects a lower retirement hazard. Since cohort effects are less likely to play a major role in male LFP, we will often concentrate on male LFP among the elderly, rather than total elderly LFP.

8.5   Direct Effect of Elderly LFP on the Young

Before turning to a more systematic exploration of the relation between elderly LFP and employment and unemployment of younger age groups, we first consider simple regressions where we regress outcomes for younger age groups on elderly LFP.

Tables 8.1 and 8.2 show the results of a number of regressions in which the dependent variable is either employment, unemployment, or the percentage in school. We show the coefficients of employment of the elderly; regressions are done in levels, in levels with a three-year lag on elderly employment, in five-year differences, and in five-lear log differences (i.e., of the form: $\ln X[t] - \ln X[t-5]$). Moreover, regressions are repeated with and without other covariates (which are not reported in the table). The other covariates include GDP per capita, the growth in GDP per capita, and the share of manufacturing in the economy.

If early retirement of the elderly age group were to have a beneficial effect on the employment of the younger age group, then the effect of elderly employment on employment of younger age groups should be negative, while on unemployment it should be positive. When elderly employment decreases, employment of the young should increase, while unemployment should decrease.

In specifications without other covariates we find for the young (twenty to twenty-four) and the prime aged (twenty-five to fifty-four) that the effects of elderly employment on unemployment are statistically significant but with the "wrong" sign. That is, lower labor force participation of the elderly seems to generate higher unemployment of the young. There are various possible explanations for this. One explanation is the existence of complementarities between employment of different age groups. A second explanation is endogeneity of policies: if unemployment soars, policymakers may increase incentives for elderly workers to retire. We will return to this possibility later.

When regressing employment of the younger age groups, the picture is a little more mixed. The effect of employment of the elderly on employment of the young tends to be positive or insignificantly negative (in the case where we use a three-year lag).

Once covariates are introduced, more coefficients become insignificant and sometimes change sign. In this case, regressions of employment in the prime age group on employment of the elderly suggest a potential beneficial effect of early retirement of the elderly on employment of prime aged

Table 8.1   Direct relationship between elderly employment and unemployment, unemployment, and education of young and prime age persons, men and women combined

Specification	Youth, 20 to 24			Prime age, 25 to 54	
	Unemployment	Employment	School	Unemployment	Employment
No controls					
Levels	-0.537	0.451	-0.602	-0.301	-0.163
	(0.095)***	(0.177)***	(0.217)***	(0.028)***	(0.245)
Three-year lag on elderly employment	-0.131	-0.253	-0.964	-0.204	-0.724
	(0.141)	(0.216)	(0.167)***	(0.050)***	(0.223)***
Five-year difference	-0.733	0.869	-0.317	-0.332	0.362
	(0.141)***	(0.158)***	(0.108)***	(0.047)***	(0.080)***
Five-year log difference	-3.277	0.466	-0.839	-3.216	0.173
	(0.520)***	(0.085)***	(0.258)***	(0.340)***	(0.042)***
With controls					
Levels	-0.228	0.105	-0.755	-0.259	-0.299
	(0.088)***	(0.096)	(0.095)***	(0.039)***	(0.057)***
Three-year lag on elderly employment	-0.163	-0.006	-0.715	-0.248	-0.317
	(0.093)	(0.096)	(0.096)***	(0.039)***	(0.052)***
Five-year difference	0.300	-0.088	-0.183	0.067	-0.239
	(0.260)	(0.302)	(0.265)	(0.095)	(0.157)
Five-year log difference	-3.014	0.290	-0.257	-2.382	0.055
	(0.666)***	(0.109)***	(0.433)	(0.571)***	(0.062)

Note: Standard errors in parentheses.
***Significant at the 1 percent level.

Table 8.2 Direct relationship between male elderly employment and unemployment, employment, and schooling of young and prime age persons, men and women combined

Specification	Youth, 20 to 24			Prime age, 25 to 54	
	Unemployment	Employment	School	Unemployment	Employment
	No controls				
Levels	−0.186	0.011	−0.518	−0.127	−0.370
	(0.057)***	(0.094)	(0.072)***	(0.019)***	(0.100)***
Three-year lag on elderly employment	−0.002	−0.236	−0.521	−0.065	−0.468
	(0.064)	(0.088)**	(0.051)***	(0.025)**	(0.077)***
Five-year difference	−0.437	0.425	−0.429	−0.249	0.204
	(0.210)**	(0.249)	(0.113)***	(0.077)***	(0.114)
Five-year log difference	−3.224	0.460	−0.904	−3.307	0.170
	(0.572)***	(0.092)***	(0.261)***	(0.355)***	(0.045)***
	With controls				
Levels	−0.142	0.060	−0.426	−0.153	−0.168
	(0.046)***	(0.053)	(0.048)***	(0.019)***	(0.031)***
Three-year lag on elderly employment	−0.102	0.008	−0.396	−0.142	−0.171
	(0.050)**	(0.052)	(0.050)***	(0.019)***	(0.028)***
Five-year difference	−0.587	0.680	−0.258	−0.002	0.202
	(0.213)***	(0.240)***	(0.241)	(0.095)	(0.147)
Five-year log difference	−3.370	0.303	−0.404	−2.659	0.039
	(0.781)***	(0.128)**	(0.495)	(0.668)***	(0.072)

Note: Standard errors in parentheses.
***Significant at the 1 percent level.
**Significant at the 5 percent level.

workers, both for employment of the elderly and employment of the elderly with a three-year lag. However, these significant coefficients disappear once a trend term is included. In sum, the regressions so far provide little evidence that inducing elderly workers to retire will alleviate unemployment of younger age groups.

For good measure, table 8.2 gives the results when we use employment of elderly males as an explanatory variable, in an attempt to reduce the possibly confounding effects of cohort differences between age categories. By and large the conclusion does not change, with most significant coefficients suggesting complementarity between employment of different age groups or becoming insignificant once a trend term is included.

It is striking to see that in all specifications elderly employment seems to have a negative effect on the proportion of the twenty to twenty-four age group in school. By and large the signs of the various coefficients of the school variable are the same as for the unemployment variable. This suggests that when job opportunities become scarce, young people are more likely to stay in school or to return to school. We also note that when we add a number of covariates, and in particular a time trend, many of the coefficients become insignificant.

8.6 Causality Tests on Differenced Variables

Dickey Fuller tests suggest that all variables of interest in the analysis have unit roots. Hence, the subsequent analysis is in terms of first differenced variables. Table 8.3 presents an overview of Granger causality tests for the various variables of interest.[3] We note that the two incentive variables (wbar and Wminpv) are Granger caused at least by employment of the young.[4] This confirms the historical description in section 8.2 that worsening employment of the young was a major factor in creating incentives for the elderly to leave the labor force. It also means that regressing youth unemployment on the incentive variables cannot reasonably be interpreted in a causal way. Employment of elderly males also appears to be Granger caused by youth employment.

The GDP per capita does not seem to be Granger caused by any of the other variables (although jointly they have a significant effect). The same is true for the percent of twenty to twenty-four in school (although that is Granger caused by GDP per capita). Based on these outcomes, we will use lagged values of GDP per capita and of percent of twenty to twenty-four in school as instruments in a regression of youth employment (and unemployment) on employment of the elderly.

---

3. The maximum number of lags used in the test is equal to two. Model selection criteria for choosing the number of lags favored from one to four lags, with relatively minor changes when the number of lags increased from two to four.

4. See the appendix for a description of the construction of these variables.

Table 8.3   **Granger causality tests**

Equation	Excluded	chi2	df	Prob > chi2
Employment (youth)	School (youth)	28.911	2	0
	Employment (prime age)	23.983	2	0
	Employment (elderly males)	2.9919	2	0.224
	Minimum wage	7.6467	2	0.022
	GDP per capita	2.2315	2	0.328
	Wbar	10.709	2	0.005
	Wminpv	5.6097	2	0.061
	All	71.332	14	0
School (youth)	Employment (youth)	3.2844	2	0.194
	Employment (prime age)	5.8738	2	0.053
	Employment (elderly males)	1.806	2	0.405
	Minimum wage	3.8917	2	0.143
	GDP per capita	11.046	2	0.004
	Wbar	0.9598	2	0.619
	Wminpv	1.8559	2	0.395
	All	21.294	14	0.094
Employment (prime age)	Employment (youth)	62.752	2	0
	School (youth)	43.08	2	0
	Employment (elderly males)	16.301	2	0
	Minimum wage	16.97	2	0
	GDP per capita	9.0657	2	0.011
	Wbar	17.017	2	0
	Wminpv	5.3358	2	0.069
	All	184.74	14	0
Employment (elderly males)	Employment (youth)	22.585	2	0
	School (youth)	4.3938	2	0.111
	Employment (prime age)	14.617	2	0.001
	Minimum wage	14.913	2	0.001
	GDP per capita	1.8118	2	0.404
	Wbar	7.3343	2	0.026
	Wminpv	4.6874	2	0.096
	All	67.96	14	0
Minimum wage	Employment (youth)	21.025	2	0
	School (youth)	3.2539	2	0.197
	Employment (prime age)	20.69	2	0
	Employment (elderly males)	3.5881	2	0.166
	GDP per capita	7.14	2	0.028
	Wbar	33.363	2	0
	Wminpv	22.309	2	0
	All	155.06	14	0
GDP per capita	Employment (youth)	3.0733	2	0.215
	School (youth)	1.7618	2	0.414
	Employment (prime age)	5.4397	2	0.066
	Employment (elderly males)	5.2948	2	0.071
	Minimum wage	2.8439	2	0.241
	Wbar	2.0804	2	0.353
	Wminpv	1.2416	2	0.538
	All	48.775	14	0

Table 8.3   (continued)

Equation	Excluded	chi2	df	Prob > chi2
Wbar	Employment (youth)	12.351	2	0.002
	School (youth)	1.3399	2	0.512
	Employment (prime age)	0.02807	2	0.986
	Employment (elderly males)	1.4233	2	0.491
	Minimum wage	15.078	2	0.001
	GDP per capita	6.485	2	0.039
	Wminpv	2.124	2	0.346
	All	67.719	14	0
Wminpv	Employment (youth)	30.749	2	0
	School (youth)	20.214	2	0
	Employment (prime age)	24.462	2	0
	Employment (elderly males)	0.72476	2	0.696
	Minimum wage	24.757	2	0
	GDP per capita	3.4185	2	0.181
	Wbar	17.809	2	0
	All	66.617	14	0

Table 8.4   **The effects of elderly employment (first difference specification)**

	Explaining youth employment or unemployment			
	Employment, OLS (1)	Unemployment, OLS (2)	Employment, IV (3)	Unemployment, IV (4)
Emp(elderly males)	0.591	−0.557	1.140	−3.039
	(0.163)***	(0.356)	(0.643)	(1.884)
GDP per capita	2.54e-06	−0.0000123	−0.0000103	0.0000435
	(7.98e-06)	(0.0000175)	(0.0000172)	(0.0000503)
Constant	0.005	0.073	0.014	0.036
	(0.005)	(0.011)***	(0.012)	(0.034)
Observations	32	32	31	31
R^2	0.39	0.15	0.15	

Note: Standard errors in parentheses.
***Significant at the 1 percent level.

8.7   Instrumental Variable Specifications

Table 8.4 presents four regressions. The first two regressions simply regress (first differences of) youth employment and youth unemployment on (first differences of) employment of the elderly, similar to tables 8.1 and 8.2. We include GDP per capita as an additional control variable. The second two regressions use the same specification but now use lagged variables of GDP per capita and of percent twenty to twenty-four in school as instruments.

We note that the effect of elderly employment on youth employment is significant for ordinary least squares (OLS) and marginally significant for instrumental variables (IV). For youth unemployment we find marginally significant effects. In none of the cases do the signs of the elderly employment variable support the notion that reducing elderly employment will help to improve the chances of younger people in the labor market.

8.8   Discussion: Employment of the Young and the Inducement to Retire

In previous phases of the International Social Security (ISS) Project, we have shown that the incentives to retire play an important role in explaining the LFP of the elderly. To check the direct effect of these incentives on the employment and unemployment of the young, we would like to use some average measure of the incentives to retire as explanatory variables for explaining the employment or unemployment of the young. We find that these incentive variables are plausibly Granger caused by youth unemployment, rather than the other way around. This is consistent with a description of the history of labor market policies in the eighties and nineties of the last century.

We do find, however, that both in ordinary regressions and in IV regressions employment of the elderly has a (marginally significant) positive effect on employment of the young and a negative effect on unemployment of the young. This suggests that attempts to improve the labor market perspectives of the young by encouraging the elderly to leave the labor market are likely to be counterproductive (or at least not effective). Altogether, we confirm the suspicion of the originator of the "old for young" idea that the strong increase in early retirement has not had an appreciable positive effect on the employment of the young.

Appendix

Incentives to retire have been approximated by considering a representative male elderly person who is aged a (between fifty-five and sixty-five), married, and a single earner, who worked at age fifty-four with median earnings but was retired from the labor market in year t. Since the person was faced with the decision to retire from the labor force or not from age fifty-five until his actual retirement age, his incentive to retire is calculated as a weighted average of the incentive to retire at the respective ages between fifty-five and a, weighted with the proportion of persons still in employment. Next, a weighted average of these incentives (aggregating over all ages a between fifty-five and sixty-five) is calculated where the weights are determined by the respective numbers of retired individuals with age fifty-five, fifty-six, and so forth. In these calculations, early retirees are assumed to have been eligible for early retirement; and the disabled are assumed to have been eligible for disability benefits. Thus, the variables used are a weighted average of the incentive to retire via ER and DI, where the weights depend on age and year (since no exact information by year is available for the whole period, the gradual introduction of ER between 1974 and 1984 has been approximated). The incentives have been approximated from 1973 onward (with earliest retirees having retired in 1963; however, since the tax schedule before 1973 is problematic, changes in the tax schedule between 1963 and 1973 have not been taken into account).

The incentive variables that we calculate in this way are wbar—a weighted average of the social security wealth of the retirees in question   as well as Wminpv, social security wealth minus the peak value, the highest obtainable SSW.

References

Sociale Verzekeringsbank (SVB). 2007. Vijftig Jaar AOW. Available at: http://www .svb.nl.

Van Oorschot, W. 2007. Narrowing pathways to early retirement in the Netherlands. *Journal of Poverty and Social Justice* 15 (3): 247–55.

Vrijzinnig Protestantse Radio Omroep (VPRO). 2004. Andere Tijden: De geboorte van de VUT. Available at: http://geschiedenis.vpro.nl/programmas/2899536/ afleveringen/19273461/.

9

Social Security Incentives, Exit from the Workforce, and Entry of the Young

Michele Boldrin, Pilar García-Gómez, and
Sergi Jiménez-Martín

9.1 Introduction

Beginning in the late 1970s, Spain has witnessed dramatic social, economic, and demographic changes. Life expectancy has increased substantially, and fertility rates have dropped to some of the lowest levels in the European Union (EU). The Spanish public system of social insurance, of which the public pension system (*Seguridad Social*) is the main component, underwent a major reform in the middle 1980s and is now substantially more comprehensive and generous than it used to be. Finally, Spanish per capita income has grown continuously since the middle 1980s, on average at about a percentage point faster than the rest of the EU, and the growth has been comparatively higher since the late 1990s. During the same period, a large share of the older workers population have been dismissed and lead to retire earlier, while the population unemployment rate soared first and then, since 1996, declined steadily to reach average European levels in the last three years.

Quite often during the last three decades, policies that favor early retirement are supported and promoted with the justification that they may induce a reduction in youth unemployment rates. The basic idea is that because jobs are a scarce resource available in a fixed number, retiring an older worker would "free" the same job for a younger, most likely unemployed, one.

Michele Boldrin is the Joseph Gibson Hoyt Distinguished Professor of Economics in Arts and Sciences and Department Chair at Washington University in St. Louis, and a research fellow of CEPR in London and of FEDEA in Madrid. Pilar García-Gómez is an assistant professor at the Erasmus School of Economics at Erasmus University Rotterdam. Sergi Jiménez-Martín is associate professor of economics at Universitat Pompeu Fabra and Director of the LaCaixa-FEDEA chair on Health Economics.

We are grateful to MEC projects SEJ2005-08783-C04-01 and EC02008-06395-C05-01 for financial support.

We have found a number of references to this issue in the press during the early eighties. Just as an example, we mention the preamble of the national employment agreement of 1981 (*Acuerdo nacional sobre empleo; El País,* July 6, 1981) describing a special retirement scheme (*Sistema especial de jubilaciones*):[1]

Las partes firmantes del acuerdo han examinado los posibles efectos sobre el empleo del establecimiento de un sistema que permita la jubilación con el 100% de los derechos pasivos de los trabajadores al cumplir 64 años de edad y la simultánea contratación por parte de las empresas de trabajadores jóvenes o perceptores del Seguro de Desempleo en número igual al de las jubilaciones anticipadas que se pacten con contratos de igual naturaleza que los que se sustituyen. El Gobierno elaborará, en el plazo de 2 meses, una norma estableciendo la regulación de un sistema que, por la vía de los convenios colectivos o del acuerdo entre empresas y trabajadores, permita las sustituciones a que se refiere el párrafo anterior.

[The signed parties of the agreement have examined the possible effects on employment of a system that allows retirement with 100 percent of the liability rights of the workers when they become sixty-four years old and the simultaneous hiring from the firm of young workers or receivers of unemployment benefits with contracts of the same nature as the ones to be substituted in equal number as the early retirees agreed. The Government will devise, in a two months period, a rule establishing the regulation of a system that, via collective agreements or agreement between employers and employees, allows the substitutions referred above.]

In fact, the 1985 pension system reform, which gave shape to the system currently in place,[2] introduced several specific programs to favor the substitution of older by younger workers. Especially relevant are the *Jubilación Especial* (special retirement scheme) at age sixty-four and the *Jubilación Parcial* (partial retirement). The first one has been always very marginal, with an incidence varying from 1 to 4 percent of the total number of retirees. The second has not been used until very recent years, after the 2002 reform. In fact, the incidence of this scheme was negligible until 2002. Since then, it has increased very rapidly (4.24 percent in 2002 and 13.27 percent in 2007). See table 9A.1 for recent information about the distribution of the retirement pensions awarded in recent years. Unfortunately, a large share of this time period is out of our sample and cannot be taken into consideration.

1. Other mentions of the issue can be found in International Labor Organization (ILO) documents (*Medidas de la OIT para luchar contra el desempleo.* El Pais, 17/08/1982. http://www.elpais.com/articulo/economia/PAISES_INDUSTRIALIZADOS/ORGANIZA CION_INTERNACIONAL_DEL_TRABAJO_/OIT/Medidas/OIT/luchar/paro/elpepiecco/ 19820817elpepieco_10/Tes; also in an article on *El País* (Artículo de opinión en El País 26/11/1983 de Daniel Gil. http://www.elpais.com/articulo/opinion/edad/jubilaciones/elpepiopi/ 19831126elpepiopi_10/Tes. More recently, in 2002, we have found another reference to the issue in Trade unions news: http://www.ugtrioja.org/web/actualidad/cp/cp219.htm.

2. There have been three reforms after 1985: 1997, 2002, and 2007. However, the shape of the system has remained unaltered since the 1985 reform.

Our goal is to understand the relationship between the employment (or exit from the labor force) of the old and the employment/unemployment of the young. To do this, we first estimate the statistical impact of the labor force participation (LFP) of the old on the employment/unemployment of the young, and also of the middle-aged individuals. However, changes in the LFP of the old may be due to factors other than changes in pension incentives, which may also be correlated with the labor conditions of the young, thus giving biased estimates. Therefore, one would like to estimate the direct effect of retirement policies.

More precisely, we would like to estimate at the aggregate level the direct relationship between the incentive for the old to leave the labor force and the employment of the young. In order to do so, we need a simple aggregate indicator of the incentive to retire. However, to obtain such an index may be complicated, especially recognizing the need to account for some key aspects of the inducement to retire: the eligibility age, the benefit level given eligibility, and the change in the benefit if the receipt of benefits is delayed (the option value/peak value [OV/PV] idea, essentially the actuarial adjustment if retirement is delayed); and the necessity to aggregate them for all the individuals "at risk" in a given year.

Methodologically, our approach is very simple: we collect time series information of the main indicators of the Spanish labor market for the key groups of the population; in parallel, we construct synthetic incentive measures for the at risk population in a given year. To do this, we combine data from the Spanish Labor Force Survey and the *Muestra Continua de Vidas Laborales* (MCVL2006).

Previous works on the relationship between employment of the young and exit of older workers in Spain (Jiménez-Martín 1999) and Europe (Boldrin et al. 1999) have found no systematic evidence of any significant correlation. Jiménez-Martín (1999) analyzes the relationship between young's entry and older's exit from the labor market in Spain using data from the panel data version of the Spanish Labor Force Survey in the 1987 to 1997 period. He analyzes the individual decision to enter the labor market (transitions into the "market") while controlling for individual and household characteristics as well as local market indicators. Among the latter, he highlights the fraction/amount of exit from the labor market on the part of older individuals, especially those aged fifty-five to sixty-four. He finds little evidence of any relationship between entry of the young and exit of older individuals.

Boldrin et al. (1999) collected various labor market observations for a sample of 260 Nomenclature of Territorial Units for Statistics (NUTS) II and NUTS III European regions over the years 1986, 1991, and 1996.[3] They expect that, if any effect is visible, it should be detectable at this level of

---

3. They represent relatively small areas, which happen to be the territorial units at which the European Commission targets its employment policies and for which national governments tend to devise the early retirement plans we mentioned earlier.

geographical disaggregation. Figures 2 and 3 in Boldrin et al. (1999) plot, separately for men and women, the relationship between the exit rates from the labor force of people born between 1931 and 1940, and the changes in the unemployment rates over 1991 to 1996 of people aged between twenty-one and thirty. Under the substitution hypothesis, we should expect a negative relationship. Neither for men nor for women, the estimated regression lines turn out to be significantly negatively sloped. For alternative specifications, controlling for cohort effects or using different lags, the results hardly change. Thus, they conclude that early retirement of older workers does not come together with a reduction of unemployment among younger people.

The rest of this document goes as follows. In section 9.2, we document the main macroeconomic facts of the last decades. In section 9.3, we describe the social security background. Data and sources are commented in section 9.4. In section 9.5, we discuss the trends of the labor force during the period of study. In section 9.6 we present the methodology and the construction of the inducement-to-retire measure and, in section 9.7, the empirical framework used to test the relevant hypothesis. The empirical results are described in section 9.8. Finally, section 9.9 offers some concluding remarks.

9.2   The Facts

9.2.1   Macroeconomic Context

Table 9.1 summarizes the Spanish macroeconomic evolution, in relation to the EU's average, since 1975. The basic facts for Spain are as follows.[4] In the period immediately after the oil shock, 1975 to 1985, which coincides with the death of Francisco Franco and the beginning of the democratic transition, both the gross domestic product (GDP) growth rate and the level of employment were well below the European average. This period corresponds to a dramatic "structural transition" in which a few million jobs were eliminated and the unemployment rate skyrocketed to levels substantially above 20 percent. This was only partially a consequence of the two oil shocks; the collapse of the Franco regime led to a spontaneous and unplanned "opening" of the economy, which preceded and anticipated the entrance into the EU by almost a decade. As a consequence of this broad restructuring process, productivity growth in Spain was by far more intense than the European average until the second half of the 1980s. In the period since 1985, the opposite happened: productivity growth in Spain is slightly but persistently below the EU average, while GDP and employment grow, on average, faster than in the rest of Europe. The last thirteen years, in particular, have seen a spectacular increase in Spanish employment (more

4. Source material is from Eurostat.

Table 9.1 The macroeconomic scenario (annual percentage growth rates)

	Spain				European Union			
	1975–1985	1985–1990	1990–1999	1999–2004	1975–1985	1985–1990	1990–1999	1999–2004
GDP real growth	1.7	4.5	2.3	2.9	2.3	3.2	1.8	2.2
Number employed	-1.6	3.3	1.0	2.2	0.1	1.4	0.2	1.0
Average hours worked	—	-0.2	-0.2	-1.2	—	-0.4	-0.3	-0.9
GDP/no. employed	3.3	1.2	1.3	—	2.2	1.7	1.6	—
GDP/total hours worked	—	1.4	1.6	—	—	2.1	1.9	—
Consumer prices	15.4	6.5	3.9	3.1	10.3	4.4	3.0	2.2
Average earnings	17.2	7.9	4.9	2.6	11.6	6.4	4.1	2.4
Average real earnings	1.6	1.4	0.9	—	1.2	1.9	1.1	—
Average real labor costs	2.1	0.5	0.6	3.2	1.5	1.4	1.1	2.8
Real unit labor costs	-1.1	-0.7	-0.7	-1.0	-1.1	-0.8	-0.7	-0.1

Note: Dashes indicate "not available."

than eight million additional jobs out of a total employment, in 1995, of about twelve million), which has, nevertheless, come together with a very slow rate of growth in labor productivity. Inflation, on the other hand, has been slightly above the European average during the whole period, although the differential has been reduced in recent years, following the implementation first of the Maastricht pact and then of the Euro. Finally, real unit labor costs have been decreasing at about the EU average during the whole period.

What are the implications of these macroeconomic facts for our purposes? Basically, that the relative economic position of Spain, and of the average Spaniard, has improved substantially, vis-á-vis that of the average European, during the last thirty years. The natural question to ask, therefore, is: did this improvement in the economic well being of the average Spaniard translates also into an improvement of the economic conditions of the elderly? Figure 9.1 reports the ratio of pension expenditure to GDP since 1965. It is apparent that this ratio has grown substantially for about thirty years and has flattened out and then slightly decreased during the last ten years or so.

9.2.2   Labor Market Reforms since the 1970s

There have been substantial changes in employment protection legislation over the last three decades. The following chronology describes the major ones:

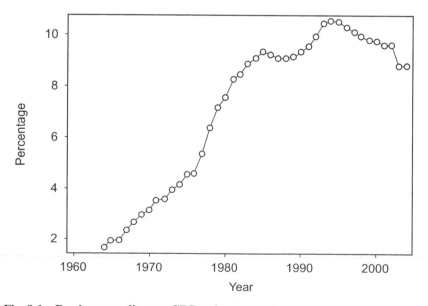

Fig. 9.1   Pension expenditure to GDP ratio

- 1978: Following the transition to democracy, Spain introduced labor legislation restricting dismissals and adding high dismissal costs.[5]
- 1980: The parliament passed the Workers' Statute including the Strike and Collective Bargaining regulation. At the same time, early retirement provisions and the notion of "disability due to economic reasons" are introduced.
- 1984: First reform of the labor market with the objective of reducing dismissal cost. Temporary contracts are introduced that became very popular since (as shown in table 9.2). As a result of the 1984 reform, the proportion of employees under temporary contracts increased from 10 percent during the 1980s to over 30 percent in the early 1990s. The temporary contracts generated a dual labor market: unstable low-paying jobs and stable high-paying jobs under the old regulation. It did not reduce unemployment until the recovery of 1994 (Kugler, Jimeno, and Hernanz 2002). Not surprisingly, reducing firing costs has been one of the recurrent recommendations of national and international organizations, although actual reforms had only a limited scope (Organization for Economics Cooperation and Development [OECD] (2005).
- 1994: Second major reform of the labor market, with the objective of introducing limitations to the use of temporary contracts.
- 1997: Third important reform of the labor market (actualized in 2001). The purpose of this reform was to further limiting the incentive to use temporary contracts by reducing dismissal cost of certain groups of workers. The most noted aspect of the reform was the introduction of a new permanent contract, with reduced severance payments. This contract was targeted to two groups: the population most exposed to unemployment (i.e., the youth, the long-term unemployed, and women and men above age forty-five) and workers on a temporary contract who

---

5. This legislation established that firms could dismiss workers for "personal reasons," in which case the firm had to prove the worker's incompetence or absenteeism, and "economic reasons," in which case the firm had to prove its need to reduce employment due to technological, organizational, or productive causes. Dismissals justified by "economic reasons" required advance notice. Workers dismissed for "personal reasons" could appeal to labor courts. The severance payment awarded depended on whether judges ruled the dismissal as "fair" or "unfair." A dismissal was ruled as "fair" if the employer was able to prove the worker's incompetence or absenteeism and "unfair" otherwise. In case of fair dismissals, firms had to pay twenty days out of the salary per year of seniority, with a maximum of twelve months. In the case of unfair dismissals, firms had to pay forty-five days per year of seniority out of the salary, with a maximum of forty-two months. Severance payments for "economic reasons" were the same as for fair dismissals under "personal reasons." In practice, this legislation turned out to be very stringent because judges ruled dismissals as unfair in the majority of cases. Moreover, approval for dismissals under "economic reasons" was often granted only when there was an agreement between employers and workers, which was achieved in most cases by raising severance payments above the legally established amounts. The Spanish government introduced the first reform designed to reduce dismissal costs in 1984. Because an across-the-board reduction of dismissal costs was politically impossible, the reform liberalized the use of temporary contracts (from Kugler, Jimeno and Hernanz 2002).

Table 9.2   Distribution of the share of temporary employment in total employment

	1985	1990	1991	1992	1993	1994	1995	1996	1997	1998	1999	2000
EU-15	9.0	10.2	10.4	10.9	10.6	11.0	11.5	11.8	12.2	12.8	13.2	13.4
Belgium	6.9	5.3	5.1	4.9	5.1	5.1	5.3	5.9	6.3	7.8	10.3	9.0
Denmark	12.3	10.8	11.9	11.0	10.7	12.0	12.1	11.2	11.1	10.1	10.2	10.2
Germany	10.0	10.5	10.1	10.5	10.3	10.3	10.4	11.1	11.7	12.3	13.1	12.7
Greece	21.1	16.5	14.7	10.2	10.4	10.3	10.2	11.0	10.9	13.0	13.0	13.1
Spain	15.6	29.8	32.2	33.5	32.2	33.7	35.0	33.6	33.6	32.9	32.7	32.1
France	4.7	10.5	10.2	10.5	10.9	11.0	12.3	12.6	13.1	13.9	14.0	15.0
Ireland	7.3	8.5	8.3	8.7	9.4	9.5	10.2	9.2	9.4	9.4	9.4	4.6
Italy	4.8	5.2	5.4	7.5	6.0	7.3	7.2	7.5	8.2	8.6	9.8	10.1
Luxembourg	4.7	3.4	3.3	2.9	3.0	2.9	—	2.6	2.1	2.9	3.4	3.4
The Netherlands	7.5	7.6	7.7	9.7	10.0	10.9	10.9	12.0	11.4	12.7	12.0	14.0
Austria	—	—	—	—	—	—	6.0	8.0	7.8	7.8	7.5	7.9
Portugal	14.4	18.3	16.4	11.0	9.8	9.4	10.0	10.6	12.2	17.3	18.6	20.4
Finland	10.5	11.5	12.0	13.1	12.7	12.9	16.5	17.3	17.1	17.7	18.2	17.7
Sweden	11.9	10.0	9.8	10.5	11.5	11.5	12.5	11.8	12.1	12.9	13.9	14.7
United Kingdom	7.0	5.2	5.3	5.5	5.9	6.5	7.0	7.1	7.4	7.1	6.8	6.7

Note: Dashes indicate "not available."

converted to an indefinite one during the one-year period following the approval of the new legislation.
- 2006: Fourth important labor market reform. Previous reforms had failed to reduce the fraction of temporary contracts; a new attempt was made by introducing strong restrictions on the extension of contracts or replacement of temporary workers.

9.2.3   Background on the Spanish Social Security System

Mandatory insurance for job related accidents was introduced in 1900, through a bill that also authorized the creation of some funds, for public employees only, paying disability and retirement pensions. In 1919, mandatory retirement insurance (*Retiro Obrero Obligatorio*) was introduced for private-sector employees aged sixteen to sixty-five whose total annual salary was below a certain threshold. In 1926, a universal pension system for public employees (*Régimen de Clases Pasivas,* or RCP) was established, which still exists under the same name. By the late 1930s, most Spanish employees were covered, in one form or another, by some minimal, government mandatory retirement insurance program.

With the end of the Republic and the advent of Franco's regime, a number of changes were implemented. In 1939, Workers' Retirement (*Retiro Obrero*) was replaced by Old Age Insurance (*Seguro de Vejez*). While the former was based upon a capitalization system, the latter was from the beginning a completely unfunded pay-as-you-go scheme. By 1950, the system had acquired its basic organization in two pillars, which remained essentially unchanged until the mid 1970s. Public servants were all covered by the RCP, while private-sector employees with annual earnings below a certain ceiling were covered by the Old Age Insurance. The 1963 reform created a very large number of special funds (*Régimenes Especiales*) next to the general scheme (*Régimen General*), generating a jungle of special treatments that is still being dismantled.

In 1977, a reform bill made a first attempt at harmonizing the many existing funds, by reducing the differences in the treatment they offered and by putting (in 1979) the administration of the whole system under the newly created National Social Security Institute (*Instituto Nacional de la Seguridad Social,* or INSS). Overall, this process increased the percentage of workers covered by the public social security system.

The key rules before the 1985 reform (see Barrada [1999] or Boldrin, Jiménez-Martín, and Peracchi [1999] for a complete description) were the following:

1. The Normal Retirement Age is set at sixty-five and the Early Retirement Age, for those that started contributing before 1967, at sixty.
2. Eligibility: ten years of contributions, of which two years should be in the last seven years preceding the date of retirement.

3. Amount of pension: 50 percent of the "benefit base" with ten years of contributions, plus 2 percent for each additional year of contributions, up to 100 percent with thirty-five years.

The reform process, which came to shape the current regime, introduced a few important changes: eligibility criteria for disability pensions were tightened; the minimum number of years of contributions required to obtain an old-age pension was increased from eight to fifteen; and the number of years entering the computation of the benefit base was increased from two to eight. On June 26, 1997, many of the parameters used for the computation of benefit bases and pensions were modified. The number of contributory years over which the benefit base is computed was increased from eight to fifteen (by year 2001). The formula for the computation of the replacement rate α (see the following) was also made less generous, whereas the 8 percent per-year penalty applied to early retirees between the ages of sixty and sixty-five was reduced to 7 percent for those individuals with forty or more contributory years at the time of retirement.

Currently, the Spanish social security offers two pathways to regular retirement:[6] early retirement and normal retirement. Early retirement is possible starting at age sixty, while the normal retirement age is sixty-five, although some professional groups have lower normal retirement ages (miners, military personnel, policemen, and fishermen are the main ones). Collective wage settlements often impose mandatory retirement at age sixty-five, facilitate retirement at sixty-four with full benefits, or encourage retirement between sixty and sixty-three through lump-sum payments.

Public pensions are provided by the following programs:

- The "General Social Security Scheme" (*Régimen General de la Seguridad Social,* or RGSS) and the "Special Social Security Schemes for Self-Employed" (*Régimen Especial de Trabajadores Autónomos,* or RETA). They cover, respectively, the private-sector employees and the self-employed workers and professionals. The RGSS covers also the members of cooperative firms, the employees of most public administrations other than the central governments, and all unemployed individuals complying with the minimum number of contributory years when reaching sixty-five.
- The scheme for government employees (*Régimen de Clases Pasivas,* or RCP) includes public servants employed by the central government and its local branches.

In what follows, we provide a brief summary of key regulatory changes in the Spanish social security system.

---

6. That is to say, in the absence of disability or long-term unemployment in late age.

- 1973: Social Security Act: Introduction of the tax base (not linked to wages) but to categories.
- 1974: Social Security Bill: Effectively linked the tax base to wages. Loosened significantly the eligibility criteria. Common replacement rates.
- 1977: Harmonization Process: Caused a significant increase of coverage.
- 1985: First major pension system reform. It included restrictions in the access to invalidity very frequent in the period 1980 to 1985. It introduced several Early Retirement programs: *Jubilación Parcial, Jubilación Flexible,* and *Jubilación Especial a los 64.* Consistent increase of the Minimum Pension to the Minimum Wage since then.
- 1997: Second Pension Reform. Following the Toledo Pact (1995). Very little effect on either incentives or pension expenditure.
- 2002: Third Pension Reform. Early Retirement up to sixty-one (but not affecting current workers). Very little effect on either incentives or pension expenditure in the short run. The incentives to use the partial retirement program were increased, and this program has been increasingly used as an exit route.
- 2007: Fourth Pension Reform (Ley 40/2007). Marginal changes on eligibility for retirement options. Important changes on eligibility (change to fifteen years or 5.475 days of effective contributions), conditions for allowing for partial retirement, and formula for disability insurance (DI) benefits.

See the appendix for a detailed description of the system rules from 1985 onward.

9.3   Description of Data and Sources

We start by providing an index of the data sets that are currently available. One important limitation should be noticed: there is no single data set covering the whole period 1975 to 2005. Most time series, therefore, will be constructed by splining data from different sources, creating obvious problems of consistency, which, while less dramatic than one might expect, are nevertheless substantial.

9.3.1   Data Sources

Employment

Data about employment and labor force participation come from the *Encuesta de Población Activa* (EPA). The EPA is a rotating quarterly survey carried out by the Spanish National Statistical Institute (*Instituto Nacional de Estadística,* INE). The planned sample size consists of about 64,000 households with approximately 150,000 adult individuals. Although the survey has been conducted since 1964, publicly released cross-sectional files are available only from 1977. The 1977 questionnaire was modified in 1987 (when a set of retrospective questions was introduced) and again in the first quarter of 1992. In both cases, the lengthening of the questionnaire led to increased nonresponse rates. Further modifications have been introduced in 1999 and 2004.

The EPA provides fairly detailed information on labor force status, education, and family background variables but, as with most European-style labor force surveys, no information on earnings and other sources of income. The reference period for most questions is the week before the interview.

Wage Profiles and Incentive Variables

Both wage profiles and monetary incentive variables are constructed using data from: (a) *Historiales Laborales de la Seguridad Social,* 1998 (old version): a sample of about 250,000 of working careers (Social Security numbers) taken at the end of 1997 (See Boldrin, Jiménez-Martín, and Peracchi 2001, 2004) for a description); complete working histories up to 1998 and monthly covered wages for employees in the 1986 to 1995, which allows us to construct year of birth × gender × region wage profiles and, thus, incentives. (b) *Muestra Continua de Vidas Laborales* (MCVL2006): a sample of about 1,000,000 of working careers (Social Security numbers) taken at the end of 2005; complete working histories up to 2006 and monthly covered wages for employees in the 1980 to 2005 period, which allows us to construct year of birth × gender × region wage profiles and, thus, incentives.

9.3.2   Labor Force Trends from 1977 to 2005

In this section, we present some descriptive and graphical evidence on labor force trends by gender for the groups under study. We also show a first glimpse of the relationship between the labor status of the different groups and the different labor and social security reforms. Figure 9.2 shows the evolution of the labor force participation, the employment rate, and the unemployment rate for the population aged sixteen to sixty-nine by gender. It can be seen that there has been an important increase in the female labor force participation since the mid-1980s, while the employment and unemployment rate of both males and females have been moved in parallel, decreasing (increasing) the employment (unemployment) rate during the mid-1980s, and an increase (decrease) in employment (unemployment) rates after the mid-1990s.

Figures 9.3 and 9.4 present some data to set the stage. They show how the employment and unemployment rate of the youth and the prime age individuals relate to the labor force participation of the older group (fifty-five to sixty-nine) and whether the labor market or social security reforms can play any role. The employment and unemployment figures of young

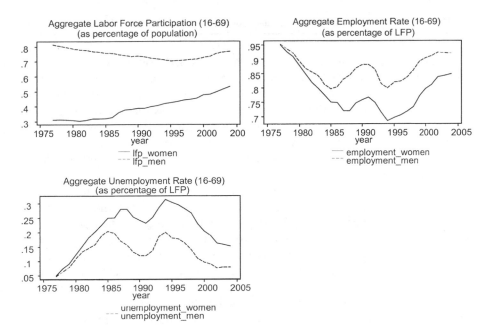

Fig. 9.2   Labor market trends by gender

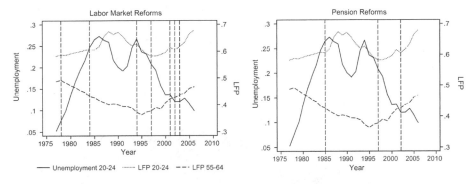

Fig. 9.3   Labor market trends of old and young individuals and labor and pension reforms

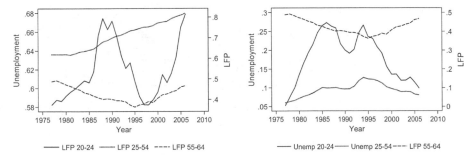

Fig. 9.4   Relationship of young and prime age individuals labor market outcomes and labor force participation of the old

and prime age individuals behave similarly during the observational period independently on whether we define young individuals to be younger than twenty-five or thirty. However, the unemployment rate of young individuals is always higher. At the same time, the figures show that there is no clear association between the labor force participation of the older group and the employment or unemployment of the other two groups. Moreover, the observed changes in this association are hard to relate with any specific policy change.

To highlight the importance of employment and unemployment for the labor force participation of older workers, figures 9.5, 9.6, and 9.7 show the labor force participation, the employment rate, and the unemployment rate for four different age groups by gender. The behavior of both the labor force participation and the employment rate is more stable during the period than the unemployment rate. We observe a decrease in both the LFP and the employment rate of individuals aged older than sixty, and a slight increase of the same measures for women aged fifty to fifty-four.

On the other hand, there has also been an important increase on the schooling rates of the Spanish population during the period under study. Figure 9.5 shows the percentage of individuals aged twenty to twenty-four who are unemployed, employed, or in school. First notice that the total amount can exceed 100 percent as there can be some individuals who are either employed or unemployed while in school. It can be appreciated that while there has been a decrease in the percentage of young individuals in

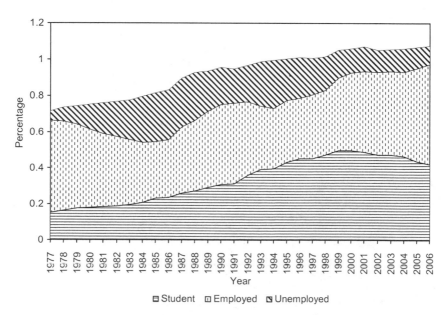

Fig. 9.5   Labor and schooling trends of young individuals in Spain, 1977–2006

unemployment and an increase in the percentage in employment, the biggest change can be seen in the percentage of individuals who declare being still at school, as it increases from less than 20 percent at the beginning of the period to over 40 percent in the last years.

9.4 Regressions

As stated before, the main purpose of this paper is to analyze the link between employment for the young and retirement from the labor force of the elderly population, and, in particular, the link between employment of the young and pension system regulations. Following an independent variable (IV) approach, we want to establish whether social security reforms have been set with the purpose to increase availability of jobs for the young and, of course, whether they have been successful.

We begin with ordinary least squares (OLS) regressions of labor market outcomes for nonelderly on labor market outcomes of the "old." With the purpose to examine as broadly as possible the relationship between LFP of the old and employment of the nonold fraction of the population, we consider the following five dependent variables: Unemployment and Employment for prime age (individuals aged twenty-five to fifty-four) and Unemployment, Employment, and Schooling for the youth (individuals aged twenty to twenty-four). The independent variable is the LFP of the old workers (individuals aged fifty-six to sixty-four). And all the variables are expressed as rates over total population of the relevant age group. We consider two versions of such regressions: levels and differences of order 5. Let us first introduce the levels regression:

$$Y_t = \alpha + \beta \text{LFPO}_t + \delta X_t + \varepsilon_t,$$

where Y denotes either Employment, Unemployment, or Schooling, and X is a set of economic controls (per capita GDP, GDP growth, and share of manufacturing in GDP) in order to control for labor market characteristics associated with both LFP of the old and employment or unemployment of either young or prime age individuals. The five-year differences equation to be estimated is analogous, but both independent and dependent variables are expressed as a five-year difference.

In summary, for each dependent variable, we carry out the following exercises: levels and differences; two age groups (young and prime age), with and without the selected covariates.

9.5 Measures of Retirement Incentives

However, as stated in the introduction, there can be some further labor market conditions beyond social security incentives that can affect both the labor force participation of the older workers and the employment and unemployment situation of either young or prime age workers. In order to solve this limitation, we construct a synthetic measure of the incentives faced by older workers.

The purpose of this section is to present the methodology and the assumptions made to construct a synthetic measure of the (monetary or financial) inducement to retirement that the population at retirement risk faces. That is we want to have an aggregate measure of the strength with which the social security spells out representative workers from the labor force. We want this index to account for the various factors influencing retirement decisions: the eligibility age, the benefit level given eligibility, and the change in the benefit if the receipt of benefits is delayed (the idea of the OV (Stock and Wise 1990) and the PV (Coile and Gruber 2000), essentially the actuarial adjustment if retirement is delayed). In order to do so, we first present the standard monetary incentives measures (Gruber and Wise 1999). Then we present the synthetic indicator(s) and the assumptions made in computations.

9.5.1   Social Security Incentives Measures

For a (representative) worker of age a, following Gruber and Wise (1999), we define social security wealth (SSW) in case of retirement at age $b \geq a$ as the expected present value of future pension benefits:

$$\text{SSW}_h = \sum_{s=h+1}^{S} \rho_s B_s(h).$$

Here S is the age of certain death, $\rho_s = \beta^{s-a}\pi_s$, with β denoting the pure time discount factor and π_s the conditional survival probability at age s for an individual alive at age a, and $B_s(h)$ the pension expected at age $s \geq h + 1$ in case of retirement at age s.

Given SSW, we define three incentive variables for a worker of age a: the accrual at horizon 1 (SSA), the implicit tax/subsidy rate (TAX), the optimal horizontal peak value (PV), and the option value (OV). The definition of these incentive measures, for an individual of age $t = 55, \ldots, 69$ are as follows:

- Accrual at horizon 1: $\text{SSA}_t = \text{ssw}_{t+1} - \text{ssw}_t$.
- Implicit tax/subsidy rate: $\text{TAX}_t = \text{SSA}_t / E_t(w_{t+1})$, where E_t is the expectation operator based upon the information available up to time t.
- Accrual at the optimal horizon h^* or peak value: $\text{PV}_t = \max_h(\text{ssw}_{t+h}) - \text{ssw}_t$, $h = 1, \ldots, R - t$, where R is the mandatory retirement age (the latter does not exist in Spain, but given the retirement evidence, we find it reasonable to assume that $R = 70$).
- *Option Value* $\text{OV}_a = \max_h(V_h - V_a)$, $h = a + 1, \ldots, R$, where

$$V_h = \sum_{s=a+1}^{h} \rho_s W_s^\gamma + \sum_{s=h+1}^{S} \rho_s [kB_s(h)]^\gamma ,$$

and p_s is the survival probability, S is age of (certain) death, W stands for earnings, and B stands for pension benefits.

We have imposed that $\beta = .97$, $\gamma = 1$, and $k = 1.25$. Note that under these assumptions:

$$V_h = \sum_{s=a+1}^{h} p_s W_s + 1.25\,\mathrm{SSW}_h.$$

9.5.2 A Summary Measure of the Incentive to Retire

To obtain such an index can become somewhat complicated, especially recognizing the need to account for the key aspects of the inducement to retire: the age of eligibility, the benefit level given eligibility, and the change in the benefit if the receipt of benefits is delayed (the OV/PV idea, essentially the actuarial adjustment if retirement is delayed). Here, we consider the development of a summary measure of the inducement to retire. We begin with a suggested summary measure of the inducement implicit in the present value of social security benefits. Then we discuss how this sort of measure might be extended to develop a single summary measure that incorporates each of the three aspects of the inducement to retire.

We will be using the incentive measure in time series regressions, so we need to think about the inducement to retire with respect to all older persons who are out of the labor force in a given year. We will consider several alternatives.

First, we want to summarize the SSW faced by persons who are out of the labor force in year t. For simplicity, we assume a rather narrow age range for illustration, but the actual age range could be much broader. Assume the first eligibility age is fifty-five. Consider the "average" social security wealth W of all persons aged fifty-five to R ($R = 70$, for example) retired in 1980. Those fifty-five in 1980 must have retired in 1980, and we want the W of fifty-five-year-olds in 1980. Those fifty-six in 1980 could have retired at fifty-five in 1979 or at fifty-six in 1980, so we need $W(55, 1979)$ and $W(56, 1980)$. And we need to weight these wealth numbers by $q(55, 1979)$ and $q(56, 1980)$, where q measures the odds of exposure to those retirement incentives at each age/year. Those fifty-seven in 1980 could have retired at fifty-five in 1978, or fifty-six in 1979, or at fifty-seven in 1980. So we need $W(55, 1978)$, $W(56, 1979)$, and $W(57, 1980)$. And we need to weight these wealth numbers by $q(55, 1978)$, $q(56, 1979)$, and $q(57, 1980)$, respectively.

So, in general, when we consider all feasible retirement ages,

$$\overline{W}(y) = \left[\sum_{a=55}^{R} \frac{P(a,y)}{\sum_{b=55}^{R} P(b,y)} \right] \left[\frac{\sum_{t=0}^{a-55} W(a-t, y-t)\, q(a-t, a-t)}{\sum_{t=0}^{a-55} q(a-t, a-t)} \right],$$

where $R = 64$, $P(a, y)$ is the proportion of retired persons at age a in year y and $q(a, y)$ is the labor force participation of person of age a in year y.

9.5.3   A More General Inducement Measure

The disadvantage of the approach laid out in the preceding is that it captures only one of the three aspects of the inducement to retire (the benefit level), while ignoring two others (the first eligibility age and the PV/OV). We would like to consider a more inclusive index that captures all three aspects of how social security systems affect retirement as well as discounting of future benefits. The generalized inducement to retirement measure, $\bar{I}$ is constructed by replacing $W(a; y)$ in the preceding formula by:

$$I(a,y,\alpha) = W(a,y) + \alpha[W(a,y) - \text{PV}(a,y)],$$

where $0 \leq \alpha \leq 1$ is a discounting factor that may vary with age. Note that when $\alpha = 1$, the same weights are given to the terms $W(a,y)$ and $W(a,y) - \text{PV}(a,y)$, and, when $\alpha = 0$, we get the W index. Note the eligibility is taken into account, under borrowing constraints, by setting $W(a,y)$ equal to zero for those ages in which the individual is not eligible to retirement. So, finally, we get the following formula:

$$\bar{I}(y) = \left[\sum_{a=55}^{R} \frac{P(a,y)}{\sum_{b=55}^{R} P(b,y)} \right] \left[\frac{\sum_{t=0}^{a-55} I(a-t,y-t)q(a-t,a-t)}{\sum_{t=0}^{a-55} q(a-t,a-t)} \right]$$

9.5.4   Assumptions Made in Incentives Calculus

We compute social security incentives for stylized individuals representing cohorts born between 1910 (age seventy in 1980) and 1970 (age thirty-five in 2005). In order to compute the preceding incentives, we need several ingredients: wage and contributions history and family characteristics.

As regards wage and contributions history, we proceed as follows:

- From every year-of-birth and gender cohort in the ECVL2006 sample, we construct (when available) the median wage distribution in the period 1981 to 2005. For example, for the group of individuals born in 1940, we recover covered wages from age forty-one to sixty-five. In general for individuals born in year j we recover wages from ages $1981 - j$ to $2005 - j$.
- Given this information, we regress the observed data against age and its square and region.
- Then we predict backward and forward in order to obtain a complete year of birth-gender-region wage profiles in the twenty to seventy age range.
- We consider that the representative individual has contributed for thirty years at age fifty-five, that is, they have contributed for thirty-five years at sixty (the early retirement age) and forty by age sixty-five (the normal retirement age).

Regarding the family and other characteristics, we assume:

1. For the male cohorts in sample, we initially assume that (a) they are married with a nonworking spouse, (b) their wife is three years younger, and (c) their mortality corresponds to the baseline male mortality from the official data (INE 1995).

2. For every female cohort in sample, we initially assume that (a) they are married with a retiree or a worker entitled to retirement benefits, (b) their husband is four years older, and (c) their mortality is the baseline female mortality from official data (INE 1995).

3. In addition, for both men and women, we assume that (d) starting at age fifty-five and until a person reaches sixty-five, there are three pathways into retirement: unemployment benefits for individuals older aged at least fifty-two (UB52+), disability insurance (DI) and early retirement (ER). At each particular age, the individual has an age-specific probability of going into retirement using any of these three programs. However, we have to take into account the following restrictions.

As for eligibility, we assume:

1. A person has no access to the ER program before age sixty.

2. After age sixty, a person cannot claim UB52+ and can only claim ER or DI benefits.

Finally, the participation and employment rates, as well as the fraction of retirees, are obtained from the *Encuesta de Población Activa* (EPA) in the period 1977 to 2006. Moreover, we have used the relative male/female employment rates to build up gender-aggregated incentive measures.

Combining Several Programs

Figure 9.6 shows the percentage of individuals aged fifty-five to sixty-four that have most likely exit from the labor force, either through normal retirement, disability, or unemployment schemes. It can be seen that the percentage that exits through other routes rather than normal retirement is nonnegligible; thus, in order to estimate a summary measure of the incentives faced by older workers in order to exit their employment, we should also include the incentives that come from other sources.

We would like to weigh the incentives to exit through the different routes using the actual taking rates. Unfortunately, we can only observe the percentage of individuals that are at each state each year, so we have approximated the corresponding weights as follows. We have first selected those individuals who are either employed, unemployed, or on a disability scheme. Then the weight assigned to SSW (normal retirement) is equal to the percentage that employed individuals represent on this selected population. Accordingly, the weight assigned to SSW (unemployment) has been approximated by the

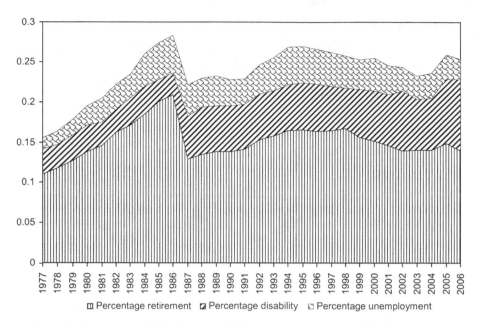

Fig. 9.6   **Percentage of individuals aged fifty-five to sixty-four that declare to be retired, unemployed, or in a disability scheme**

proportion that unemployed individuals represent on that population and the weight assigned to SSW (disability) as the proportion that individuals on a disability scheme represent on this selected population. We have further restricted the probability of receiving unemployment SSW to zero for individuals older than sixty and calculate two different indexes depending on whether retirement wealth was assumed to be zero earlier than the retirement age.

9.5.5   Description of Variation

Figure 9.7 presents the time trend of the incentive variable $\bar{I}$ assuming that alpha equals 2.5 under different assumptions regarding on one hand the effects of different routes into retirement and on the other the value of pension social security wealth before the legal retirement age of sixty. The first index (Ibar250_1) assumes that pension social security wealth before the age of sixty equals 0 and that there is only normal retirement as a route into retirement. The different assumption in the second index (Ibar250_2) is that wealth before age of sixty is different from zero. Both the third (Ibar250_3) and the fourth (Ibar250_4) indexes include different routes into retirement, but while the third assumes that social security wealth before the age of sixty is equal to 0, the fourth doesn't.

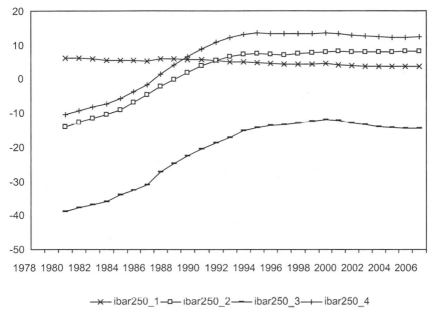

$$\longleftarrow \text{ibar250\_1} \quad \square \quad \text{ibar250\_2} \quad \text{ibar250\_3} \quad + \quad \text{ibar250\_4}$$

Fig. 9.7   Trends of Ibar under different assumptions on routes into retirement

9.5.6   Incentives Regression

In addition to the relationship between the employment of the old and the unemployment of the young, as described in the preceding, we would like to estimate the direct relationship between the inducement for the old to leave the labor force and the employment of the young. So we add to the regressions the synthetic measure of the inducement to retirement. In this case, the model to be estimated is the following:

$$Y_t = \alpha + \beta \bar{I}_t + \delta X_t + \varepsilon_t$$

9.6   Results

We finally come to the empirical findings. In order to test whether the old and young Spanish workers are complement or substitute, we follow a two-step procedure. In the first step, we test if there is any direct relationship between the labor force participation of the old and the employment and unemployment levels of the young. We estimate both sets of regressions in levels and in five-year differences, with and without covariates to control for the economic cycle. In the second step, we analyze how the incentives to retire faced by the old directly influence the employment outcomes of the young. However, before obtaining the second set of estimates, we compute empirically the value of alpha to be used to weigh the two components of the *I*-index. The analysis is carried out using data aggregated to the cells in the period 1977 to 2006 ($N = 30$).

9.6.1   Direct Effects of LFP of the Old

Table 9.3, 9.4, and 9.5 report the results about the direct effect of the labor supply of older workers on the employment outcomes of the young; the models have been estimated in levels and in fifth differences. The evidence is mixed, although it mostly rejects the substitutability hypothesis. On the other hand, the complementarity hypothesis is also rejected in some specifications, especially when the full set of economic covariates is included.

On the basis of this evidence, one could argue that there exists a positive relationship between the labor force participation of older workers and the employment rate of prime age individuals, while the association between unemployment and labor force participation is negative. Moreover, there is no evidence supporting the hypothesis that old and young workers are substitute; if anything, they are complement.

One may argue that, in Spain, the entry into active labor market participation takes place later than in most countries; hence, individuals aged twenty-five to twenty-nine should be treated as "young" and not considered within the prime age group. In order to test the sensitivity of our results to age grouping, we have replicated the analysis treating people from twenty to twenty-nine as young and redefining the prime age group accordingly (thirty to fifty-four). The results are shown in table 9.4 and are consistent with those in table 9.3.

The results shown in table 9.5 exploit the regional variations available in

Table 9.3   **Estimates of the direct effect (older [55+] workers labor force participation)**

	Levels			5-year differences		
	Coefficient	SE	R^2	Coefficient	SE	R^2
Covariates: GDP per capita, GDP growth, % manufactures						
Employment young	0.809	0.301	0.738	−0.477	0.284	0.338
Unemployment young	0.298	0.329	0.888	0.618	0.292	0.325
Students	−1.981	0.350	0.964	−0.171	0.365	0.287
Employment prime	0.437	0.077	0.988	−0.271	0.077	0.679
Unemployment prime	−0.609	0.127	0.918	0.422	0.063	0.6346
No covariates						
Employment young	1.061	0.194	0.378	−0.378	0.282	0.058
Unemployment young	−1.176	0.168	0.477	0.391	0.314	0.048
Students	−1.736	0.370	0.311	0.108	0.346	0.006
Employment prime	0.195	0.265	0.014	−0.272	0.083	0.283
Unemployment prime	−0.900	0.052	0.911	0.354	0.084	0.289

Notes: SE = standard error.

Table 9.4   **Estimates of the direct effect (older [55+] workers labor force participation)**

	Levels			5-year differences		
	Coefficient	SE	R^2	Coefficient	SE	R^2
Covariates: GDP per capita, GDP growth, %manufactures						
Employment young	0.734	0.194	0.896	−0.456	0.170	0.674
Unemployment young	−0.143	0.260	0.905	0.611	0.190	0.517
Students	−1.653	0.300	0.953	−0.359	0.397	0.146
Employment prime	0.425	0.074	0.991	−0.221	0.087	0.434
Unemployment prime	−0.603	0.112	0.910	0.413	0.066	0.651
No covariates						
Employment young	0.828	0.251	0.199	0.548	0.178	0.220
Unemployment young	−1.296	0.129	0.652	0.493	0.224	0.121
Students	−1.271	0.261	0.324	−0.034	0.398	0.001
Employment prime	0.134	0.266	0.007	−0.184	0.088	0.131
Unemployment prime	−0.783	0.051	0.890	0.319	0.082	0.282

Notes: SE = standard error.

Table 9.5   **Estimates of the direct effect (older [55+] workers labor force participation) exploiting regional variation**

	Levels			5-year differences		
	Coefficient	SE	R^2	Coefficient	SE	R^2
Covariates: GDP per capita, GDP growth, %manufactures						
Employment young	0.541	0.238	0.290	0.017	0.134	0.073
Unemployment young	−0.460	0.093	0.541	0.044	0.120	0.047
Students	−0.403	0.245	0.709	−0.150	0.127	0.042
Employment prime	0.534	0.063	0.889	0.060	0.044	0.035
Unemployment prime	−0.343	0.099	0.486	−0.029	0.036	0.041
No covariates						
Employment young	0.682	0.231	0.217	0.061	0.083	0.002
Unemployment young	−0.618	0.139	0.280	−0.051	0.092	0.002
Students	−0.737	0.174	0.127	−0.025	0.078	0.000
Employment prime	0.444	0.099	0.130	0.051	0.045	0.009
Unemployment prime	−0.434	0.101	0.429	−0.010	0.032	0.001

Note: See table 9.3 notes.

Spain. We estimate the previous models (in levels and in five-year differences, with and without covariates) using information at the autonomous communities level. The results are consistent with the evidence reported previously. Once again, the evidence differs depending on the set of results analyzed (levels versus five-year differences), but the R^2 values suggest a better fit from the equation in levels. In this case, we can see that, regardless of the use of covariates, the evidence suggests a positive association between employment of the young and of prime age individuals and the labor force participation

Table 9.6   Estimates of the indirect effect (coefficients of the incentive variable $\bar{I}$)

	Levels			5-year differences		
	Coefficient	SE	R^2	Coefficient	SE	R^2
Covariates: GDP per capita, GDP growth, %manufactures						
LFP older	−0.005	0.000	0.984	−0.006	0.004	0.228
Employment young	−0.001	0.002	0.723	0.019	0.003	0.670
Unemployment young	−0.002	0.002	0.888	−0.025	0.003	0.750
Students	0.010	0.002	0.953	0.003	0.004	0.2875
Employment prime	−0.002	0.001	0.987	0.004	0.001	0.565
Unemployment prime	0.003	0.001	0.910	−0.004	0.002	0.398
No covariates						
LFP older	−0.002	0.000	0.286	−0.002	0.003	0.020
Employment young	0.002	0.001	0.104	0.011	0.004	0.214
Unemployment young	−0.002	0.001	0.100	−0.012	0.005	0.207
Students	0.011	0.001	0.9176	0.008	0.003	0.138
Employment prime	0.005	0.001	0.462	0.001	0.001	0.010
Unemployment prime	0.002	0.000	0.269	−0.001	0.002	0.010

Notes: Definitions of population groups: young = 20–24; prime = 25–54; ERA = earle retirement age; older = 55+. Assumptions: $\alpha = 2.5$ and $\gamma = 1$, pre-ERA wealth is set to zero and combining exit routes. SE = standard error; LFP = labor force participation.

of the old. The same is true for the unemployment rates of these two age groups. Moreover, the percentage of students in the young group is also negatively associated with the labor force participation of the old.

9.6.2   Effects from the Incentives to Retire

Table 9.6 presents the key result from the analysis both in levels and five-year differences. First, results vary substantially depending of the specification (levels or five years differences). Second, the Ibar variable is much more significant in the specification in levels (with and without covariates). Third, in the specification with covariates, the incentive variable works in the correct direction for the LFP of the old, and it is insignificant for the behavior of the young. On the other hand, in the specification with no covariates, the effect of the incentive variable indicates substitutability between the young and the old workers.

9.7   Conclusions

The Spanish pension system has witnessed relatively few changes during the period 1975 to 2005. In fact, only the changes in the pension formula introduced in 1985 are of some relevance. The recent reform (2002, further modified in 2007) introduced some important changes, but the key ones are to be phased out during several years, and a very large fraction of the active workers can still retire under the 1997 rules. This is particularly true for the change in the ERA (from sixty to sixty-one).

The most important changes have been the increase in the generosity of both the minimum and survival pensions, and the introduction (in 1990) of noncontributive pensions. However, these changes only affect the low-skilled workers, which are, in practice, scarcely substitutable by younger, and usually much more educated, workers. The pension incentives faced by the average and high earners, who are relatively more substitutable by the educated young, have remained relatively stable since 1985.

This defines a context of "unimportant" reforms (except, perhaps, for the 2006/2007 changes that we cannot study), which severely limits the variation in data. Either for this reason or because there is actually no correlation whatsoever between the two variables, we have found only some (very weak) evidence of a positive relationship between the employment level of the young and the exit from the labor force of older workers.

An interesting potential avenue for further analysis may be the consideration of the regional dimension of the Spanish labor market, which is likely to introduce substantial additional variation in the data.

Appendix
The Spanish Pension System since 1985

The rules governing the old age and survivors pensions in the RGSS in 1985 are described in the following. The changes introduced by the 1997 reform (R97) and the 2002 (A02) amendment will be illustrated as we go along. A summary of the basic technical aspects of the pre- and post-1997 systems can be found in table 9A.2.

Financing and Eligibility

The RGSS is a pure pay-as-you-go scheme. Contributions are a fixed proportion of covered earnings, defined as total earnings, excluding payments for overtime work, between a floor and a ceiling that vary by broadly defined professional categories. Currently, eleven categories are distinguished, each one with its own ceiling and floor for covered earnings. The current RGSS contribution rate is 28.3 percent, of which 23.6 percent is attributed to the employer and the remaining 4.7 percent to the employee. A tax rate of 14 percent is levied on earnings from overtime work.

Entitlement to an old age pension requires at least fifteen years of contributions. As a general rule, recipiency is conditional on having reached age sixty-five and is incompatible with income from any kind of employment requiring affiliation to the social security system.

Table 9A.1   Distribution of retirement pension awards in the 2002–2007 period

	2002		2003		2004		2005		2006		2007	
	No.	%	No.	%	No.	%	No.	%	No.	%	No.	%
Before 65	68,486	40.49	76,292	43.83	86,265	49.58	89,667	42.00	98,350	46.47	51,371	45.43
With penalties	53,786	31.8	57,228	32.87	58,740	33.76	57,609	26.98	59,655	28.18	30,178	26.69
≤ 60 years	28,668	16.95	30,504	17.52	28,767	16.54	27,727	12.99	25,588	12.09	11,643	10.30
61 years	6,092	3.6	6,419	3.69	7,850	4.51	8,145	3.81	9,217	4.35	4,823	4.27
62 years	8,192	4.84	7,226	4.15	7,098	4.08	8,058	3.77	8,964	4.24	4,682	4.14
63 years	5,238	3.1	8,171	4.69	7,273	4.18	7,190	3.37	8,789	4.15	4,699	4.16
64 years	5,596	3.31	4,908	2.82	7,752	4.46	6,489	3.04	7,097	3.35	4,331	3.83
Without penalty	2,836	1.68	3,398	1.95	4,491	2.58	4,943	2.32	4,834	2.28	2,598	2.30
Special 64	5,045	2.98	4,799	2.76	7,294	4.19	6,187	2.90	6,052	2.86	3,590	3.17
Partial	6,819	4.03	10,867	6.24	15,740	9.05	20,928	9.80	27,809	13.14	15,005	13.27
65+	100,653	59.51	97,788	56.17	87,710	50.42	123,839	58.00	113,311	53.53	61,710	54.57
Total	169,139	100.00	174,080	100.00	173,975	100.00	213,506	100.00	211,661	100.00	113,081	100.00

Source: Seguridad Social Española (www.seg-social.es).

Benefit Computation

When eligibility conditions are met, a retiring worker receives an initial monthly pension, P_t, equal to

$$P_t = \alpha_n BR_t,$$

where the benefit base (*base reguladora*) BR_t is a weighted average of covered monthly earnings over a reference period that consists of the last eight years before retirement until the 1997 reform. Therefore, the BR_t using eight years as the number of contributed years is calculated as:

$$\frac{1}{96}\left(\sum_{j=1}^{24} BC_{t-j} + \sum_{j=25}^{96} BC_{t-j} \frac{I_{t-25}}{I_{t-j}} \right)$$

where W_{t-j} and I_{t-j} are earnings and the consumer price index in the jth month before retirement. Pensions are paid in fourteen annual installments, hence the division by 112 in the previous formula. The replacement rate α_n depends on the age of the retirees and on the number of years of contribution. When age is below sixty, $\alpha_n = 0$ for all n. For age equal or greater than sixty-five, α_n is equal to

$$\alpha_n = \begin{cases} 0, & \text{if } n < 15, \\ .6 + .02(n - 15), & \text{if } 15 \leq n < 35. \\ 1, & \text{if } 35 \leq n. \end{cases}$$

In the case of early retirement, that is, for ages between sixty and sixty-five, α_n is determined by the previous formula multiplied by a penalization factor. The latter is equal to 0.60 at sixty, and increases of .08 each year, until reaching the value of 1.0 at age sixty-five.

$$BR_t = \frac{1}{112}\left(\sum_{j=1}^{24} W_{t-j} \sum_{j=25}^{96} W_{t-j} \frac{I_{t-25}}{I_{t-j}} \right)$$

Beginning in 1997, the number of reference years used for computing BR_t has been increased by one every year until 2003, to reach a total of fifteen years. The formula for computing α_n has been changed to the following:

$$\alpha_n = \begin{cases} 0, & \text{if } n < 15 \\ .5 + .03(n - 15), & \text{if } 15 \leq n < 25 \\ .8 + .02(n - 25), & \text{if } 25 \leq n < 35 \\ 1, & \text{if } 35 \leq n. \end{cases}$$

The penalization factors have, basically, remained the same, with an exception made for workers with forty or more years of contributions (details

Table 9A.2   Technical aspects of the system before and after the 1997-reform

	RGSS System	
	1985–1996	After 1997
A. Basic ingredients	*Provisions affecting all individuals*	
A1. The benefit base formula	$\dfrac{1}{96}\left(\sum_{j=1}^{24}\mathrm{BC}_{t-j}+\sum_{j=25}^{96}\mathrm{BC}_{t-j}\dfrac{I_{t-25}}{I_{t-j}}\right)$	$\dfrac{1}{180}\left(\sum_{j=1}^{24}\mathrm{BC}_{t-j}+\sum_{j=25}^{180}\mathrm{BC}_{t-j}\dfrac{I_{t-25}}{I_{t-j}}\right)$
Contribution period	8 years	15
Fraction actualized	6 years	13
A2. Fiscal system		
Income tax	(progressive)	id.
Labor tax	linear (regime and group specific)	id.
B. Replacement rates		
Function of contributive years	$\begin{cases}0, & \text{if } n<15,\\ .6+.02(n-15), & \text{if } 15\le n<35,\\ 1, & \text{if } 35\le n.\end{cases}$	$\begin{cases}0, & \text{if } n<15,\\ 5+.03(n-15), & \text{if } 15\le n<25,\\ .8+.02(n-25), & \text{if } 25\le n<35,\\ 1, & \text{if } 35\le n.\\ \quad\text{exception for } n\ge 40:\end{cases}$
Function of age	$\begin{cases}0, & \text{if } a<60,\\ .6+.8(a-60), & \text{if } 60\le a<65,\\ 1, & \text{if } 65\le a.\end{cases}$	$\begin{cases}0,\text{if } a<60,\\ .65+.07(a-60), & \text{if } 60\le a<65,\\ 1,\text{if } 65<a.\end{cases}$
C. Income tax exemptions	*Provisions affecting particular individuals*	
Max pension exempted	∝ Minimum wages	id.
Max income exempted	∝ Minimum wages	id.

D. Min./Max. contributions		
Min level of contribution	(specific for 12 group)	id.
Max level of contribution	(specific for 12 group)	id.
E. Min. and max. pensions		
Min. pension	$\propto$ minimum wages and family specific	id.
Max. pension	4.3 minimum wage (in 1995)	id.
F. Age bonuses	Yes (occupation specific)	id.
G. Survivor benefits	0.45×(benefit base)	
H. Dependant benefits	18, 22 (means tested)	18, 23 (means tested)
Eligibility	2 years contrib. last 10 years	2 out of last 15 years
Pension computation	$b_t = \max\{\min\{\bar{b}_t[n, e, BR(BC, I)], \bar{b}_t\}, \underline{b}_t\}$	

where $\underline{b}_t$ is the pension in A + B and

$\bar{b}_t$ and $\underline{b}_t$ are respectively the maximum and minimum pension.

2002 Amendment

Scheme for early retirement:

$$\begin{cases} 0, & \text{if } a < 61, \\ \alpha_n = 1 - \kappa(a - 60) & \text{if } 61 \le a < 65, \text{ where } \kappa = \\ 1 & \text{if } 65 \le a. \end{cases} \begin{cases} 0.08 & \text{if } n = 30 \\ 0.075 & \text{if } 31 \le n \le 34 \\ 0.07 & \text{if } 35 \le n < 37 \\ 0.065 & \text{if } 38 \le n \le\, < 39 \\ 0.06 & \text{if } 40 < n. \end{cases}$$

Premium for late retirement: $\alpha_n = 1 + 0.02(a - 65)$ if $n \ge 30$

Social Security contributions: No contributions for workers 65+, provided $n \ge 35$

Survivor benefits: $0.46 \times$ (benefit base)

in the next subsection). The A02 amendment allows for the possibility of α_n being greater that one when people are above sixty-five years of age, that is,

$$\alpha_n = 1 + .02(a - 65), \quad \text{if } 65 \leq a \text{ and } n \geq 35.$$

Outstanding pensions are fully indexed to price inflation, as measured by the consumer price index. Until 1986, pensions were also indexed to real wage growth.

Early Retirement

The normal retirement age is sixty-five but early retirement at age sixty is permitted under fairly common circumstances (sixty-one from the 2002 reform, but phased out to those who have not contributed before January, 1 1967). The replacement rate for early retirees is reduced by 8 percentage points for each year under age sixty-five. Starting from 1997, workers who retire after the age of sixty with forty or more contributive years are charged a penalty of only 7 percent for each year under age sixty-five. The 2002 amendment has modified further the rules determining the replacement rate. It now reads as follows:

$$\alpha_n = \begin{cases} 0, & \text{if } a < 61 \\ 1 - \kappa(a - 60), & \text{if } 61 \leq a < 65 \\ 1, & \text{if } 65 \leq a, \end{cases}$$

where

$$\kappa = \begin{cases} 0.08 & \text{if } n = 30, \\ 0.075 & \text{if } 31 \leq n \leq 34 \\ 0.07 & \text{if } 35 \leq n \leq 37 \\ 0.065 & \text{if } 38 \leq n \leq 39 \\ 0.06 & \text{if } 40 \leq n. \end{cases}$$

Unless a collective labor agreement prescribes mandatory retirement, individuals may continue working after age sixty-five. Before 2002 there were no incentives to work past age sixty-five. As mentioned, the 2002 legislation now allows for:

$$\alpha_n = 1 + .02(a - 65), \quad \text{if } 65 \leq a \text{ and } n \geq 35$$

and eliminates social security contributions for workers meeting the eligibility criteria for full normal retirement ($a \geq 65$ and $n \geq 35$) and who continue working. About 10 percent of the workers enrolled in the RGSS are actually exempt from reduction in the replacement rate in case of early retirement.

Maximum and Minimum Pension

Pensions are subject to a ceiling, legislated annually and roughly equal to the ceiling on covered earnings. The 2000 ceiling corresponds to about 4.3 times the minimum wage (*salario mínimo interprofesional,* or SMI) and about 1.6 times the average monthly earnings in the manufacturing and service sectors. If the initial old age pension, computed as in the preceding, is below a minimum, then the minimum pension is paid. The latter is also legislated annually. Other things being equal, minimum pensions are higher for those who are older than sixty-five or have a dependent spouse.

In Spain, the annual value of the minimum guaranteed is discretionarily chosen by the government. In 2005, 2.25 millions of contributory pensions topped up (which represents 28.4 percent of all pensions (21.7 percent in RGSS and 38 percent of RETA, 28.2 percent of all old age pensions (36.5 percent of widowhood). The percentage of RGSS retirees receiving a minimum pension has been declining steadily, from over 75 percent in the late 1970s to 27 percent in 1995. The ratio between the minimum old age pension and the minimum wage has been increasing steadily from the late 1970s (it was 75 percent in 1975) until reaching almost 100 percent in the early 1990s. In 2007, the ratio of the minimum benefit for pensioners above +65 (with a dependant spouse) to the minimum wage was 108, or 92 percent of the average pension. The real rate of growth of the minimum pension in 1990/2007 was 1.1 percent and 3.86 in the first term of Zapatero, 2004/2007.

Minimum pensions are also very popular for their redistributive properties: "atendiendo al principio de solidaridad que inspira la redistribución de rentas en el sistema de seguridad social español, los mecanismos establecidos son la garantía de pensión mínima en la esfera contributiva y las pensiones no contributivas" (Spanish Ministry of Labor and Social Affairs 2005).

Family Considerations

A pensioner receives a fixed annual allowance for each dependent child that is younger than 18 or disabled. In 2000, this allowance was equal to 48,420 pesetas for each child under 18, and to 468,720 pesetas (45 percent of the annualized minimum wage) for each disabled child.

Survivors (spouse, children, and other relatives) may receive a fraction of the benefit base of the deceased if the latter was a pensioner or died before retirement after contributing for at least 500 days in the last five years. The surviving spouse gets 45 percent of the benefit base of the deceased (46 percent after the 2002 amendment, a fraction that will be increased further in the forthcoming years). Such pension is compatible with labor income and any other old age or disability pension, but is lost is the spouse marries.

Each of the surviving children gets 20 percent of the benefit base until the age of eighteen (amount raised to 23 percent in 1997). An orphan who is sole beneficiary may receive up to 65 percent of the benefit base. If there are several surviving children, the sum of the pensions to the surviving spouse (if any) and the children cannot exceed 100 percent of the benefit base.

A Spanish peculiarity is the "pension in favor of family members." This pension entitles other surviving relatives (e.g., parents, grandparents, siblings, nephews, etc.) to 20 percent of the benefit base of the principal if they satisfy certain eligibility conditions (older than forty-five, do not have a spouse, do not have other means of subsistence, have been living with and depending economically upon the deceased for the last two years). To this pension, one may add the 45 percent survivors pension if there is no surviving spouse or eligible surviving children.

Rules for the Self-Employed

In this section, we sketch the main differences between the RGSS and the RETA. Beside differences in the Social Security tax rate and the definition of covered earnings, the people affiliated to RETA and who are not miners or sailors have no early retirement option.

While the Social Security tax rate is the same for the RETA and the general scheme (28.3 percent in 2000), covered earnings are computed differently, as the self-employed are essentially free to choose their covered earnings between a floor and a ceiling legislated annually. Not surprisingly, in light of the strong progressivity of Spanish personal income taxes, a suspiciously large proportion of self-employed workers report earnings equal to the legislated floor until they reach about age fifty to fifty-five. After that age, one observes a sudden increase in reported covered earnings. This behaviors exploits the "finite memory" in the formula for the calculation of the initial pension and appears to be fading after the 1997 legislation increased the number of years used in that calculation from eight to fifteen.

A crucial difference with respect to the general scheme is that, under the RETA, recipiency of an old age pension is compatible with maintaining the self-employed status. Other important provisions are the following: RETA only requires five years of contributions in the ten years immediately before the death of the principal in order to qualify for survivors pensions. Under RETA, the latter is 50 percent of the benefit base. If the principal was not a pensioner at the time of death, the benefit base is computed as the average of covered earnings over an uninterrupted period of five years chosen by the beneficiary among the last ten years before the death of the principal.

Rules for Central Government Employees (RCP)

We now describe briefly the main differences between the general scheme and the RCP, the pension fund for the employees of the central government.

Public servants are divided into five categories, labeled from A to E, corresponding loosely to decreasing school levels: A for college graduates, B for people holding certain kinds of college diplomas, C for high school graduates, D for junior high school diplomas, and E for individuals with lower education levels. For each of these categories, the budget law defines every year a theoretical Social Security wage, which is used to compute Social Security contributions and pensions. The implied wage scale has remained relatively constant since 1985. The top to bottom ratio never exceeded 2.5.

The basic monthly pension of a public servant who retires in month t after contributing for n years to RCP is computed as $P_t = \alpha_n \text{BR}_t$, where the dependence of α_n upon the numbers of years worked has changed frequently over time. For $n \geq 15$, the last table of proportionality factors, legislated in 1990, can be reasonably (but not exactly) approximated by:

$$\alpha_n = \min[1, 1 - 0.0366(35 - n)].$$

The differences with respect to the general scheme are various. First, while the entitlement to a pension still requires at least fifteen years of contributions, the replacement rate (the ratio of the pension to the benefit base) increases somewhat irregularly with seniority up to 100 percent after thirty-five years. So, for example, fifteen years of service give right to a pension equal to only 26.92 percent of the benefit base, against 60 percent of the general scheme. After thirty years, the same ratio has increased to 81.73 percent, against 90 percent for the general scheme.

Second, the benefit base is computed as a weighted average of covered earnings upon which the worker paid the contributions, with weights equal to the percentage of the career spent at each level, that is,

$$\text{BR}_t = \sum_i p_i H_{it},$$

where p_i is the fraction of the career spent on level i and H_{it} are the covered earnings corresponding to level i, as determined by the current law at time t.

Third, unlike the general scheme, the RCP imposes mandatory retirement at age sixty-five. Exceptions are made for a few special categories, such as university professors and judges. On the other hand, the RCP allows for early retirement at the age of sixty, without any penalty for public servants with at least thirty years of service (twenty for military personnel).

A fourth important difference with respect to the general scheme is compatibility between RCP pension recipiency and income from continuing to work. In a number of special cases, RCP pensioners are allowed to keep a public-sector occupation, as long as this does not provide them with a "regular flow of income" (for example, this is the case of members of legislative bodies). More important, the legislation allows RCP pensions to be cumulated with earnings from employment in the private sector.

References

Barrada, A. 1999. Public expenditure in social welfare in Spain from 1964 to 1995. Madrid: Fundación BBV.

Boldrin, M., J. Dolado, J. F. Jimeno, and F. Peracchi. 1999. The future of European pension systems. *Economic Policy* 29:289–320.

Boldrin, M., S. Jiménez-Martín, and F. Peracchi. 1999. Social security and retirement in Spain. In *Social security programs and retirement around the world,* ed. J. Gruber and D. Wise, 305–54. Chicago: University of Chicago Press.

———. 2001. *Pensions system and labor market in Spain.* Madrid: Fundación BBVA.

———. 2004. Micro-modeling of retirement behavior in Spain. In *Social security and retirement around the world: Microestimations,* ed. J. Gruber and D. Wise, 499–578. Chicago: University of Chicago Press.

Coile, C., and J. Gruber. 2000. Social security incentives for retirement. NBER Working Paper no. 7651. Cambridge, MA: National Bureau of Economic Research.

Gruber, J., and D. A. Wise. 1999. *Social security programs and retirement around the world.* Chicago: University of Chicago Press.

Instituto Nacional de Estadística (INE). 1995. *Projections of the Spanish population.* Madrid: INE.

Jiménez-Martín, S. 1999. Young's entry and older's exit from the labor force: What relationship, if any? Universidad Carlos III de Madrid. Unpublished Manuscript.

Kugler, A., J. F. Jimeno, and V. Hernanz. 2002. Employment consequences of restrictive permanent contracts: Evidence from Spanish labor market reforms. IZA Working Paper no. 657. Bonn, Germany: Institute for the Study of Labor.

Organization for Economic Cooperation and Development (OECD). 2005. OECD economic surveys: Spain. Paris: OECD.

Social Security, working histories continuous sample, since 2005. 2006. Available at: http://www.seg-social.es/Internet_1/Lanzadera/index.htm?URL=82.

Spanish Ministry of Labor and Social Affairs. 2005. Spanish strategy report regarding the future of the pension system. Madrid.

Stock, J. H., and D. A. Wise. 1990. Pensions, the option value of work, and retirement. *Econometrica* 58 (5): 1151–80.

University of Ottawa
Université d'Ottawa

Check Out / Prêt

29003005457800   16:33   2010/09/16

1. Social security programs and retirement around the
world : the relationship to youth employment / ed
39003026101468   Due / Dû: 10-12-15

Total 1 article(s).

Incentives to Retire, the Employment of the Old, and the Employment of the Young in Sweden

Mårten Palme and Ingemar Svensson

10.1 Introduction

The idea that unemployment among younger people in a society could be counteracted by inducing exit from the labor market of older workers has been used as an argument for providing generous social security programs. In times of high unemployment rates among younger workers, or in connection to firm closures, the public disability insurance program has been used in order to "save the jobs for the young." Creating jobs for the young has even been the explicit motivation for a special government program, the so-called Age-Shift Allowance, which provided more generous retirement options for an older worker requiring a younger worker to fill the position of the retired worker.

The validity of the argument that retirement of older workers increases the possibilities for younger workers of finding a job depends critically on two factors. First is the substitutability between younger and older workers in the production process. If older workers are not fully replaceable by younger ones, it will, of course, counteract any effect on the unemployment rate of younger workers. Second, retirement of older workers will decrease the production in the economy. This will, in turn, decrease the overall demand in the economy and ultimately the demand for younger workers.

In this paper, we empirically examine the hypothesis that the increasing generosity of the social security system has decreased labor force participation among the elderly. We then investigate whether labor force participation among older workers affects employment among younger workers.

Mårten Palme is professor of economics at Stockholm University. Ingemar Svensson is a senior researcher at the Division for Research at the Swedish National Social Insurance Board.

The paper is organized as follows. Section 10.2 gives an short description of the history of Sweden's pension schemes. Section 10.3 investigates policies based on the argument for providing job opportunities for the young. Section 10.4 analyzes to what extent program provisions affect employment of older workers. Section 10.5 presents the results from the analysis of the relation between labor force participation of older workers and employment of the young. Section 10.6 concludes.

10.2   A Short History of Swedish Pensions

In this section, we give a summary description of the different components of pension programs in Sweden and their development. More details pertaining to the period of our employment data series and a descriptive analysis of the relationship between program provisions and the labor market participation of older workers are provided in section 10.4.

10.2.1   The Public Old Age Pension System

The first public pension system was legislated in 1913 and implemented in January 1914.[1] The process leading to this decision started in 1884. The law covered old age, disability, as well as survivor's pensions. The benefit had two components, a funded, contribution-defined part and a means-tested part. The system covered all citizens, not just workers like some other pension systems at that time.

In 1937, the funded and contribution-defined pensions were replaced by a basic pension (a fixed amount) financed according to the pay-as-you-go principle, and, in 1938, the means-tested benefits were raised and differentiated according to living costs in different municipalities.

The next major reform was implemented in 1948. The basic pension was significantly raised, and the relative importance of the means-tested component was reduced, and it was transformed to a means-tested housing allowance. The pension costs with these changes were expected to increase by more than 100 percent. Before the reform, a significant share of pensioners, especially in the major cities, was still dependent on poverty relief from the municipalities. The goal of the reform was to more or less eliminate poverty among pensioners.

From 1949, the basic pension has been price indexed. Between 1953 and 1968, the real value of the basic pension was also raised, thus giving all pensioners a share of the rapidly rising incomes of the working population during this period.

Even with these improvements of pension benefits, the replacement rates in the 1950s were low, except for low-income workers. Other small groups with significant replacement rates (around 65 percent) were government employees and some white-collar workers in the private sector, who had

1. The account until the early 1960s is based on Elmér (1960) and Molin (1965).

earnings-related pension insurance. For these reasons, the issue of how to supplement the national basic pension with some kind of earnings-related pension insurance became important on the policy agenda. After a series of government investigations and reports, starting in 1947, and after a referendum in 1957 and an extraordinary election in 1958, the decision was finally taken in 1959 about the design of the supplementary pension system—the ATP scheme.

It was a mandatory system covering all employees. Self-employed could choose to stay outside the system. Basically the system was pay-as-you-go, but during the first decades, significant funds were built up in order not to depress national savings. Contributions to the new system were paid on earnings starting in 1960, and the first pensions were paid in 1963. The benefit was based on an average of the best fifteen years of earnings. Initially, a full pension benefit required earnings above a threshold of one basic amount for twenty years.[2] From cohort 1915, the required number of years was then raised by one year for each successive cohort up to thirty years. The implication of this transition rule was that until 1980, it was not possible to get a full ATP pension benefit, and, until 1990, it was necessary to have earnings above the threshold each year between 1960 and retirement to receive a full benefit.

After 1968, the real value of the basic pension was kept approximately constant, but in 1969 a new benefit was introduced—the pension supplement—in order to increase pension benefits for individuals without any or with only low ATP benefits. Thus, also during the 1970s, the minimum pensions were rising just like the ATP benefits were due to the maturing of the ATP scheme during the 1960s and 1970s.

During the 1990s, the major parties in the parliament agreed about a reform to replace the basic pension and the ATP schemes with a new scheme combining a funded contribution-defined part with a pay-as-you-go contribution-defined part. The contribution rate for the former is 2.5 percent of earnings and for the latter 16 percent. These earnings-related benefits are supplemented by a guarantee pension for residents in Sweden, obtainable from the age of sixty-five.

The reform was legislated in stages between 1994 and 2001. The new rules for pension entitlements were implemented in 1999, and the first pensions from the new scheme were paid in 2003 (except for some early pensions during 2001 and 2002).

10.2.2   Occupational Pension Insurance

Already before the introduction of the public pension scheme in 1914, central government employees had significant pension benefits, financed by contributions divided between the employer and the employee. In the early

---

2. The basic amount is closely linked to the Consumer Price Index and was introduced in the ATP reform as a means for the price indexing of benefits and pension entitlements.

twentieth century, similar schemes were also introduced for local government employees.

Also, in the private sector, some employees were covered by voluntary pension insurance provided by the employer. Until the end of the 1950s, the coverage was however low, especially among blue-collar workers, and the schemes often provided low benefits. Still, in the beginning of the 1950s, an occupational pension solution with better coverage was considered both by the Employer's Confederation and the major unions as an alternative to a national supplementary pension scheme. In 1954, the Employer's Confederation proposed a system organized through collective contracts, with fees paid entirely by the employers and without any involvement from the state (Molin 1965, 192). At this time, the Swedish Trade Union Confederation (LO) had however opted for a mandatory public system.

In 1959, the same year as the ATP supplementary pension reform was decided by the Swedish parliament, negotiations started between the Employer's Confederation and the major unions for white-collar workers in the manufacturing sector about how to adjust the existing employer-provided pension insurances to the new situation. The result was a new occupational scheme, the ITP scheme, to be implemented in 1960. Consequently, from 1960, most white-collar workers in the private sector were covered both by the new national ATP scheme and the ITP scheme. The ITP agreement provided additional benefits to ATP and had a much higher ceiling than the public supplementary pension scheme. The retirement age also was lower than sixty-seven, which still applied to the ATP scheme. Men could retire at age sixty-five with a benefit of 65 percent of the final salary. The pension age of women was originally sixty but was later raised to sixty-five.

In the beginning of the 1960s, the retirement age within the occupational schemes for government employees was also below sixty-seven—between sixty and sixty-five depending on occupation. With the introduction of the ATP scheme, a rule for coordination was introduced in both schemes for government employees: the ATP pension was deducted from the benefits provided by the occupational schemes, that is, the occupational schemes were changed to give supplements to the growing public ATP pensions.

Finally, beginning in July 1973, blue-collar workers in the private sector also were covered by an occupational scheme negotiated between the Employer's Confederation and the Swedish Trade Union Confederation (LO). This new STP scheme provided benefits between age sixty-five and the national retirement age of sixty-seven until the latter was changed to sixty-five in 1976. In addition to this decrease of retirement age, the scheme provided lifelong benefits in addition to the public pensions just like the other three large occupational schemes with about the same replacement rate (10 percent). In this case, however, there were no benefits replacing earnings above the ceiling within the ATP scheme.

The four large negotiated occupational schemes still remain in place but have undergone several revisions since their introduction. In 1977, the ITP scheme and, in 1991, the scheme for central government employees got supplementary-funded and contribution-defined components. During the last decade, there has been a general transition from defined-benefit pay-as-you-go schemes to funded defined-contribution schemes.

10.2.3   Disability Pensions

As mentioned at the outset, the 1913 pension law also contained regulations for a disability (invalidity) pension. Until 1948, the old age and disability pensions were closely related in terms of financing and benefit rules. The difference was the eligibility criterion—age respective invalidity. An individual was entitled to pension benefit before the age of sixty-seven if his or her working ability permanently was reduced by at least two-thirds due to sickness or disability.

With the 1948 reform, the benefit rules for old age and invalidity pensions became significantly different. While the means-tested component within old age pensions was significantly reduced, the main part of the disability pension was still means tested. The implication of these rules was that a disabled person could earn labor income up to one-third of normal earnings of an individual of his education and place of residence without losing the right to disability pension, but the benefit was reduced accordingly. In 1948, a temporary disability benefit (*sjukbidrag*) was also introduced for individuals who had lost their working ability for a significant amount of time but not permanently.

Means testing as a way of providing partial benefits for individuals whose working ability was not completely lost was replaced by fixed categories of partial benefits in the next major reform of disability insurance, which was implemented in 1963. This reform also coordinated the disability rules within the basic pension scheme and the new supplementary ATP pension scheme. From 1963, the law required that at least half of the individual's working ability was lost and partial benefits of one-third and two-thirds were introduced for cases with some remaining working ability. As previously described, a full ATP pension by the old age pension transition rules was not possible until 1980. By the disability pension rules, however, an individual could receive a considerable supplementary ATP pension already in the beginning of the 1960s because "assumed pension points" from the year of pensioning until normal retirement age were added to pension points based on actual earnings. Thus, the economic incentives to retire with disability pension changed quickly with the 1963 reform and the introduction of the ATP supplementary scheme.

The next reform was implemented in July 1970, implying softer eligibility requirements for elderly workers. In the application of the law, workers aged sixty-three or more were initially considered as elderly, but the age limit was lowered to sixty in 1975. The initiative to this reform came from the Swedish Trade Union Confederation (LO). The proposal was to increase the possibilities to take labor market reasons into account in addition to the medical condition, and also to decrease the medical requirements when deciding about disability pension for elderly workers.[3] The purpose was to provide better income security for elderly workers displaced by structural change and for elderly workers with demanding working conditions. In the 1970 reform, the lowest partial benefit was also raised from one-third to one-half of full pension.

In July 1972, the eligibility criteria were extended even more. From this date, elderly long-term unemployed could receive a disability pension without any impairment of working ability due to sickness or disability.[4] The original age limit of sixty-three was lowered to sixty in January 1974.

Already, in 1979, the government expressed concern about the fact that male employment was decreasing in ages above sixty and that the employment of women in these ages did not increase in the same rate as for younger women. A commission was appointed to investigate what could be done in terms of labor market regulations, labor market policy, working conditions, pension policy, marginal tax rates and marginal effects from the benefit systems, and the attitudes to work at high ages to increase employment among elderly workers.[5] The commission delivered its report in 1983. No specific policy proposals to promote employment of the elderly were put forward. The economic recession and the high unemployment rates in all ages at that time were stated as motives for this decision.

The growing use of labor market reasons within the disability pension system, well beyond the original social reasons for the rules, was, however, the subject of growing concern during the 1980s, and, finally, these rules were abolished in October 1991. This policy was part of a series of measures to extend the traditional "work principle" within Swedish labor market policy also to sickness and disability insurance.[6] However, it was still possible to take labor market considerations into account in decisions about disability pension for workers above age sixty according to the rules introduced in July 1970. In January 1997, these special rules for elderly workers also were abolished.

In 2003, a major revision of disability insurance was implemented, in part due to necessary adjustments because of the reform of old age pensions. The rules for calculation of the earnings-related benefit that had been in place since 1963 were replaced with new rules meant to insure current income

3. To some extent, this was true also for nonelderly workers.
4. From this date, the term "disability pension" is, of course, misleading because the system for elderly workers now is a combined disability and unemployment insurance. After the 1963 reform, the system was in Swedish called *Förtidspension,* which literally translated means "early retirement pension."
5. See SOU (1983:62, 11–12).
6. See Prop. 1988/89:150. Prop. 89/90:62 and SfU 1989/90:12.

rather than historical income. Disability insurance was transferred from the pension to the sickness insurance scheme. The reform also introduced different rules for individuals aged nineteen to twenty-nine and thirty to sixty-four. These changes were made to emphasize that disability insurance was not meant to provide lifelong benefits, especially not for the young.

10.3   Job Opportunities for the Young as an Argument in Swedish Pension Policy

Ever since 1884, the pension system has been subject of more or less constant analysis, debate, and reform. Reforms of both the old age and disability pension systems have been prepared in government committees, normally with members from all the major parties in the parliament and often including ambitious empirical research. The schemes and reforms have often also been the subject of heated political debate. At two occasions, in 1936 and 1958, pension policy was also major issues in the elections.

The arguments that have been important are those about affordability considering other needs, coverage, funded versus nonfunded, and voluntary versus mandatory systems and the principles and details of benefit calculation. Reforms have been driven mainly by concerns about income security and income standard of older workers and pensioners and the effects of different options on the economy.

As far as we know, the argument that retirement of older workers should be facilitated in order to increase job opportunities for the young have been put forward among legislators only on two occasions in Sweden: in the 1930s and in the 1990s. On both occasions, the economy was severely depressed, with high unemployment rates, especially among young workers. During the 1990s, long-term unemployment peaked in 1996 (except for male young workers where the peak was already in 1993) and then decreased gradually until year 2000.

In the 1930s, the idea of replacing old by young workers was put forward by some members of the parliament from the Conservative party headed by professor Gösta Bagge (Molin 1965, 8).[7] The proposal was that the state should subsidise employers to provide pensions for workers above age sixty-five. In 1935, a liberal member of the parliament proposed mandatory supplementary pensions for all private sector employees, again with decreasing unemployment among young workers as one of the purposes (Molin 1965, 8–9). Neither of these proposals found support in the parliament.

In 1998, the Social Democratic government introduced a new program among the many active labor market programs tried during the 1990s: the Generational Switching Allowance. The scheme made it possible for

---

7. Gösta Bagge was professor of Social Policy and Economics at *Stockholms Högskola* and leader of the Conservative party from 1935 to 1944.

a worker aged at least sixty-three to retire with a benefit corresponding to the unemployment benefit if the employer agreed to employ a long-term unemployed individual aged twenty to thirty-five. The employer was also required to contribute to the financing with 25 percent. Application for the allowance was only possible during 1998. Only around 840 individuals used the allowance.

Neither the proposal from the Conservatives in the 1930s, nor the Generational Switching Allowance was about major program provisions of old age or disability insurance like retirement ages or other eligibility criteria. They were specific subsidies meant to be temporary.

However, it seems clear that labor market conditions for the young due to the business cycle had an impact on policy. The decision to abolish pure labor market reasons in disability insurance was taken not in 1983, when there was a serious recession and the Swedish industry was subject to large-scale structural change, but in 1989, when there was an exceptional boom in the Swedish economy.

Also, the idea that early retirement of the old might improve job opportunities among the young apparently has some appeal among the general population. The idea of a Generational Switching Allowance was put forward in 1997 by a government commission for the review of youth policies in Sweden.[8] The commission organized local meetings with around 1,800 young Swedes and also ordered a survey among the population aged fifteen to twenty-five. A decrease of the retirement age was a frequent proposal at the meetings and also found support in the survey. The commission argued against a general decrease of retirement ages with the argument that such measures in Denmark, Holland, and France has not helped to reduce unemployment, but argued for retirement through generational switching and also for subsidized career breaks if the employer gives job to an unemployed worker.[9]

10.4   Program Provisions and the Employment of Older Workers

As in most other industrialized economies, the increasing female labor force participation and the decreasing labor force participation of older male workers are two of the main changes of Sweden's labor force in recent decades. Figure 10.1 shows the development of labor force participation rates in different age groups for male and female workers, respectively. An apparent change in the labor force is the long-term decline of the share of the male group aged between sixty and sixty-four as well as a decline in male

8. See SOU (1997:40).
9. Subsidized career breaks were introduced in twelve municipalities in 2002 and for the whole country in 2005. An evaluation of this policy is in Nordström Skans and Lindqvist (2005).

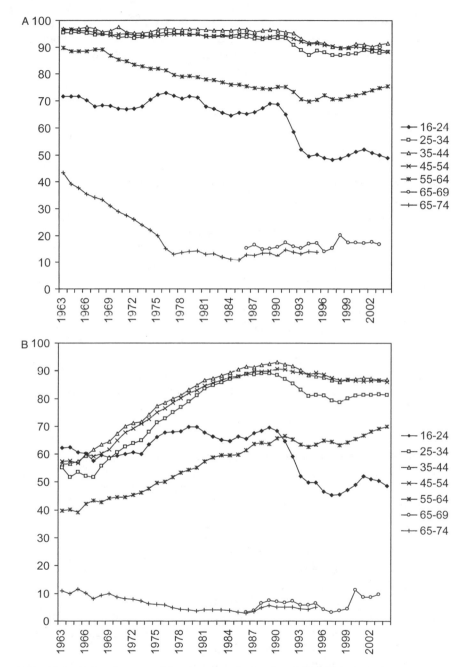

Fig. 10.1   Labor force participation rates in Sweden 1963–2006: *A*, Males by different age groups; *B*, Females by different age groups

Source: Various reports of the Swedish Labor Force Survey, provided by Statistics Sweden.

labor force participation of those older than age sixty-five in the 1960s and early 1970s. An apparent candidate for the explanation to this development is the build up of the Swedish income security system since the early 1960s. In this section, we investigate how these changes affected economic incentives to leave the labor market.

10.4.1   The Old Age Public Pension System and Occupational Pensions

The introduction and maturity of the supplementary pension program (ATP) and the lowering of the normal retirement age are the two most important changes for old age pensions in Sweden during the period under study. Because white-collar workers in the private sector as well as employees in the public sector did have negotiated pension plans before ATP was implemented, the ATP reform did primarily affect blue-collar workers in the private sector. This development is revealed in figure 10.2, which shows the development of average pension benefit and different pension sources by year of birth for cohorts retired between 1955 and 1982, estimated from a cross section in 1983. Each panel shows one of the four occupational pension groups.

For the earlier cohorts, the sampling error is large, and there is probably an upward bias due to differential mortality by income. Still the results in figure 10.2 reveal a clear pattern. For former employees in the public sector, the introduction of the supplementary pension program is to a large extent crowded out by lower occupational pension benefits. This is because of the rules for coordination between the ATP and occupational schemes described in section 10.2. For former white-collar workers in the private sector, there is much less of "crowding out" from the occupational pension scheme. However, the largest relative improvement is for blue-collar workers in the private sector, who before the introduction of ATP in general had no or very low occupational pension benefits.

Also, the level of the basic pension has increased since the early 1960s. Figure 10.3 shows this development for both the old age and the disability pension benefits. Most of the increase can be attributed to the introduction of the special supplement benefit, which is a benefit targeted at pensioners with no or very low supplementary benefit. The divergence of the two graphs in figure 10.3 represents the introduction of a double special supplement for the disability pension benefit.

Table 10.1 shows normal, early, and delayed retirement ages in the national old age pension system. Before the introduction of ATP, pension could only be claimed from age sixty-seven. When the income-related ATP scheme was introduced, both the basic and the supplementary part became accessible starting from age sixty-three with a 0.6 percent actuarial reduction for each month of early withdrawal before age sixty-seven. In 1976, the normal retirement age was decreased to sixty-five and the actuarial reduction lowered to 0.5 percent per month. However, as described in section 10.2, the

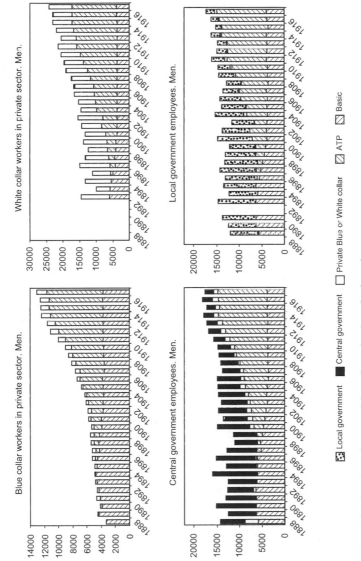

Fig. 10.2 Levels and composition of pension benefits by cohort

Notes: Each panel shows one of the main occupational pension groups. Birth for cohorts retired between 1955 and 1982 are estimated from a cross section in 1983.

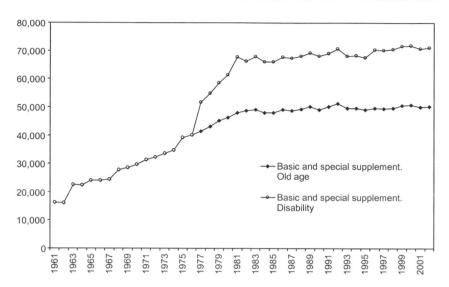

Fig. 10.3   Level of basic pension benefit from the national pension scheme

Table 10.1   Normal, early, and delayed retirement ages along with actuarial
                    adjustment factors in the national old age pension system

Period	NR	ER	UR	Reduction per month, % of benefit	Increase per month, % of benefit
1914–1962	67				
1963–1976 (June)	67	63	72	0.6	0.6
1976 (July)–1990 (June)	65	60	70	0.5	0.5
1990 (July)–1997	65	60	70	0.5	0.7
1998–	65	61	70	0.5	0.7

Note: NR = normal retirement; ER = early retirement; UR = delayed retirement.

change in the normal retirement age did only affect workers not covered by
the main occupational pension programs, such as farmers and homemak-
ers. White-collar workers in the private sector had an agreement on normal
retirement age at sixty-five already in 1960 and public-sector workers' retirement ages between sixty and sixty-five, depending on type of occupation.
Finally, blue-collar workers in the private sector had an agreement in 1973
on normal retirement age at sixty-five.

The effect of the changes in the normal retirement ages is apparent in
figure 10.1, showing the development of labor force participation rates in
different age groups. The graph for the group aged between sixty-five and
seventy-four declines rapidly in the 1960s and early 1970s, that is, during the
period when the lower retirement ages were introduced in different sectors

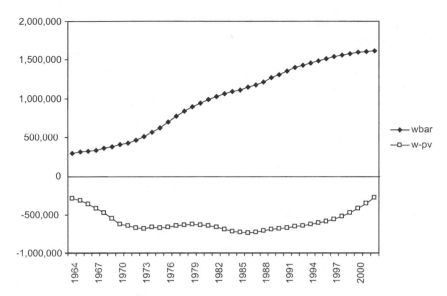

Fig. 10.4   **The development social security wealth and social security wealth minus peak value**

of the economy. After 1976, the labor force participation rate has remained on a very low level in this age group.

The introduction of an income-related supplementary pension system, the increase of the minimum pension level, and the lowering of retirement ages are likely to have two contradictory effects on incentives to remain on the labor market. First, for at least some workers, because the benefit levels are substantially increased, it will create a wealth effect toward earlier exit from the labor market, provided that leisure is a normal good. The lowering of the normal retirement ages had similar effect. Second, because the supplementary pension system, as opposed to the prereform basic pension, is related to the contributions made to the scheme the gain from remaining in the labor force increases during the years of maturity of the ATP scheme. Both the basic and the ATP schemes also include an actuarial reduction for those who start to claim benefits before the normal retirement age and an actuarial addition for those who delay retirement. This will create an incentive to remain in the labor force.

The resulting time series indexes of the average incentives faced by persons who retire in each year are shown in figure 10.4. This graph summarizes all changes in the social security system described in the preceding. It has, as expected, an upward trend in social security wealth illustrating the greater incentives to retire earlier through an income effect from the various reforms in the recent decades. The growth of the economy also contributed to the increasing trend for social security wealth. But also the gain to postponing retirement, measured by the peak value, increases, at least in the beginning of the period.

To sum up, we have two contradictory effects over time on incentives to remain on the labor market, and, as figure 10.1 reveals, the trend for labor force participation of men and women go in the opposite direction. For reasons explained in the next subsection, there is also reason to believe that the decreasing labor force participation of elderly male workers is related to the provisions within the disability scheme rather than to the incentives created by the old age pension scheme.

Our conclusion from these facts is that it is hard to find any connection between the time series of incentives to retire and the labor force participation of elderly workers. This is, however, not contradicting our previous results where we find significant effects with the expected signs of incentives on retirement behavior in a cross section of individuals, where there are many sources of identifying variation in the data (Palme and Svensson 2004). Also, the result is consistent with the cross-country analysis in Gruber and Wise (1999). The incentives from the earnings-related old age pension scheme with actuarial adjustments for early and postponed retirement help keep the average retirement age through the old age pension pathway comparatively high (it has been around sixty-five since the middle of the 1970s, i.e., close to the normal retirement age).

10.4.2   The Disability Insurance Program

In section 10.2, we described how the eligibility rules for disability pension changed significantly in 1970 and how the system was transformed into a combined sickness and unemployment insurance in 1972. The 1972 rules were abolished in 1991 and the 1970 rules in 1997. This development is summarized in table 10.2.

Figure 10.5 shows the available data on the number of new disability pensions per year during the period 1961 to 2006. There was a very big increase in connection with the 1970 reform. There was again an increase in the

Table 10.2   Eras of different eligibility rules in the Disability Insurance

Period	Medical reasons	Possibility to take labor market and social conditions into account	Favorable rules for older workers	Labor market reasons
–1962	Yes	Very small	No	No
1963–1970 (June)	Yes	Some	No	No
1970 (July)–1972 (June)	Yes	Yes	Yes, aged 63–66	No
1972 (July)–1974 (June)	Yes	Yes	Yes, aged 63–66	Yes, aged 63–66
1974 (July)–1976 (June)	Yes	Yes	Yes, aged 60–66	Yes, aged 60–66
1976 (July)–1991 (Sept)	Yes	Yes	Yes, aged 60–64	Yes, aged 60–64
1991 (Oct)–1996	Yes	Yes	Yes, aged 60–64	No
1997–	Yes	Very small	No	No

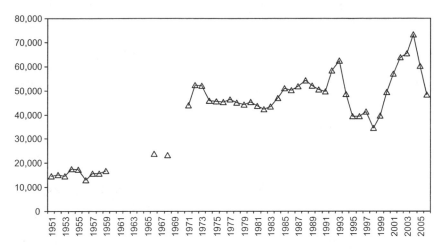

Fig. 10.5   Annual number of new disability pensions, 1951–2006

middle of the 1980s. This coincided with a more extensive use of the pure labor market reasons introduced in the 1972 law. The use of these reasons peaked in 1985 when around 20 percent of the new pensions were for reasons without any medical condition. After 1990, the rates have fluctuated a lot, but the average number of new pensioners has been on the same level as during the late 1980s.

Figure 10.6 shows that the growth of the stock of disability pensioners among males aged fifty-five to sixty-four corresponds closely to the growth of males outside the labor force in the same age group in the period 1968 to 1990. Although there is some mismatch between these series due to partial disability benefits, the correspondence between these series of data motivates the conclusion that disability pension was the dominating pathway to retirement below age sixty-five during these decades.

After the eligibility rules for labor market reasons were abolished in 1991, the task of providing unemployment insurance was taken over by the occupational systems. Between 1991 and 1994, the number of individuals in the age group fifty-five to sixty-four having occupational pension benefits as their main income source increased from 1.3 to almost 4 percent, thus accounting for a significant part of the gap between the stock of disability pensioners and the total number of individuals outside the labor force that appeared at that time according to figure 10.6.[10] After 2002, the number of men on occupational pension decreased, but the number of women remained around 4 percent still in 2005.

After 1998, the labor force participation among males aged fifty-five to

10. This is defined as at least 80 percent of total annual income from work or transfer payments. The estimate is from our own calculations on income statistics provided by Statistics Sweden (the LISA database).

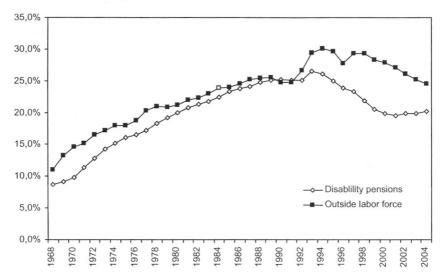

Fig. 10.6   Share with disability pension (including partial pensions) and share outside the labor force, males aged 55–64

sixty-four has increased significantly. This change coincides in time with the abolition of the special eligibility rules for elderly workers introduced in 1970. As we have shown elsewhere (Karlstrom, Palme, and Svensson 2008), at least initially there was no positive effect on the number of individuals actually working from this reform. In the first few years after the reform, the number of long-term unemployed and the number of individuals with long sickness benefit periods increased. The first and often also the second of these groups are included in the labor force along with those who are actually working.

10.5   Is there a Relation between Employment of Older and Younger Workers?

To investigate the potential relation between employment of older and younger workers, let us first take a look at the development of the aggregate series. Figure 10.7 shows labor force participation rates for male and female worker aged between fifty-five and sixty-four as well as between sixteen and twenty-four, respectively, along with unemployment rates for the younger age group from 1963 and onward. The main changes in the income security programs are marked with vertical lines in the figure. The changes in the old age pension program, marked with solid lines, include the introduction of the supplementary pension program in 1963 and the decrease in the normal retirement age from age sixty-seven to sixty-five in 1976.

The development of labor force participation for the age group fifty-five to sixty-five shows a slight positive trend from around 65 percent in the early 1960s to almost 75 percent by the end of the period under study. The driving force behind this increase is the rapid overall increase of female labor force participation in the Swedish economy. There is no apparent effect of any of the changes in the income security programs marked in figure 10.7 on the labor force participation rates of the older workers. However, such changes may be masked by the overall increase in the female labor force participation.

For the labor force participation rate of the younger age group, there is a sharp drop in the economic recession in the early 1990s, when it drops from around 70 to around 50 percent. A similar shift can be seen for the unemployment rate for this age group. However, as opposed to the labor force participation rate, the unemployment rate decreases to a lower level after the initial increase, although the postrecession level is substantially higher than the stable level before the recession. The main reason behind the lower labor force participation rate for the young age group is that the education programs introduced in the recession tended to be permanent as well as a major build up of higher education starting in the early 1990s.

There is no apparent covariation between the development of labor force participation of the older workers and the unemployment rate of the young. Although the increase in youth unemployment in the 1970s is accompanied with a slight increase in labor force participation of the elderly, the decline in youth unemployment in the 1980s was not accompanied by a decline in labor force participation of the elderly. Also, the huge increase in youth unemployment in the early 1990s was apparently driven by the economic recession rather than changes in labor force participation of the older workers.

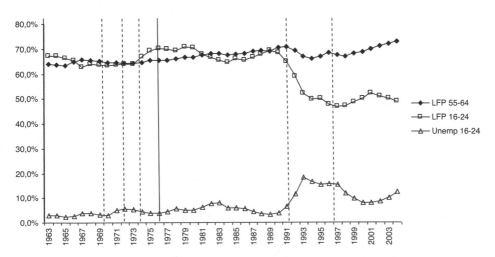

Fig. 10.7   LFP of older workers, LFP of younger workers, unemployment of the young, and major changes in the income security systems: Males and females pooled

Figure 10.8 shows the same development as in figure 10.7, but now the data is confined to male workers in order to exclude the effect of the trend in female labor force participation. The development of the labor force participation rate for the older age group can be interpreted as an effect of changes in the income security programs: the decline starting in the early 1970s follows the more generous eligibility rules implemented in the early 1970s. The slight increase follows in particular the abolition of the special eligibility rules for older workers in the Disability Insurance. Again, it is not possible to interpret the changes in the development of youth unemployment to be driven by changes in labor force participation of the old.

The relation between labor force participation rates of older workers and unemployment rates in younger age groups are further investigated in figure 10.9, which shows labor force participation rates for the age group fifty-five to sixty-five, along with the development of the unemployment rate for young workers aged sixteen to twenty-five, as well as that of prime aged workers aged between twenty-five and fifty-four. To facilitate the interpretation of covariations, the unemployment rate is measured on the right-hand scale, and the labor force participation rate is shown on the left-hand one.

The results in figure 10.9 shows that the unemployment rate among prime aged workers is much less volatile than that of younger workers. Also, the trend toward an increased youth unemployment starting in the early 1960s until the early 1980s is not present for the prime aged workers. Thus, the trend toward a higher labor force participation rate among older workers was not reflected in a corresponding trend of higher unemployment rate among the prime aged. The development since the early 1990s is also hard to interpret as supporting the view of a covariation between the labor force participation of the old and the unemployment rates of the younger age groups.

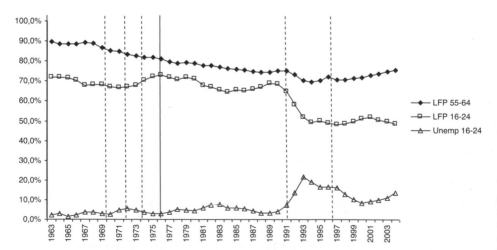

Fig. 10.8   LFP of older workers, LFP of younger workers, unemployment of the young, and major changes in the income security systems: Males

Figure 10.10 shows the development of labor force participation rates for the three main age groups. The slight increase in labor force participation rates for both older workers and the prime aged can be attributed to the very large increase in female labor force participation. Again, it is not possible to interpret the data as the development of labor force participation of the old are related to that of any of the other groups.

Another way to study the relation between labor force participation of the old and employment of younger workers is through regression analysis. We depart from the specification:

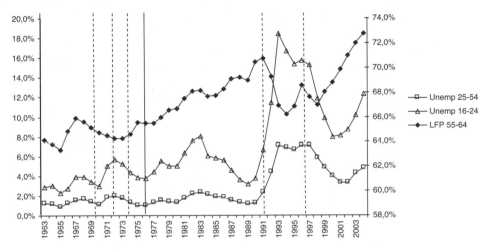

Fig. 10.9   LFP of older workers, unemployment rates of younger and prime age workers: Males and females pooled

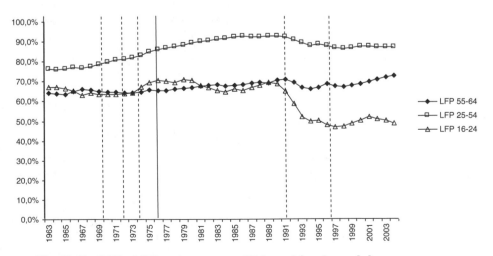

Fig. 10.10   LFP of different age groups: Males and females pooled

(1) $$U_{\text{young},t} = \alpha + \beta \text{LFP}_{\text{old},t} + \delta X_t + \varepsilon_t,$$

where $U_{\text{young},t}$ measures the unemployment rate in the young age group, $\text{LFP}_{\text{old},t}$ is the labor force participation rate among older workers, X_t other observable characteristics also likely to affect the unemployment rate of the young, and, finally, ε_t measuring unobservable characteristics and functional form deficiencies affecting the dependent variable.

Table 10.3 shows the results where different specifications of equation (1) have been estimated when the data on males and females have been pooled. The upper panel of table 10.3 shows the results from specifications where the vector of controls has been excluded and the lower panel from those where it has been included. Each column represents one outcome variable. For the young age group, we have three different outcomes: the unemployment rate (UE), the employment rate (EMP), and the share in schooling (SCH). For the prime aged group, we have only two outcomes: the unemployment rate (UE) and employment (EMP). Table 10.4 shows the corresponding results to the upper panel of table 10.3 for males and females separately, that is, when controls are excluded, and table 10.5 shows the results separately for males and females corresponding to the lower panel of table 10.3, that is, when controls are included in the specification.

Table 10.3   Direct relationship between the elderly labor force participation and the employment and unemployment of young and prime age individuals (men and women combined)

	Youth 16–24			Prime 25–54	
	UE	EMP	SCH	UE	EMP
Levels	0.129	–0.579	0.698	0.112	0.337
	(0.024)	(0.129)	(0.080)	(0.020)	(0.059)
3-year lag on elderly employment	0.135	–0.680	0.741	0.129	0.227
	(0.025)	(0.128)	(0.073)	(0.021)	(0.069)
5-year difference	–0.136	1.612	–0.728	–0.222	1.058
	(0.146)	(0.440)	(0.234)	(0.105)	(0.164)
5-year log difference	–1.001	1.625	–1.001	–3.578	0.720
	(0.470)	(0.465)	(0.470)	(1.961)	(0.105)
	With controls				
Levels	0.225	0.043	0.236	0.153	0.655
	(0.159)	(0.722)	(0.424)	(0.142)	(0.292)
3-year lag on elderly employment	0.374	–1.541	1.071	0.372	–0.326
	(0.087)	(0.395)	(0.213)	(0.072)	(0.189)
5-year difference	–0.048	1.231	–0.474	–0.096	1.052
	(0.096)	(0.338)	(0.197)	(0.053)	(0.172)
5-year log difference	0.506	0.999	–0.789	–1.397	0.665
	(1.022)	(0.242)	(0.454)	(0.968)	(0.089)

Notes: UE = the share of the population unemployed; EMP = the share of the population in work; SCH = the share of the population in school and not in work. Standard errors are in parentheses.

Table 10.4   **Regression results on the direct effect between labor force participation of older workers and employment of younger workers (males and females separately, no controls)**

	Youth 16–24			Prime 25–54	
	UE	EMP	SCH	UE	EMP
Levels					
Men	–0.291	1.375	–1.096	–0.241	0.549
	(0.041)	(0.182)	(0.123)	(0.036)	(0.074)
Women	0.092	–0.362	0.724	0.098	1.030
	(0.020)	(0.131)	(0.078)	(0.019)	(0.080)
3-year lag on elderly employment					
Men	–0.240	1.312	–1.090	–0.219	0.529
	(0.047)	(0.185)	(0.113)	(0.040)	(0.076)
Women	0.095	–0.480	0.767	0.113	0.849
	(0.021)	(0.138)	(0.073)	(0.019)	(0.098)
5-year difference					
Men	–0.560	1.324	–0.514	–0.472	0.621
	(0.175)	(0.554)	(0.281)	(0.131)	(0.206)
Women	–2.304	2.363	–1.468	–5.216	1.348
	(0.165)	(0.431)	(0.490)	(1.827)	(0.151)
5-year log difference					
Men	–8.583	2.331	–1.448	–9.789	0.611
	(2.656)	(0.784)	(0.769)	(3.260)	(0.175)
Women	–3.513	2.323	–1.715	–6.291	1.007
	(1.197)	(0.263)	(0.333)	(1.237)	(0.139)

Note: See table 10.3 notes.

The first row shows the specification where the rates in levels have been used for both the dependent and the independent variables. As can be seen in the results of the upper panel in table 10.3, when excluding the controls, there is a positive and significant relation between the unemployment rate of the young and labor force participation of the old. This result is in line with the idea that the labor force participation of the old indeed crowd out employment possibilities for younger workers, resulting in a higher unemployment rate in this age group. The results for the other two outcome measures, employment rate and share in schooling, in this age group also give similar results. The results in table 10.4 show that relation can be attributed to the female subsample. For males, the results reveal a completely reversed relation, that is, that a higher labor force participation among older workers tends to decrease the unemployment rate among younger workers. The results also show that when we add controls to the specification, the significance of the pooled sample as well as the female subsample is lost. However, the inverse relation for the male subsample is robust for including controls.

The results for the prime aged age group are somewhat different. For the

Table 10.5   Regression results on the direct effect between labor force participation of older workers and employment of younger workers (males and females separately, with controls)

	Youth 16–24			Prime Age 25–54	
	UE	EMP	SCH	UE	EMP
Levels					
Men	−0.501	1.622	−0.923	−0.474	0.761
	(0.112)	(0.444)	(0.257)	(0.094)	(0.174)
Women	0.214	0.600	0.166	0.112	1.755
	(0.149)	(0.823)	(0.502)	(0.142)	(0.351)
3-year lag on elderly employment					
Men	−0.391	1.483	−0.938	−0.438	0.726
	(0.169)	(0.626)	(0.349)	(0.142)	(0.252)
Women	0.338	−1.638	1.248	0.346	0.080
	(0.080)	(0.446)	(0.246)	(0.072)	(0.264)
5-year difference					
Men	0.296	−1.650	0.822	0.224	−0.461
	(0.129)	(0.382)	(0.238)	(0.075)	(0.140)
Women	0.008	1.702	−0.577	−0.097	2.000
	(0.095)	(0.372)	(0.208)	(0.055)	(0.284)
5-year log difference					
Men	1.838	−0.835	1.033	3.895	−0.080
	(1.687)	(0.407)	(0.739)	(1.816)	(0.098)
Women	1.606	1.407	−0.879	−0.769	1.365
	(1.088)	(0.284)	(0.478)	(1.038)	(0.178)

Note: See table 10.3 notes.

pooled sample and the specification without controls, the results on the unemployment and employment rates as dependent variable are contradictory. The results in table 10.4 show that the result for unemployment, indicating a positive relation between the unemployment rate of the prime aged workers and the labor force participation rate of the older, can be attributed to the female subsample. Again, this result loses significance in both the pooled and the female subsample when controls are added to the specification. However, the positive relation between the employment rate among the prime aged and the labor force participation rate of the elderly applies in both the male and female subsamples and are robust to adding controls in all samples.

The second row in table 10.3 shows the results of the regression in levels, but when the independent variable, the labor force participation rate of the older workers, is lagged by three years. As for the previous set of results, there is a positive relation between the labor force participation of the old and the unemployment rate of the young that can be attributed to the female subsample. In the male subsample, the relation is reversed. In this specification, the results are generally robust for including controls.

Any causal relation between the labor force participation of the old and unemployment of the young is likely to show up if we relate changes, rather than levels, that is, the following model:

$$(2) \quad \ln U_{\text{young},t+1} - \ln U_{\text{young},t} = \alpha + \beta(\ln \text{LFP}_{\text{old},t+1} - \ln \text{LFP}_{\text{old},t})$$
$$+ \delta(\ln X_{t+1} - \ln X_t) + \varepsilon_{t+1} - \varepsilon_t.$$

We use five-year lags and show results from levels as well as logged data.

For the differenced data, the results indicate complimentarity between the labor force participation of the old and employment of the young or prime aged. This applies for the specifications without controls for both the male and female subsamples. However, the statistical significance of the results is, in most cases, lost when controls are included in the specifications. In some cases, the sign is reversed and still significant when controls are included in the male and female subsamples.

10.6   Conclusions

As in most other industrialized economies, there has been a gradual decrease in the labor force participation of older male workers in Sweden since the beginning of the 1960s. At the same time, the income security system has gradually become more generous, primarily through the introduction and maturity of the income-related national supplementary pension system (ATP) and more generous eligibility rules in the Disability Insurance program. It has been hypothesized that the access to the more generous income security system for older workers could explain the development toward a lower labor force participation in this group. In this paper, we have tried to get empirical support for this hypothesis. Moreover, we have tried to link the labor force participation rate among older workers to the employment rate among younger workers.

On some aspects, we have found empirical support for a relation between the development of the income security system and labor force participation rates among older workers. First, the changes in the normal retirement ages did have an apparent effect on the labor force participation rates of workers older than age sixty-six. Second, the more generous eligibility rules in the Disability Insurance program and the opening of the possibilities to be awarded Disability Insurance for labor market reasons seem to have an effect on the labor force participation rate in the group aged between sixty and sixty-four. Third, the stricter eligibility rules in the Disability Insurance in the beginning of the 1990s did at least affect the inflow to the Disability Insurance program although it is unclear if it in the end affected the labor force participation rates among the older workers.

On the other hand, we did not find unambiguous empirical support for the hypothesis that the more generous pension benefits in the national system did have an effect on labor force participation rates. Although there are relatively few who claim old age pension benefits before the normal retirement age, the more generous benefits may have affected the inflow to the Disability Insurance. If this was the case, however, we would have witnessed an increase in this inflow much earlier, already in the beginning of the 1960s, than in the early 1970s when it actually happened.

On the second research question, to what extent a high labor force participation rate among older workers tends to "crowd out" employment possibilities for the younger, we find no empirical support for this being the case. On the contrary, most of the empirical results suggest a positive relation between labor force participation of older workers and employment of the young.

There are at least two reasons to believe that regression models where the labor force participation is used as explanatory variable and different measures of employment of younger workers as dependent variable will give biased results. First, there may be a spurious regression effect through unmeasured business-cycle effects driving both higher labor force participation rates among the older workers and lower unemployment rates among young workers. Second, for at least some eras covered by the period under study, a secular trend toward higher female labor force participation and a trend toward higher youth unemployment may have affected the results.

The different sources of potential bias go in different directions, and the labor force trends differ for men and women. To resolve this, which calls for further research, some form of exogenous variation in labor force participation is needed.

References

Elmér, Å. 1960. *Folkpensioneringen i Sverige* (with a summary in English). Lund, Sweden: C. W. K. Glerups.
Gruber, J., and D. Wise, eds. 1999. *Social security and retirement around the world.* Chicago: University of Chicago Press.
Karlstrom, A., M. Palme, and I. Svensson. 2008. The employment effect of stricter rules for eligibility for DI: Evidence from a natural experiment in Sweden. *Journal of Public Economics* 92:2071–82.
Molin, B. 1965. *Tjänstepensionsfrågan. En studie i svensk partipolitik.* Lund, Sweden: C. W. K. Glerups.
Nordström Skans, O., and L. Lindqvist. 2005. Causal effects of subsidized career breaks. IFAU Working Paper no. 2005:17. Uppsala, Sweden: Institute for Labour Market Policy Evaluation.
Palme, M., and I. Svensson. 2004. Income security programs and retirement in Sweden. In *Social security and retirement around the world: Micro-estimates,* ed. J. Gruber and D. Wise. Chicago: University of Chicago Press.

11   Releasing Jobs for the Young? Early Retirement and Youth Unemployment in the United Kingdom

James Banks, Richard Blundell, Antoine Bozio, and Carl Emmerson

11.1   Introduction

Previous volumes of the International Social Security project at the NBER have shown convincingly that the incentives provided by pension schemes provisions have had a strong negative impact on labor force participation at older ages (Gruber and Wise 1999, 2004). Many countries increased the generosity of their state pension provision in the 1970s, despite the fact that demographic changes (both differences in cohort sizes and higher life expectancy) would subsequently pose serious threats to the financial viability of those pension schemes. In many instances, it was stressed that changes to pension provisions have somehow been made with the idea to "release jobs" for the young. Indeed, with unemployment increasing after the 1970's oil shocks, it is perhaps unsurprising that European governments were implementing various reforms aimed at reducing unemployment, and youth unemployment in particular. In other words, increased incentives to retire early may have been motivated by this expected impact of early retire-

James Banks is professor of economics at University College London and deputy research director of the Institute for Fiscal Studies (IFS), where he also directs the Centre for Economic Research on Ageing. Richard Blundell is the Ricardo Professor of Political Economy at University College London, and research director of the Economic and Social Research Council (ESRC) Centre for the Microeconomic Analysis of Public Policy at the Institute for Fiscal Studies. Antoine Bozio is a senior research economist at the Institute for Fiscal Studies. Carl Emmerson is deputy director of the Institute for Fiscal Studies.

This paper forms part of the International Social Security project at the National Bureau of Economic Research (NBER). The authors are grateful to the other participants of that project. We are also grateful to the ESRC-funded Centre for the Microeconomic Analysis of Public Policy at the IFS (grant number RES-544-28-5001) for funding this project. Material from the Family Expenditure Survey (FES) and the Labour Force Survey (LFS) was made available by the UK Data Archive. Any errors are the responsibility of the authors alone.

ment: less unemployment among the young only at the expense (and benefit) of more leisure time among the old.[1]

This chapter tries to take this claim seriously and assess whether we have any empirical evidence of links between early retirement and youth unemployment. Most economists would today dismiss the idea immediately as another version of the naive "lump-of-labor fallacy."[2] In its most basic form, this proposition holds that there is a fixed supply of jobs and that any reduction in labor supply will reduce unemployment by offering jobs to those who are looking for one. Taken to the extreme, this view would support that the idea that a high *level* of employment of one group of individuals can only be at the expense of another group: if, for instance, were the population of a country to increase, younger individuals would be unemployed as older individuals would not "release" enough jobs for the new entrants. The absurdity of this view in the long term is simply seen by considering the fact that the size of a country does not bear any relation to the *share* of population unemployed.

There might be, however, a subtler claim, that is, that controlling for population size (and overall demand), the employment *rate* of younger workers might be affected by the share of older workers employed. Older and younger workers might have different characteristics in terms of qualifications, skills, and productivity and, therefore, be more or less substitutable depending on the degree of flexibility of labor markets. Some economists have suggested that specific policies to encourage employment of the old might end up being counterproductive if, for instance, productivity declines markedly with age and if the wages of older workers end up above their productivity. Mulligan and Sala-i-Martin (1999) suggest provocatively that negative externalities of older workers might lead to the incentives for early exit from the labor force.

Given that changes in pension systems should be, and usually are, for the very long term, our interest is to look for a long-term relationship between labor force participation rates of the old and employment rates of the young: it is very likely that labor markets take time to adjust to changes in age or sex composition and that substitution effects could be seen in the very short term. Hence, we will cover labor markets and policies in the United Kingdom over more than forty years and provide empirical evidence on programs abandoned a long time ago. This historical background will prove essential to provide empirical evidence for a relationship (or absence of relationship) intrinsically difficult to uncover.

The challenges when estimating a causal relationship between the employment rates of different age groups rest on a combination of endogeneity and general equilibrium effects. At the micro level, controlling for enough fac-

---

1. Evidence on the impact of pension arrangements on the public finances and on the welfare of older individuals can be found in Gruber and Wise (2007 and forthcoming, respectively).

2. Other versions include capping weekly hours of paid work, limits to immigration, or increased incentives for mothers to stay at home, all as means to reduce unemployment.

tors, a degree of substitution must indeed be apparent. Workers of similar qualification, skill, ability, experience, and other characteristics should be at least partly substitutable if one controls for total output. This micro-substitution is of particular interest for labor economists but does not lead to specific conclusions on the overall employment relationship between older workers and younger ones. The question we would like to answer is *unconditional,* that is, does a higher (lower) rate of labor force participation of older worker increase (decrease) unemployment of the younger ones, not controlling for the fact that output might be higher (lower)?

At the macro level, where the macro-substitution is to be found, one is faced with the problem of endogeneity. Changes in the employment of the old are not exogenous and react, with youth unemployment, to general changes in labor demand, following, for example, the ups and downs of business cycles. These shifts in labor demand may be hard to control for. Moreover, they are usually measured by changes in gross domestic product (GDP), that is, by changes in measured output. Interpretations of an absence of substitution at the macro level will, therefore, be hard to distinguish from simultaneity issues.

The first step in our analysis is to examine the importance of incentives to retire on older labor force supply in the United Kingdom over the last forty years. We describe the reforms to pension system and early retirement schemes to assess in what respect are the changes in financial incentives exogenous from the labor market situation. The UK case is very interesting in that respect, as most of the pension reforms—and, arguably, all of the major reforms in the 1980s and 1990s—were motivated more by public finance considerations (both short and long run) than by unemployment. Section 11.2 describes the debates concerning the relationship between the number of older and younger workers in the United Kingdom and discusses in what respect they led to changes in policies to foster early exit of older workers. Section 11.3 contains descriptive figures comparing the labor force participation of older individuals in the United Kingdom with the evolution of employment for younger individuals as well as a cross-country comparison of the French and the UK experience. Section 11.4 describes in detail the Job Release Scheme (JRS), the major UK early retirement scheme of the late 1970s and early 1980s, and presents estimations of what could be considered to be a "natural experiment" of specific incentives to encourage early retirement. Section 11.5 describes the methodology of comparable regressions both at the micro level and in times series of the relationship between young and old labor force participation. Section 11.6 concludes.

11.2   Debates and Policies in the United Kingdom

Compared to many continental European countries, the United Kingdom has not developed extensive policies to encourage older workers to leave jobs for the young. This does not mean that debates and policies about the "lump of labor" have been absent from the United Kingdom, quite the contrary. The debate about work sharing started in nineteenth century United Kingdom about working-time regulations. Walker (2007) traces back the first appearance of the expression "lump-of-labour fallacy" to an article from the UK economist David F. Schloss (1891) and suggests that it is the London-based magazine *The Economist* that has lately popularized the phrase by repeatedly denouncing the "fallacy."[3] If the debate about work sharing was mostly confined to hours of work, the idea that reducing the labor supply of older workers could help mitigate the rise in unemployment was most keenly put forward in the aftermath of the late 1970s oil shock (Laczko and Phillipson 1991).

The first policy that led to the growth of early exit from the labor force was the Redundancy Payments Act of 1965, which required employers to make lump-sum payments to workers who lost their jobs. The idea was not to fight unemployment but to help reduce overstaffing in UK industries by securing greater acceptance of these restructuring and facilitating workers' mobility to new jobs. In practice, however, the Act was used by companies to get rid of older workers and, thus, to encourage early exit. Early retirement packages by private companies have been used extensively in the late 1970s, but comprehensive information is very scarce about these private schemes.

Pension reforms in the United Kingdom have not been influenced heavily by concerns about unemployment of the young (see box 11.1 for a chronology of UK pension reforms from 1975 to the present).[4] The UK pension debate has largely been focused on the trade-off between social assistance, that is, providing a minimum income to the elderly, and social insurance, that is, increasing the contributory principle of pension provision. Concerns about the cost to the public finances have tended to reduce this latter objective to a minimum. The 1975 Social Security Act (applied from April 1978) increased the generosity of the Basic State Pension (BSP) scheme and introduced the State Earnings-Related Pension Scheme (SERPS), to provide higher benefits, related to earnings, for those employees who were not a member of an employer's defined benefit pension arrangement. Two years later, in 1980, the generosity of state pensions was reduced with an indexation in line with the growth in prices instead of the greater of the growth in prices or earnings. This reduced generosity took place while unemployment was increasing and concerns for the labor market implications were clearly not motivating these reforms. Since then, overall state spending on pensions remained at a roughly constant share of UK GDP, as figure 11.1 provides clear evidence.

The main policy that explicitly had the goal to reduce elderly employment

---

3. Walker (2007) expresses a sceptical view of the idea that economists have been able to prove the "lump-of-labor" to be a fallacy indeed.

4. For an overview of the pension system in the United Kingdom, see Blundell and Johnson (1998), Dilnot *et al.* (1994), Dilnot, Kay, and Morris (1984), and Disney and Emmerson (2005).

Box 11.1	**Reforms to the U.K. State Pension System, 1975 to present day**
Social Security Act 1975	Basic State Pension (BSP) made more generous for those with certain formal caring responsibilities from April 1978. Married women no longer given the choice of opting out of the BSP from April 1977.
	State Earnings-Related Pension Scheme (SERPS) introduced for all employees not in a defined benefit employer arrangement from April 1978. Entitlement based on the best twenty years of earnings (between a lower and an upper earnings limit set) uprated to retirement by growth in average earnings. Accrual rate set at 25 percent.
Social Security Act 1980	State pension payments to be increased by growth in prices instead of the greater of growth in prices or earnings from November 1980.
Social Security Act 1986	Entitlement to SERPS to be calculated on the basis of earnings over entire working life (sixteen to state pension age) rather than across the best twenty years phased in for those reaching the state pension age from April 2000 onward.
	The accrual factor on SERPS to be reduced from 25 percent to 20 percent of earnings between the lower and upper earnings limits. This is being phased in for those reaching the state pension age between April 2000 and March 2008, although accrued entitlement from before April 1988 is protected.
	Surviving partners of those dying after April 2000 to inherit 50 percent of their spouse's state pension instead of 100 percent. (This change was later put back to October 2002 after the Department for Social Security failed to correctly inform some individuals of this change and now relates to year reached state pension age rather than year died).
Social Security Act 1995	State pension age for women to be increased from sixty to sixty-five gradually between 2010 and 2020 (by one month every two months).
	Technical change made to the formula used to calculate SERPS entitlement. This reduced the generosity of SERPS to those reaching the state pension age after April 1999, with both retrospective and prospective SERPS rights reduced.
Child Support, Pensions and Social Security Act 2000	The State Second Pension (S2P) to replace SERPS from April 2002 onward. This is more generous to lower earners and to some individuals with caring responsibilities.
Pension Act 2007	Both the level and the coverage of the BSP to be increased. The level is to be earnings (rather than price) indexed from some point between 2012 and 2015. For those reaching the state pension age from April 2010 onward, the number of qualifying years needed to receive a full BSP reduced from thirty-nine for women and forty-four for men to thirty years for both. Accrual of S2P to be reduced for higher earners to claw back some of the increase in BSP.
	State pension age to be increased from sixty-five to sixty-eight gradually between 2024 and 2046.

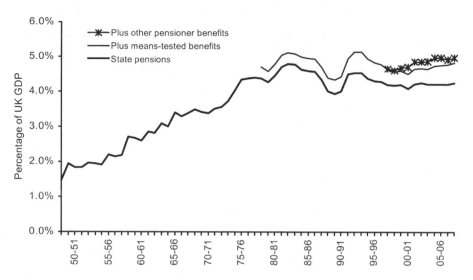

Fig. 11.1   State spending on financial transfers to pensioners in Great Britain, 1948–1949 to 2007–2008

Source: Emmerson, Tetlow, and Wakefield (2005).

in order to reduce youth unemployment was the JRS. It was introduced in 1977 and was described as "a measure which allows older workers to retire early in order to release jobs for the registered unemployed" (Department of Employment 1978). The debates in Parliament about the scheme were not so much about its effectiveness (substitution between older workers and younger ones was assumed to be very high) but about the gross cost of such a scheme. The following exchange in the House of Commons in 1979 is very revealing of the debate in the United Kingdom in the late 1970s:[5]

> Mr. Atkins, MP: "In view of the large numbers of people involved, would not even a phased reduction of the age to sixty provide many thousands of jobs for younger people? Is it not a fact that there is an even more urgent need because of the rapid development of microcomputer technology?"

> Mr. Grant, The Undersecretary of State for Employment: "This is a cost-effective way of dealing with the problem. Nevertheless, it entails additional resources and, therefore, must be looked at in the light of overall priorities. However, it is being considered further.

The scheme appeared at the time to be limited in its achievement due to the fact that the take-up rate remained low (Makeham and Morgan 1980). The allowance being unrelated to earnings, the incentives for an early exit was confined to low-wage earners and those who could draw an occupational

5. House of Commons, 20th February 1979, Hansard, vol. 963 cc228-9.

pension alongside the JRS allowance. In 1984, suggestions by some MPs to make the scheme earnings-related were rejected on the ground of cost.[6] Until the end of the scheme in 1988, there were repeated claims from some MPs to increase the scope of the scheme by reducing the age at which an individual could take opportunity of it (we will see in the next section that the scope was indeed changed many times). Calls for expansion of the scheme can be seen as late as the 1987 Labour Party general election manifesto.[7]

> We will extend the voluntary Job Release Scheme to men over 60 so that those who want to retire early vacate jobs for those who are currently unemployed. This could take as many as 160,000 people out of unemployment and into work.

Similar claims—albeit on a smaller scale—can be found in the 1987 Liberal/Social Democratic Party (SDP) manifesto: "For the long-term unemployed we will provide a guarantee of a job through (. . .) an expanded job release scheme, opening up 30,000 jobs by allowing men to benefit from the scheme at 62 years of age."

In the early 1980s, the government's main policy toward the elderly was to reduce their labor supply in order to reduce the numbers on the unemployment register (Brown 1990). In 1981, men aged sixty and over who had been unemployed for one year could claim the long-term supplementary benefit rate provided they ceased to register for unemployment. In 1983, this possibility was extended to all men aged sixty and over. These measures were not expected to release jobs for the young but simply to reduce the formal unemployment count.

In the same period, it was debated whether to reduce state pension age for men from sixty-five to sixty in order to make it the same for men and women. Interestingly a large part of the debate was about the real ex post cost of such a measure, the advocates of the move insisting that due to the substitution between older workers and younger unemployed, the ex post cost would be small. The first costing of this proposal rested on the assumption of a substitution rate of 75 percent (i.e., 75 percent of jobs vacated would be filled by individuals who would otherwise had been unemployed).[8] An Institute for Fiscal Studies research paper by Hammond and Morris (1985) estimated variants of these costs according to different estimations of the degree of substitution between older workers and younger ones. They used a substitution rate of 50 percent as benchmark but stressed the importance of the assumption: "the numbers of people taken from the unemployment register or placed on the unemployment register following a change in the

6. Debates in the House of Commons, 20th November 1984.
7. UK general election manifestos can be found online at http://www.psr.keele.ac.uk/area/uk/man.htm.
8. Department of Health and Social Security (DHSS) evidence to Social Services Committee (1982).

age at which men and women become eligible for a state pension is a much more crucial determinant of the final cost to government revenues" (34).

By 1988, the JRS had been phased out for new claimants, and, in the 1990s, the idea that reducing the labor supply of older workers could help mitigate unemployment was dropped altogether from the UK policy debate. The Social Security Act of 1986 reduced the generosity of SERPS by computing benefits on the basis of earnings over the entire working life rather than across the best twenty years. The reform was phased in between 2000 and 2008. Figure 11.2 illustrates these reductions in generosity, first to the BSP and then to SERPS.

In recent years, the case against policies that aimed at encouraging earlier retirement seemed to generate consensus among UK economists. Layard, Nickell, and Jackman (1991) rephrased the "lump-of-labor" fallacy as a "lump-of-output" fallacy (i.e., early retirement can reduce unemployment only if one assumes that output is constant) and summarized the view of many on early retirement policies. The very recent pension reforms are solely concerned with the adequacy of individual retirement saving decisions, with recognition that for those with inadequate provision, a combination of increased saving and later retirement might be the most appropriate solution. In April 2002, the State Second Pension (S2P), a scheme more generous to low earners, replaced SERPS. With the 2007 Pension Act, requirements to qualify for a BSP have been reduced and the level of the BSP increased, while state pension age is planned to increase from age sixty-five to age sixty-eight. This dramatic increase did not lead to fears of rising youth unemployment.

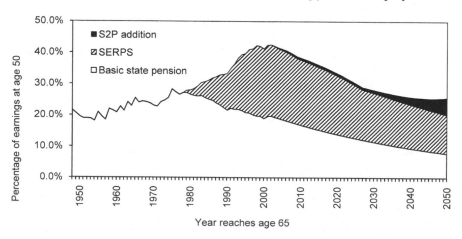

Fig. 11.2   State pension entitlement for male with median (age-specific) earnings, full employment history, 1948–2050

Source: Disney and Emmerson (2005).

Notes: Calculations for individuals with full contribution history with median male age specific earnings and 2 percent annual economywide real earnings growth. The 2007 Pension Act is not included in these computations.

Interestingly, a major document from the Labour government, dedicated to the elderly and titled *Winning the Generation Game* (Cabinet Office 2000), contains a specific box denouncing the "lump of labour fallacy":

> The lump of labor fallacy is difficult to dispel because it feels true in individual cases and requires a wider understanding of the labor market to understand why it is not. It is particularly insidious in relation to older people who are detached from the labor market and it should not be allowed to influence policies towards this group. (40)

Today's consensus in the United Kingdom seems to be at the opposite end of the spectrum from the early 1980's consensus.

11.3   Descriptive Analysis

This section describes trends over time in the economic activity of older and younger individuals. Figures 11.3 and 11.4 contrast the evolution of labor force participation of the old (defined as those aged fifty-five to sixty-four to the evolution of the unemployment and employment share of the young (defined as those aged twenty to twenty-four) and of those of the prime age (defined as those aged twenty-five to fifty-four). We use data from

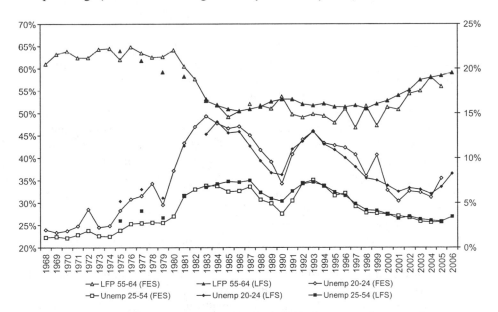

Fig. 11.3   Labor force participation of older individuals compared to unemployment of younger individuals

Sources: LFS (1975, 1977, 1979, 1981, and 1983 to 2006) and FES (1968 to 2005).

Notes: Unemployment is expressed as a share the population in the age group (and not as a share of the active). The right-hand axis corresponds to the unemployment series, whereas the labor force participation series can be read on the left-hand axis.

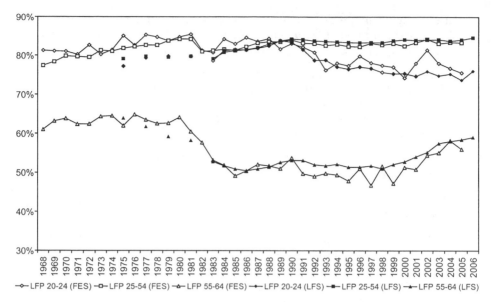

-◇-LFP 20-24 (FES) -□-LFP 25-54 (FES) -▲-LFP 55-64 (FES) -◆-LFP 20-24 (LFS) -■-LFP 25-54 (LFS) -▲-LFP 55-64 (LFS)

Fig. 11.4   Labor force participation of older individuals compared to employment of younger individuals
Sources: LFS (1975, 1977, 1979, 1981, and 1983 to 2006) and FES (1968 to 2005).

the Labour Force Survey (LFS) from 1975, 1977, 1979, 1981, and 1983 to 2006 (inclusive) and the Family Expenditure Survey (FES) from 1968 to 2005 (inclusive). Both surveys show very consistent evolution of both employment and unemployment rates.

Figure 11.3 illustrates clearly the massive structural shocks of the late 1970s and early 1980s in the United Kingdom: a massive rise in youth unemployment, a strong rise in unemployment for prime age individuals, and a massive drop in labor force participation of older workers (a drop of more than 10 percentage points). Unemployment rates of the young and prime age were quicker to decline than older workers' labor force participation, which stayed stable until the end of the 1990s. The last period exhibits a reversal in these trends, with increased participation of the old and substantial reductions in unemployment of the young and prime aged. Figure 11.4 provides a similar picture, adding the fact that employment of the prime aged have trended upward during the period with the increase in female labor force participation, while youth employment has recently been falling with increasing participation in higher education.

Figure 11.5 illustrates on one graph the major changes to the various public retirement schemes and the labor force participation of older individuals against the labor participation and unemployment of the young. The introduction of SERPS in 1978 increased the generosity of pension provisions, while the indexation of state pensions to growth in prices (rather

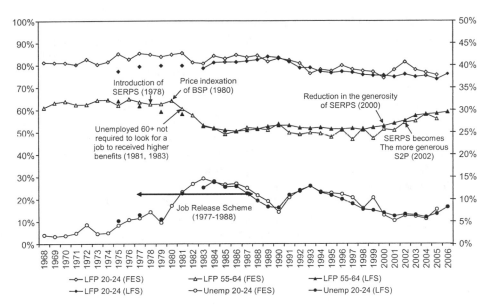

Fig. 11.5   Program changes and labor force participation of young and old (1968–2006)

Sources: LFS (1975, 1977, 1979, 1981, and 1983 to 2006) and FES (1968 to 2005).

Notes: Unemployment is expressed as a share of the population in the age group (and not as a share of the active). The right-hand axis corresponds to the unemployment series, whereas the labor force participation series can be read on the left-hand axis.

than the greater of growth in prices or earnings) from 1980 onward went in the opposite direction. These two reforms predate the large drop in labor force participation of the old but hardly explain it. The JRS was introduced in 1977 when unemployment of younger individuals had been increasing for five years continuously. The unemployment continued to increase while the scheme was extended. Youth unemployment started to decline when the scheme was reduced in scope.

From 1984 onward, and up to 1998, the labor force participation of the old remained stable in the United Kingdom. Since then, it has been increasing, from 51 percent in 1998 to 59 percent in 2006. It is hard to link directly this sizable rise to changes in the pension system. While the generosity of SERPS was reduced in 2000, the introduction of S2P from 2002 represented an increase in generosity and would be expected to have the opposite impact on labor force participation. The planned increase in the state pension age is not due to take place before 2010 for women and 2024 for men. Most UK commentators have stressed that the increase in elderly employment in recent years is largely attributable to the upturn in the economic cycle since the mid-1990s (Disney and Hawkes 2003).

When considering labor force participation in the United Kingdom, one has also to acknowledge the rise in the numbers claiming incapacity benefits. After the end of the JRS, the Invalidity Benefit scheme (later reformed into the Incapacity Benefit) has seen the number of its recipients increase dramatically. Figure 11.6 shows the number of recipients of the Invalidity/Incapacity Benefit for the fifty to sixty-four age group (both male and female). These schemes became, over the decade from the mid-1980s onward, a major path of early exit from the labor force. From April 1995, the Invalidity Benefit was replaced by the Incapacity Benefit for new recipients, with the latter having a more stringent health test. The reform stopped the growth in recipients but did not reverse the trend. The replacement of Incapacity Benefit with the Employment Support Allowance from October 2008, which again is intended to have a more stringent health test, is expected by the Government to reduce the number of beneficiaries.

Figure 11.7 illustrates the various paths toward retirement in the United Kingdom and the importance of the "sick or disabled" route. The massive drop in employment rates in the late 1970s is again very clear. First unemployment increases, then the share of older individuals reporting that they are retired or that they are "sick or disabled" increases considerably. The number reporting that they are "sick or disabled" only starts falling in the period from 1995 onwards, during which an increase in employment and a fall in unemployment are also observed. The proportion reporting that they are retired is little changed over the period from the late 1980s onward.

So far the descriptive evidence hardly supports the claim that older work-

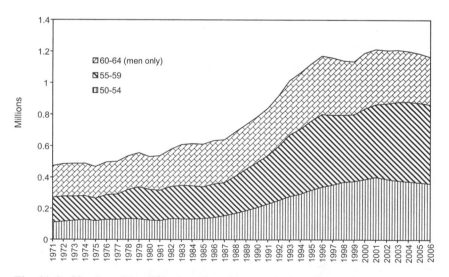

Fig. 11.6   Number of invalidity benefit and incapacity benefit recipients aged 50 to the state pension age, 1971–2006

Source: Computations from the authors using the EIRNI database (Anyadike-Danes and McVicar 2008).

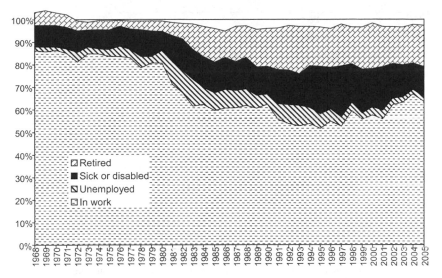

Fig. 11.7   Employment status of older men (55–69 years old)
Source: FES (1968 to 2004)

ers crowd out younger ones. The UK case seems to highlight that both old and young workers react to the general economic conditions. In times of relative economic hardship, youth unemployment rises while older labor force participation is reduced; in times of economic expansion, the employment level of both groups increases. To understand better the possible relationship between retirement incentives and youth unemployment, one can advantageously undertake a cross-country comparison—which is, finally, the raison d'être of this volume.

We thus present in figure 11.8 a France–United Kingdom comparison of employment rates of older workers over the 1968 to 2005 period. This comparison is very interesting because both countries are of similar size and have relatively similar economies. Both have had significant and aging primary and secondary industries that were hit by the 1970s oil shocks and restructured in the 1980s in part with the help of early retirement schemes. Both countries have experienced large drop in employment rates of those fifty-five years old and above until the mid-1980s. Even though France had lower employment rates among both sixty to sixty-four-year-olds and fifty-five- to fifty-nine-year-olds before these macroeconomic shocks, the UK-France difference is no different in 1983 to that seen in the late 1960s. Both countries have used early retirement schemes even if public subsidies for these schemes were far more developed in France than the United Kingdom, where only the JRS can be seen as a public early retirement scheme. Early retirement schemes in France also started as private schemes but have been progressively extended to become public policies.

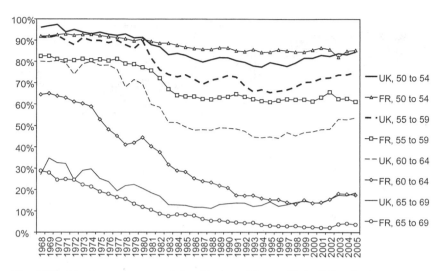

Fig. 11.8   Employment rates of the older men (France–United Kingdom)

Sources: FES (1968 to 1982) and LFS (1983 to 2005) for the United Kingdom, Enquête Emploi for France.

While the JRS was designed to be—and turned out to be—temporary, the French government decided to stabilize the trend toward the use of early retirement vehicles by introducing permanent changes to the pension system, that is, by lowering the retirement age from sixty-five to sixty. The idea was that the need for early retirement schemes (i.e., schemes that were not part of the formal pension system) would thus disappear and that by providing pensions earlier to every retiree, it would be more fair. From 1983 onward, trends in employment rates of the French and UK elderly began to diverge markedly. While the UK employment rate of those sixty to sixty-four years old remained stable at 50 percent, the French one went on falling, down to 14 percent in 2000. While the difference for this age group was only 15 percentage points in 1968, it is now more than 35 percentage points apart. The 1983 French pension reform also reduced the incentives to work for those sixty-five and above. The employment rate of those sixty-five to sixty-nine years old, at roughly the same level up the mid-1980s, started also to diverge. French employment males past age sixty-five is now almost non-existent, while close to 20 percent of UK males aged sixty-five to sixty-nine were still working in 2006, with a clear trend over the last ten years toward increased employment among this group.

A comparison between youth unemployment in France and in the United Kingdom is shown in figure 11.9. The share of the twenty to twenty-four age group unemployed according to International Labour Organization (ILO) definition is compared across both countries over the same period as in figure 11.8. First, it should be noted that this is not the unemployment rate usually

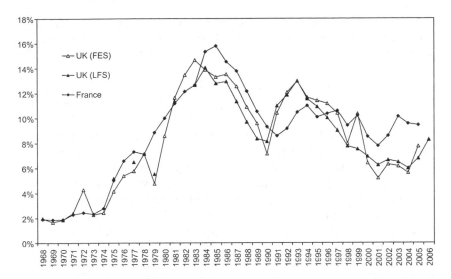

Fig. 11.9   Share of the 20–24 age group unemployed (France-United Kingdom)
Sources: FES (1968 to 1982) and LFS (1983 to 2005) for the United Kingdom. Enquête Emploi for France.

presented (i.e., the unemployed as a share of the active). Given the marked differences between the two countries in terms of the share of the twenty to twenty-four age group in education, unemployment rates might not be considered as directly comparable. The striking fact emerging from figure 11.9 is that youth unemployment shares are very similar in both countries and do react strongly to changes in general economic conditions. When LFP of the old was declining similarly in both countries (up to the early 1980s as shown in figure 11.8), youth unemployment was rising almost identically. The higher intensity of early retirement policies in France and the divergence in LFP of the old described in figure 11.8 did not seem to have led to any significant decrease of youth unemployment in France relative to that seen in the United Kingdom. If anything, youth unemployment has been higher in France than in the United Kingdom in recent years.

All these descriptive analyses do not provide causal evidence in any sense, but they suggest convincingly that over the long term, higher (lower) labor force participation of the old is not related to higher (lower) unemployment of the young.

11.4   An Evaluation of the Job Release Scheme

The only public policy in the United Kingdom with the aim to reduce unemployment by enticing older workers to retire is the JRS. This section describes its implementation in detail and presents estimates of its possible effect using a difference-in-differences methodology. The goal is to assess whether this specific policy has had a measured positive impact on youth employment in the short term, irrespective of its long term and wider impact.

The JRS was introduced in the United Kingdom in 1977 by a Labour government and was expanded in the early 1980s under the Conservative government of Margaret (now Lady) Thatcher. It was supposed to be temporary and very selective (contrary to examples in continental Europe of general early retirement schemes). It was first limited to employees within one year of the state pension age (fifty-nine for women and sixty-four for men) in some specific areas of the country (Assisted Areas) where unemployment was more prevalent. The scheme required the employer to provide a job to an individual from the unemployment register. A JRS claimant must agree not to take another job, nor set up a self-employed business.

The scheme was changed at multiple times as figure 11.10 exemplifies. Very soon after its introduction, it was limited to full-time employees. In April 1977, it was extended nationwide, then extended temporarily to younger men (aged sixty-two and sixty-three) in 1979 to 1980 (but not younger women), then restricted for new claimants to sixty-four-year-old men (with fifty-nine-year-old women still eligible), then again extended in 1982 to 1984 to men and women within three years of the state pension age before being restricted for new claimants once more to just those within one

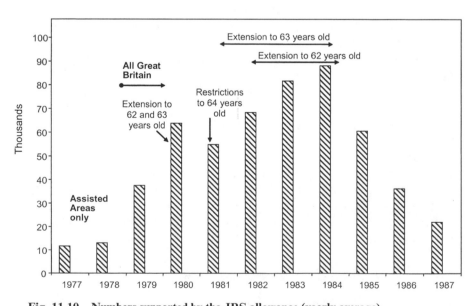

Fig. 11.10   Numbers supported by the JRS allowance (yearly average)

Sources: House of Commons Session 1988–1989; Employment Committee 2nd report "The Employment Patterns of the Over 50s," table 6.2, page 95.

year of the state pension age. It was closed in early 1988. A similar scheme applied to part-time jobs (the Part-Time JRS). Its take-up rate was much lower than the full-time scheme, with only a few thousand recipients.

The JRS offered a flat rate allowance (described in detail in appendix A) and, therefore, was more attractive to low earners or individuals that could claim a private occupational pension alongside a JRS award. If the allowance was low relative to average earnings, it was 40 percent higher than the flat rate BSP (available at age sixty-five for men) and 70 percent higher than the unemployment benefit. Surveys of recipients of JRS show that, indeed, many individuals received an occupational pension alongside the scheme allowance (Makeham and Morgan 1980).

The JRS was put in place in times of rising youth unemployment. Figure 11.11 shows the rise in the share of youth unemployed compared to the numbers supported by the JRS. The scheme was (generally) expanded until 1984 and was reduced in scale in 1985, just when youth unemployment stopped rising. The high correlation between the expansion of the JRS and unemployment highlights the estimation difficulties encountered in this volume. It is impossible to attribute any success to the JRS in reducing youth unemployment, and, in addition, it appears clear that the introduction of this scheme was prompted by rising youth unemployment.

The fact that the conditions to qualify for this scheme changed so many times is a dream scenario for economists willing to evaluate a policy. It

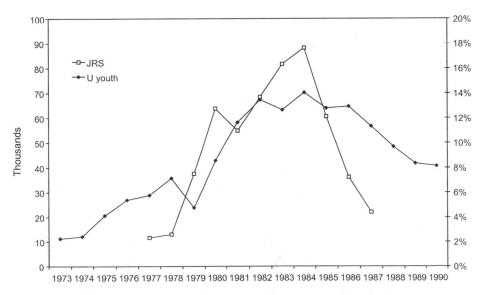

Fig. 11.11   Youth unemployment and numbers supported by the JRS (1973–1990)
Sources: See figure 11.3 for youth unemployment and figure 11.10 for numbers on JRS.
Notes: Youth unemployment as a share of population is shown in the right-hand axis, while numbers supported by the JRS are to be read in the left-hand axis (in thousands).

generates many treated and control groups. Unfortunately, no specific data are available to study the individuals possibly affected—the scheme took place a long time ago, at a time policy evaluations were far from being as developed as today. Nevertheless, we can use the LFS for the years 1975, 1977, 1979, 1981, and 1983 to 1989 (inclusive) to study the impact of the JRS on the employment of the old. Our methodology will rely on estimating difference-in-differences impact on the employment of the old using changes in the age threshold.

We use each change in the rules determining eligibility to JRS as pseudo natural experiment. We estimate the effect of being eligible to the JRS on employment rates of males controlling for age dummies and year dummies. Results are presented in table 11.1. The expansion of the scheme seemed to lead to a reduction in the employment rates of the age group concerned (specifications [1] and [3]), but neither of the two periods of restriction of the scheme lead to a statistically significant increase in employment (specifications [2] and [5]). The estimation using all the changes in scheme eligibility (specification [4]) leads to a 3.6 percentage point decline in the employment rate of sixty-two- to sixty-four-year-old men as a result of the JRS (from a base of 44 percent). A causal interpretation is possible only under the common trend assumption, that is, that 61-year-olds have had no change in employment prospects from sixty-two-year-olds during this period, except through the impact of the JRS. This might be a strong assumption. Older

Table 11.1   Estimated impact of the Job Release Scheme on employment of the old and the young

	Old					Young
	(1)	(2)	(3)	(4)	(5)	(6)
Coefficient	−0.035*	−0.014	−0.056***	−0.036***	0.007	0.038***
	(0.021)	(0.028)	(0.017)	(0.007)	(0.021)	(0.003)

Notes: Specification (1) corresponds to the introduction of the Job Release Scheme (JRS) to 62, 63, and 64 years old in 1979 as compared to 61 years old in 1977 (unaffected in both years). Specification (2) corresponds to the restriction of the JRS to 63 years and above in 1981. We compare 63 years old to 62 years old in both years. The coefficient presented is the interaction between being 62 years old in 1981. If the removal of the JRS led to increase in employment rate of 62 years old, we would expect a positive and significant sign. Specification (3) corresponds to the expansion of the JRS to 62 and 63 years old in 1983 and 1984; 61 and 64 years old are used as controls. Specification (4) corresponds to a general analysis of the effect of JRS over the entire period, controlling for age and period dummies. Specification (5) corresponds to the restriction of the scheme after 1984 to the 64 years old, using 63 years old as controls. If the removal of the JRS had had a positive impact on employment of the 63 years, we would have expected a negative sign. Specification (6) corresponds to the coefficient on JRS variable in a regression of youth unemployment status with sex and age dummies as controls (period 1975–1989). Standard errors in parentheses.

***Significant at the 1 percent level.
*Significant at the 10 percent level.

workers might be more likely to reduce their labor force participation in times of rising unemployment, even without early retirement schemes. The fact that we do not find statistically significant reversal of the trend when eligibility to the scheme is restricted adds to this possible weakness.

Even if we accept the result that the JRS had a negative impact on employment of the old, we cannot directly apply this methodology to assess its impact on youth labor status. The difference-in-differences methodology rests on comparing alike older individuals, but no young can be deemed unaffected as "jobs released" by sixty-three or sixty-two-year-olds can be filled by any young unemployed. The only strategy left for us is to use the variation in eligibility to the scheme over time and compare the periods of increased eligibility to periods of restrictions. We run a regression on unemployment probability of those aged twenty to twenty-four, controlling for age and sex dummies adding the number of jobs presumably released as a share of youth population (specification [6]).[9] The results lead to significantly positive coefficients of the JRS eligibility variable, that is, an increase in the numbers supported by the JRS is associated with a 2 percentage points *increase* in the unemployment probability of the young, controlling for year, age, and sex. We do not interpret this result as causal—we have shown that the JRS eligibility was linked to expansion of youth unemployment and to the political need to expand this policy.

Even when looking at one specific early retirement scheme, which was conditioned on hiring unemployed, we do not find conclusive evidence of at least some substitution between young and older workers. This does not, again, prove that these schemes have had no effect on the youth unemployment, but despite our best effort, we have not been able to identify, even in the short run, their presumed positive (negative) impact on youth employment (unemployment).

11.5 Regression Analysis

In this section, we present regression analyses based on data from the United Kingdom covering the entire period, that is, from 1968 to 2005. Table 11.2 presents the results of ordinary least squares (OLS) regressions that exhibit simple correlations between employment of the old and labor status of the young. These estimations have been done following similar specifications in every country of this volume to facilitate comparisons. The table reproduces the coefficients on the employment rate of those aged fifty-five to sixty-four. The top part of the table shows pure correlations between labor market status of the young and employment rate of the old. Four specifications are presented, in "levels," that is, rates of population regressed on rates,

---

9. We use the number of claimants of the JRS as a proxy for the number of "jobs released."

Table 11.2   **Direct relationship between the elderly labor force participation and the unemployment or employment of younger individuals**

	Youth 20–24			Prime age 25–54	
	UE	EMP	SCH	UE	EMP
	No controls				
Levels	−0.53***	1.10***	−0.84***	−0.27***	0.15***
	(0.07)	(0.15)	(0.25)	(0.03)	(0.05)
3-year lag	−0.21**	1.01***	−1.10***	−0.15***	0.06
	(0.10)	(0.14)	(0.20)	(0.04)	(0.05)
5-year differences	−0.68***	0.51***	0.22	−0.32***	0.44***
	(0.11)	(0.18)	(0.15)	(0.05)	(0.08)
5-year log differences	−2.85***	0.30**	0.13	−2.91***	0.23***
	(90.60)	(0.12)	(0.24)	(0.51)	(0.04)
	With controls				
Levels	−0.18***	0.37***	−0.24**	−0.20***	0.22***
	(0.06)	(0.13)	(0.13)	(0.04)	(0.07)
3-year lag	−0.06	0.09	−0.08	−0.11***	0.07
	(0.06)	(0.13)	(0.12)	(0.04)	(0.07)
5-year differences	−0.28**	0.56**	−0.09	−0.21***	0.54***
	(0.11)	(0.25)	(0.22)	(0.07)	(0.11)
5-year log differences	−1.00*	0.34*	−0.22	−1.75***	0.22***
	(0.53)	(0.19)	(0.38)	(0.56)	(0.06)

Notes: Reported is the coefficient on elderly employment (55–64 years old), with its standard error in parentheses. The dependent variable is mentioned at the top of each column, that is, for the first columns, it is the share of unemployment of youth aged 20–24 regressed on the employment rate of those aged 55–64. UE = the share of the population unemployed; EMP = the share of the population in work; SCH = the share of the population in school and not in work.

***Significant at the 1 percent level.
**Significant at the 5 percent level.
*Significant at the 10 percent level.

"three years lag," "five years differences," and "five years log differences." The bottom part of the table presents the same regressions including a set of controls, that is, a constant, GDP per head, growth of GDP per head, and the share of manufacturing within GDP.

Results of correlations without any controls show strong positive association between employment of the young and employment of the old and strong negative association between employment of the old and youth unemployment. In other words, when labor market conditions are good for the old, they are typically also good for the young.

Once controls are included, the magnitude of this strong association is reduced but remains largely statistically significant. Even controlling for GDP and its variations, there remains a positive association between employment rates of the old and employment rates of the young. These correlations are not necessarily causal effects. They suggest simply that in the long term in the United Kingdom, one does not find changes in employment rates of one age group at the expense of the other.

Even after adding the controls for the aggregate effects of GDP growth and so on in table 11.2, it may well be that the elderly labor force is endogenous. One option is to exploit the incentive measures to retire as computed in previous volumes of the International Social Security (ISS)-NBER project (see Gruber and Wise 1999). We have established in section 11.2 of this chapter that pension reforms in the United Kingdom were not influenced by concerns relative to youth unemployment (early retirement scheme like the JRS were cautiously kept out of social security elements). In that case, incentives measures that are good predictors of the probability to retire seem like reliable instruments to assess the impact of labor force participation on youth unemployment. The difficulty is that the macroeconomic nature of the estimation problem makes it impossible to remain at the microeconomic level. Effects on youth unemployment can only be assessed at the times series level (because it is not possible to apply the financial incentives to work faced by older individuals to the employment prospects of younger individuals at any more disaggregated level). It is, therefore, necessary to build incentives measures that do confidently explain labor force participation of older individuals in the times series dimension.

Table 11.3 contrasts the impact of our incentives measures at the micro level and at the aggregated level (times series) on the probability to retire. Specifications (1) and (2) are based on estimation on micro data at the year, age, and sex level. The standard model of Social Security Wealth (SSW) and Peak value (PV) is estimated with a variant in the definition of the peak value (PV*). Detailed information on these incentives measures can be found in

Table 11.3 Incentives measures and the probability to retire

	Micro-level estimation		Times series estimation	
	(1)	(2)	(3)	(4)
SSW	0.0030**	0.0054**	−0.0005	−0.0007
	(0.0014)	(0.0024)	(0.0006)	(0.0022)
PV	−0.0022**		0.0001	
	(0.0011)		(0.0018)	
PV*		−0.0024**		0.0001
		(0.0011)		(0.0018)

Notes: Controls are constant, gross domestic product (GDP) per head, growth in GDP per head, and share of manufacturing in the economy. SSW = social security wealth; PV = peak value; PV* = a variant in the definition of the peak value. Standard errors are in parentheses.
**Significant at the 5 percent level.

appendix B. Controls include age, year, and sex dummies as well as inter-actions between sex, age, and year. At the micro level, both incentives are statistically significant with the expected sign. Higher SSW leads to higher probability to retire, while higher peak value, that is, how much it is worth to delay retirement, leads to lower retirement probability.

The results in times series are presented in specifications (3) and (4). Incentives and the dependent variable are aggregated at the year level. Controls include the same set of variables than in table 11.2, that is, constant, GDP, growth of GDP, and share of manufacturing within GDP. All the effect of the incentives vanishes completely at the times series level. There are important reasons that can account for this. First, both retirement incentives and employment rates vary greatly by sex and age within the same year. Estimating the impact of precise incentives on micro data makes use of these important variations. Changes in times series are per se much smoother. Second, the time variations that may account for changes in economic environment are fully taken into account at the micro level (through the inclusion of year dummies) without concern but need to be carefully controlled for in the time series regressions with all the caveats that entails.

The incentive variables, therefore, do not provide powerful instruments for the older labor force variable in the regressions of table 11.2. Consequently, our results have to rest on the discussion of policy experiments in section 11.4 and the regressions in table 11.2. We find no evidence that changes in employment rates of older workers adversely affect the employment rate of the young.

11.6   Conclusion

Policies to foster early retirement to release jobs for the young have been limited in the United Kingdom. Pension provisions have been more influenced by constraints on the public finances, a desire to "privatize" the system, and, more recently, with concerns with the adequacy of retirement saving than by youth unemployment. However the example of the JRS (1977 to 1988) shows that a desire to increase youth employment opportunities was also present in the United Kingdom at some stage. Looking precisely at the impact of this scheme, we find some evidence that it reduced employment of the old but no positive effect can be found on youth employment. When looking at the entire 1968 to 2005 period, labor force participation of the old is positively associated with employment of the young. Controlling for the business cycle reduces the magnitude of the correlation but does not alter this positive association.

Overall, we find no evidence of long-term crowding out of younger individuals from the labor market by older workers. The evidence, according to a variety of methods, points always in the direction of an absence of such a relationship.

Appendix A
Job Release Scheme Allowance

Table 11A.1   Weekly allowance of the full-time Job Release Scheme (in pounds sterling)

	Tax-free (men aged 64, women aged 59)			Taxable allowance (disabled men 60–63, able men aged 62 or 63)		
	Normal rate	Married with spouse with low income	Threshold for spouse income	Normal rate	Married with spouse with low income	Threshold for spouse income
01/01/1977	23.00	—	—	—	—	—
01/11/1977	26.50	—	—	—	—	—
01/07/1978	26.50	35.00	8.50	—	—	—
01/04/1979	31.50	40.00	8.50	—	—	—
06/04/1980	36.00	45.50	10.00	43.00	53.00	10.00
01/04/1981	40.00	50.50	11.00	47.50	59.00	11.00
01/04/1982	43.50	55.00	12.00	52.00	64.00	12.00
11/04/1983	45.70	57.75	13.00	54.60	67.20	13.00
01/04/1984	48.00	60.75	13.00	57.35	70.55	13.00
01/04/1985	49.95	63.00	13.00	58.35	71.15	13.00
01/04/1986	51.95	65.50	13.00	60.65	74.00	13.00
01/04/1987	53.90	67.55	13.00	61.15	74.50	13.00
01/04/1988	56.05	70.25	13.00	62.15	75.50	13.00

Sources: Makeham and Morgan (1980); Tolley's Social Security and State benefits, 1981, 1982, 1983–1984, 1985, 1986, 1987–1988; Written answers March 1979, House of Commons; Special employment measures 1980–1981, 14 February 1980, House of Commons; Speech 12 June 1985, House of Commons; Written answers 10 July 1985, House of Commons; Written answers 19 March 1986, House of Commons; Written answers 1 April 1987, House of Commons; Written answers 30 March 1988, House of Commons. Dashes indicate no specific allowance.

Table 11A.2   Weekly allowance of the part-time Job Release Scheme (in pounds sterling)

	Tax-free (men 64, women 59)			Taxable allowance (disabled men 60–63, able men aged 62 or 63)		
	Normal rate	Married with spouse with low income	Threshold for spouse income	Normal rate	Married with spouse with low income	Threshold for spouse income
03/10/1983	22.85	28.90	13.00	27.30	33.60	13.00
01/04/1984	24.00	30.35	13.00	28.65	35.30	13.00
01/04/1985	28.95	35.55	13.00	33.80	10.70	13.00
01/04/1986	30.10	37.00	13.00	35.15	42.35	13.00
01/04/1987	31.15	38.05	13.00	35.80	43.00	13.00
01/04/1988	—	—	—	37.25	44.70	13.00

Sources: Tolley's Social Security and State benefits, 1983–1984, 1985, 1986; Written answers 19 March 1986, House of Commons; Written answers 1 April 1987, House of Commons; Written answers 30 March 1988, House of Commons. Dashes indicate no allowance.

Appendix B

Incentives Measures

The incentives we have computed for this volume follow the ones described in Gruber and Wise (1999, 2004). As each exercise leads to variants of these incentives measures, we detail in this appendix the exact computations done in this chapter.

For an individual aged t, we first compute Social Security Wealth at age t (SSW_t). The value of the Social Security Wealth depends on the age, $t' \geq t$, at which the individual decide to retire and is given by:

$$SSW_{t,t'} = \sum_{s=t'}^{T} \beta^{s-t} \pi\left(\frac{s}{t}\right) B_s(t'),$$

with $B_s(t')$ the expected level of pension at age s for an individual who retired at age t', π (s/t) the probability of surviving up to age s for an individual aged t, and T the maximal age at death. The SSW incentive in this volume includes benefits paid to the survival spouse, but no other schemes than the state pensions (BSP, SERPS, and S2P). In particular, it does not include the Invalidity Benefit or Incapacity Benefit, benefits from the JRS, or benefits targeted at those on low incomes. Social Security Wealth does not include social security contributions (or other taxes) either.

The second incentive, the Peak Value (PV), is the absolute value of the difference between the maximum of the Social Security Wealth associated to all possible ages at retirement and Social Security Wealth in case of an immediate retirement:

$$PV_t = \left| \text{Max}_s(SSW_{t,s}) - SSW_{t,t} \right|$$

A variant of the Peak Value (PV*) is the maximum present value of the Social Security Wealth associated to all possible ages at retirement beyond the current year:

$$PV_t^* = \text{Max}_{s \geq t+1}(SSW_{t,s})$$

To compute these incentives, we simulate pensions at each age and in each year for three different types (men with full working life, women with full working life, and women with reduced working life) and for each decile of the earnings distribution. Earnings profiles are estimated on the 1923 cohort and then earnings growth is applied to all other cohorts. Going forward, we assume 2.5 percent inflation and 2 percent real growth in earnings.

Average incentives by year, sex, and age, as well as at the year level, are computed using weights computed from the FES.

References

Anyadike-Danes, M., and D. McVicar. 2008. Has the boom in incapacity benefit claimant numbers passed its peak? *Fiscal Studies* 29 (4): 415–34.

Blundell, R., and P. Johnson. 1998. Pensions and labor market participation in the UK. *American Economic Review* 88 (2): 168–72.

Brown, J. 1990. *Victims or villains? Social security benefits in unemployment.* London: Policy Studies Institute.

Cabinet Office, Performance and Innovation Unit. 2000. *Winning the generation game. Improving opportunities for people aged 50–65 in work and community activity.* London: Stationary Office.

Department of Employment. 1978. Measures to alleviate unemployment in the medium term: Early retirement. *Department of the Employment Gazette* (March): 283–85.

Dilnot, A. W., R. Disney, P. Johnson, and E. Whitehouse. 1994. Pensions policy in the UK. London: Institute for Fiscal Studies.

Dilnot, A. W., J. A. Kay, and C. N. Morris. 1984. The reform of social security. Oxford, UK: Oxford University Press.

Disney, R., and C. Emmerson. 2005. Public pension reform in the United Kingdom: What effect on the financial well-being of current and future pensioners? *Fiscal Studies* 26 (1): 55–82. http://www.ifs.org.uk/publications.php?publication_id=3334.

Disney, R., and D. Hawkes. 2003. Why has employment recently risen among older workers in Britain? In *The labour market under new labour,* ed. R. Dickens, P. Gregg, and J. Wadsworth, 53–69. Basingstoke, UK: Palgrave Macmillan.

Emmerson, C., G. Tetlow, and M. Wakefield. 2005. Pension and saving policy. Election Briefing Note no. 12. London: Institute for Fiscal Studies. http://www.ifs.org.uk/bns/05ebn12.pdf.

Gruber, J., and D. Wise, eds. 1999. *Social security programs and retirement around the world.* Chicago: University of Chicago Press.

———. 2004. *Social security programs and retirement around the world: Microestimation.* Chicago: University of Chicago Press.

———. 2007. *Social security programs and retirement around the world: Fiscal implications of reform.* Chicago: University of Chicago Press.

———. Forthcoming. *Social security programs and retirement around the world: Welfare of the elderly.* Chicago: University of Chicago Press.

Hammond, E., and N. Morris. 1985. An exploration of the cost implications of changing the age of retirement. IFS Working Paper no. 92. London: Institute for Fiscal Studies.

Laczko, F., and C. Phillipson. 1991. Great Britain: The contradictions of early exit. In *Time for retirement: Comparative studies of early exit from the labor force.* ed. M. Kohli, M. Rein, A-M. Guillemard, and H. van Gunsteren, 222–51. Cambridge, UK: Cambridge University Press.

Layard, R., S. Nickell, and R. Jackman. 1991. *Unemployment. Macroeconomic performance and the labor market.* Oxford, UK: Oxford University Press.

Makeham, P., and P. Morgan. 1980. Evaluation of the job release scheme. Department of Employment Research Paper no. 13. London: Department of Employment.

Mulligan, C., and X. Sala-i-Martin. 1999. Gerontocracy, retirement, and social security. NBER Working Paper no. 7117. Cambridge, MA: National Bureau of Economic Research, May.

Schloss, D. F. 1891. Why working-men dislike piece-work. *Economic Review* 1 (3): 312–26.

Social Services Committee. 1982. Third report, Session 1981–1982, Vol. II: Minutes of evidence and appendices. London: HMSO.

Walker, T. 2007. Why economists dislike a lump of labor. *Review of Social Economy* 65 (3): 279–91.

Do Elderly Workers Substitute for Younger Workers in the United States?

Jonathan Gruber and Kevin Milligan

The Social Security program has been the single biggest social insurance program in the United States for decades. It is viewed as a vital piece of the nation's safety net, providing security and well-being for the elderly. Yet it is also a program with a long-run fiscal shortfall that soon will be spending more than it collects and that by roughly 2050 will have no savings left from the existing trust funds to finance that benefit shortfall. As a result, there is a wide ranging policy discussion over reform to the program. Suggestions range from the straightforward (raising the payroll tax that finances the program) to the more exotic (private savings accounts to replace the existing system).

A number of the policy options considered would impact the labor force decisions of the elderly, as discussed in Coile and Gruber (2004, 2007). For example, Coile and Gruber (2004) estimate that raising both the early and normal retirement age by three years would lead to significantly lower retirement rates, with the odds of participating in the labor force at age sixty-five rising by as much as 20 percentage points.

One question that is often raised in international discussion is whether such an increase in the labor supply of the elderly will lead to a reduction in the labor supply of young and prime age workers. A common view expressed in the international context is the "lump of labor" view that there are a fixed

Jonathan Gruber is professor of economics at the Massachusetts Institute of Technology and director of the Program on Health Care at the National Bureau of Economic Research, where he is a research associate. Kevin Milligan is associate professor of economics at the University of British Columbia, and a faculty research fellow of the National Bureau of Economic Research.

This paper was prepared as part of the National Bureau of Economic Research's (NBER) International Social Security project, organized by Jonathan Gruber and David A. Wise. We thank Natalija Novta for research assistance with the incentive calculator.

number of jobs, so that if more of those jobs are taken by the nonretiring elderly, there will be fewer such jobs for the young. This view is commonly disputed by economists, however, who argue that the labor market is not a fixed box but is rather a dynamic market that can adapt to large changes in labor supply. In the U.S. context, this view appears to dominate, as there has been little discussion of the "crowding out" of the young by older workers.

In this paper, we investigate the extent of such "crowding out" in the United States over time. We begin by documenting time series trends in labor supply by age group. We then turn to a more formal regression analysis of those trends. Finally, we develop a measure of the variation over time in the incentives for retirement of the elderly and relate that to the labor supply of both the elderly and younger workers. Overall, our data suggest little substitution across these groups.

12.1   Background

12.1.1   Institutional Features of Social Security

As this paper focuses on labor supply responses to Social Security reform, a brief overview of the Social Security program is necessary to understand how the program affects retirement; see Diamond and Gruber (1998) for a more detailed review. An individual is entitled to retired worker benefits once he or she has worked forty quarters in covered employment. Benefits are calculated in several steps. Annual earnings are indexed by an average wage index, and the thirty-five highest years of earnings are used to compute the average indexed monthly earnings (AIME).[1] A progressive formula is applied to the AIME to obtain the primary insurance amount (PIA). Finally, the PIA is adjusted to obtain the monthly benefit amount based on when benefits are first received. Individuals claiming at the normal retirement age (NRA, legislated to grow slowly from sixty-five to sixty-seven) receive the PIA. Individuals can receive benefits as early as age sixty-two (the early retirement age, or ERA) or can delay until age seventy. Benefits are reduced by 6.67 percent for each year of receipt prior to the NRA and are increased by a delayed retirement credit of 3 percent to 8 percent for each year receipt is postponed past the NRA, depending on the worker's birth year.[2] Benefit receipt is subject to an earnings test before age sixty-five, whereby earnings above a floor amount reduce benefits currently and cause them instead to be paid out (with an actuarial adjustment) upon full retirement. Spouses of beneficiaries also receive a dependent benefit equal to 50 percent of the

1. Earnings after age sixty are in nominal dollars, increasing the incentive to work at these ages.
2. The delayed retirement credit (DRC) is rising from 3 percent for workers born prior to 1925 to 8 percent for workers born after 1942. For workers with an NRA above sixty-five, benefits are reduced 5 percent per year for receipt more than three years before the NRA.

worker's PIA or a survivor benefit equal to 100 percent of the worker's PIA although the spouse receives only the larger of this and his or her own retired worker benefit. Benefits are funded with a payroll tax of 12.4 percent, paid half by employers and half by employees.

Additional work affects Social Security wealth in several ways. First, the additional year of earnings may replace an earlier year of zero or low earnings in the AIME calculation, raising the monthly benefit. Second, work beyond age sixty-two implies a delay in claiming benefits (if earnings are significantly above the earnings test floor). Benefits are foregone for a year, but future benefits are higher due to the actuarial adjustment. Finally, additional work results in additional payroll taxes. The combination of these three effects determines whether the Social Security system provides a return to additional work that is more or less than actuarially fair.

12.1.2   Concerns over "Crowding Out" of Labor Supply of Young

The United States has really had only two major reforms of its Social Security system over the past thirty years. The first was the "Greenspan Commission" in 1983, called in to solve an impending fiscal crisis for the program. Part of the Commission's recommendations, which were adopted into law, was extending the "normal retirement age" from age sixty-five to age sixty-seven over a period of many years. As Coile and Gruber (2007) estimate, such a reform has a relatively modest impact on retirement decisions because the actuarially fair U.S. system makes incentives roughly neutral around retirement ages. Perhaps as a result, there is no evidence of a significant discussion about the labor market consequences of this bill for the nonelderly. A detailed literature search found only one article from this entire era addressing the issue. Hicks (1977, 33) writes "Increasing the retirement age may cost the unemployed as many as 150,000 to 200,000 jobs a year, plus delaying the promotions of those already working."

The second major reform was the removal of the "earnings test" for Social Security after age sixty-five, which was legislated in 2000. Once again there was little discussion of possible substitution of the labor supply of the elderly for that of the young. Smith (2003) titled her article "Senior Citizens Are among Teenagers' Job Competition," but the article itself contains little discussion of this point. Congressman Jim Bunning, in announcing a hearing on the future of Social Security, did say about options to raise the retirement age, "But retirement income might be lower for those who cannot work longer due to employers continuing to provide incentives for older workers to retire and make room for younger workers" (Committee on Ways and Means 1998).

This is only a very modest set of comments on an issue that is a major source of discussion in other nations. Somehow, the "lump of labor" view does not appear to have taken hold in a meaningful way in the United States.

12.2   Time Series Trends

Our analysis of the labor market impacts of changing elderly labor force participation uses data from the nation's largest annual labor market survey, the Current Population Survey (CPS). We use data from the annual March supplement to the CPS, for most years from 1962 through 2007.[3] This supplement includes detailed questions about labor force participation that are fairly constant over time. We divide our sample into three age groups: those twenty to twenty-four (the "young"), those twenty-five to fifty-four ("prime age"), and those fifty-five to sixty-four (the "elderly"). We examine several variables of interest: labor force participation (LFP), employment, and unemployment. We take averages of these measures for each age group over time using the provided survey weights. The analysis is presented in each case first for both sexes pooled together, then for males and females separately.

Time series comparisons of the trends across age groups are shown in panel A of figure 12.1. The labor force participation (LFP) of the elderly displays a gentle U-shaped pattern, dropping until the late 1980s before rising through to 2007. The LFP of the young is rising through time, likely because of increasing participation by females. Finally, the unemployment rate of the young hits its highest points in the late 1970s and early 1980s when elderly LFP is at its lowest. This does not appear consistent with the crowd-out hypothesis.

We break this analysis down by sex in panels B and C of figure 12.1. The LFP of young males is fairly constant at around 80 percent over the entire span. Participation by elderly men rebounds only slightly in the late 1990s and does not reach the levels seen in the 1960s. In contrast, the LFP of both young and older women increases over the time period studied here. For younger women, the increase is concentrated in the first two decades of the sample up to the mid-1980s. In contrast, the LFP of the elderly women does not begin to rise until the mid-1990s, when it rises substantially. Finally, the cyclicality of male youth unemployment appears to exceed that of females.

Panel A of figure 12.2 displays the LFP of the elderly against the unemployment rate for the young and the prime-aged. The most noticeable pattern here is the cyclicality of the unemployment rate for the youth, which is mirrored in a muted way for the prime-aged. Panels B and C of figure 12.2 for males and females demonstrate again that males and younger individuals show more cyclicality. However, nowhere here is there any evidence of crowd out. When unemployment is at its highest in the early 1980s, elderly LFP is near its lowest.

Finally, panel A of figure 12.3 shows the employment rates of the youth

3. We are missing data from 1963, 1965, 1970, 1976, and 1994.

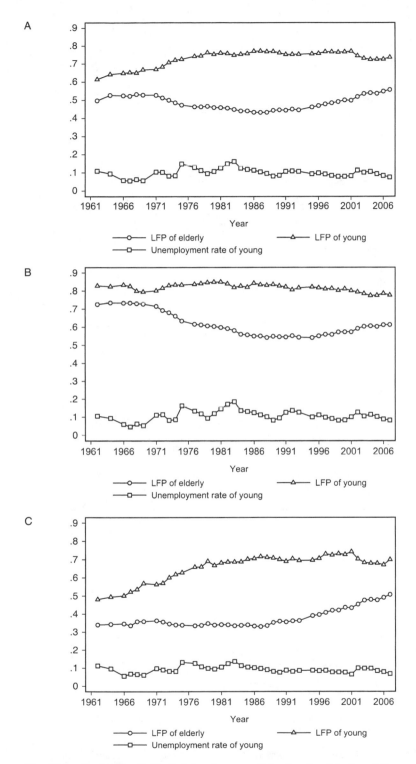

Fig. 12.1 Evolution of elderly labor force participation for elderly and the young:
A, Both sexes; *B*, Males; *C*, Females

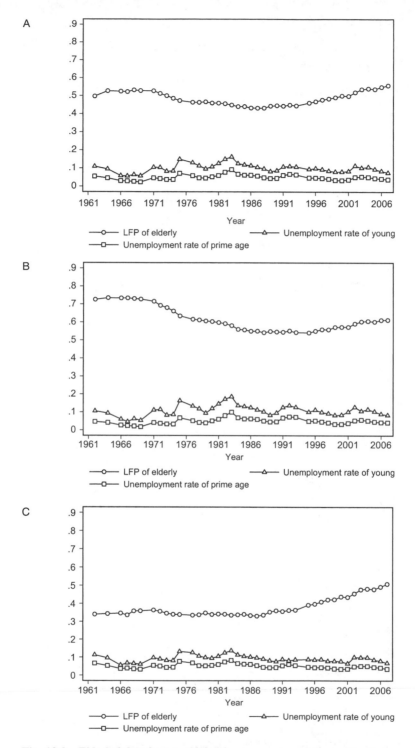

Fig. 12.2   Elderly labor force participation versus unemployment for the young and prime age: *A*, Both sexes; *B*, Males; *C*, Females

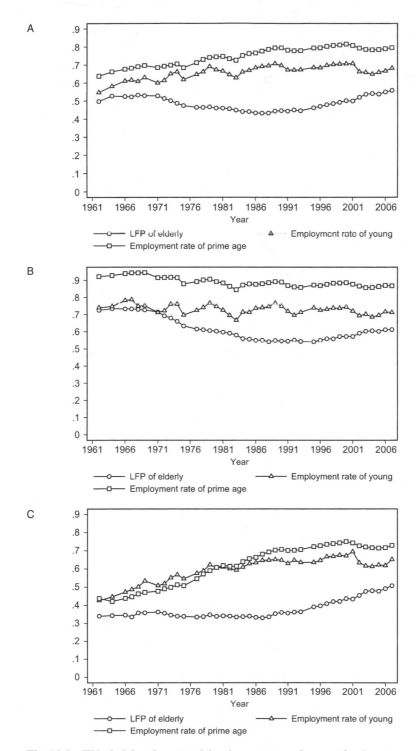

Fig. 12.3 Elderly labor force participation versus employment for the young and prime age: *A*, **Both sexes;** *B*, **Males;** *C*, **Females**

and prime-aged against the LFP of the elderly. The employment rates trend upward over this time period. The breakdown by sex reveals in panel B of figure 12.3 that male employment rates do not trend (but are cyclical) and that there is a very strong upward trend for both youth and prime-aged female employment. Nowhere, however, is there sign of any crowd-out effect.

To summarize the graphical analysis, we find gentle U-shaped trends in the LFP of the elderly, but the labor market behavior of the youth and prime-aged is best described as cyclical for the males, and as following a secular upward trend for the females. The cyclicality and secular trend appear to be much stronger than any crowd-out effect.

12.3   "Direct" Crowding-Out Regressions

In this section, we formalize the graphical analysis of Section 12.2 by running time series regressions of the labor supply of the young and prime age on that of the elderly. We estimate time series regressions of the form:

$$Y_t = \beta_0 + \beta_1 \, \text{ELDERLYEMP}_t + X_t \beta_2 + e_t.$$

For both the young and the prime age groups, we use unemployment rate and the employment rate as dependent variables (Y_t). The key independent variable in each regression is the rate of elderly employment (ELDERLYEMP_t). The additional control variables (X_t) that we use in some specifications include the level of gross domestic product (GDP) per capita, and the growth rate of GDP per capita.

We employ four different specifications, in common with the other countries in this project. Each of these four is repeated first without any extra control variables and then with the extra X_t control variables. For the first specification, we use the simple levels of elderly employment and the dependent variables. Next, we lag elderly employment by three years in order to try to avoid the impact of any contemporary shock affecting both sides of the equation. Third, we take the fifth difference of all the variables in the equation. Finally, we log both elderly employment and the dependent variable and take the five-year log difference.

Table 12.1 displays the results for men and women pooled together. Each cell reports the coefficient on elderly employment from a separate regression. Looking at unemployment rates in the first column, we expect an increase in elderly employment to increase youth unemployment if there is crowd out. However, the coefficients down the column are strongly negative. The –0.402 coefficient in the first row can be interpreted as follows: a 1 point increase in the elderly employment rate is predicted to decrease youth unemployment by 0.402 points. The coefficients, with one exception, are statistically significant. This evidence is against the crowd-out hypothesis.

The second column has the results for youth employment. Here, we expect a negative coefficient if elderly employment crowds out youth employment.

Table 12.1   **Direct regressions of labor market crowdout: both sexes**

	Youth		Prime	
	UE	EMP	UE	EMP
	No controls			
Levels	−0.402	−0.297	−0.258	−0.136
	(0.065)	(0.174)	(0.040)	(0.237)
3-year lag on elderly employment	−0.224	−0.507	−0.192	−0.488
	(0.097)	(0.138)	(0.058)	(0.221)
5-year difference	−0.486	−0.105	−0.337	−0.110
	(0.127)	(0.240)	(0.084)	(0.157)
5-year log difference	−4.062	−0.065	−5.189	−0.078
	(1.025)	(0.206)	(1.126)	(0.118)
	With controls			
Levels	−0.415	−0.468	−0.277	−0.439
	(0.066)	(0.098)	(0.038)	(0.067)
3-year lag on elderly employment	−0.223	−0.545	−0.195	−0.558
	(0.098)	(0.094)	(0.059)	(0.055)
5-year difference	−0.104	−0.875	−0.065	−0.539
	(0.119)	(0.213)	(0.069)	(0.162)
5-year log difference	−3.192	−0.246	−3.991	−0.163
	(1.137)	(0.138)	(0.776)	(0.088)

Notes: Reported in each cell is the coefficient on elderly employment in separate regressions with the dependent variable listed in the column headings. The standard error is beneath each estimate in parentheses. The different specifications appear in each row of the table. The specifications are explained in the main text. UE = the share of the population unemployed; EMP = the share of the population in work.

Without controls in the top panel, three of four coefficients fail to attain statistical significance, but all are negative. In the bottom panel, with controls, all four coefficients are statistically significant at conventional levels, and all are negative. This suggests that more elderly employment leads to a decrease in youth employment, which is consistent with crowd out. Moreover, the coefficients are large. For example, with controls, the five-year difference specification yields a coefficient of −0.875, which is the predicted drop in the youth employment rate with a 1 point increase in the elderly employment rate. This is somewhat confusing because the unemployment rate and the employment rate are moving in the same direction. This is possible, though, if there is a large increase in labor force exits. However, these estimates might be tainted by the secular trend increase in female employment through this period. We will check this further in the male-only results that follow.

The third and fourth columns of the table investigate the impact of elderly employment on the labor market behavior of the prime-aged twenty-five to fifty-four-year-olds. The same pattern emerges as for the youth—negative impacts for the unemployment rate and the employment rate across all specifications, with most attaining statistical significance.

Table 12.2   **Direct regressions of labor market crowdout: males only**

	Youth		Prime	
	UE	EMP	UE	EMP
	No controls			
Levels	−0.182	0.197	−0.141	0.369
	(0.055)	(0.058)	(0.031)	(0.028)
3-year lag on elderly employment	−0.024	0.070	−0.072	0.275
	(0.073)	(0.072)	(0.043)	(0.044)
5-year difference	−0.597	0.382	−0.400	0.417
	(0.151)	(0.218)	(0.095)	(0.101)
5-year log difference	−4.913	0.378	−6.214	0.328
	(1.327)	(0.211)	(1.386)	(0.081)
	With controls			
Levels	−0.415	0.150	−0.277	0.323
	(0.063)	(0.088)	(0.035)	(0.041)
3-year lag on elderly employment	−0.260	−0.051	−0.222	0.238
	(0.101)	(0.111)	(0.058)	(0.069)
5-year difference	−0.072	−0.403	−0.054	0.009
	(0.143)	(0.216)	(0.085)	(0.082)
5-year log difference	−3.498	0.157	−4.236	0.227
	(1.438)	(0.206)	(1.018)	(0.055)

Note: See table 12.1 notes.

To check on the impact of the different trends experienced by males and females over this forty-five-year time period, we break out the results for males only in table 12.2. The results for the unemployment rates are the same in direction as was seen in table 12.1. The magnitudes are sometimes higher and sometimes lower, and statistical significance fails in some cases. However, for the males, the message is clear that the youth and the prime-aged unemployment rates drop when elderly employment increases. In contrast to the pooled sex results, the impact on youth is mixed and for prime-aged employment is strongly positive. For the youth, two positive estimates attain statistical significance at the 10 percent level, and there is one significant negative result. The rest are not statistically significant. For the prime-aged, seven of the eight are positive and statistically significant. The difference between these results and table 12.1 may be driven by the increasing female employment rates through time that contrast with the downward trend in elderly employment over this period. When just males are used, this effect is absent.

12.4   Incentive Regressions

In this section, we explore the use of an index capturing the incentive for elderly workers to retire. By using this index, we hope to use variation in the work behavior of the elderly that is related to policy changes rather than potentially endogenous economic shocks that might affect all parts of the economy. The index, described in more detail in the appendix, attempts to encapsulate in one number for each year in the data set the overall incentives faced on average by elderly labor market participants. This may be a somewhat difficult task to undertake because the time series variation in benefits is not large—as discussed earlier, the reforms of the system have been few, especially compared with many European countries.

A graph of the index values against elderly employment rates appears in figure 12.4. The Ibar line represents the full index, capturing both the wealth and dynamic incentive effects. The Wbar line shows the average value of Social Security Wealth among those still in the labor force. (Again, more details are in the appendix.) There are no sharp jumps in Wbar through time, so the growth in Wbar reflects wage growth across cohorts and through time. The sharp increase in Ibar after 1971 reflects the influence of the well-known "notch" in Social Security benefits. The impact of the notch lives on into the 1980s in this calculation because we average over the incentives faced by active labor market participants, and the "notch generation" was still active into the mid-1980s.

How should the index results be interpreted? When the index increases, it should decrease the labor force participation of the elderly. This means that we expect to see negative coefficients for the employment of the elderly when regressed on this measure. Following through, if there is less employment among the elderly, a positive coefficient among the youth or prime-aged would indicate that there is evidence of crowding out.

Table 12.3 begins the analysis, using the same eight specifications as in the direct analysis in tables 12.1 and 12.2. The top panel shows results without

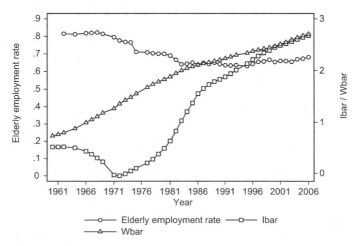

Fig. 12.4   Elderly employment rate, $\bar{I}(y)$ and $\bar{W}(y)$

Table 12.3   Impact of retirement incentives on the employment of the elderly, prime-aged, and young: both sexes

	Elderly		Youth		Prime	
	UE	EMP	UE	EMP	UE	EMP
	No controls					
Levels	0.000	0.005	0.000	0.024	0.002	0.045
	(0.001)	(0.005)	(0.003)	(0.005)	(0.002)	(0.004)
3-year lag on elderly employment	−0.001	0.015	−0.006	0.022	−0.001	0.043
	(0.001)	(0.006)	(0.003)	(0.006)	(0.002)	(0.005)
5-year difference	0.000	−0.007	−0.016	−0.003	−0.002	0.013
	(0.004)	(0.012)	(0.010)	(0.016)	(0.007)	(0.010)
5-year log difference	0.100	−0.025	0.047	−0.004	0.114	0.011
	(0.103)	(0.010)	(0.071)	(0.015)	(0.095)	(0.008)
	With controls					
Levels	0.005	−0.027	−0.005	0.004	0.008	0.026
	(0.003)	(0.018)	(0.010)	(0.014)	(0.006)	(0.010)
3-year lag on elderly employment	0.000	0.029	−0.032	−0.012	−0.011	0.005
	(0.003)	(0.018)	(0.009)	(0.014)	(0.007)	(0.012)
5-year difference	0.001	−0.009	−0.014	−0.004	0.001	0.014
	(0.003)	(0.010)	(0.006)	(0.015)	(0.004)	(0.010)
5-year log difference	0.217	−0.064	0.069	0.015	0.191	0.025
	(0.094)	(0.015)	(0.087)	(0.017)	(0.092)	(0.010)

Notes: Reported in each cell is the coefficient on the retirement incentive index in separate regressions with the dependent variable listed in the column headings. The standard error is beneath each estimate in parentheses. The different specifications appear in each row of the table. The specifications are explained in the main text. UE = the share of the population unemployed; EMP = the share of the population in work.

additional controls, and the bottom panel shows similar results from specifications with control variables. The first two columns contain the results for the impact of the index on the elderly. The results, mostly, are statistically insignificant. The five-year log difference specification does show statistical significance in the expected direction, with higher unemployment and lower employment indicated in years with higher values for the retirement incentive index.

A scatter plot of the fifth difference of the Ibar index and the elderly employment rate appears in figure 12.5. In this scatter plot, there is no clear relationship between the two variables. This may explain the lack of consistent findings in the first two columns of table 12.3.

For youth and prime-aged individuals, the results in table 12.3 are mixed. The youth columns show two statistically significant negative results for unemployment and two positive results for employment. If there were crowd out, this is the direction we would expect these coefficients to go. For the prime-aged, there is one positive coefficient for unemployment and several

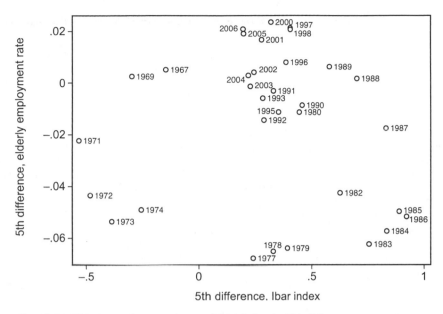

Fig. 12.5   **Elderly employment rate and $I(y)$ index in fifth differences**

positive coefficients for employment. The stronger results for prime-aged employment are consistent with the idea of crowd out—higher retirement incentives for the elderly appear to be related to more employment by the prime-aged.

For these results, the caveat discussed earlier about the long-run upward trend of female employment again becomes important. For this reason, we again investigate the results just for men in table 12.4. In the first two columns for the elderly, the results are mildly stronger than the pooled men and women results, with several statistically significant findings. The positive relationship between the incentive index and unemployment—and the negative relationship of the index with employment—indicates that the incentive index is somewhat predictive of the labor market behavior of the elderly.

The results for the youth and the prime-aged, however, show no consistent pattern. There are a few statistically significant results across the table, but the signs are not clearly in one direction or the other. For example, the second row with the three-year lag on elderly employment shows a significant –0.015 drop for a one unit increase in the index. However, when controls are introduced in the sixth row of the table, the coefficient is now negative and significant at the 10 percent level. The overall impression of this table, however, is of no statistically significant relationship between the incentive index and the employment of young and prime-aged men.

Table 12.4   **Impact of retirement incentives on the employment of the elderly, prime-aged, and young: males only**

	Elderly		Youth		Prime	
	UE	EMP	UE	EMP	UE	EMP
No controls						
Levels	−0.001	−0.048	−0.002	−0.010	0.002	−0.019
	(0.001)	(0.007)	(0.004)	(0.004)	(0.003)	(0.003)
3-year lag on elderly	−0.002	−0.037	−0.010	−0.006	−0.002	−0.015
employment	(0.001)	(0.009)	(0.004)	(0.005)	(0.003)	(0.004)
5-year difference	0.002	−0.008	−0.022	0.020	−0.002	0.007
	(0.006)	(0.014)	(0.014)	(0.018)	(0.010)	(0.010)
5-year log difference	0.147	−0.028	0.057	−0.006	0.130	−0.005
	(0.102)	(0.009)	(0.088)	(0.014)	(0.112)	(0.006)
With controls						
Levels	0.008	−0.041	−0.003	0.006	0.012	−0.008
	(0.004)	(0.023)	(0.014)	(0.013)	(0.008)	(0.010)
3-year lag on elderly	0.001	0.033	−0.039	0.021	−0.012	0.019
employment	(0.005)	(0.025)	(0.013)	(0.014)	(0.009)	(0.010)
5-year difference	0.004	−0.012	−0.017	0.015	0.004	0.003
	(0.004)	(0.011)	(0.008)	(0.014)	(0.005)	(0.005)
5-year log difference	0.306	−0.061	0.087	0.015	0.264	−0.005
	(0.110)	(0.016)	(0.098)	(0.021)	(0.099)	(0.007)

Note: See table 12.3 notes.

12.5   Conclusions

In this chapter, we have investigated the impact of elderly employment on the youth and prime-aged labor markets. In the "direct" regressions, we find some evidence that movements in elderly employment are negatively related to prime-aged employment. However, our males-only evidence suggests that these findings may be tainted by the inclusion of women, who experienced a large secular increase in employment over this period. Using the incentive index, we find little evidence of crowd out. But our incentive index is not strongly predictive of the labor market behavior of the elderly, so this may reflect more on the difficulty of exploiting the available policy variation in a time series study.

Our conclusion, therefore, is relatively weak. We find no consistent evidence of an impact of the employment of the elderly on the young or prime-aged in our sample. This evidence for one country alone may not be conclusive. However, when placed in the context of the other countries in this project, it is possible that stronger conclusions may be drawn—again highlighting the potential power of the multicountry analysis.

Appendix
Incentive Index Construction

Please note that this discussion is drawn from the Canadian chapter because the construction of the index followed very similar methodology and computer programs.

The goal of the exercise is to arrive at a single incentive number for each calendar year to be used in the time series regressions. We begin with a profile of median earnings for a central cohort. This earnings profile is then shifted for inflation forward and backward to generate equivalent real wage profiles for all birth cohorts. This method ensures that the only difference in incentive measures across years will be in changes in benefit formulas and not cross-cohort differences in wages.

These cohort age-earnings profiles are next pushed through a detailed calculator for Social Security benefits. At each age from fifty-five to sixty-nine, we calculate the capitalized value of future benefits (Social Security Wealth, or SSW) and also the "peak value" concept found in Coile and Gruber (2004, 2007). The peak value represents the difference between current SSW and its highest value in the future, given current information for a forward-looking individual.

To collapse this down to an annual time series, we start by recognizing that an individual viewed at age *a* has faced retirement incentives at age a, $a-1$, $a-2$, . . . back to the first age of eligibility. We, therefore, average the incentives within a cohort across ages (from the current age back to age fifty-five), using the aggregate age-year-sex specific labor force participation as weights. We generate the age-year-sex labor force participation rates from the CPS. Because this survey only goes back to 1962 and is also missing some years, we fill in missing years and extrapolate backward using an assumption of constant age-sex labor force participation rates. This calculation gives us an average exposure to retirement incentives for each cohort in each year of interest.

The final step involves collapsing the average incentive measures to a single number for each year. This means we must average the incentive measures faced by each cohort in a given year. To do this, we weight by the proportion of the population represented by each age in a given year.

To enrich the measurement of incentives, we assign a weight to the SSW component and the peak value component. We determined these weights using an iterative technique, finding weights that maximized the fit of a regression of elderly LFP on the incentive measure.

The foregoing can be expressed mathematically as follows. The incentive measure I at age a and year y can be expressed as:

$$I(a, y) = \{\gamma W(a, y) + \alpha[W(a, y) - \text{PV}^*(a, y)]\},$$

where $W(a, y)$ is the SSW at age a and year y, $PV^*(a, y)$ is the peak value of SSW, and α and γ are the weighting parameters for the wealth level and peak value difference, respectively. These $I(a, y)$ terms are then summed across all previous ages, within cohort:

$$\bar{I}(a, y) = \sum_{a=55}^{a=69} \left(\left\{ P(a,y) \times \left[\frac{\sum_{t=0}^{a-55} I(a,y) \cdot LFP(a-t, y-t-1)}{\sum_{t=0}^{a-55} LFP(a-t, y-t-1)} \right] \right\} / \sum_{a=55}^{a=69} P(a,y) \right),$$

where $LFP(a - t, y - t - 1)$ is the labor force participation rate for a member of the cohort in a previous year. The extra minus 1 accounts for the fact that we want the labor force participation rate at the beginning of the year, not during the year. Finally, we average across all cohorts in a particular year, where $P(a, y)$ is the population of the cohort in a given year. This $\bar{I}(y)$ term is the incentives index used for the regressions appearing in tables 12.3 and 12.4.

We also make use of $\bar{W}(y)$, which is calculated by substituting the SSW of the individual at age a and year y, $W(a, y)$, in for $I(a, y)$. This $\bar{W}(y)$ term calculates the average pension wealth across individuals in a given year.

References

Coile, Courtney, and Jonathan Gruber. 2004. The effect of Social Security on retirement in the United States. In *Social Security programs and retirement around the world: Micro-estimation.* ed. Jonathan Gruber and David A. Wise, 691–730. Chicago: University of Chicago Press.

———. 2007. Future social security entitlements and the retirement decision. *Review of Economics and Statistics* 89 (2): 234–46.

Committee on Ways and Means. 1998. Bunning announces eighth hearing in series on "The future of Social Security for this generation and the next," Committee on Ways and Means, Subcommittee on Social Security, Advisory no. SS-13, February 13, 1998.

Diamond, Peter, and Jonathan Gruber. 1998. Social Security and retirement in the United States. In *Social security and retirement around the world,* ed. Jonathan Gruber and David A. Wise, 437–73. Chicago: University of Chicago Press.

Hicks, Nancy. 1977. Retirement—Giving it five more years—Who wins, who loses? *Black Enterprise* 8 (5): 33.

Smith, Erika. 2003. Senior citizens are among teenagers' job competition. *Akron Beacon Journal,* May 12, 2003.

Contributors

Michael Baker
Department of Economics
University of Toronto
150 St. George Street
Toronto, Ontario M5S 3G7 Canada

James Banks
Department of Economics
University College London
Gower Street
London WC1E 6BT, England

Melika Ben Salem
Paris School of Economics (INRA)
48 Bd Jourdan
75014 Paris, France

Paul Bingley
Department of Economics
The Danish National Centre for Social
   Research
Herluf Trolles Gade 11
1052 Copenhagen K, Denmark

Didier Blanchet
INSEE-Timbre G201
B.P. 100-15 Bd Gabriel Péri
92244 Malakoff Cedex, France

Richard Blundell
Department of Economics
University College London
Gower Street
London WC1E 6BT, England

Michele Boldrin
Department of Economics
Washington University in St. Louis
Campus Box 1208
St. Louis, MO 63130-4899

Axel Börsch-Supan
Mannheim Research Institute for the
   Economics of Aging
University of Mannheim
D-68131 Mannheim, Germany

Antoine Bozio
Institute for Fiscal Studies
7 Ridgmount Street
London WC1E 7AE, England

Agar Brugiavini
Department of Economics
Universita' Ca' Foscari Venezia
S. Giobbe, 873
30121 Venice, Italy

Nabanita Datta Gupta
Department of Economics
Aarhus School of Business
Aarhus University
Frichshuset
Hermodsvej 22, 1st and 2nd floors
8230 Aabyhoej, Denmark

Carl Emmerson
Institute for Fiscal Studies
7 Ridgmount Street
London WC1E 7AE, England

Pilar García-Gómez
Universitat Pompeu Fabra
Department of Economics and
    Business
c/ Ramon Trias Fargas, 25-27
08005 Barcelona, Spain

Jonathan Gruber
Department of Economics, E52-355
Massachusetts Institute of Technology
50 Memorial Drive
Cambridge, MA 02142-1347

Sergi Jiménez-Martín
Department of Economics
Universitat Pompeu Fabra
Ramon Trias Fargas 25-27
08005 Barcelona, Spain

Alain Jousten
HEC-Management School
University of Liège
Bldg. B31, Boulevard du Rectorat 7
4000 Liège 1, Belgium

Adriaan Kalwij
Utrecht School of Economics
Vredenburg 138
3511BG Utrecht, The Netherlands

Arie Kapteyn
RAND Corporation
1776 Main Street, P.O. Box 2138
Santa Monica, CA 90407-2138

Mathieu Lefèbvre
GATE
University of Lyon
93 Chemin des Mouilles
69130 Ecully, France

Kevin Milligan
Department of Economics
University of British Columbia
#997-1873 East Mall
Vancouver, B.C., Canada V6T 1Z1

Akiko Sato Oishi
Faculty of Law and Economics
Chiba University
1-33 Yayoi-cho, Inage-ku
Chiba-shi 263-8522, Japan

Takashi Oshio
Graduate School of Economics
Kobe University
2-1 Rokko-dai, Nada-ku
Kobe 657 8501, Japan

Mårten Palme
Department of Economics
Stockholm University
SE-106 91 Stockholm, Sweden

Peder J. Pedersen
Economics Department
Aarhus University
Bartholins Allé, bygning 1322
DK - 8000 Århus C, Denmark

Franco Peracchi
Faculty of Economics
Tor Vergata University
via Columbia, 2
00133 Rome, Italy

Sergio Perelman
HEC-Management School
University of Liège
Bldg. B31, Boulevard du Rectorat 7
4000 Liège 1, Belgium

Pierre Pestieau
HEC-Management School
University of Liège
Bldg. B31, Boulevard du Rectorat 7
4000 Liège 1, Belgium

Muriel Roger
Paris School of Economics (INRA)
48 Bd Jourdan
75014 Paris, France

Reinhold Schnabel
Universität Duisburg-Essen, Campus
    Essen
Universitätsstr. 12
45117 Essen, Germany

Satoshi Shimizutani
Institute for International Policy
    Studies
Toranomon 30 Mori Bldg., 6F
Toranomon 3-2-2
Minato-ku, Tokyo 105-0001, Japan

Ingemar Svensson
National Social Insurance Board
Adolf Fredriks Kyrkogata 8
S-103 5 1 Stockholm, Sweden

Klaas de Vos
CentERdata
PO Box 90153
5000 LE Tilburg, The Netherlands

David A. Wise
Harvard University and NBER
1050 Massachusetts Avenue
Cambridge, MA 02138-5398

Author Index

Subject Index